I0357736

False Facts and True Rumors

Lashon HaRa in Contemporary Culture

Michael Scharf
Publication Trust
Yeshiva University Press

מגיד
MAGGID

Rabbi Daniel Z. Feldman

False Facts and True Rumors

Lashon HaRa in Contemporary Culture

The Michael Scharf Publication Trust of
Yeshiva University Press
Rabbi Isaac Elchanan Theological Seminary

The RIETS Halakhah Series

Maggid Books

False Facts and True Rumors
Lashon Hara in Contemporary Culture

First Edition, 2015

The Michael Scharf Publication Trust
of Yeshiva University Press

Maggid Books
An imprint of Koren Publishers Jerusalem Ltd.

POB 8531, New Milford, CT 06776-8531, USA
& POB 4044, Jerusalem 9104001, Israel
www.korenpub.com

Cover Design: Daniel Bar-Lev

The publication of this book was made possible
through the generous support of *Torah Education in Israel.*

ISBN 978-1-59264-748-4, *paperback*

Library of Congress Control Number: 2017275221

A CIP catalogue record for this title is
available from the British Library

Printed and bound in the United States

Dedicated in memory of my father,
Rabbi Dr. David M. Feldman,
who epitomized lashon tov in so many ways

Contents

Acknowledgments xi

Foreword xvii

SECTION ONE: THE THEORY

Introduction: The Mysterious Peddler 3

The Textual Case Against Lashon HaRa: From Concept to Precept 11

But Words Will Never Hurt Me? Identifying the Harm of Lashon HaRa 25

- Damage to the Subject 26
- Damage to the Speaker 31
- Damage to Society 35

Is It Really True? 43

- The Possibility of Subjectivity and Error 44
- The Fallibility of Memory 48
- The Illusion of Confidence 52
- Cognitive Biases and Disproportionate Influence 54
- The Fundamental Attribution Error 55
- Ambiguity, Intolerance, and the Availability Heuristic 58
- The Halo/Devil Effect 60
- Confirmation Bias 63

Pattern Seeking and Anchoring 67
Group Polarization 71
Disproportionate Impact 76
Blindness to Bias 77
Defining the Prohibition: A Forbidden Character Trait or Prohibited Behavior? 83

SECTION TWO: THE APPLICATION

Permitted Lashon HaRa: Purposeful and Beneficial Speech 93
Defining the Concept 93
The Conditions of the *Ḥafetz Ḥayim* 97
Therapy 104
Potential Marriage Partners (*Shiddukhim*) 107
Further Considerations of *Lashon HaRa* and *Shiddukhim* 114
Educational Issues 119
Business Issues 124
Contentious People (*Baalei Maḥaloket*) 127
Additional Issues of "Purpose" and Self-Defense 130
"Accepting" Lashon HaRa 133
Defining the Prohibition 133
What Does It Mean "to Accept"? 139
A Prohibition to Listen? 146
When Listening Is Necessary 150
Credibility Factors 151
Lashon HaRa that Is Public Knowledge, in the Subject's Presence, and Indirect 159
"In the Presence of Three" (*Apei Telata*) 159
In the Presence of the Subject 167

The "Dust" of *Lashon HaRa* 172
Purim Plays 176
Widely Spread Public Knowledge 180
Privacy and Confidentiality 181
Contemporary Culture: Journalism, the Internet, and Politics 189
Journalism 189
The Internet and Social Media 193
Checking of Information 194
Group Polarization 196
The Cost of Speed 197
The Online Disinhibition Effect 198
Further Aspects of Anonymity 203
Tone Misreading 207
Adjustment of Expectations 208
"Acceptance" Issues 209
Other Issues of *Lashon HaRa* and the Internet 212
Privacy Issues 214
The Political Culture and Negative Campaigning..............217
Further Aspects of the Dual Nature of Lashon HaRa 221
No Names 221
When the Subject Doesn't Care 223
Lashon HaRa About Oneself 224
"Harmless" *Lashon HaRa* and Unknown Benefit...............226
Speech About Groups 226
Speech About Things 228
Speaking Ill of the Dead.......................................228

Fixing It: Reparations, Repentance, and Redemption 231
Financial Restitution 231
Asking Forgiveness: The Controversy 234
Personal Repentance for *Lashon HaRa* 243
Epilogue: Remembering Miriam 247

Halakhic Rulings by Rabbi Hershel Schachter 257
Halakhic Rulings by Rabbi Mordechai Willig 259
List of Sources Cited 263
Glossary 303
Index of Topics and Names 305
Index of Biblical and Rabbinic Sources 325
Index of References to the Works of the Ḥafetz Ḥayim 331
About the Author 335

Primary Hebrew sources for this book can be found at
www.yutorah.org/_materials/lashon-hara-sources.pdf.

Acknowledgments

With deep gratitude to the *Ribbono shel Olam,* I humbly tender this work to the reading public.

This work is being published through the auspices of Yeshiva University Press and the Michael Scharf Publication Trust, where I have the privilege of working with Rabbi Yona Reiss, who shares his erudition and insight on all of our YU Press projects, and who thoroughly reviewed this work, offering a wealth of greatly helpful comments and perspectives; and Dr. Jeffrey Gurock, whose participation and enthusiasm has done so much to enable the publication of Torah literature through our yeshiva. Our projects are carried out under the banner of the Rabbi Isaac Elchanan Theological Seminary (RIETS), which has the good fortune of being led with wisdom and creativity by Rabbi Menachem Penner, the Max and Marion Grill Dean, and by President Richard M. Joel, both of whom have always made themselves available to me on a personal level as well as on a professional level and have provided deeply appreciated guidance.

This book, like so many of our projects, is produced in partnership with Maggid Books, and we greatly appreciate the wonderful work of Matthew Miller, Rabbi Reuven Ziegler, Shalom Dinerstein and Tomi Mager. Gratitude is extended to Shifra Schapiro for her wonderful indexing work and to Rabbi Moshe Schapiro for all of his assistance and input.

I thank my senior *ḥevrusas* and mentors Rabbi Baruch Simon and Rabbi Zvi Sobolofsky for their constant advice and guidance. I extend deep thanks to my revered *rebbe,* Rabbi Hershel Schachter, whose world-famous *shiurim* I have been privileged to hear and grow from for several years, for all of his influence and counsel, and for his warm and kind encouragement. Rabbi Mordechai Willig, from whom I have been fortunate to hear *shiurim* and draw influence for many years in many contexts, has always made himself available to advise and assist in all ways big and small, and I am immensely grateful to him for that, and for so much more.

I express my profound gratitude to my *rebbe,* Rabbi Menachem Mendel Blachman of Yeshivat Kerem B'Yavneh, for all of his support. I also acknowledge the continuing influence of the founding Rosh Yeshiva of Kerem B'Yavneh, Rabbi Chaim Yaakov Goldvicht, *z"l.*

Rabbi Dr. Norman Lamm, Chancellor Emeritus of Yeshiva University, has been a source of support and advice from my earliest days on campus, as has Rabbi Zevulun Charlop, who served for almost four decades at the helm of RIETS, and Rabbi Kenneth Brander, Vice President for University and Community Life. A special thanks goes to Rabbi and Mrs. Hershel Reichman for all they have done for me and my family.

I thank Mrs. Bella Wexner *a"h* and, *tibadel leḥayim,* Ms. Susan Wexner, for their generous sponsorship of the Bella and Harry Wexner Kollel Elyon at Yeshiva University, in which I was privileged to learn for four years at RIETS, and to hear *shiurim* and gain direction from Rabbi Willig and Rabbi Michael Rosensweig.

I wish to express my appreciation to the leaders of the schools that currently give me the opportunity to teach Torah under their auspices, including President Joel, Rabbi Lamm, Rabbi Charlop, Rabbi Reiss, Rabbi Penner, and to the administration of RIETS; to Dr. Moses Pava and the Sy Syms School of Business; and to Dr. Saul Andron and the Wurzweiler School of Social Work. I wish to express my appreciation as well to all of the synagogues, schools, and other institutions that have hosted my lectures, including Congregation Beth Aaron of Teaneck, New Jersey, and its wonderful Rabbi Laurence Rothwachs, whose friendship I deeply cherish. And to my students and participants at these institutions, I offer my thanks for listening, challenging me, and helping me to gain a clearer understanding of all I would hope to teach.

To the wonderful people of Ohr Saadya of Teaneck, and all who have joined with us in various stages throughout the years, I convey my gratitude, my pride and my appreciation in our shared experiences and endeavors, and the blessing that the future bring only success and happiness in the fulfillment of our goals and aspirations.

This work greatly benefited from extensive comments from Dr. David Pelcovitz and Dr. David Shatz, and from conversations with Rabbi Lord Jonathan Sacks. Joel Markin did wonderful work in assisting in many aspects of the project, providing both valuable insight and long hours of careful attention. My friend and frequent collaborator Rabbi Isaac Rice kindly offered comments and references characteristic of his broad erudition.

I would like to thank the good friends who were always available to discuss issues relevant to the content and format of this project, including Chaim B. Hollander, Avi Shmidman, Rabbi Benjamin G. Kelsen, Rabbi Steven Burg, Daniel Benovitz, Dr. Isaac Schechter, Rabbi Dr. Meir Soloveichik, Menachem Butler, Rabbi Gil Student, and so many others.

I extend a very special thank you to Mr. Terry D. Novetsky, who with great patience, insight, and graciousness with his time made it possible for previous efforts to get to print.

I would like to express deep gratitude to our friends Warren and Esther Feldman, whose generosity, care, and foresight has done so much to further our efforts and those of so many others.

My brother Rabbi Jonathan and his wife Rachel and their family are constant and invaluable sources of love, insight, and support. My sister Rebecca, together with her husband Dr. Tal Becker and their family, extends her wise counsel and warm compassion with consistency and devotion, and I am a most fortunate beneficiary.

As the book was being completed, my family was deeply saddened by the loss of my beloved father, Rabbi Dr. David M. Feldman, *z"l*. When I write that this book would not exist without him, I mean that in far more than the usual sense. Of course, I owe all that I am and that I do to him and to my noble and devoted mother, Rebbetzin Aviva. In many more specific ways, this book and all of my writings owe a particular debt to my father and his legacy. With his own writings, he was a pioneer in the field of writing English-language books that dealt with advanced rabbinic literature, doing so with clarity, sophistication, and deep scholarship, and thus set a model for so many after him to follow. More personally, he was always ready to give of his time to review my own writings, and would constantly go above and beyond through several cycles of careful and patient attention to the manuscripts.

Even more specifically, though, it is the subject matter of this book – the power of speech and the necessity of care in its usage – that most closely reflects my father's essence. He had an endless love for good words, and the true and lasting goodness that words can do and can bring about. He was a master of language, and had a deep appreciation for the power of words to educate, to inspire, to inform, to console, to gladden, to teach, to comfort, to cheer, to edify, and to elevate the world in God's image. He infused words with kindness, compassion, sensitivity, and generosity of spirit, and served as an exemplar of how the defining attribute of humanity, the power of speech, can be a benefit to the world rather than its undoing. It is most fitting that this work, arriving in anticipation of his first *yahrtzeit,* be dedicated in his memory. It is my fervent prayer that it will do honor to his legacy, and that his equal partner in all things, my mother, finds in it comfort and solace.

I extend my profound gratitude to my father-in-law, Rabbi Mordechai Feuerstein, for all of his kind support and encouragement, and we will forever be inspired and guided by the memory and the lifework of my extraordinary mother-in-law, Rebbetzin Shaindel Feuerstein, *a"h.* We are deeply fortunate to have the love and guidance of my wife's esteemed grandmother, Mrs. Shirley Feuerstein, and of so many beloved aunts, uncles, and cousins on both sides of the family.

In particular, I express tremendous gratitude for the constant support and guidance of my uncle and aunt, Rabbi Meyer and Goldie Fendel, and their entire family, and for that of my aunts and uncles Drs. Miriam and Ben Landau, Trude B. Feldman, and Ruth and Colin Lever.

It is an immense blessing that our children are guided by the life and legacy of two sets of grandparents who, following their own parents, placed the vision of *ḥesed* at the forefront of all that they ever did, and crowned their many accomplishments with kindness, compassion, and boundless communal service.

Finally, nothing I do would begin to be possible without my wife Leah; and still nothing can begin to be expressed, as her modesty combines with the limitations of language in preventing me from saying even a fraction of what should be said. I will only express my continued gratitude that our children, Adina, Ya'akov, Miriam, Shaindel, and Tehilla, have the role model they have in all the ways of life, and that a beacon of *ḥesed* lights their path.

Foreword

We are pleased to present to the public this new volume on the laws of *lashon hara* (derogatory speech) authored by Rabbi Daniel Feldman, who serves as a Rosh Yeshiva at the Rabbi Isaac Elchanan Theological Seminary (RIETS) and is also the executive editor of the RIETS Press. This book is an important contribution to the RIETS Halakha Series, which seeks to educate the public in a sophisticated and comprehensive fashion regarding the application of Jewish law to modern day life.

The topic of *lashon hara* is well known throughout the Jewish world, but is often muddled in mystique and misunderstanding. On the one hand, it is not in consonance with the culture of the Jewish people to take monastic vows of silence. On the other hand, whenever words are uttered, the possibility of uttering some form of *lashon hara* seems virtually like a *pesik reishei* – an inevitable consequence of normal human discourse. Indeed, the Talmud (*Bava Batra* 165a) states that one of the three areas of transgression that no human being can escape each day is *avak lashon hara* – the "dust" of derogatory speech. As King Solomon proclaimed, *kol hadevarim yege'im – lo yukhal ish ledaber* – "all words are wearisome; one becomes speechless" (Eccl. 1:8; see Yoma 19b).

Nonetheless, Rabbi Yisrael Meir Kagan, who authored the seminal work *Ḥafetz Ḥayim* concerning the myriad prohibitions related to *lashon hara* and the numerous types of speech and communication that are interdicted, was reputed to have talked constantly.[1] While there are numerous pitfalls, if someone truly understands and masters the laws of *lashon hara,* it is perfectly possible to engage in regular conversation without violating any transgressions. Along these lines, the purpose of this volume is precisely to explain and elucidate the rules in a fashion that will enable a reader to both appreciate the guidelines and engage in more edified discourse.

Additionally, what is often overlooked is that there are many occasions when Jewish law actually requires the dissemination of negative information that would normally be prohibited as *lashon hara.* In fact, some authorities have bemoaned the phenomenon that sometimes people will freely share derogatory information when prohibited, such as in the context of trivial conversation, but will adamantly refuse to share such information when required under Jewish law, such as to warn others against an unwise marriage proposal or a treacherous business partnership.[2] It is therefore imperative to understand all of the nuances of the laws of *lashon hara* not only to avoid negative speech, but to know when the halakha actually requires the sharing of negative information.

One major problem is that people are often wont to tackle the symptoms rather than the causes of *lashon hara.* It is not uncommon to observe campaigns waged not to speak *lashon hara* for a certain period of time, such as by designating a "*lashon hara* awareness day." With tremendous sincerity, communities of people unite in their resolve to avoid *lashon hara* during that time frame. However, what often happens is that murky situations arise, and despite the best of intentions, individuals fall back into their customary patterns.

---

1. See Rabbi Yissocher Frand, www.torah.org, on *Parashot Tazria–Metzora,* transcribed by David Twersky in the name of Rabbi Berel Wein in the name of his father-in-law, Rabbi Layzer Levine, who grew up in the house of Rabbi Kagan.
2. See *Ḥafetz Ḥayim, Laws of Rechilut, klal* 9.

In contrast, this book cuts to the core of the issue. Rabbi Feldman not only spells out the multitudinous scenarios of prohibited speech but also penetrates to its root causes from a psychological and emotional perspective, marshaling both rabbinic and secular sources to explore the motivations and underpinnings of the desire to engage in *lashon hara*. In clear and systematic fashion, Rabbi Feldman demonstrates how the exercise of *lashon hara* is almost always counterproductive in terms of attaining the very goals sought by the speaker in the first place.

Finally, Rabbi Feldman includes a groundbreaking examination of the dangers of the Internet and social media in the context of *lashon hara* laws, analyzing notions such as the disinhibition effect that makes people more prone to engage in irresponsible dialogue when sitting alone next to a computer and releasing toxic messages into the amorphous and anonymous cloud of cyberspace. For anyone trying to navigate the challenges of communication in the contemporary world, this book is truly indispensable.

Our Sages teach us that *deva'ei ḥayim belishanei* (Arakhin 15b) – proper speech, grounded in words of Torah, provides the elixir for life. Yeshiva University and RIETS are fortunate to be led by President Richard M. Joel, who has constantly urged students and faculty to use their speech in an ennobling fashion, thus enabling a meaningful and purposeful existence. Former Rosh Yeshiva Rabbi Norman Lamm, Dean Emeritus Rabbi Zevulun Charlop, and Rabbi Menachem Penner, Dean of RIETS, have all contributed mightily towards the life-affirming atmosphere of our yeshiva, and have served as role models in using their speech to inspire and educate others. Finally, we are most indebted to Rabbi Daniel Feldman for sharing with us not only his expository excellence, but also his vast talmudic and academic erudition in fashioning this monumental work.

It is our hope and expectation that all those who read this volume will gain both a better understanding of the intricacies of the laws of *lashon hara* as well as the wherewithal and *weltanschauung* to weather and withstand its challenges.

Rabbi Yona Reiss
Director, RIETS Press
Tevet 5775

Section One:
The Theory

Introduction: The Mysterious Peddler

Many hundreds of years ago, a traveling peddler arrived in the Galilean town of Tzippori (Sepphoris), proclaiming, in the style of the day, the wares he had to offer. The peddler announced to all who would listen, "Who wishes to purchase the elixir of life?" As a crowd gathered, the peddler was exhorted to provide the enticing brew he was advertising. Finally, the peddler reached into his bag, but what he revealed was not a potion, but a parchment. He was holding a biblical text – specifically, the Book of Psalms – and, with great drama, he read from it: "Who is the man who desires life, and loves days, that he may see good?Guard your tongue from evil, and your lips from speaking deceitfully. Turn from evil, and do good; seek peace, and pursue it" (34:13–15).

Apparently, the peddler was not simply reciting biblical verses; nor were his prospective customers disappointed. Even great scholars, such as the venerable R. Yannai, were deeply impressed. He was moved to exclaim that King Solomon, the son of the psalmist King David, had made a similar statement: "One who guards his mouth and his tongue guards his soul from troubles" (Prov. 21:23). R. Yannai stated nonetheless that he had studied this verse in Psalms all his life, and never fully appreciated its scope until the peddler opened his eyes.[1]

The tale of the peddler captured the attention of many rabbinic commentators, who offer varying insights as to the thrust of its message. To some, the significance of the story is not to identify the transgression of malicious speech – that prohibition, as we will see, is thoroughly expressed throughout the entire development of Jewish law, in the Torah and in the rabbinic writings, in narrative sections as well as in legal declarations, in admonishments of character refinement, and in prophetic condemnations.

Rather, the intent of the peddler's message is to convey the havoc that gossip wreaks upon life in this world, the here and now – not only the spiritual devastation that is imposed, and the guilt incurred, but the damage inflicted upon day-to-day life. Thus, the question is "who desires life": not only the eternal life of the soul, but the physical life of the social being on this earth.[2]

Others feel that the story conveys a positive, proactive perspective on the unsavory subject of malicious gossip. The devastating impact of evil speech is well known – the shattered reputations, the destroyed relationships, and the devastated psyches cannot go unnoticed. But the idea that vigilance in this area can be presented not only as a cautionary exhortation, but as an affirmative worldview, as a recipe for a rich and meaningful existence, an "elixir of life"; this is innovative and invigorating. Thus, not only does the verse emphasize "turn from evil," but equally, "do good; seek peace, and pursue it."[3]

1. Versions of this story appear in Leviticus Rabba 16:2 and in *Yalkut Shimoni* 11:767. A different version, involving R. Alexandri, can be found in Avoda Zara 19b. The presentation here is a composite of these versions. For a harmonization of the various versions, see Rabbi Yaakov Shechter, *Divrei Yaakov,* Prov. 4:3, n. 5. See also Maharal of Prague, *Netivot Olam* 2, *Netiv HaLashon,* ch. 1, and Rabbi Reuven Schwartz, *Emek HaLashon* 23.
2. See, for example, Rabbi Betzalel Rudinsky, *Mishkan Betzalel,* Leviticus, pp. 114–15; see also Rabbi Yosef Greenwald, *Vayeḥi Yosef,* Genesis, p. 57, and *Kokhav MiYaakov,* cited in Rabbi Yoel Menaḥem Mendel Saḥarov, *Menaḥem Yisrael,* in *Otzar Tehillot Yisrael,* p. 346.
3. On the exact reading of this verse, see *Tosafot* to Yevamot 109b, s.v *atia.*

This positive emphasis carries a further message: not only can the ethic of speech be addressed in a life-affirming fashion, but perhaps it must be done so; maybe the only successful approach in this realm is one that centers on the promise of a rich, optimistic life rather than a fearful existence of silence. Thus, the exemplar of the message is not a cloistered monk, but a gregarious, talkative salesman.[4]

In fact, the salesman seems to be a deeply ironic choice. The word used to identify him – the *rokhel* – describes the very same occupation the Torah uses to *prohibit* malicious speech: "You shall not go about as a *rokhel* among your people" (Lev. 19:16). In this verse, the peddler is seen as representative of one who travels from place to place with his "wares," the salacious tales he has gleaned about others. In the verse in Psalms, the peddler plays the opposite role, leading some major thinkers to conclude that he represents a penitent former gossip, infused with the zeal of the converted.[5] He is one who has been deeply affected by the corrupting effects of disparaging others and has come out on the other side, transformed and imbued with a passionate appreciation for positivity and a desire to share that with others. This is, in effect, his penance – to serve as the apostle for elevated speech, to engage others in his new vision of what life can be like.[6]

More than one hundred years ago, a humble yet revered Polish rabbi by the name of Yisrael (Israel) Meir Kagan (1838–1933) took up both the charge and the language of the mysterious peddler. Rabbi Kagan

---

4. See, along these lines, Rabbi Avraham Shmuel Binyamin Sofer, *Ketav Sofer* to Leviticus, *Parashat Metzora*; Rabbi Natan Gestetner, *Lehorot Natan*, to Leviticus; *Mishkan Betzalel*, Leviticus, pp. 103–11; and the approbation of Rabbi Isser Zalman Meltzer to Rabbi Shmuel Hominer, *Ikkarei Dinim*. See also Rabbi Asher Weiss, *Minḥat Asher*, Leviticus, pp. 478–79 and *BeYad HaLashon*, pp. 307–10. See also Rabbi Yeḥiel Libshitz, *HaMidrash VeHaMaase* 111, *Parashat Metzora* 1, who explains accordingly the difference between *shemira* and *netzira*.
5. This was the view of Rabbi Tzaddok HaKohen of Lublin.
6. For further analysis of this story, see also the discussions in Rabbi Yosef Tzvi Dushinsky, *Torat Maharitz*, Leviticus, and Rabbi Yaakov Kaminetsky, *Emet LeYaakov*, *Parashat Metzora*, as well as the interpretation of Rabbi Barukh Meir Klein, *Imrei Barukh* to *Parashat Metzora*, and Rabbi Yosef Oḥayon, in the journal *HaMaor*, Kislev–Tevet 5773, p. 29, citing the work *Yoshev Ohalim*. See also Rabbi Barukh Mordekhai Ezraḥi, *Birkat Mordekhai* to *Parashat Metzora*.

published a volume, first issued in 1873, that revitalized the study of the Jewish laws of speech, taking his title from the phrase that the peddler emphasized: *Ḥafetz Ḥayim*, or "Desirer of Life." In doing so, the rabbi, who came to be known by the title of his work, placed the principles of careful speech at the forefront of the awareness of a broad section of the population, and sparked a movement that continues to grow to this day, inspiring Jews all over the world to devote their energies to "guarding their tongue."[7] In this, he gave magnificent realization to the message of the peddler, which, according to some thinkers, was that the well-known and ancient precepts of speech needed to be actively brought to the attention of the public, and that doing so is the elixir of life to which the verse refers.[8]

The Jewish prohibition against malicious gossip – known by the Hebrew phrase *lashon hara* (lit., evil tongue), is at once simple and complex, easy to observe and irresistibly difficult, intuitive and shocking, obvious and deeply mysterious.

The prohibition of *lashon hara* may have the distinction of being the quintessential Jewish precept. Rooted firmly in the realm of interpersonal law, it is not a ritual statute, but is accessible to human understanding. Yet, it builds on a somewhat nonintuitive element that places it just beyond the range of laws that society would be assumed to innovate, absent divine command.[9]

Often rendered as "slander,"the term "*lashon hara*" in contemporary usage is generally exclusive of that term. Slander is a false allegation, which in Jewish law is termed *motzi shem ra*. *Lashon hara*, by contrast, disparages by conveying true information. This is one area in which the

7. For emphatic rabbinic endorsements of the study of this work in different generations, see *Sedei Ḥemed, Maarekhet HaLamed, klal* 63, and Rabbi Yisrael Yaakov Kanievsky, *Karyana DeIgarta* 111:846.
8. See *Lehorot Natan*, Leviticus, and see also Rabbi Yitzḥak Arama, *Akedat Yitzḥak*, Leviticus, *shaar* 62. See also the commentary of *Maharzu* to the Leviticus Rabba, 16:2, who notes that the main lesson of the verse can be identified in the dramatic presentation "who wishes to purchase the elixir of life?" rather than a more prosaic formulation such as "life can be attained through guarding one's tongue."
9. In fact, the editor of *BeYad HaLashon* (pp. 291–93) suggests that the lesson that R. Yannai learned from the peddler is that the precepts of *lashon hara* are not self-evident, and require a knowledgeable teacher to convey them.

novelty of the halakha (Jewish law) manifests itself. The wrongdoing of slander is self-evident, and thus the offense is subject to civil sanction, along with its written correlate, libel. However, in the realm of slander and libel, truth is an absolute defense. The notion that a statement could be true, and yet still be forbidden, is profoundly innovative. Granted, indulgence in gossip is unsavory; nonetheless, it is presumed that a divide exists between the nasty and the criminal.

It is here, then, that the halakha makes a unique contribution. An action perceived to be mean-spirited, but permissible, instead displays the interconnectedness between malice of thought and legislated prohibition. As such, Jewish law guides the individual toward an elevated perception of interpersonal sensitivity. Thus, there is as well a unique opportunity in this subject matter: to unite elements of thought, attitude, and philosophy with deed and effect, all deeply and richly guided by the Torah and rabbinic literature, toward an integrated and effective personality. Perhaps this is the message of the peddler: amid all the other rules and precepts of Jewish practice, here is an area where particular attention can yield the key to "life."[10]

From the time of the Talmud until this very day, Jewish legal literature has focused its attention on comprehending the prohibition of *lashon hara* and its many related precepts. Its parameters have been defined, over the course of much (continuing) debate and rabbinic exchange; its nature has been probed; its damage has been assessed; and its effect has been analyzed and decried, the subject of equal measures of cold legal analysis and hot ethical excoriation. At the same time, this transgression has been understood as a corruption of character rather than commission, an element of personality more than practice.

Therefore, it is worth examining the relationship of thought to deed in regard to the prohibition of *lashon hara,* and the extent to which this relationship is manifest in the legal underpinnings of the precept. To do so, we must consider the roots and the values of *lashon hara* and its related concepts.

---

10. See *Ḥiddushei HaRadal* to Leviticus Rabba, 16:13, and compare Rabbi Simḥa Bunim Sofer, *Shaarei Simḥa, Parashat Metzora,* s.v. *BiHaMedrash.*

A number of glaring questions present themselves, for example:

- As mentioned above, *lashon hara* certainly includes, if not exclusively, stating true facts. Are we bidden then, to conceal the truth, to be in any sense less than honest? How can a religious system built on truth, commanded by a God whose "seal is truth" (Shabbat 55a), tolerate, let alone demand, an embargo on factual revelation?
- Not only is it prohibited to speak gossip, there is an equal (perhaps greater) prohibition of "receiving," which might be understood as "believing," such gossip. How can one be expected to control his beliefs? More pointedly, if the information is indeed true and factually accurate, would not refusing to believe be an act of willful ignorance and self-deception? Can Jewish law actually demand such a perspective?
- Further, does a reluctance to speak and believe the truth not expose the public to terrible danger from those who would seek to do them harm? How can the undeniable and crucial mandate to protect the innocent accept such restrictions? How does Jewish law expect danger to be avoided, and society to be healed of its ills, let alone progress to be made in any area, if negative speech is to be banned?
- Why should such a severe prohibition be attached to mere speech, with no accompanying "sticks and stones"? This is particularly surprising in light of the fact that all human beings at some time or another are irresistibly tempted by at least minor gossip: Is an impossible standard being demanded, against an inevitable element of life?

In the contemporary era, these questions have become only more complex and more urgent. We live now in an era of unprecedented connectedness, where the global village is smaller than ever. The benefits of the information age are widely recognized, and the ability of an informed citizenry to both protect its interests and advance its aspirations is deeply appreciated. Advances in technology together with the accomplishments of many fields of social sciences and arts have brought new value to openness and disclosure. Increasing awareness of horrible crimes and offenses that have been perpetrated under the veil of secrecy and concealment has further indicated that there exists today a greater access to vital information that has not always been forthcoming.

At the same time, the potential for devastation from a misplaced item of information or innuendo has reached unprecedented heights. The speed and ease with which utter personal destruction and irreparable social division – whether the result of malice, misinformation, or well-intentioned miscalculation – can be brought about through the transmission of words is staggering. The need for a deeper appreciation of all of the conflicting values and realities in this realm is manifestly self-evident.

In the coming pages, we will attempt to address these questions. Clearly, any effort to do so sits under an enormous shadow, cast by the giant who influences every discussion of the topic, in general or on any specific point, the *Ḥafetz Ḥayim*. The contribution of the *Ḥafetz Ḥayim* provides us with much more than a compendium of sources and rulings; the very existence of his work, just as that of the midrash that recounts the peddler's mission, serves as a vital foundation for further discussion.

Over the past two centuries, objections have been raised against the *Ḥafetz Ḥayim*'s methodology, particularly regarding the risks inherent in converting principles that seem to be directed toward character into rules of practice, and, further, the codification of regulations in an area that involves highly variable situations with subjective interpretations and conflicting imperatives.[11] However, it is our premise that the *Ḥafetz Ḥayim*'s works represent a crucial step in the communal discussion, establishing that this area, so often perceived as outside the arena of conventional halakha, is in fact a deeply mandatory and regulated realm treated as such by the Torah, the Talmud, and great medieval halakhic codifiers such as Maimonides. Such awareness, however, need not ignore the complexities raised by the objectors. It may, though, necessitate a different approach of halakhic discussion: one that integrates an exploration of the theory of the concept; a consideration of the relevant psychological, sociological, and interpersonal realities; and a traditional

11. See Benjamin Brown, "From Principles to Rules and from Musar to Halakhah: The *Hafetz Hayim*'s Rulings on Libel and Gossip," *Dine Israel* 25 (2008): 171–256.

analysis and survey of the legalistic material in the hope of emerging with a refined sensitivity to the issues at hand. This, in turn, should result in a more ideal realization of the practical commandments of the Torah. It is our aspiration in the coming pages to take at least a few small steps in this direction, and it is our hope that in doing so, we can give further expression to the promises of King David, the mysterious peddler, and the *Ḥafetz Ḥayim*, for a better life.

The Textual Case Against Lashon HaRa: From Concept to Precept

The sheer weight of condemnation that Jewish tradition places on *lashon hara* is staggering. It begins with several commandments in the Torah, along with at least one cautionary tale and one punitive disease; and extends through numerous harshly worded statements in rabbinic literature, continuing into the extensive codification and devoted attention of the past century.

The phrase "*lashon hara*" does not appear in the Torah itself, although it appears frequently in rabbinic literature. The primary prohibition in the Torah addressing *lashon hara* is the verse, "You shall not go about as a *rakhil* among your people" (Lev. 19:16). In this verse, the word *rakhil* – the same word used to describe the mysterious peddler discussed in the introduction[1] – is generally rendered in this context

1. There is a slight difference in the word form; see Nahmanides to Lev. 19:16, and see also his extensive discussion of the translation of Onkelos.

as a "gossipmonger"[2] or "talebearer"[3] or "gossiper."[4] The connotation is one who travels from place to place offering merchandise, and thus the imagery is one who carries all the latest gossip to hungry ears far and wide.

Maimonides, in his classic legal code,[5] describes a *rakhil* as one who "collects information and [then] goes from person to person."[6] Following this description, he appears to identify four categories of transgressors that are addressed by this verse:[7]

1. The first category, related to the default term of *rekhilut* (the gerund form of *rakhil*), is one who relates to people what has been said about them: "This is what so-and-so said. This is what I heard about so-and-so." Even if the statements are true, relating them "destroys the world."
2. The second category, which refers to the classic *lashon hara*, is one who speaks to the disparagement of his fellow, "even though he speaks the truth."

---

2. Artscroll translation.
3. Hertz and Koren translations.
4. *The Living Torah* translation. The Jewish Publication Society (JPS) translation renders the phrase, "Do not deal basely with your countrymen," with a footnote noting that the meaning of the word *rakhil* is not known.
5. *Mishneh Torah, Laws of Personal Development* 7:2.
6. This phrasing appears in Y. Pe'ah 1:1; and similar language is in *Sifra, Parashat Kedoshim* 40; see Rabbi Menaḥem Krakowsky, *Avodat Melekh* to *Mishneh Torah, Laws of Personal Development* 7:1.
7. This listing is based on Maimonides's statements as understood by his primary commentator Rabbi Yosef Karo in *Kesef Mishneh,* and thus avoids certain ambiguities in Maimonides's own language. In particular, Maimonides does not clearly state that *rekhilut* is relayed to the subject of the speech. This is, however, stated explicitly in *Sefer Mitzvot Gadol,* prohibition 9 and the *Sefer HaḤinnukh* 236; and may be inferred from Sanhedrin 31a, as discussed above. See also *Kiryat Sefer* to *Mishneh Torah, Laws of Personal Development* and *Sefer HaBattim, azhara* 301.
   See the commentary *Daat UMaḥashava* to *Mishneh Torah, Laws of Personal Development,* who suggests that Maimonides understands *rekhilut* to be gossip that is not inherently negative, in contrast to *lashon hara,* and cites as well an interpretation of Rabbi Ḥayim Vital, that *lashon hara* is what is spoken by the first party, while those who continue to spread the item are engaged in *rekhilut.* See also *Leḥem Yehuda,* to *Mishneh Torah, Laws of Personal Development,* and *Emek HaLashon* 14. See also the analysis in Rabbi Mordekhai Tzvi Zilber, *Zikhron David,* pp. 109–10.

3. The third category is the slanderer, known as *motzi shem ra.*
4. The fourth category is one who is a habitual gossip, one who "sits" and shares all kinds of derogatory information, whom Maimonides terms a "*baal lashon hara.*"[8] It is this individual, he writes, who is referred to in Psalms 12:4: "God shall cut off all equivocating (lit., smooth) lips, and the tongue that speaks boastfully (lit., great things)."

It is this taxonomy that originated the contemporary usage according to which *lashon hara* refers to true information, and *mozti shem ra* to slander.[9] However, this distinction should not be taken as absolute. While both phrases appear in the Talmud, it is not obvious that they are distinguished in this manner,[10] and it is not clear that Maimonides means to indicate that *lashon hara* contains total and unadulterated truth.[11] What is clear, though, is that truth is not a defense against an accusation of *lashon hara.*

8. There is some ambiguity as to whether this is actually a fourth category, distinct from *lashon hara;* see Rabbi Yitzḥak Ratzabi, *Einei Yitzḥak,* p. 333–34n7, and *Kodesh Yisrael,* 2:3. See also Rabbi Ephraim Greenblatt, *Responsa Rivevot Ephraim* IV:35 and the extensive analysis in *Emek HaLashon* 46.
9. Maimonides also makes this distinction in his commentary to Pirkei Avot 1:7. Nahmanides, in his biblical commentary (Num. 13:32), writes that the term *motzi dibba* is used for a false report, whereas *mevi dibba* is used for a true report. See also *Pardes Yosef HaḤadash,* Deuteronomy, p. 943, sec. 91, and *Iyyunim BaParasha,* Leviticus, pp. 90–91.
10. See *Avodat Melekh* and *Ḥafetz Ḥayim, Laws of Lashon HaRa* 1:1, for suggestions as to the talmudic basis for the distinction.
11. See, particularly, *Migdal Oz,* to *Mishneh Torah, Laws of Personal Development,* and see also Rabbi Eliyahu Katz, in *Har HaMelekh,* vol. v, *Laws of Personal Development* 7:2 and Rabbi Barukh Reuven Shlomo Shlesinger, *Birkat Reuven Shlomo,* Sota, sec. 30. There are many references in the Talmud and rabbinic literature using the term *lashon hara* that seem to refer to falsehoods – see for example Shabbat 33b; Pesaḥim 118a (see Rabbi Elazar Kalir, *Or Ḥadash,* loc. cit.); Sota 35a; *Yalkut Shimoni, Parashat Shelaḥ* 13:87; Rashi to Taanit 7b, s.v. *ruaḥ,* and *Tosafot* s.v. *panim;* Rashi to Shabbat 118b, s.v. *lo;* Rashi to Sanhedrin 103a, s.v. *lo* (and *Margoliyot HaYam,* to to Sanhedrin 103a, cit. no. 12) and elsewhere. See Rabbi Reuven Margoliyot, *Nefesh Ḥayya, Oraḥ Ḥayim* 156:12 and Rabbi Yehoshua of Kutno, *Me'at Tzari* in *Yeshuot Malko* to *Mishneh Torah, Laws of Personal Development* 7:2. Rabbi Ḥayim Ḥizkiyahu Medini, *Sedei Ḥemed, Maarekhet HaLamed, klal* 63, concludes that at least in talmudic

Further, the distinction between *rekhilut* and *lashon hara,* with the former referring to information told directly to the subject regarding what has been said about him, is also not explicit in the Talmud. However, it may be inferred from a passage in the Talmud (Sanhedrin 31a) in which the prohibition of "peddling" is invoked to prohibit one member of a rabbinic tribunal from informing a litigant that he had voted in his favor, but was outvoted by the majority.[12] Such disclosure has the effect of telling the subject that other individuals spoke against him, thus arousing his ire at those specific people. This ruling might provide the basis for the understanding of Maimonides and others that conversation of this nature constitutes the essence of *rekhilut.* Similarly, the *Ḥafetz Ḥayim* asserts that the prohibition covers not only

language, *lashon hara* refers both to truth and falsehoods, as does the Maharsha to Shabbat 33b, *Ḥiddushei Aggadot,* s.v. *VeHaMelekh.* Similarly, Rabbi Menaḥem Troyesh, in his *Oraḥ Meisharim* 8:4, asserts that the distinction is not found in the Talmud, and Maimonides created it in order to facilitate memory by assigning appropriate categories. See also *Zikhron David,* pp. 25–26, and Rabbi Ḥayim Kanievsky, *HaSam Orḥotav* 6. Rabbi Tzvi Hirsch Frimer, *Responsa Eretz Tzvi* 1:4, puts forward an innovative theory: in his formulation, *lashon hara* includes and prohibits both true and false statements, as long as the derogatory statements are of a general nature not connected to actual substantive guilt. However, if the reference is to an actual spiritual or moral transgression, then the prohibition of *lashon hara* forbids only a false allegation, but not a true one, which should still be concealed (assuming it is not harmful to do so) as a matter of good policy and piety but not as an absolute prohibition. Concerning the specific question addressed by Rabbi Frimer (one who intentionally witnesses the misdeed of another, or calls it to the attention of another to witness), compare Rabbi Nissim Karelitz, *Ḥut Shani,* p. 336, and Rabbi Yosef Shalom Elyashiv, *Kovetz Teshuvot* II, 20:4.

Rabbi Avraham Yosef Ehrman, *Kodesh Yisrael* 3, interprets Rabbeinu Yonah's position to be that *motzi shem ra* is distinguished from *lashon hara* in that the former is more public and necessarily changes the status of the subject from one with a positive reputation to one with a negative reputation.

12. See Sanhedrin 31a and *Mishneh Torah, Laws of the Sanhedrin* 22:7–8. Note also that there are variant texts suggesting that the source for this ruling is actually Prov. 11:13. See Rabbi Tzvi Yehuda ben Yaakov, *Mishpatekha LeYaakov* III, 31:15, regarding the classification of this ruling; as to whether the other judges can grant permission for this revelation, see *Responsa Az Nidberu* XIV, 66:11. See also the discussion in *Kodesh Yisrael* 8. Regarding a situation in which one judge feels the ruling is in error and feels obligated to inform the litigant so he can pursue corrective action, see *Tur* and *Shulḥan Arukh, Ḥoshen Mishpat* 19:1, with *Baḥ, Knesset HaGdola,* and *Tummim.*

information that the listener does not know; *rekhilut* is committed even if the speaker is merely "riling up" the listener concerning a fact already known, as this causes conflict.

Maimonides further distinguishes between *rekhilut* and *lashon hara* by maintaining that the latter is far worse. He does not, however, explain why this is so, and thus the task is left to the commentaries to take up. One suggestion is made by Radbaz (Rabbi David ben Zimra, 1480–1589), who notes that *rekhilut,* addressed to the subject of the gossip, is an attempt to curry favor with the subject by providing information relevant to him.[13] *Lashon hara,* which does not have even that potential of self-interest for the speaker, is thus the result of pure malice.[14] It is noteworthy that Raavad (Rabbi Avraham ben David of Posquières), Maimonides's frequent interlocutor, takes issue with his ranking, and appears to assert that *rekhilut* is actually the greater offense. There is much discussion in the later works as to the substance and the details of their dispute,[15] but one general approach is to interpret *rekhilut* and *lashon hara* as representing two categories of damage brought about through speech: *rekhilut* provokes fights between people, while *lashon hara* involves disparaging an individual.[16] Within such an

---

13. *Responsa Radbaz* I, *LeLeshonot HaRambam* 1.
14. See also Rabbi Avraham Yitzḥak HaKohen Kook, *Orot HaRambam,* in *Bein Shenei Kohanim Gedolim,* p. 138.
15. For analysis of their debate, see *Avodat Melekh, Ben Yedid, Beit Leḥem Yehuda, Mirkevet HaMishna* (Rabbi Aharon Alpandari), and *Shalal David* to *Mishneh Torah, Laws of Personal Development;* Rabbi Avraham Yitzḥak HaKohen Kook (of Rechovot) in the journal *HaBe'er* (Sanz), vol. XXIV, pp. 47–50; and Rabbi Binyamin Ehrentrau in the journal *Kol Torah* XL, p. 119–22. Many of these commentaries suggest that Maimonides and the Raavad define the terms differently from each other. See also Rabbi Naphtali Tzvi Yehuda Berlin, *Haamek She'ela* 28:3, who associates the view of Rabbi Aḥai Gaon with that of the Raavad.
    See also *Emek HaLashon* 15, who, in addition to analyzing the debate, suggests a number of practical ramifications, including the question of whether one may speak *lashon hara* in order to avoid a conflict being provoked by *rekhilut.*
16. See *Ḥafetz Ḥayim, Laws of Lashon HaRa, klal* 3, *Be'er Mayim Ḥayim* 6, and Rabbi Zevulun Shuv, *Shaarei Zevulun, Yoreh De'ah* 76. This characterization of *rekhilut* is built upon the assumption that it involves relating conversations to their original subjects; as noted, this is not explicit in Maimonides's words, although it is inserted by the *Kesef Mishneh.* The original language, which is missing that detail, may

understanding, Maimonides and Raavad differ as to which infliction of harm is more egregious.

While the "peddler verse" (Lev. 19:16) is well known as a source for the *lashon hara* prohibition, there is actually a dispute about the issue in the Talmud,[17] with an opinion locating the prohibition elsewhere: "You shall guard yourself against every evil thing" (Deut. 23:10), with the last word, *davar*, interpreted in the sense of the related word meaning "speech."[18] If the verse is indeed read that way, that is, "You shall guard yourself against every evil speech," it is then the closest the Torah comes to actually using the phrase *lashon hara* (lit., evil speech).

In his biblical commentary, Nahmanides understands the prohibition as specific to the context of the opening of the verse: "When you shall go out as a camp against your enemies." According to this explanation, there is an additional prohibition on derogatory speech

---

simply refer to the revelation of secrets, which "destroys the world" by eroding the elements of trust between people, but not necessarily by provoking dispute. See *Kodesh Yisrael,* 2:1.

Regarding the assumption that *rekhilut* is about provoking disputes, see *Shaarei Avraham,* pp. 324–25, for other scenarios in which speech is likely to evoke conflict and thus should be prohibited as some form of *rekhilut.*

A possible halakhic distinction premised on this categorization is considered by Rabbi Shmuel Ḥayim Lafier in the journal *Kol Torah* LV, pp. 61–65. If one is put on the spot by an inquiry that would require an answer that would be *rekhilut* or *lashon hara,* is one permitted to avoid the transgression by answering falsely, per the license of the Talmud (Yevamot 65b) to deviate from the truth in order to preserve harmony? While the *Ḥafetz Ḥayim* does allow this in *Laws of Rekhilut* 1:8, it is not clear that this would be the case regarding *lashon hara.* The explanation for a distinction between the two would be that *rekhilut* is about provoking conflict, so avoiding that transgression may be included in a mandate to preserve harmony, as opposed to *lashon hara,* which has a different focus and may not be included. However, see also *Ḥelkat Binyamin,* p. 50, who independently considers and rejects this distinction. For more on speaking falsehood to avoid *lashon hara,* see *Emek HaLashon,* pp. 125–26.

17. Ketubot 46a; in this passage, the term "*motzi shem ra*" is used; in Y. Pe'ah 1:1, the term "*lashon hara*" is used. See *Mishneh Torah, Laws of the Virgin Maiden* 3:1, with *Kesef Mishneh.*
18. Concerning this derivation, and its relationship to the "peddler verse," see *Penei Yehoshua* to Ketubot, and Rabbi Yaakov Ḥayim Sofer, *Torat Yaakov,* pp. 303–11 and Rabbi Shlomo Schneider, *Divrei Shlomo* IV, pp. 532–33.

during wartime, so as not to increase internal divisions at a dangerous time. The great twentieth-century commentator Rabbi Meir Simḥa of Dvinsk suggests both verses have their applications: the "peddler verse" prohibits internal *lashon hara,* while the verse in Deuteronomy warns against the exposure of sensitive secrets to the outside world.[19] It is also noteworthy that at least one major authority considers *motzi shem ra* to be proscribed by the biblical injunction, "And a man shall not wrong his fellow" (Lev. 25:17), a phrase understood by the Talmud (Bava Metzia 58b) to refer to verbal oppression.[20]

Not only is there a prohibition against spreading *lashon hara,* there is also a prohibition against "accepting" (*kabbala*) it. According to the Talmud, this prohibition is located earlier in the Torah, in a verse that is complicated to translate but appears to prohibit the "bearing" (*lo tissa*) of a report (*shema*) that is *shav* (Ex. 23:1), which is translated either as "false" or "unnecessary."[21] In that same talmudic passage, it is suggested that this verse addresses the speaker of *lashon hara* as well, as the report is "borne" by both the receiver and the transmitter.

In his assessment of the Torah's legislation against *lashon hara,* the *Ḥafetz Ḥayim* notes that there are numerous other negative and positive precepts, many of which are dependent on circumstances, that may also be contravened when malicious speech is spoken, and when relevant contribute to the severity of the offense. For example, he notes that the speaker may also be profaning the divine name; and may be guilty of separate interdictions involving arrogance, hatred, vengeance, entrapment, flattery, and humiliation,[22] and may also be disrespecting his parents or elders, or the sanctity of a synagogue or similar location.[23]

---

19. *Meshekh Ḥokhma* to Deuteronomy. See, at length, the analysis of these derivations in Rabbi Eliezer Yehuda Waldenberg, *Responsa Tzitz Eliezer* XX:6.
20. Rabbi Moshe Isserles, *Darkei Moshe, Ḥoshen Mishpat* 228:2.
21. *Pesaḥim* 118a. See also *Mishneh Torah, Laws of the Sanhedrin* 21:7.
22. See also the comment of Rabbi Avraham Yitzḥak HaKohen Kook on this point, together with the commentary of Rabbi Menaḥem Aryeh Kampinsky, *Be'er LaḤai Ro'i,* in *Bein Shenei Kohanim Gedolim,* pp. 101–5.
23. On this, see Rabbi Meir Peretz, in the journal *HaBe'er* (Sanz), XXIV, pp. 70–73.

In the Torah's presentation, the *lashon hara* interdict is backed up by more than law; there is a bodily affliction connected as well. The Torah (Lev. 13–14) speaks extensively of a malady known as *tzaraat*, a physical ailment which, the Sages explain, is brought about by spiritual deficiencies.[24] While there are a number of such failings that are blamed for this manifestation, the most prominent and commonly identified is that of malicious speech.[25] In line with this understanding, this section of the Torah constitutes not only a warning against the dangers of such speech, but a prohibition as well. The Torah later commands, in language utilized for prohibitions, a vigilance against allowing oneself to fall subject to this malady: "Take heed concerning the *tzaraat* affliction" (Deut. 24:8). Accordingly, that verse is considered yet another specific prohibition against engaging in malicious speech.[26]

More pointedly, the Torah tells of Miriam, sister of Moses, who spoke against her brother and was punished with this same ailment.[27] Yet again, a specific verse in the Torah (Deut. 24:9) mandates remembering

24. See *Tanḥuma, Metzora* 2, where, in the context of many negative statements regarding *lashon hara,* a linguistic relationship is related regarding *metzora* and *motzi shem ra.* Rabbi Yeshaya HaLevi Horovitz, known as the *Shla* (*Shenei Luḥot HaBrit*), Pesaḥim, *derush* 3 for *Shabbat HaGadol,* suggests there is a dual meaning to this relationship: not only is *motzi shem ra,* in the sense of slander, the cause of *metzora,* but one who finds himself a *metzora* must respond by being *motzi* the *shem ra* from himself; i.e., he must remove the tendency toward disparaging speech from his character.

25. Rabbi Barukh Dov Povarsky, in *Bad Kodesh, Parashat Metzora,* pp. 50–51, suggests that according to a popular theory that spiritual impurity corresponds to the loss of life potential, the significance of *tzaraat* to *lashon hara* is premised on the unique potential of the spiritual-physical synthesis represented by speech; he also explains the promise of the "mysterious peddler" in this way. A similar approach is used to explain the purification process of the *tzaraat*-inflicted individual in R. Avraham Elyashuv, *Bikkurei Avraham, Parashat Metzora,* pp. 272–73.

26. *Sifra, Parashat Beḥukkotai* 1. See also *Mishneh Torah, Laws of Contamination from Tzaraat* 16:10. The Maharil (*Minhagim, Laws of the Ten Days of Repentance, ot* 14, p. 309) understands this verse to constitute the main prohibition of *lashon hara.*

27. As to whether Miriam's speech was technically *lashon hara* or *motzi shem ra,* see Leviticus Rabba 16:1; *Haamek Davar* to Lev. 12:11 and Deut. 24:9; Rabbi Moshe

her transgression and its consequence. Some great authorities, such as Nahmanides, understand that verse to be an actual commandment,[28] one that obligates vigilance against such speech.[29]

Following this tradition, the Talmud (Arakhin 15b) states that one who engages in negative speech will be subject to "afflictions," narrowly taken as a reference to this ailment, but also interpreted as a general statement regarding punishments.[30]

Indeed, while the above reflects the legal mandates as set forward in the text of Scripture itself, the Talmud, through a number of statements and interpretations, adds very significantly to the condemnation of one who speaks *lashon hara.*

Among these statements are understandings of seminal events in biblical history in the context of forbidden speech. The snake in the Garden of Eden, which brought about the fall of Adam and Eve, engaged in *lashon hara* against God, portraying Him as a jealous deity who simply wanted to prevent Adam and Eve from sharing in His knowledge.[31] Later, Moses understands that the Jews, enslaved in Egypt, deserve their exile due to the maliciousness of their talk, as they mischaracterize his efforts to protect them.[32]

More recently, the ongoing exile of the Jewish people is blamed on their negative attitude toward one another, as well as their negativity towards the Land of Israel and God's gifts, as exemplified by the

---

Sofer, *Torat Moshe, Parashat Ki Tetzeh,* s.v. *zakhor;* Rabbi Shlomo Zalman Kook, *Mitzva Shelema,* p. 143:4; and *Ḥelkat Binyamin, Laws of Lashon HaRa* 1:5.

28. Biblical commentary, Leviticus, and glosses to Maimonides's *Sefer HaMitzvot,* positive commandment 7.
29. Nahmanides also implies that this is the core commandment regarding *lashon hara,* casting a question on his understanding of the "peddler verse"; see Rabbi Naḥum Brobovsky, *Shalmei Naḥum,* pp. 553–60.
30. See Rabbi Aharon Elḥanan Neubert, *Erekh HaḤayim,* Arakhin 15b; see also Rabbi Avraham Yisrael Moshe Solomon, *Netivot HaKodesh* to Arakhin.
31. See Genesis Rabba 20:1. As to whether the snake's claims were true or false, see Nahmanides to Gen. 2:9.
32. Exodus Rabba 1 and *Tanḥuma, Shemot* 10; see also Rashi to Ex. 2:14. Note the comments of the Lubavitcher Rebbe in *Shaarei Ahavat Yisrael,* pp 259–71, and particularly in *Likkutei Siḥot* XXXI, *Parashat Shemot* 2, and see also Rabbi Avigdor Parnes, *Lev Tahor,* pp. 334–35, and *Emek HaLashon* 11–12.

Sin of the Spies (Num. 13–14), who disparaged the Promised Land and began a spiral of descent into homelessness.[33] Interestingly, one talmudic passage (Arakhin 15a) considers the story of the spies to be yet another exhortation against *lashon hara,* stating that if their transgression, committed against an inanimate land ("sticks and stones"), deserved such punishment, it can be logically inferred that speaking about human beings, who have emotions and reactions, must be understood as a far worse violation.

Beyond these narrative interpretations, the Talmud and rabbinic literature are replete with general statements of condemnation of gossip and slander, clearly placing these offenses on a unique level of prominence within the pantheon of egregious spiritual violations.

A brief sampling of some of these statements would yield declarations that *lashon hara* is equivalent in severity to the three cardinal transgressions that demand martyrdom[34] (despite itself not having that requirement[35]); the speaker has no portion in the World to Come[36] and will not receive the Divine Presence (Sota 42a); the speaker has denied God and has sinned in a manner whose severity ascends to the heavens (Arakhin 15b); rains are held back from the world because of *lashon hara;*[37] the speaker is worthy of being thrown

33. The Talmud (Yoma 9b) attributes the destruction of the Temple to baseless hatred, which is presumably manifested in *lashon hara;* see introduction to *Ḥafetz Ḥayim,* and Rabbi Ḥayim Yudchik, *Shemuot Ḥayim,* Arakhin, ch. 3:22, as well as *Zikhron David,* p. 14, in a footnote.

34. Y. Pe'ah 1:1. For several explanations as to why this apparently extreme comparison is apt, see *Shaarei Teshuva* 3:203–9. See also *Zikhron David,* pp. 40–41.

35. See *Responsa Rivash* 171; *Shaarei Teshuva* 3:202, and Maharsha, Arakhin 15b; see also *Shemuot Ḥayim,* Arakhin 15b, and *Zikhron David,* pp. 41–42.

36. *Pirkei DeRabbi Eliezer,* ch. 52, *Mishneh Torah, Laws of Personal Development* 7:3. The *Ḥafetz Ḥayim, Laws of Lashon HaRa* 1:4, and *Be'er Mayim Ḥayim* 6 understands that this and similar statements mentioned above refer only to one who regularly engages in *lashon hara* (in Maimonides's parlance, the *baal lashon hara*). See also *Daat UMaḥashava* 7:2; Rabbi Yitzḥak Meir Patziner, *Parashat HaMelekh* to *Laws of Personal Development,* and *Emek HaLashon* 20, and pp. 104–5.

37. Taanit 7b; See also *Keren Ora,* and Rabbi Meir Leibush Malbim, *Ḥiddushei HaMalbim* to Taanit.

to the dogs;[38] and the speaker is considered to have violated all five books of the Pentateuch (Leviticus Rabba 16:6) and will not find atonement (Zevaḥim 88b). Many other condemnatory statements are presented by the Sages.[39]

This attitude extends into the liturgy as well. For example, in the litany of specific confessions recited in conjunction with Yom Kippur, sins connected to *lashon hara* occupy at least ten spaces.[40]

Much has been added to these condemnations in the later literature as well, but of particular note is a tradition that one who speaks badly of others will find himself, on the Day of Judgment, having absorbed all of the sins of his subject, while the subject will have himself taken on all of the merits of the speaker. This notion is conveyed by Rabbeinu Baḥya ibn Pekuda in his *Ḥovot HaLevavot*,[41] and has been widely commented upon in later literature. Among these later commentators is the twentieth-century ethicist Rabbi Eliyahu Dessler, who notes that the justice in this consequence derives from the fact that the offense is aggravated by the personal stature of the speaker: the positive reputation of the speaker lends weight to his words, thus enabling them to do more damage.[42] Accordingly, that stature is transferred from the offender to the victim.[43] Furthermore, Rabbi Dessler asserts that the

---

38. Pesaḥim 118a and Makkot 23a; for homiletic interpretations of this statement, see Rabbi Meir Eisenstatter, *Imrei Yosher*, p. 34; Rabbi Avraham Binyamin Silverberg, *Ḥemdat Binyamin* to Makkot; *BeYad HaLashon*, pp. 159–62; Rabbi Natan Gestetner, *Natan Piryo* to Makkot, p. 217.

39. See Rabbi Ḥayim Palagi, *Nefesh Ḥayim, Maarekhet HaLamed* 17 for a list of forty negative statements about *lashon hara* from the rabbinic literature. An extensive listing of many spiritual calamities that befall one who speaks *lashon hara* can be found in Rabbi Yitzḥak Zahler, *Yalkut Yitzḥak, mitzva* 237.

40. See Rabbi Avraham Yaakov Pam, *Moreh Tzedek*, p. 175, and Rabbi David Kronglass, *Siḥot Ḥokhma UMusar* 20.

41. *Shaar HaKniya, shaar* 6, ch. 7. See also *Orḥot Tzaddikim, shaar haanava*. The *Ḥafetz Ḥayim, Shemirat HaLashon, shaar hazekhira*, ch. 7, traces the idea to *Midrash Shoḥer Tov, mizmor* 42; see also Rabbi Tzvi Hirsch Frimer, *Responsa Eretz Tzvi* II, *derush* 2, who in a lengthy excursus challenges this source and suggests an alternative. See also Rabbi Eliezer Adirim, *Ateret Zahav*, pp. 65–68.

42. *Mikhtav MeEliyahu*, vol. IV, *biurim baagada* at end of ch. 1.

43. Similarly, see Rabbi Moshe Sternbuch, *Responsa Teshuvot VeHanhagot* V:396.

speaker is motivated by a desire to gain esteem through the degradation of his subject; thus, that effort is frustrated by his assuming of the subject's deficiencies.[44]

It emerges, quite bluntly, that throughout the development of Jewish law, from the Torah to the modern era, an extraordinary emphasis

---

44. See also Rabbi Ḥayim Friedlander, in the journal *Marpei Lashon* IV, pp. 59–62. See Rabbi Yosef Tzvi Dushinsky, *Torat Maharitz,* Leviticus, p. 23b, who connects this notion to the "peddler" tale, as does Rabbi Raphael Hamburger, *Marpei Lashon, Ammud HaYira,* sec. 2. See also Rabbi Barukh Tzvi Moskowitz, *Nishba LaAvotekha,* Avot, ch. 4, pp. 220–21, who explains the justice in this notion by noting the interconnectedness of the Jewish nation: one who interprets the behavior of others positively partakes of that positivity, and vice versa. See also the alternative explanations suggested by Rabbi Mordekhai Potash in the journal *Marpei Lashon* V, pp. 79–82, and by Rabbi Shalom Tzvi Shapiro in VII, pp. 129–32.

See also *Birkat Reuven Shlomo,* Sota, 30:18–22, and *Responsa* V:49, who analyzes this notion and considers whether it is a reference only to one who regularly speaks maliciously, or even does so only once; as well as whether repentance reverses the effect. See as well Rabbi Yisrael Yaakov Fisher, *Responsa Even Yisrael* IX:164. Rabbi Binyamin Yehoshua Zilber, *Responsa Az Nidberu* XIV:69, assumes that repentance could restore the merits, but only a complete repentance, while a lesser level may be effective for other purposes, such as avoiding punishment; see also Rabbi Moshe Sofer, *Derashot, derasha* for seventh of Adar, p. 170b, and *Torat Moshe, Parashat Tetzaveh,* p. 64a; *Ben Ish Ḥai* III, *derush* 3 for *Shabbat HaGadol,* p. 42; and Rabbi Yosef Tzvi Adler, *Al Pi HaTorah,* Leviticus. ch. 10: 72.

Strikingly, Rabbi Avraham Price, *Mishnat Avraham* to *Sefer Ḥasidim* 92:1, attributes a practical application to this transference. Commenting on a statement of the *Sefer Ḥasidim* 92:1 that one is not obligated to judge favorably a speaker of *lashon hara,* he explains that in general an individual has both merits and demerits, and thus one is obliged to give the benefit of the doubt; however, one who speaks *lashon hara* no longer has any merits.

This general idea of transference of merit and liability is surveyed in Rabbi Aharon Leib Shteinman, *Ayelet HaShaḥar,* Gen. 42:37. See also Rabbi Ḥayim Yosef David Azulai, *Zeroa Yamin* to Pirkei Avot 2:4; *Ḥiddushei Ḥatam Sofer,* Megilla 11a; and Rabbi Ḥayim Ḥizkiyahu Medini, *Sedei Ḥemed. Maarekhet HaAlef* 38. See also Rabbi Moshe Sternbuch, *Taam VeDaat* to Lev. 24:20; Rabbi Aryeh Mizraḥi, *Kerem Aryeh,* Ḥagiga 15a and Keritot 6b; Rabbi Ḥayim Mordekhai Gottlieb, *Derashot Yagel Yaakov,* p. 24; Rabbi Daniel Shteinshneider, *Divrei Daniel,* ch. 1:5, p. 1; Rabbi Nissim Dayan, *Zekukei Nura,* p. 33; Rabbi Asher Weiss, *Minḥat Asher,* Leviticus, p. 480; Rabbi Eliyahu Shlesinger, *Eila HaDevarim,* Leviticus, pp. 30–32; Rabbi Mordekhai Benedict, *She'arim Metzuyanim al HaTorah,* pp. 458–59; and Rabbi Yaakov Ḥayim Sofer in the journal *Or Yisrael* XL, p. 100ff.

has been put on offenses of speech, characterizing them as egregious, uniquely malicious, particularly harmful, strictly prohibited, degrading of character, far-ranging in their effect, and indeed standing at the forefront of every major sorrow that has befallen the Jewish people and all of humanity.[45] Clearly a message is being sent; the task remains to understand its substance.

45. One notable anomaly within this process has been the fact that the primary code of Jewish law, the *Shulḥan Arukh,* which follows the section arrangement of its predecessor the *Tur* (Rabbi Yaakov ben Asher, ca. 1270–1340) has neither a section nor even an individual paragraph directly recording the prohibition of *lashon hara.* However, as so much of the literature does reflect the prohibition, this omission poses a question more to the *Shulḥan Arukh* than to the place of *lashon hara* within the legal corpus. Discussions of this issue can be found in *Responsa Birkat Reuven Shlomo* I:109, and in the journal *Or Yisrael* (XXXII, p. 161, and XXXIV, p. 130, quoting Rabbi Shammai Kehat Gross in *Alim LiTrufa* 381), and Rabbi Gamliel Rabinowitz surveys various explanations in the journal *HaBe'er* (Sanz) XXIV, pp. 74–75.

But Words Will Never Hurt Me? Identifying the Harm of Lashon HaRa

All we have seen so far begs the question: What, in fact, is so terrible about *lashon hara*? Yes, slander is a vicious personal attack – but *lashon hara* is not limited to slander. Yes, gossip is nasty and unkind – but nasty and unkind is a far cry from the condemnation we have seen.

The literature offers many theories to address this question. It would seem that the question itself can be asked in two ways. First, what is so damaging about *lashon hara,* that it deserves such critical attention? Second, what is it within the human psyche that draws one into such behavior?

One noteworthy and oft-quoted passage from the Talmud (Arakhin 15b) may help to frame the discussion. *Lashon hara,* we are told, is uniquely damaging in that it "kills" three people: the one who speaks [the *lashon hara*], the one who accepts it [i.e., the listener], and the subject [the one about whom it is said]. While there is much to debate as to the exact intent of this passage, it conveys at least as a starting point the notion that the harm wrought by malicious speech is multifaceted, and prompts us to consider the multiple ways in which various principal players, and society itself, are affected.[1]

DAMAGE TO THE SUBJECT

The most obvious of the victims of *lashon hara* is the subject of the information. As the one being derogated, he or she is the first site of damage when targeted by malicious speakers. It would appear that the harm involved could be broken down into two distinct, but related, areas.

One approach is to focus on the value of an individual's reputation, and to work from an assumption that there exists a right to have one's reputation protected. This right is especially noteworthy in that it apparently protects the subject not only from false attacks, which is more easily understood, but even from statements of truth.

Understanding reputation as a right, or as a form of property, has strong foundation both in Jewish and in secular legal philosophy. The mishna (Avot 4:13) states that while there are many "crowns" that confer stature upon an individual, the "crown of a good name" is the most valuable. Indeed, much of Jewish law operates through the principle of *ḥazaka,* which might be roughly translated in this context as "presumption" but derives from a word that also means "to hold." A prominent example of this concept is *ḥezkat kashrut,* or the presumption of decency that an individual "possesses," due to a history of good behavior or at least the absence of bad behavior.

Similarly, from a legal perspective it has been posited that reputation is itself a form of property, the esteem of others earned by "the fruit of personal exertion," in the words of law professor Robert Post.[2] Thus,

1. It should be noted that there is much complexity as to the application of this phrase, and there is extensive discussion among the commentaries to the *Mishneh Torah, Laws of Personal Development* 7:2 as to its subject of reference, i.e., whether it is what has become known as *lashon hara* or as *rekhilut,* and the effect of the aforementioned dispute between Maimonides and the Raavad; see also Rashi and *Tosafot* to Arakhin, and *Oraḥ Meisharim* 8:1. We will not detail all of the various positions and interpretations here. See also *Emek HaLashon* 24.
2. Robert C. Post, "The Social Foundations of Defamation Law: Reputation and the Constitution" 74 *California Law Review* 691, 694 (1986).

as Daniel Solove notes in his book *The Future of Reputation*, "people work hard at building a reputation in society; and it can often be among a person's most valuable assets. One reason to protect reputation, then, is to preserve the years of effort people put into developing it."[3]

Post further suggests that reputation is an essential component of human dignity: "The dignity that defamation law protects is thus respect (and self-respect) that arises from full membership in society." Human dignity, while subject to varying definitions, is a hallowed principle in Jewish legal philosophy, an axiom that emanates from the creation of man in the image of God and one that has a tremendous impact on the priorities of Jewish law.[4] Specifically, the great medieval legal codifier Rabbeinu Asher (Rosh) writes that the embarrassment that comes from slander and other verbal offenses is far greater than that which comes from any physical humiliation.[5]

It must be emphasized that the above perspective posits reputation as an end in and of itself, inherently valuable and deserving of protection. The second type of personal damage from *lashon hara* is distinct from the first, yet flows directly from it: the concern that the spread of the item will result in actual material loss to the subject. Once the individual has been painted in a certain light, there is a clear and direct line towards all sorts of harm in every arena of life, whether in the dismantling of current realities or in the deprivation of future opportunities, or any combination thereof.[6]

Of course, in the case of both forms of damage, there are times when such impact is fair, necessary, and appropriate. Indeed, gossip, in the judgment-neutral form of the word, has from the dawn of humanity played an important role in the functioning of society, protecting the innocent while facilitating the advancement of its shared goals.[7]

---

3. Daniel J. Solove, *The Future of Reputation: Gossip, Rumor, and Privacy on the Internet* (New Haven, CT: Yale University Press, 2007), p. 34.
4. See Berakhot 19b; Shabbat 81b, 94b; Megilla 3b; and Eiruvin 41b.
5. Rosh, *Bava Kamma* VIII, 15.
6. For a discussion of legal remedies toward the protection of reputation, see Solove, *Future of Reputation*, 114–24.
7. For "defenses" of gossip, see Emrys Westacott, *The Virtue of Our Vices: A Modest Defense of Gossip, Rudeness, and Other Bad Habits* (Princeton, NJ: Princeton

In an environment of limited information, reputation is a crucial tool to allow the safe and productive progression and maintenance of the societal structure.

Further, reputation is as valuable as it is largely because it is not automatic or resistant to conflicting data, and because it does play a necessary part in influencing the actions of others. From the perspective of game theory, which analyzes the decisions made and affected by the evaluation of what others are likely to do, one author writes, "The importance of reputation explains why human language became important – so people could gossip. Gossip spreads reputation, making altruistic behavior based on reputation more likely.... Reputation breeds cooperation because it permits players in the game of life to predict the actions of others."[8] Similarly, Michael McCullough writes in his book *Beyond Revenge*: "These reputations have cash value: if you have a good reputation, people will be inclined to cooperate with you and treat you with respect. If you have a bad reputation, people will steer clear of you or actively work against you.... Reputations are used to establish cooperation not through direct reciprocity... but through indirect reciprocity."[9] In other words, bad behavior is punished not through retaliating with similar behavior, but through spreading the word so that the bad actor is punished through disassociation with others.

Similarly, the concern for preserving one's reputation is a crucial motivator of behavior, ensuring that an individual acts in a socially acceptable fashion so as to maintain his stature among others. In fact, from some perspectives, reputation is the single most effective tool

University Press, 2012), pp. 53–99; John D. Mayer, *Personal Intelligence: The Power of Personality and How It Shapes Our Lives* (New York: Scientific American; Farrar, Straus and Giroux, 2001), pp. 197–99; Solove, *Future of Reputation*, 63–65; and Nicholas DiFonzo, "The Gossip Paradox" at http://www.psychologytoday.com/blog/around-the-watercooler/201002/the-gossip-paradox.

8. Tom Siegfried, *A Beautiful Math: John Nash, Game Theory, and the Modern Quest for a Code of Nature* (Washington, DC: Joseph Henry, 2006), p. 87.
9. Michael McCullough, *Beyond Revenge: The Evolution of the Forgiveness Instinct* (San Francisco: Jossey Bass, 2008), pp. 107–9. See also Paul J. Zak, *The Moral Molecule: The Source of Love and Prosperity* (New York: Dutton, 2012), p. 72, and David DeSteno, *The Truth About Trust* (New York: Hudson Street Press, 2014), p. 15.

toward this end. In Plato's *Republic*, the author is asked by his brother, Glaucon, to consider the effect of the mystical ring of Gyges, which would confer invisibility upon its wearer. Could it still be expected that the bearer would continue to act honorably, knowing that his reputation was secure, as no one would perceive his bad behavior? While one would hope that there are other motivating factors, and indeed, that was Plato's response, there is much empirical evidence to endorse Glaucon's skepticism. In the words of Jonathan Haidt, who emphatically advocates this attitude in his book *The Righteous Mind,*[10] this reflects the realization that "the most important principle for designing an ethical society is to make sure that everyone's reputation is on the line all the time, so that bad behavior will always bring bad consequences."

Thus, it would seem unreasonable and unjust to insist that reputation be protected irrespective of the worthiness of the subject and his actions. Accordingly, no such insistence is made, nor should it be. Nonetheless, assessing what is fair, just, and necessary must begin by first acknowledging the importance of reputation, both as a means in and of itself and as a portal to both harm and benefit. If it is deemed imperative or justified to speak of a subject in a manner that will harm his reputation, the information that the speaker conveys about the subject should be accurate and necessary, and the damage caused to the subject should be proportionate.

One may object to any regulation in the area of expression, citing the hallowed principle of freedom of speech. However, a number of points must be noted regarding the interaction of this right with the prohibition of *lashon hara.* First and perhaps foremost, freedom of speech is a governmental right, while the ban on *lashon hara* is a religious and moral precept. To say this is not to demean the former to the benefit of the latter; it is merely to note that the two systems have different priorities. A government, such as that of the United States, must balance its obligations towards serving and protecting its citizens with protecting their liberties, in particular those that have been deemed most integral to the values of the nation. The axiom

10. Jonathan Haidt, *The Righteous Mind: Why Good People Are Divided by Politics and Religion* (New York: Pantheon, 2012), pp. 72–74 and throughout.

that a government may not interfere with a citizen's free speech in no way absolves the speaker of moral responsibility for his speech, or in any way exonerates the content of the speech, nor does it exempt the speaker from criticism, even from the perspective of the government itself.

Moreover, from a religious perspective the premise that religious precepts address all areas of life is a fundamental belief. Indeed, Rabbeinu Yonah of Gerona claims that speaking *lashon hara* is heretical because the speaker assumes that the realm of speech is outside of God's influence. This is reflected in the words of the psalmist, "God shall cut off all equivocating lips, and the tongue that speaks boastfully. Those who have said, 'with our tongues we shall prevail, our lips are with us, who is master over us?'"[11] (Ps. 12:4–5)

Second, even in regard to governmental legislation, freedom of speech is not absolute, and the degree to which it might be balanced by other considerations varies from society to society in those in which the value exists. Just as, for example, laws will not allow for slander or incitement within freedom of speech, the principle of *lashon hara* might be seen as an extension of these and other common limitations. This is particularly understandable in light of the fact that moral codes typically encompass a broader sphere of activity than that which is addressed by secular legal codes.

That being said, it need not be concluded that Jewish law discounts the value of free speech completely. In their book *The Offensive Internet: Speech, Privacy, Reputation*, Saul Levmore and Martha C. Nussbaum identify three theories of freedom of speech, and note that all three theories lend themselves to some form of regulation. They include John Stuart Mill's understanding that free speech protection is instituted to help society arrive at the truth; the notion that restriction of speech impinges on the autonomy of humans as free beings entitled to make their own choices; and the theory of Alexander Meiklejohn that free speech is important for the preservation of the open debate

11. Compare also *Tanḥuma, Metzora* 2.

necessary for democracy.[12] In line with their presentation, it may be consistent with these theories to assume the inverse: that speech that detracts from the truth, negates the dignity of others, and is irrelevant to the governing of society, is outside the realm of that which freedom of speech is intended to protect.

The damage caused by *lashon hara* described above is exacerbated by another factor that may explain some of the unusual degree of condemnation directed at *lashon hara*. The transgression is uniquely complicated to undo.[13] This complication stems from many directions: it is difficult to assess the damage, as it is generally not clear who heard the derogatory statements, or what effect they had; and even if the listeners can be identified, it is close to impossible to change the impressions they have formed based on what they heard.

Even the personal repentance of the speaker is affected by the nature of this particular sin. As it is transgressed so easily, often casually and repeatedly without much attention, it is unlikely that the offender will perceive his act to be the damaging transgression that it is, or that he will take the necessary steps to address the situation. Furthermore, the habitual nature of such behavior is of a type that does not readily lend itself to change without intense focus and motivation to change. Accordingly, the speaker of *lashon hara* is likely to continue along that path, one which is strewn with many pitfalls and dangers, as will be discussed below.

DAMAGE TO THE SPEAKER

The notion that malicious speech is harmful to the speaker as well is less intuitive, but is very real nonetheless. As a starting point, all sin is a source of harm to the sinner himself, in that through such actions the perpetrator incurs guilt and punishment. However, the sense is that this arena is unique in its impact on the actor, imposing an effect distinct from that of sin in general.

---

12. Saul Levmore and Martha C. Nussbaum, *The Offensive Internet: Privacy, Speech, and Reputation* (Cambridge, MA: Harvard University Press, 2010), p. 8.
13. Many of the difficulties are discussed by Rabbeinu Yonah of Gerona, *Shaarei Teshuva* 3:207–8. For a fuller discussion of the challenges of "repairing" *lashon hara* and other consequences of the act, see below pp. 231–245.

From a philosophical perspective, many Jewish thinkers have focused on the unique role of speech as a defining element of humanity. Speech, at least in its fully realized form, distinguishes man from animal; as an expression of thought, this is a distinction with a profound difference. This notion is reflected in the Aramaic translation by Onkelos of the phrase "and man became a living soul" (Gen. 2:7), the last words of which are rendered *ruaḥ memalela,* or "a talking spirit." In the introduction to his book, the *Ḥafetz Ḥayim* cites this phrasing in explaining why he subtitled the main section of his work *Mekor Ḥayim,* or "Source of Life."

Further, it has been noted, speech is an essentially nonphysical act with an immense impact on the physical world, and thus wields an awesome power;[14] in the words of King Solomon, "Death and life are in the power (lit., hand) of the tongue" (Prov. 18:21). Accordingly, the attribute of speech demands extreme care and sensitivity in its usage, and the abuse of this precious resource imposes an exceptional degradation on the speaker.[15]

In addition, on a level that is more psychological/moral, it is asserted that offenses of speech both reflect and deepen particularly unsavory elements of the human personality. The Talmud implies that *lashon hara* is an expression of pure malice, not benefiting the speaker in any way, while devastating the subject. The speaker is compared to a snake who bites and poisons, without the benefit of at least eating his victim, as other predatory animals do.[16] The *Ḥafetz Ḥayim* emphasizes this element in his writings,[17] and thus asserts that more than other

14. See Maharal, *Netivot Olam* 2, *netiv halashon* ch. 2, and *Shemirat HaLashon, shaar hazekhira,* ch. 1.

15. See Rabbi Moshe Schapiro, in *BeYad HaLashon,* pp. 373–79; Rabbi Mordekhai Karlebakh, *Ḥavatzelet HaSharon,* Numbers. pp. 436–38; Rabbi Eliyahu Bakshi-Doron, *Siḥot Binyan Av* II, *Parashat Metzora.*

16. Taanit 8a, commenting on Eccl. 10:11. For a discussion of this passage, see Rabbi Barukh Mordekhai Ezraḥi, *Birkat Mordekhai* to *Parashat Metzora.*

17. *Ḥafetz Ḥayim, Introduction, Prohibition* 6. In his *Be'er Mayim Ḥayim* section of that work, he adds another element to explain the unique desecration involved: In contrast to other transgressions; *lashon hara* is particularly subject to rationalization and self-justification. Accordingly, one who is accused of *lashon hara,* rather than ceasing his behavior, will continue and intensify it so as to validate

transgressions, *lashon hara* constitutes a desecration of God's name, as a sin reflective more of rebellion than of any personal motive.[18]

On the surface, this claim may seem surprising. While the speaker of *lashon hara* may often have malicious intent, this does not exclude other motives; there would seem to be many personal advantages that speakers of gossip have pursued and perhaps attained. Indeed, one towering halakhic authority, Rabbi Avraham Yeshaya Karelitz, known as the *Ḥazon Ish*, was quoted as saying that the *Ḥafetz Ḥayim*'s advancing of this claim was proof that the saintly author "never tasted the taste of *lashon hara*."[19]

While it is possible to thus argue on the *Ḥafetz Ḥayim*'s premise, it seems likely that he acknowledged the human weaknesses that indeed allow pleasures to be found in speaking *lashon hara*, but considered them either to be negligible in comparison to the harm that is inflicted (in comparison, for example, to a thief, who at least obtains items of objective value); or to be motivations that are uniquely degrading to one who indulges in them.

---

the original act. It thus emerges that this sin expands the more it is criticized, thus creating a greater desecration to God's name than do other sins. See also Rabbi Yaakov Avraham Marcus, in the journal *Marpei Lashon* II, pp. 32–38. Rabbi Mordekhai Tzvi Zilber, *Zikhron David*, p. 29, offers another aspect, citing the *Sefer Yere'im*, sec. 6, and noting that a desecration of God's name takes place when a serious transgression is treated frivolously, a reality that certainly applies to *lashon hara*.

18. Rabbeinu Yonah of Gerona (*Shaarei Teshuva* 3:200) makes a similar statement in explanation of the rabbinic equation of the speaking of *lashon hara* with heresy. See also Rabbi Meir Lembrasky, *BeShaarei HaTshuva*, pp. 388–92, and Rabbi Avigdor Nebenzahl, *Siḥot LeSefer Bemidbar*, pp. 156–57.

19. See *A'aleh BaTamar*, p. 36; for further questions on this, see Rabbi Ḥayim Rappaport in the journal *Or Yisrael* XLVIII, pp. 230–32, and see also Rabbi Nissim Karelitz, *Ḥut Shani*, pp. 333–34. See as well the detailed objection of Rabbi Yaakov Edelstein, in *KaMatar Likḥi*, vol. II, p. 102–4, who sides with the *Ḥazon Ish* against the position of the *Ḥafetz Ḥayim*, and interprets the Talmud's statement accordingly. See also the comments of Rabbi Yitzchak Hutner, *Sefer Zikkaron LeMaran Baal HaPaḥad Yitzḥak*, pp. 329–31. Rabbi Avraham Yitzḥak HaKohen Kook had a similar objection to the *Ḥafetz Ḥayim*'s position on this point; see *Bein Shenei Kohanim Gedolim*, pp. 106–9. See also Rabbi Yehonatan Rozler, *He'arot Rigshei Ḥayim*, pp. 23–25.

There are many such motivations. One might be the desire to enhance one's own status through the diminishing of the other;[20] this is known in the Talmud as *mitkabbed biklon ḥavero* and it is harshly condemned.[21] Social psychologists call this "downward social comparison," in contrast with upward comparison, which is the effort to improve by following the practices of those perceived as being superior.[22] This distinction is evocative of a story related about Rabbi Yisrael (Lipkin) Salanter, the founder of the *Musar* movement, which was devoted to personal introspection and improvement. The story describes the rabbi coming upon two children quarreling. The subject of their heated dispute was which of the two was the taller. In a final act of desperation, one child pushed the other to the ground, and, standing over him, proclaimed, "There, now I am the taller one!" Rabbi Yisrael helped the defeated child to his feet and then said to the aggressor, "There was no need to push him to the ground to prove that you were taller – all you had to do was stand on a box!"

Rabbi Eliyahu Meir Bloch, the Rosh Yeshiva of the Telz Yeshiva, commented that it is easy for one who does not want to overtly praise himself to instead claim that he is righteously bemoaning the failings of his surroundings, and thus to boost himself by comparison.[23] This desire to inflate oneself at the expense of the other may be rooted in simple self-aggrandizement, or it may target the subject specifically, either because of a preexisting antipathy, or, very commonly, because of jealousy.[24] Similarly, the very act of judging and disparaging another is an expression of arrogance, itself a character trait severely condemned in the Talmud and elsewhere.[25]

---

20. See *Divrei Yirmiyahu, Laws of Personal Development* 7:2. See also Nicholas DiFonzo, *The Watercooler Effect: A Psychologist Explores the Extraordinary Power of Rumors* (New York: Avery, 2008), p. 69, 101 for expansions on this theme.
21. Megilla 28a; Y. Ḥagiga 2:1; Genesis Rabba 1:5; *Mishneh Torah, Laws of Personal Development* 6:3, and *Laws of Repentance* 3:14.
22. John D. Mayer, *Personal Intelligence*, 198.
23. *Shiurei UPninei Daat.* See there for a listing of several other negative attributes that may be indulged when *lashon hara* is spoken.
24. See Rabbi Eliezer Geldzehler, *Torat Eliezer,* letter 1, p. 164; and Rabbi Matisyahu Solomon in the journal *Kol Torah* XL, pp. 112–15.
25. See Arakhin 15b and Sota 5a; see also Rabbi Yehoshua Heshel Ryzman, *Iyyunim BaParasha* II, p. 271, and IV, p. 40, and Rabbi Yaakov Shechter, *Divrei Yaakov*, pp. 94–95.

Further, these attitudes cannot exist without other correlating moral deficiencies. The ability to inflict reputational harm on another is indicative of a lack of empathy, signalling that this act may be only the beginning of the damage that the speaker is capable of imposing.[26]

Significantly, the speaker of *lashon hara* may, by causing such harm, manifests a bias toward negativity, a dangerous attitude which feeds upon itself and ultimately affects all that is in its purview. Maimonides writes as much in his legal code, where he notes a direct path from hearsay to heresy, noting that those who at first are merely cynical in their orientation will eventually come to disparage and deny God Himself.[27] This aspect must not be understated; the tendency toward a negative assessment, when circumstances allow for other perspectives, is profoundly corrosive and, left unchecked, can undermine the possibility of a fair treatment and appreciation for any value of life.[28]

DAMAGE TO SOCIETY

This negativity is emblematic of a harm that *lashon hara* afflicts that goes beyond the speaker and the subject. In the Talmud's statement, the third victim of *lashon hara* is the "receiver," who by "accepting" the report participates in the transgression and in many of its offenses. More broadly, it must be noted that society as a whole is hurt by the spread of gossip, in many ways, including the seepage of this negative bias in to the communal attitude.

The major identified harm that is imposed upon society is the divisiveness that is provoked by malicious gossip. Earlier, it was noted that *lashon hara* can be seen as disparaging an individual, while *rekhilut* can be understood as causing conflict between parties. Both offenses converge into communal division, as members of society are alienated

26. See *Daat Ḥokhma UMusar* I, p. 10; and Rabbi Matisyahu Solomon in the journal *Kol Torah* XL, p. 112.
27. *Mishneh Torah, Laws of Contamination from Tzaraat* 16:10.
28. For a discussion of the relationship between a general attitude of negativity and *lashon hara*, see Rabbi Avigdor Nebenzahl, *Siḥot LeSefer Shemot*, pp. 328–31.

from one another, whether because of unwarranted distrust or antipathy toward the subjects of gossip, or offense taken by the subjects themselves, as well as the subsequent retaliations.

The Talmud identifies this division as the primary consequence of *lashon hara.* The Torah prescribes that one who is afflicted with the spiritually caused physical malady of *tzaraat* be temporarily removed from the Jewish encampment (Lev. 13:46). In explaining this, the Talmud (Arakhin 16b) notes that the speaker of *lashon hara* (as discussed above, the likely cause of the affliction) separated friends from each other with his talk, and it is therefore appropriate that he be separated from the community.[29] Similarly, at one point the Talmud (16a) distinguishes between *lashon hara* that has been "successful" and that which hasn't been; Rashi,[30] in his classic talmudic commentary, defines "success" as when "people have quarreled because of it."[31] Similarly, in his biblical commentary Nahmanides (Deut. 23:10) suggests that there is an additional prohibition of *lashon hara* during wartime due to the concern that the resulting infighting will do more damage than the enemy will.[32]

In this context, it is relevant to note another Torah mandate, which is fundamentally intertwined with the precept of *lashon hara.* Immediately preceding the "peddler prohibition" (Lev. 19:16), the Torah commands, "with justice shall you judge your fellow" (v. 15), which the mishna (Avot 1:6) interprets as an obligation to give others the benefit of the doubt.[33] While the parameters of this imperative are the topic of much analysis, it is instructive to consider the reasoning behind it.[34] The intuitive assumption is that expressed by some of the great early

29. See also Rabbi Naphtali Hertz Kretzmer, *Noam HaMitzvot* 4: *mitzvot* 362–63. On the general issue of *lashon hara* and divisiveness, see also Rabbi Avraham Ḥayim of Zlotov, *Oraḥ LeḤayim, Parashat Mishpatim,* p. 175; and Rabbi Shalom Noaḥ Berezovsky, *Netivot Shalom, Parashat Tazria,* pp. 60–62.
30. Arakhin 16a, s.v *ahanu.*
31. See also Rabbi Avigdor Nebenzahl, *Siḥot LeSefer Bemidbar* 14.
32. See also *Likkutei Siḥot* XXXI, *Parashat Shemot* 2.
33. See Rashi to Leviticus, and Shabbat 127b.
34. See Maimonides, *Commentary to the Mishna,* Avot 1:6; *Shaarei Teshuva,* 3:218, and *Ḥafetz Ḥayim, Laws of Lashon HaRa* 3:7–8.

authorities, that this principle is an expression of "love your fellow as yourself" in the sense of its crucial role in the support of social harmony, as one aspect of evaluating others positively is the sense of goodwill that is evoked through the exercise of this principle.[35] The effort to bestow a generous estimation on others minimizes the grounds for animosity and strife, and thus contributes to the maintenance of the noncontentious community.[36]

Conversely, engaging in harsh judgment of others creates a quick path to communal discord, and to outright hatred. This animosity is fueled by a vicious cycle, as the subject of suspicion resents what is said about him, and the disparagement itself makes the subject an easier target for disapproval. It is noteworthy that the Torah follows the "peddler verse" immediately with the prohibition of "you shall not hate your brother in your heart" (Lev. 19:17); one twentieth-century halakhic authority asserts that the prohibition of *lashon hara* is actually a proactive safeguard, designed to protect the "hatred" prohibition from being violated.[37]

In truth, the relationship between one's actions toward another and one's feelings toward that person is indeed complex and apparently cyclical. In his autobiography, Benjamin Franklin relates how he won over an opponent by inducing that individual to do a favor for him; this phenomenon has been extensively supported in later psychological studies.[38]

35. See Rabbi Eliezer of Metz, *Sefer Yere'im* 39 and Rabbi Shlomo Luria, *Responsa Maharshal* 64. In *Sefer Ḥaredim* (chs. 12, 54), Rabbi Elazar ben Moshe Azkiri writes that this principle is fundamental to advancing the goals of "Seek peace, and pursue it" (Ps. 34:15).

36. See Rabbi Ḥanokh Zundel, *Etz Yosef* to Pirkei Avot. See Rabbi Alezander Susskind ben Moshe, *Yesod VeShoresh HaAvoda, Shaar Avodat HaLevi*, ch. 8; Rabbi Moshe Yeḥiel Elimelekh, *VaYomer Moshe, Parashat Kedoshim*; and, at length, Rabbi David Kronglass, *Siḥot Ḥokhma UMusar*, pp. 70–76.

37. Rabbi Tzvi Hirsch Frimer, *Responsa Eretz Tzvi* 1:4. It is striking that *Yalkut Shimoni* 1:933 implies the inverse: hatred is dangerous because it leads to *lashon hara*!

38. See David McRaney, "The Benjamin Franklin Effect," ch. 3 in *You Are Now Less Dumb: How to Conquer Mob Mentality, How to Buy Happiness, and All the Other Ways to Outsmart Yourself* (New York: Gotham Books, 2013). Compare also *Tanḥuma, Mishpatim* 1.

Ironically, there are those who have attributed a positive role to gossip because of the role it purportedly plays in establishing social bonds.[39] Even were this to be the case – an arguable point in and of itself – it is readily apparent that bonding in such fashion does more harm than good, establishing connections through the exclusion of others and through their possibly unjust disparagement as well. Such bonding is a major component of what is known as bullying, as the persecution of the weaker individual (in whatever form that takes) is used to strengthen group cohesion.

To be clear, social bonding is an affirmative value of great importance, and some commandments, such as the mandate to host guests (even those not in need)[40] and to send gifts of food on the festival of Purim are attributed to accomplishing that goal.[41] However, achieving such bonding through the demeaning of others fails on at least three counts. First, the ends in no way justify the egregious means. Second, the ends themselves are suspect. The acknowledged value of social bonding is not absolute, but is contingent on the assumption that upstanding individuals are uniting with like-minded people; in contrast, Scripture (Ps. 1:1) praises one who does not join a "seating of scoffers" (*moshav letzim*), and the Talmud (Sanhedrin 26a) condemns a "bond of evildoers." Third, there is no long-term viability for a bond built on the disparagement of others, as each party knows it could easily become the next target.

There is another alleged benefit to gossip that, when considered, also actually sheds some light on harm that it brings with it. In his book

39. See Robin Dunbar, *Grooming, Gossip and the Evolution of Language* (Cambridge, MA: Harvard University Press, 1996) cited and discussed by Daniel Tammet, *Embracing the Wide Sky: A Tour Across the Horizons of the Human Brain* (New York: Free Press, 2009), pp. 197–98. See also Michael Shermer, *The Science of Good and Evil: Why People Cheat, Share, Gossip, and Follow the Golden Rule* (New York: Times Books, 2004), p. 44nn24–25; and Melinda Blau and Karen L. Fingerman, *Consequential Strangers: The Power of People Who Don't Seem to Matter… but Really Do* (New York: W. W. Norton, 2009), pp. 178–80.

40. See Rabbi Ḥayim ben Betzalel, *Sefer HaḤayim, Sefer Parnasa VeKalkala* III, ch. 3.

41. See Rabbi Shlomo Alkabetz, *Manot HaLevi, Ester* 9:3, and *Responsa Ḥatam Sofer, Oraḥ Ḥayim* 196.

The Authenticity Hoax, Andrew Potter quotes (and proceeds to question) the following view:[42]

> Another defense of gossip... flags its ability to reveal to us the elusive, quirky, and shadowy truths about human nature. As philosopher Ronald de Sousa writes, "Gossip is inherently democratic, concerned with private life rather than public issues, 'idle,' in the sense that it is not instrumental or goal oriented. Yet it can serve to expand our consciousness of what life is about in ways that are effectively inaccessible to other modes of inquiry." This is the counterpart to the argument that gossip subverts traditional hierarchies: by cracking open the private sphere to general public scrutiny, gossip can be an instrument of egalitarianism and social leveling. It reminds us that everyone is flawed in some way, that we all have habits, desires, beliefs, and character traits that are unpleasant or perverted, and that we are all insecure or cowardly or vain. That we are all, in a very base and common way, human. Because of the way it can cut the legs from the public stilts we build that we might strut around a bit higher than our fellow citizens, we may want to call gossip a virtue of authenticity.[43]

It is far from obvious that such exposure is actually beneficial, or at least unreservedly so. On the one hand, there is truth to the need to prevent rank and cynical hypocrisy from infecting the leadership of society;[44] but that is a far cry from the suggestion that no gap can exist between ideals and achievement. Quite the contrary, great Jewish philosophers have suggested that the purpose of existence is to perfect one's character traits; by virtue of simply being alive, it can be taken as a given that we all have much work to do in living up to our own values.[45] The suggestion

---

42. Andrew Potter, *The Authenticity Hoax: How We Got Lost Finding Ourselves* (New York: HarperCollins, 2010), pp. 163–64.
43. See also Solove, *Future of Reputation*, 64–66.
44. See Yoma 86b, and *Ḥafetz Ḥayim*, *Laws of Lashon HaRa* 4:7 and *Be'er Mayim Ḥayim* 30. However, note also the interpretation of Rabbi Noaḥ Segal, *Responsa Olat Noaḥ, Yoreh De'ah* 5.
45. This theme was emphasized by the Vilna Gaon in his writings, such as *Even Shlomo.*

that to be human is to abandon hope of elevated behavior does great damage to the crucial notion of an aspirational existence.

Similarly, there is merit in providing a realistic perspective as to what is possible, so that spiritual strivers not be disillusioned by the seemingly unbridgeable gap between themselves and their role models. Indeed, the noted twentieth-century rabbinic thinker and Rosh Yeshiva Rabbi Yitzchak Hutner writes that the trend towards publishing hagiographies of great figures can be counterproductive to the spiritual aspirations of those who read them, as they feel they are failures if they are not born without temptation and struggle.[46] Inversely, there is also value in emphasizing human frailty to provide caution as to the temptations and weakness that threaten everyone, and thus to discourage complacency and overconfidence. (In fact, the Talmud [Bava Batra 165a] apparently does so regarding none other than the innate tendency toward *lashon hara.*)

However, these worthwhile goals are hardly the substance of most gossip, which serves, intentionally or not, the opposite ends. Painting a picture of universal venality and hypocrisy conveys the message that aspiration is pointless; and complacency is encouraged not because of success but rather because there is no one who has actually achieved success.

In this vein, it is illuminating to note that one of the great rabbinic figures of early-twentieth-century Jerusalem, Rabbi Yehoshua Leib Diskin, suggests another motivation for the mandate of judging others favorably.[47] A fundamental factor in the avoidance of sin is the embarrassment associated with iniquity. Believing that society on the whole adheres to a higher standard is essential to maintaining this attitude. Thus, it is necessary to assume that the behavior of one's social group is exemplary, at least in the aggregate. Similar thinking is evident earlier in the writings of the medieval authority Rabbi Menaḥem HaMeiri, who notes that one who suspects others of bad behavior will

46. Rabbi Yitzchak Hutner, *Paḥad Yitzhak, Iggerot UKhtavim* 128.

47. *Responsa Maharil Diskin*, end of *Pesakim*, and *Ḥiddushei Maharil Diskin al HaTorah*, Lev. 19:15.

lose respect for society as a whole and will immunize himself against their good influence.[48]

Furthermore, gossip, even when ostensibly true, creates a false impression through its overemphasis of petty details, and thus contributes to a degraded culture in which such items are the focus of attention. This concern is reflected in American privacy law as well. As Louis Brandeis and Samuel Warren wrote in 1890 in the *Harvard Law Review*, "Even gossip apparently harmless, when widely and persistently circulated, is potent for evil. It belittles by inverting the relative importance of things, thus dwarfing the thoughts and aspirations of a people."[49]

The above admonitions against gossip and portrayals of its pernicious consequences are not intended to advocate the whitewashing or ignoring of actual misdeeds or offenses; the mandate to judge favorably does not call for exonerating or overlooking improper behavior. Rather, the warnings against gossip and its ramifications show that the default effect of gossip is not necessarily the fulfillment of positive goals with which it might be theoretically associated, and that "market forces" cannot be relied upon to achieve those goals either. Accordingly, if any constructive result is to emerge from what would otherwise be called gossip (the term itself is connotative of nonconstructive conversation), it will do so not despite the laws of *lashon hara*, but rather within the framework of those limitations.

In sum, it emerges that gossip and malicious speech constitute a uniquely malevolent force, placing well-earned reputations and their possessors at significant risk; inflicting not only guilt but varied forms of spiritual, moral, and psychological corruption upon the perpetrators; and seriously undermining the structure of society through the infusion of hatred, suspicion, and division, and through the reduction of communal standards. However, there is still another element to consider in the equation: the role of truth and falsehood, and the often thin line between them.

---

48. *Ḥibbur HaTeshuva, Meshiv Nefesh, maamar* 1:4.

49. Samuel D. Warren and Louis D. Brandeis, "The Right to Privacy," 4 *Harvard Law Review* 193 (1890), discussed in Lori B. Andrews, *I Know Who You Are and I Saw What You Did: Social Networks and the Death of Privacy* (New York: Free Press, 2012), pp. 49–53.

Is It Really True?

The potential harm inherent in the slander and unjust deprecation of others is firmly established. However, it is also established that *lashon hara* is not limited to false reports, but includes truthful statements as well. Factual reporting would seem not only to be excluded from slanderous activity, but also to be often necessary for the effective functioning of society. As such, how can the transmission of true information be prohibited?

One step toward an answer involves asking a basic question: If the speaker is stating facts, is the listener actually hearing the truth? There are a number of reasons to question this assumption. From a textual perspective, it is illuminating to consider that the source in the Torah for the prohibition to "accept" *lashon hara* is the verse "You shall not bear a false (*shav*) report" (Ex. 23:1), in which the word *shav* can also be translated as "unnecessary," which would work well with a general concept of prohibition. However, a number of the most important biblical commentators render the term as "false,"[1] which makes it difficult to interpret the prohibition as including that which is factually true.[2] While there are a number of suggested interpretations,

1. For example, Onkelos and Rashi.
2. See Rabbi Yaakov Tzvi Mecklenberg, *HeKetav VeHaKabbala*, to Exodus. This will be discussed at greater length below, ch. VII.

what seems most likely is that something very significant is taking place during the transmission. Even though the speaker is saying words that may be technically true, that which reaches the listener's ears is functionally false. Accordingly, a prohibition that is addressed specifically to the listener can appropriately be understood as forbidding a "false report."

In short, it is a mistake to believe that every statement spoken by an honest person conveys complete truth to the listener, or that every utterance is either the complete truth or an intentional lie. It is well understood that not everyone is honest, and discretion must be used in whom to trust and believe. However, it is less appreciated that honest people can also transmit falsehoods, with innocent intentions. This can happen due to human failings relating to the speaker, the context, the listener, or some combination of any or all of these.

THE POSSIBILITY OF SUBJECTIVITY AND ERROR

It may also be the case that a statement made by an honest person might nonetheless be simply incorrect. On the most basic level, this can be for at least two reasons: the statement is subjective, or is just a mistake.

The first factor, subjectivity, accounts for a large portion of what could be considered *lashon hara*. The statement may be factual, and represent the honest opinion of the speaker, but yet does not represent any objective contextual truth. Thus, the utterance could not justly be termed slander, but nonetheless has no claim to actual truth. This might be exactly what Maimonides was referring to when he defined *lashon hara* as "speaking disparagingly of his fellow even though [the speaker] speaks the truth."

The subjectivity of opinion allows any fact to be expressed in a disparaging way, without regard to evidence or consistency. Gordon Allport demonstrates this in his book *The Nature of Prejudice* with this imagined conversation with an anti-Semite:

> Mr. X: The trouble with Jews is that they only take care of their own group.

> Mr. Y: But the record of the Community Chest campaign shows that they give more generously, in proportion to their numbers, to the general charities of community, than do non-Jews.
>
> Mr. X: That shows they are always trying to buy favor and intrude into Christian affairs. They think of nothing but money; that is why there are so many Jewish bankers.
>
> Mr. Y: But a recent study shows that the percentage of Jews in the banking business is negligible, far smaller than the percentage of non-Jews.
>
> Mr. X: That's just it; they don't go in for respectable business; they are only in the movie business or run night clubs.[3]

Further, context is a crucial determinant of whether any statement is able to be perceived accurately or not. This is true both on a micro level and on a macro level. On a micro level, a fact without any supporting context might simply be not understandable, or might create a false impression.

On a macro level, human beings are far more complex than any one fact or story may reflect. The *lashon hara* prohibition may be premised upon the assumption that even true information can create a false picture of the individual. Daniel Solove expresses this articulately in a chapter of his book *The Future of Reputation* appropriately entitled "The Virtues of Knowing Less":

> We grow and change throughout our lives. According to the philosopher John Dewey, the individual is not "something complete, perfect, finished, an organized whole of parts united by the impress of a comprehensive form," but is "something moving, changing, discrete and above all initiating instead of final." A person is a life process from cradle to corpse. At any given moment, we are seeing just a snapshot in time, a slice of this lifelong process. As the playwright and author Friedrich

3. Gordon Allport, *The Nature of Prejudice*, 2nd ed. (Reading, MA: Addison-Wesley, 1979), pp. 13–14, cited and discussed in Carol Tavris and Elliot Aronson, *Mistakes Were Made (but Not by Me)* (Orlando: Harcourt, 2007), pp. 61–62.

> Durrenmatt eloquently wrote, "What one commonly called one's self was merely a collective term for all the selves gathered up in the past, a great heap of selves perpetually growing under the constant rain of selves drifting down through the present from the future, an accumulation of shreds of experience and memory, comparable to a mound of leaves that grows higher and higher under a steady drift of other falling leaves." Protection against disclosure permits room to change, to define oneself and one's future without becoming a "prisoner of [one's] recorded past." Society has a tendency to tie people too tightly to the past and to typecast people in particular roles. The human personality is dynamic, yet accepting the complete implications of this fact can be difficult.[4]

There is a context not only for the presentation but for the side of the interpretation as well. In 1951, a football game between Dartmouth University and Princeton University became violent, with players on both teams ending up injured. In assessing blame, students of each school perceived the events very differently, with vastly different assessments of which team was more at fault and behaved more inappropriately. One researcher from each school, Albert Hastorf of Dartmouth and Hadley Cantril of Princeton, took the opportunity to conduct a study of the varying interpretations of the respective student populations. They showed students a film clip of the game and asked them to make a list of all the infractions that they noticed.

As Farhad Manjoo, who wrote a book about context entitled *True Enough: Learning to Live in a Post-Fact Society,* describes, "The results were remarkable. Although all students were shown the same film, each side "saw" a completely different game. The Dartmouth students found a roughly equal number of transgressions committed by each team – about four errors per side, as they counted it – although they did notice the Princeton players making many more "flagrant," as opposed to "mild," infractions. The Princeton students saw the game very differently; they watched the movie in wild-eyed anger

4. Solove, *Future of Reputation,* 73.

at the Dartmouth team's clear disregard for the rules. The Princeton students claimed to witness an average of almost ten infractions committed by Dartmouth during the game, the majority of them flagrant. The Princeton fans saw Princeton players make only half as many errors, and most were minor. The disparate reading of the film, Hastorf and Cantril found, was not a product of mere bias. The fans were not choosing to see actions in the game – or deliberately overlooking things – in a way that corresponded with their feelings. Rather, it was a matter of visual perception: their eyes were taking in the same game, but their brains seemed to be processing the events in two distinct ways."[5]

Manjoo continues:

> The phenomenon of selective exposure... involve[s] choosing your sources of information according to your preexisting biases. Hastorf and Cantril's study illustrates a different cognitive trap. Selective perception says that even when two people of opposing ideologies overcome their tendency toward selective exposure and choose to watch the same thing, they may still end up being pushed apart from each other. That's because they really won't be experiencing the "same" thing... each of them will have seen, heard, felt, and understood the "thing" vastly differently from the others who have experienced it.[6]

This principle is relevant also to the mandates of judging others favorably. Many authorities and commentators suggest that the obligation to extend the benefit of the doubt is not necessarily addressed to a discrete action, but rather to the individual as a whole; even if one act, taken individually, may be indefensible, the total picture of the individual's

5. See also Eli Pariser, *The Filter Bubble: What the Internet Is Hiding from You* (New York: Penguin, 2011), pp. 85–87; Max H. Bazerman, *The Power of Noticing: What the Best Leaders See* (New York: Simon and Schuster, 2014), p. 24; Michaek Kaplan and Ellen Kaplan, *Bozo Sapiens: Why to Err Is Human* (New York: Bloomsbury, 2009), pp. 55–56.
6. Farhad Manjoo, *True Enough: Learning to Live in a Post-Fact Society* (Hoboken, NJ: Wiley, 2008), pp. 67–71.

history, motivations, and other mitigating factors may paint a very different picture.[7]

THE FALLIBILITY OF MEMORY

Beyond the concern of subjectivity and context, it is also entirely possible that the speaker is mistaken. Much has been written about the underestimated unreliability of memory.[8] As cognitive psychologists Elizabeth Loftus and Katherine Ketcham write, memory can be affected "by succeeding events, other people's recollections or suggestions, increased under-standing, or a new context... truth and reality, when seen through the filter of our memory, are not objective facts, but subjective, interpretive realities."[9] Memory expert Ulric Neisser has demonstrated, more surprisingly, that even "flashbulb memories" – memories of major events that appear to be captured perfectly due to their significance – are often completely incorrect.[10] Sadly, this unreliability has affected the credibility of testimony in courts of law, with, at times, tragic results.[11]

---

7. This idea can be found in many commentaries to Pirkei Avot 1:6, including Rabbi Yehuda Aryeh Leib of Ger, *Sefat Emet;* Rabbi Yitzḥak Meir of Ger, *Ḥiddushei HaRim,* cited in Rabbi Yosef Patzanofsky, *Pardes Yosef,* Lev. 13:3; Rabbi Gedalya Felder, *Yesodei Yeshurun;* Rabbi Menaḥem Mendel Frankel-Teomim, *Be'er HaAvot;* Rabbi Natan Gestetner, *Lehorot Natan;* Rabbi Yaakov Yehoshua Belcrovitz, *Tiferet Yehoshua;* and Rabbi Zelig Pribelsky, cited in Rabbi Moshe Levi, compiler, *MiShel Avot.*
8. See the discussion in Tavris and Aronson, *Mistakes Were Made,* chs. 3–4; Christopher Chabris and Daniel Simons, *The Invisible Gorilla* (New York: Crown, 2010), pp. 61–79; Gary Marcus, *Kluge: The Haphazard Construction of the Human Mind* (Boston: Houghton Mifflin, 2008), ch. 2; and Claudia Hammond, *Time Warped: Unlocking the Mysteries of Time Perception* (New York: Harper Perennial, 2012), pp. 166–76, 227–36.
9. E. Loftus and K. Ketcham, *Witness for the Defense: The Accused, the Eyewitness, and the Expert Who Puts Memory on Trial* (New York: St. Martin's, 1991), p. 20.
10. U. Neisser and N. Harsch, "Phantom Flashbulbs: False Recollections Studies Hearing the News about the Challenger," in E. Winograd and U. Neisser, eds., *Affect and Accuracy in Recall: Studies of "Flashbulb"* (New York: Cambridge University Press, 1992), p. 9. See Chabris and Simons, *Invisible Gorilla,* pp. 66–76; Leonard Mlodinow, *Subliminal: How Your Unconscious Mind Rules Your Behavior* (New York: Pantheon, 2012), pp. 69–70; and Robert Alan Burton, *On Being Certain: Believing You Are Right Even When You're Not* (New York: St. Martin's, 2008), pp. 9–13; and Rolf Dobelli, *The Art of Thinking Clearly* (New York: HarperBusiness, 2013), ch. 78.
11. A particularly devastating example of this is described in Kathryn Schulz's book *Being Wrong: Adventures in the Margins of Error* (New York: Ecco, 2010), ch. 11.

German psychologist Hugo Munsterberg was inspired to study the fallibility of memory after his own experiences with providing mistaken testimony in 1907, and published his ideas in a best-selling book called *On The Witness Stand: Essays on Psychology and Crime.* Among his major findings that are generally accepted by modern researchers are, as summarized by a contemporary author, Leonard Mlodinow, "first, people have a good memory for the general gist of events but a bad one for the details; second, when pressed for the unremembered details, even well-intentioned people making a sincere effort to be accurate will inadvertently fill in the gaps by making things up; third, people believe the memories they make up."[12]

Mlodinow further discusses the findings made by Frederic Bartlett in the early part of the twentieth century. Bartlett conducted a study in which subjects were asked at repeated intervals to recollect a story that they had been told. He discovered

> an important trend in the evolution of memory: there wasn't just a memory loss; there were also memory additions. That is, as the original reading of the story faded into the past, new memory data was fabricated, and that fabrication proceeded according to certain general principles. The subjects maintained the story's general form but dropped some details and changed others. The story became shorter and simpler... Elements were added or reinterpreted so that "whenever anything appeared incomprehensible, it was either omitted or explained" by adding content.... Inaccuracy was the rule, and

---

See also Thomas Kida, *Don't Believe Everything You Think: The 6 Basic Mistakes We Make in Thinking* (Amherst, NY: Prometheus Books, 2006), pp. 211–13 (and see all of ch. 11 regarding the unreliability of memory, and discussion and citation of Loftus and Neisser, *Witness for the Defense*), and see Tavris and Aronson, *Mistakes Were Made,* ch. 5; Mlodinow, *Subliminal,* pp. 52–63; Bill Kovach and Tom Rosenstiel, *Blur: How to Know What's True in the Age of Information Overload* (New York: Bloomsbury, 2010), pp. 80–82; and Chabris and Simons, *Invisible Gorilla,* pp. 109–15. See also Ralph L. Rosnow and Gary Alan Fine, *Rumor and Gossip: The Social Psychology of Hearsay* (New York: Elsevier, 1976), pp. 67–70, regarding the work of Robert Buckhout and of Bernard Hart.

12. Mlodinow, *Subliminal,* p. 62.

> not the exception.... [Bartlett learned that] the process of fitting memories into a comfortable form "is an active process," he wrote, and depends on the subject's own prior knowledge and beliefs about the world, the "preformed tendencies and bias which the subject brings to the task" of remembering.[13]

Similarly, as Ralph L. Rosnow and Gary Alan Fine relate in their study *Rumor and Gossip: The Social Psychology of Hearsay,* "because of the natural porosity of human memory and the tendency to simplify and bring order to things, the most common rumor distortions are the result of leveling (elimination of some details), sharpening (selective attention given to particular information), and assimilation (twisting of new material to build a better overall structure)."[14]

Further, as discussed by the authors of *Sleights of Mind,* a book which analyzes magicians' tricks from a cognitive perspective, memory is subject to a "misinformation effect," which is a tendency for misleading information presented after an event to reduce the accuracy of memory of the original event.[15] They describe the net effect as follows:

> At a deeper, biological level, all your memories are fallible. The act of remembering an event from your past is not like playing back a mental videotape in your mind's home theater system. It is more like retelling a shaggy dog story that you once heard. You recall a few key phrases and junctures along with the story's overall gist, but you don't recall the exact order of words in the story. When you repeat the "same" story to another person, you reconstruct it in your own way. You freely embellish and fill in missing gaps to make the story flow smoothly. While you might repeat verbatim a few key bits of the original telling, most of the word choices are yours. Similarly, when your brain lays down a new memory, what it actually encodes is a sparse constellation of

13. Ibid., 68–69.
14. Rosnow and Fine, *Rumor and Gossip,* 36.
15. Stephen Macknick and Susana Martinez-Conde, *Sleights of Mind* (New York: Henry Holt, 2010), pp. 116–18, 121–22.

> personal details and meaningful junctures. When your brain later retrieves the memory, it uses that constellation as a scaffold for reconstructing the original experience. As the memory plays out in your mind, you may have the strong impression that it's a high-fidelity record, but only a few of its contents are truly accurate. The rest of it is a bunch of props, backdrops, casting extras, and stock footage your mind furnishes on the fly in an unconscious process known as confabulation. And it gets stranger. Sometimes a feature that was confabulated during one act of remembering gets re-remembered during the next act. In the process, the confabulation can become a permanent feature of the memory. It becomes indistinguishable from the original.[16]

Daniel L. Shachter, the chairman of the psychology department at Harvard University, wrote a comprehensive work on the failings of memory entitled *The Seven Sins of Memory: How the Mind Forgets and Remembers*. Among the "sins" relevant for our purposes that he discusses at length are transience, the weakening or loss of memory over time, and absent-mindedness, which prevents memories from being properly formed in the first place. These, as problematic as they are, are "sins of omission," and often the one forgetting is at least aware of the problem. More dangerous, though, are "sins of commission," such as the misattribution or misinformation discussed above which, he asserts, "is far more common than most people realize, and has potentially profound implications in legal settings."

Further, he maintains:

> The related sin of suggestibility refers to memories that are included as a result of leading questions, comments, or suggestions when a person is trying to call up a past experience. Like misattribution, suggestibility is especially relevant to – and sometimes

16. For more about the misinformation effect, see David McRaney, *You Are Not So Smart: Why You Have Too Many Friends on Facebook, Why Your Memory Is Mostly Fiction, and 46 Other Ways You're Deluding Yourself* (New York: Gotham Books; Penguin, 2011), ch. 32.

can wreak havoc with – the legal system. The sin of bias reflects the powerful influences of our current knowledge and beliefs on how we remember our pasts. We often edit or entirely rewrite our previous experiences – unknowingly and unconsciously – in light of what we now know or believe. The result can be a skewed rendering of a specific incident, or even an extended period in our lives, which says more about how we feel now then what happened then.[17]

THE ILLUSION OF CONFIDENCE

It is also often incorrectly assumed that it is less likely that individuals are mistaken if they are confident that they are correct. Thus, when a speaker confirms that he is "sure," the listener then considers it appropriate to accept the report as factual. However, there is in reality much less of a correlation, if not an inverse correlation at times, between confidence and accuracy.[18] Even the confidence that comes with professional expertise is not a guarantee of correctness, as has been well documented.[19]

This "confidence heuristic" is not unreasonable.[20] It is indeed likely that someone who is unsure of his position may actually be incorrect. However that does not result in a perfect record for confidence, which can be diluted by overconfidence, false confidence, and simple error.

17. Daniel L. Schacter, *The Seven Sins of Memory: How the Mind Forgets and Remembers* (Boston: Houghton Mifflin, 2001). The quoted citation is from p. 5.
18. See Kida, *Don't Believe Everything*, 194; Chabris and Simons, *Invisible Gorilla*, ch. 3, and Ian Ayres, *Super Crunchers: Why Thinking-by-Numbers Is the New Way to Be Smart* (New York: Bantam, 2007), p 114.
    It should be noted that while Jewish law does categorize definite claims (*bari*) as superior to indefinite ones (*shema*), this ranking (which is itself of limited scope) is not a function of the self-confidence of the claimant, but rather a preference for claims that are asserted from a definitive position, rather than a tentative one.
19. See, for example, David H. Freedman's book *Wrong: Why Experts* Keep Failing Us – and How to Know When Not to Trust Them: *scientists, finance wizards, doctors, relationship gurus, celebrity CEOs, high-powered consultants, health officials, and more* (New York: Little, Brown, 2010).
20. See Dan Gardner, *Future Babble: Why Expert Predictions Are Next to Worthless, and You Can Do Better* (New York: Dutton, 2011), pp. 152–56.

This tendency of the listener to over-credit confidence applies both to individual statements and to the overall personalities that people display. In her book *Quiet: The Power of Introverts in a World That Can't Stop Talking,* Susan Cain describes the exaggerated credibility given to those who talk in a more assertive fashion:[21]

> If we assume that quiet and loud people have roughly the same number of good (and bad) ideas, then we should worry if the louder and more forceful people always carry the day. This would mean that an awful lot of bad ideas prevail while good ones get squashed. Yet studies in group dynamics suggest that this is exactly what happens. We perceive talkers as smarter than quiet types – even though grade-point averages and SAT college admission exam and intelligence test scores reveal this perception to be inaccurate. In one experiment in which two strangers met over the phone, those who spoke more were considered more intelligent, better-looking, and more likable. We also see talkers as leaders. The more a person talks, the more other group members direct their attention to him, which means that he becomes increasingly powerful as a meeting goes on. It also helps to speak fast; we rate quick talkers as more capable and appealing than slow talkers. All of this would be fine if more talking were correlated with greater insight, but research suggests that there's no such link. In one study, groups of college students were asked to solve math problems together and then to rate one another's intelligence and judgment. The students who spoke first and most often were consistently given the highest ratings, even though their suggestions (and math SAT scores) were no better than those of the less talkative students. These same students were given similarly high ratings for their creativity and analytical powers during a separate exercise to develop a business strategy for a start-up company. A well-known study out of the University of California at Berkeley by organizational behavior professor Philip

21. Susan Cain, *Quiet: The Power of Introverts in a World That Can't Stop Talking* (New York: Crown, 2012). pp. 51–52.

> Tetlock found that television pundits – that is, people who earn their livings by holding forth confidently on the basis of limited information – make worse predictions about political and economic trends than they would by random chance. And the very worst prognosticators tend to be the most famous and the most confident, the very ones who would he considered natural leaders in an HBS [Harvard Business School] classroom.[22]

Overconfidence plagues listeners as well as speakers. As Nicholas Epley relates in his book *Mindwise,*

> When one group of researchers evaluated decades of studies and hundreds of experiments that measured how well people could distinguish truths from lies, they found that people's ability to spot deception was only a few percentage points better than a random coin flip: people were 54 percent accurate overall, when random guessing would make you accurate 50 percent of the time.[23]

Beyond these factors, there are multiple other concerns regarding how the item will be received on the listener's end.

COGNITIVE BIASES AND DISPROPORTIONATE INFLUENCE

One general concern is that even if what the listener hears is true and accurately presented, the impact that it has on him and his decisions is a disproportionate one, and that disproportionate impact itself is an untruth. Therefore, even if the statement is factually true, the result is falsehood. There are many reasons why such a scenario could unfold. One is the reality that individuals do not approach every decision with a completely objective and neutral evaluation of facts. Rather, they rely on certain shortcuts that are necessary to make functioning manageable,

---

22. See also Schulz, "The Allure of Certainty," ch. 8 in *Being Wrong*; and Daniel Kahneman, *Thinking Fast and Slow* (New York: Farrar, Straus and Giroux, 2011), pp. 261–63.
23. Nicholas Epley, *Mindwise: How We Understand What Others Think, Believe, Feel, and Want* (New York: Knopf, 2014), p. 8ff.

but nonetheless do not necessarily reflect a fair assessment of all elements. Nobel Prize winner Daniel Kahneman devoted to this subject an entire important book, entitled *Thinking Fast and Slow,* in which he describes two separate systems of decision making that are utilized by people in their thinking, which he terms "System 1," which is "fast, intuitive, and emotional," and "System 2," which is "slower, more deliberate, and more logical."[24]

Similarly, Cass Sunstein and Richard Thaler, in their book *Nudge,* refer to the same two systems as the "Automatic System" and the "Objective System." Regarding the easily influenced Automatic System, they assert a principle that might be appropriated by those who, sensitive to concerns of *lashon hara,* are careful about what they say and what they listen to: "Everything matters."[25]

In other words, System 1, the Automatic System, is resistant to conscious control. Instead, it is greatly affected by subconscious factors, and items that are heard will contribute to that impact, whether or not an objective evaluation would consider that effect fair or proportionate.

THE FUNDAMENTAL ATTRIBUTION ERROR

In addition, human psychology is prey to several cognitive biases that interfere with a fair assessment of material being presented to them.

One of the most well-known of these biases is described in the literature as the "fundamental attribution error." This bias, which may play a very central role in understanding the gravity of *lashon hara,* refers to the phenomenon of an individual processing negative information about others in a fundamentally different way from how he would interpret identical information about himself. When the subject is someone else, the information is considered to be entirely reflective and typical of the character of the subject. However, the same action, when relevant to the listener, would be interpreted as out of character and atypical – not reflective of any enduring personality trait (this is also known as the

---

24. See also Alex Pentland, *Social Physics: How Good Ideas Spread – the Lessons from a New Science* (New York: Penguin, 2014), pp. 235–40.
25. Richard H. Thaler and Cass R. Sunstein, *Nudge: Improving Decisions About Health, Wealth, and Happiness* (New Haven, CT: Yale University Press, 2008), pp. 19–22.

"actor-observer effect").[26] Thus, information is granted a far more judgmental quality than justice may otherwise dictate, simply because the subject is another person. In the words of Sam Sommers, who in his book about the importance of context terms this tendency as "what you see is what you get,"[27] "We see others' missteps as indicating deficient personality, but we chalk up our own feelings to external causes. When the customer in front of you lines his pockets with the extra change the cashier mistakenly gives him, you view him as dishonest; when you do the same thing, it's because the cashier was rude, you're in a hurry, and you're pretty sure the store is marking up prices to begin with."[28]

This tendency has been implicated in much human conflict, including road rage. In that context, author Tom Vanderbilt, in his book *Traffic: Why We Drive the Way We Do (And What It Says About Us)*, cites speculation as to the underlying explanation: "Psychologists theorize that the actor-observer effect may stem from one's desire to feel more in control of a complex situation, like driving in traffic. It also just might be easier to chastise a 'stupid driver' for cutting you off than to fully analyze the circumstances that caused this event to occur."[29]

More fundamentally, this disposition can also be explained by the reality that the one judging is committed to preserving his own reputation, while he has no such commitment to the reputation of others. If

---

26. See Lee Ross, "The Intuitive Psychologist and His Shortcomings: Distortions in the Attribution Process," *Advances in Experimental Social Psychology* 10 (1977); and Harold Kelley and John Michella, "Attribution Theory and Research," *Annual Review of Psychology* 31(1980): 477–78, both cited in Robert Mnookin, *Bargaining with the Devil: When to Negotiate and When to Fight* (New York: Simon and Schuster, 2010), p. 16nn4–5.
27. Sam Sommers, *Situations Matter: Understanding How Context Transforms Your World* (New York: Riverhead Books, 2011), pp. 17–20, 139.
28. For more regarding the fundamental attribution error, see Clay Shirky, *Cognitive Surplus: Creativity and Generosity in a Connected Age* (New York: Penguin, 2010), pp. 122–23; McRaney, *You Are Not So Smart*, ch. 39; Dobelli, *Thinking Clearly*, ch. 36; and DeSteno, *Truth About Trust*, p. 102 and throughout.
29. Tom Vanderbilt, *Traffic: Why We Drive the Way We Do (and What It Says About Us)* (New York: Knopf, 2008), pp. 23–24, citing Thomas Britt and Michael Garrity, "Attributions and Personality as Predictors of the Road Rage Response," *British Journal of Social Psychology* 45 (2006): 127–47.

such concern were indeed extended to the subjects of *lashon hara,* they might also be judged more favorably. In this vein, one homiletic interpretation of the Torah's commandment to love one's fellow "as yourself" is that just as one is always able to excuse one's own faults, with a little empathy that same "love of oneself" could be directed toward others as well.[30]

Setting aside the double standard regarding others, the thrust of the error in this bias is the assumption that any glimpse of another's personality is a complete picture of the individual. As Sommers puts it, "we are easily seduced by the notion of stable character. So much of who we are, how we think, and what we do is driven by the situations we are in, yet we remain blissfully unaware of it." The emphasis on "situation," at least for our purposes, is not to absolve the bad actor of blame and to deny free will, but rather to emphasize that the behavior may well be discrete and not indicative of any other characteristic.

Not only may an individual action not be representative of one's true personality, such an analysis is elusive at its very core. Stanford Prof. Walter Mischel, in his 1968 book *Personality and Assessment,* argues that while we might perceive others as consistent, this perception is an illusion; we classify others by using "prototypes" of people, similar to the stereotyping of entire groups. As John D. Mayer puts it in his book *Personal Intelligence* (which does argue for the role of personality in assessment and evaluation) "once we have pegged someone as a particular 'type,' we continue to see him through that lens:[31] if we believe someone is 'emotional and dramatic,' we will fit whatever he does into an 'emotional' template, forgetting the many times he has behaved in a perfectly calm fashion."[32]

---

30. See, for example, *HaKetav VeHaKabbala* to Lev. 19:18; see also *Ḥafetz Ḥayim,* positive commandment 2.
31. Mayer, *Personal Intelligence,* 15–18.
32. See also Gino, Francesca, *Sidetracked: Why Our Decisions Get Derailed, and How We Can Stick to the Plan* (Boston: Harvard Business Review Press, 2011), pp. 157–58, regarding "correspondence bias," and see also David DeSteno and Piercarlo Valdesolo, *Out of Character: Surprising Truths About the Liar, Cheat, Sinner (and Saint) Lurking in All of Us* (New York: Crown Archetype, 2011).

AMBIGUITY, INTOLERANCE, AND THE AVAILABILITY HEURISTIC

Further, people tend to prematurely and possibly inaccurately rush to an assessment due to a bias known as "ambiguity intolerance" (sometimes known as "uncertainty intolerance"). This refers to the tendency of ambiguity to instill discomfort and anxiety to such a degree that a false or incomplete certainty becomes preferable, either consciously or subconsciously.[33]

A similar tendency, with comparable effects, is known as the "availability bias" or the "availability heuristic."[34] This refers to the mistaken belief that whatever information is available to someone at any given moment is necessarily the most reflective information or the complete picture, when in reality such an item of information, even if it is true, is only one among many equally significant pieces of information. Such a bias can easily lead to negative information, even if independently true, having a distorted and misrepresentative impact.

Another common evaluative error is described by Dylan Evans in his book *Risk Intelligence*:

> A common error in judgment... first documented by Dale Griffin and Amos Tversky. They discovered that people tend to put more emphasis than they should on the strength of the evidence and not enough on its credibility, so when the evidence points strongly to one conclusion but the source credibility is low, overconfidence is likely to result. The strength of the evidence refers to the relative support that the evidence gives to one hypothesis as opposed to another. Credibility, on the other hand, refers to the ability of the evidence to lend support to any hypothesis at all. When evaluating a job reference for a potential employee, for

---

33. See Dylan Evans, *Risk Intelligence: How to Live with Uncertainty* (New York: Free Press, 2012), pp. 50–53, and note his distinction between ambiguity and uncertainty intolerance.

34. See Thaler and Sunstein, *Nudge*, 24–26; David DiSalvo, *What Makes Your Brain Happy and Why You Should Do the Opposite* (Amherst, NY: Prometheus Books, 2011), pp. 213–14: Dobelli, *Thinking Clearly*, ch. 11; McRaney, *You Are Not So Smart*, ch. 9; Kaplan and Kaplan, *Bozo Sapiens*, 42–43.

> example, managers may consider both how positive the reference is and how well the referee knows the candidate. The first question refers to the strength or extremeness of the evidence, whereas the second refers to its weight or credibility. Griffin and Tversky suggest that people attend first to the strength of the evidence and then make some adjustments in accordance with its weight. Crucially, however, the adjustment is generally insufficient. In the case of a positive job reference, for example, employers might be overly impressed by the warmth of the recommendation and not make enough allowance for the fact that the writer has known the candidate for only a few months.[35]

The availability bias and the mistaken assessment of credibility often converge when an individual is asked to comment on a potential *shiddukh*, or candidate for dating and marriage. It frequently happens that the "experts" consulted draw their authority merely from being the only connection the inquiring party has to the potential match. Little attention is paid to the fact that the lack of a better source for the inquirer does not make the responder well acquainted with the subject.

Mistaken evaluations of credibility can often be discerned through what, upon reflection, seems to be a clear logical fallacy. If someone makes a statement, the listener can either believe the speaker or not. However, if the speaker says, "don't take my word for it, I heard it from a very honest/reliable (unnamed) person," the listener will be likely to assign the statement much more credibility. However, all that has happened is that the speaker now has to be believed on several issues: the truth of the statement; the honesty or reliability of the individual he is quoting; and whether or not that individual actually made the statement, and whether or not it is being quoted completely accurately. Logic would dictate that if the speaker was not to be automatically believed on one item, adding more necessary premises would make it even less believable; however, this is not the automatic reaction most people would have.

---

35. Evans, *Risk Intelligence,* 80–83.

THE HALO/DEVIL EFFECT

Another related bias is known as the "halo effect," or, alternatively, the "devil effect." In this instance, it is assumed that the one quality that is known about an individual is completely definitive, and therefore all other traits can be assumed to be consistent with that impression. One good trait will grant an individual a "halo" placing all else about him in an angelic light, while a negative trait will do the opposite, branding the subject a "devil." This effect was observed in 1920 by Edward Thorndike, a psychologist in the US Army who noted that a soldier who made a positive first impression on a military officer was likely to get good scores in all categories of an evaluation, whereas the opposite was true for a soldier who made a negative first impression. Once again, an item that may by itself be true will have a greatly disproportionate effect.

The halo effect magnifies the impact of reputation, extending its effect beyond the area in which it was earned (justly or unjustly). As Michael Fertik and David Thompson put it in their book *Wild West 2.0*, "the halo effect makes this form of social reputation even more powerful: just as most people would not play poker against a gambler with a reputation as a cheater, most people also would not trust him to watch their children."[36] Accordingly, as reputation is the target of *lashon hara*, this effect obtains particular relevance.

The impact of the halo effect is significant, and it is particularly sensitive to order and sequence. As Daniel Kahneman puts it, "sequence matters.... Because the halo effect increases the weight of first impressions, sometimes to the point that subsequent information is mostly wasted."[37] He notes that he himself was placed at a disadvantage by this effect early in his teaching career, when he eventually realized that, when grading papers, if the first question was answered well, he gave the student the benefit of the doubt for the following questions, in a manner that was not extended to other students.[38]

---

36. Michael Fertik and David Thompson, *Wild West 2.0: How to Protect and Restore Your Online Reputation on the Untamed Social Frontier* (New York: Amacom, 2010), p. 20.
37. Kahneman, *Thinking Fast and Slow*, pp. 82–85. See also p. 206.
38. For more on the halo effect, see Phil Rosenzweig, *The Halo Effect... and the Eight Other Business Delusions That Deceive Managers* (New York: Free Press, 2007), throughout, and in particular chs. 4–6; Duncan J. Watts, *Everything Is Obvious Once*

Further, the devil effect, which presumably concerns us in this discussion more than the halo effect, is also very likely the stronger force. Humans commonly have a "negativity bias," assigning more credibility, as well as more weight, to information that is negative in nature. For example, the assessment of psychologist John Gottman that a successful marriage requires a ratio of five compliments for every criticism has been associated with this bias.[39] This point was made by a group of psychologists in a paper entitled "Bad Is Stronger Than Good," who wrote, "Bad emotions, bad parents, and bad feedback have more impact than good ones, and bad information is processed more thoroughly than good. The self is more motivated to avoid bad self-definitions than to pursue good ones. Bad impressions and bad stereotypes are quicker to form and more resistant to disconfirmation than good ones."[40]

The evaluative impressions people make of one another have a deep impact that is not always perceptible on a conscious level. In their book *Blind Spot: Hidden Biases of Good People,* Mahzarin R. Banaji and Anthony G. Greenwald cite studies that even amnesiacs, who were completely incapable of remembering details that had been provided them about individuals, could very accurately recall the positive or negative impressions they had formed about those individuals.[41]

This phenomenon is intensified if the subject is already labeled as an enemy of some sorts, as we are always desirous of believing that our enemies are evil, with no redeeming qualities, so as to justify our opposition. This tendency combines the two halves of the

---

You Know The Answer (New York: Crown Business, 2011), pp. 219–224; Dobelli, *Thinking Clearly,* ch. 38; Marcus, *Kluge,* 42–44; and McRaney, *You Are Now Less Dumb,* ch. 5.

39. See Jonah Lehrer, *How We Decide* (Boston: Houghton Mifflin Harcourt, 2009), p. 81 and Kahneman, *Thinking Fast and Slow,* p. 302.

40. Roy F. Baumeister, Ellen Bratslavsky, Catrin Finkenauer, and Kathleen D. Vohs, "Bad Is Stronger Than Good," *Review of General Psychology* 5 (2001): 323, cited in Kahneman, *Thinking Fast and Slow,* p. 302. He also cites on this subject Paul Rozin and Edward B. Royzman, "Negativity Bias, Negativity Dominance, and Contagion," *Personality and Social Psychology Review* 5 (2001): 296–320. See also Gardner, *Future Babble,* p. 140.

41. Mahzarin R. Banaji and Anthony G. Greenwald, *Blind Spot: Hidden Biases of Good People* (New York: Delacorte Press, 2013), pp. 63–64.

"fundamental attribution error" into one process: the opponent has committed misdeeds that wholly define him as irredeemably evil, while the victim, who may have performed similar acts, did so as isolated events under understandable circumstances. As Roy F. Baumeister writes in his book *Evil*:

> The myth of pure evil depicts malicious, alien forces intruding on the world of well-meaning, unsuspecting, virtuous people. The victims are thus freed from any blame or responsibility for their own misfortune. Their problems are not entirely solved by such an explanation, of course, but it is comforting in at least one respect: They do not have to feel guilty, stupid, or otherwise responsible.[42]

A 1943 study conducted by Syracuse University social psychologist Floyd H. Allport and Milton Lepkin concluded:

> When an individual is hostile toward something, or toward somebody, he is all the more ready to believe unfounded statements to the discredit of that object or person. He seizes upon something he can use as a "justifiable reason" for his hostility; and at the same time he has an opportunity, through belief in the damaging rumor, to attack the object he dislikes and vent his feelings upon it. The belief in rumors derogatory to racial or religious groups might, perhaps, be found to be based upon a similar motive.

Nicholas DiFonzo, who discusses this study in his book *The Watercooler Effect*, adds, "In other words, a hostile attitude may predispose someone to reason that a false rumor is possible, plausible, and perhaps even likely. Believing the rumor then allows one to spread the rumor and in so doing vent one's feelings of hostility."[43]

---

42. Roy F. Baumeister *Evil: Inside Human Cruelty and Violence* (W. H. Freeman, 1997), pp. 89–90.
43. DiFonzo, *Watercooler Effect*, 132–33.

CONFIRMATION BIAS

A vicious cycle is created by what is commonly known as "confirmation bias," among other names. This refers to the tendency individuals have to believe more readily that which is consistent with their previously formed opinions, and to discount information that is contradictory.[44] What's worse, this bias is apparently not corrected by increased levels of education or intelligence. Researcher David Perkins performed an experiment in which individuals were presented with a social issue and asked to write down their initial judgments. They were then asked to think about the issue further and to write down all relevant factors on either side of the issue. In the words of Jonathan Haidt:

> The findings get more disturbing. Perkins found that IQ was by far the biggest predictor of how well people argued, but it predicted only the number of "my-side" arguments. Smart people make really good lawyers and press secretaries, but they are no better than others at finding reasons on the other side. Perkins concluded that "people invest their IQ in buttressing their own case rather than in exploring the entire issue more fully and evenhandedly."[45]

Another version of this tendency is "diagnosis bias," which likewise refers to the tendency to uphold one's original assessment of the situation. Further, the initial diagnosis, even when made by others, has an impact on perceptions that is difficult to overcome. Ori Brafman and Ron Brafman, who discuss diagnosis bias throughout their book *Sway: The Irresistible Pull of Irrational Behavior*, describe a study that was done at

---

44. For discussions of this topic, see, for example, the entire book *Mistakes Were Made* by Tavris and Aronson; Kahneman, *Thinking Fast and Slow,* pp. 80–81; Gardner, *Future Babble,* pp. 85–86, 202–6; Watts, *Everything Is Obvious,* pp. 41–42; Evans, *Risk Intelligence,* pp.84–91; Barbara Oakley, *Evil Genes* (Amherst, NY: Prometheus Books, 2007), pp. 190–92; Gary Marcus, "Cognitive Humility," in John Brockman, ed., *This Will Make You Smarter,* (New York: Harper Perennial, 2012), pp. 39–40 and his *Kluge,* pp. 53–55; Dobelli, *Thinking Clearly,* chs. 7–8; Elaine Fox, *Rainy Brain Sunny Brain* (New York: Basic Books, 2012), pp. 151–52 (and see pp. 12–14 and throughout regarding cognitive biases in general).

45. Haidt, *Righteous Mind,* pp. 79–80. See also pp. 89–90, 92.

the Massachusetts Institute of Technology, in which a substitute teacher was described in a bio given out to students. Half the students received a paragraph-long bio which, among many other details, described the teacher as a "very warm person." The other half of the students received the identical bio, with just two words changed: in this case the teacher was described as "rather cold." The authors describe the results of the study as follows:

> At the end of the period, each student received an identical questionnaire about the sub. Upon seeing the results, you'd think the students were responding to two completely different instructors. Most students in the group that had received the bio describing the substitute as "warm" loved him. They described the instructor as "good natured, considerate of others, informal, sociable, popular, humorous, and humane." Although the second group sat in the exact same class and participated in the exact same discussion, a majority of them didn't really take to the instructor. They saw him as "self-centered, formal, unsociable, unpopular, irritable, humorless, and ruthless." This one word, "warm" or "cold" – albeit irrelevant in the larger scheme of things – made students assign a high or low value to the professor.[46]

To take this effect one step further, a study described by Melinda Blau and Karen L. Fingerman in their book *Consequential Strangers: The Power of People Who Don't Seem to Matter... but Really Do* is instructive. In this case, student volunteers at Princeton University were given a written description of a fictitious fellow undergraduate student, called "Donald." They were then given the task of relaying his characteristics to other students, who they knew in advance had either a positive or negative opinion of Donald. The authors report the findings as follows:

> The results might remind you of social life in the seventh grade. When students were told ahead of time that the other guy... liked

46. Ori Brafman and Ron Brafman, *Sway: The Irresistible Pull of Irrational Behavior* (New York: Doubleday, 2008), pp. 71–73.

> Donald, they described him as if they liked him, too. They barely mentioned Donald's negative traits and put a positive spin on ambiguous qualities – for instance, portraying him as "confident." But when they thought the other guy didn't like Donald, the volunteers' descriptions again mirrored their audience. They flipped the ambiguous traits – now Donald was conceited – and relayed mostly the negative information they had read. The fact is, most of us play to our audiences and, therefore, selectively disclose what we know. We also begin to believe our own spin. A week later, when asked their own impressions of Donald, volunteers tended to remember what they had *said* about him – the tailored version, not what they had read. They actually felt that way about Donald, too. In effect, saying was believing.[47]

Perhaps even more disturbing is the phenomenon that the subjects of the diagnosis themselves are inclined to take on the characteristics assigned to them. The Brafman brothers cite an experiment done in Israel, in which trainees in an army commander training program were randomly given classifications assessing their leadership potential. Despite the fact that these classifications did not actually reflect the real data, fifteen weeks later, when tested on their new knowledge, there was a significant correlation between performance on the test and the original labels given to the trainees. As the researchers describe further:

> This molding process becomes self-perpetuating: when we take on characteristics assigned to us, the diagnosis is reinforced and reaffirmed. Take a look at what happened with the Israeli soldiers and officers. When [the researcher] ... informed the trainers that the command potential scores had actually been fabricated and assigned randomly, they staunchly disagreed. In a desperate attempt to prove their point, they offered up evidence that the high-potential soldiers indeed performed better on the exit exams. This, of course, is circular logic. The exit tests confirmed

47. Blau and Fingerman, *Consequential Strangers*, 176–79.

> the initial diagnosis; the trainees had merely molded their abilities to the diagnoses ascribed to them.[48]

In fact, the confirmation bias is even more impactful than it seems. Social scientists Brendan Nyhan and Jason Reifle performed an experiment in which they discovered what amounts to a "backfire effect." Their results essentially demonstrated that once one is predisposed to a certain view, not only will new information not sway him from his position, but it will further entrench the position and will be interpreted as additional proof to that original view.[49] This effect has a particularly pernicious application in the area of *lashon hara*: since the moral decisions of the speaker are on the line, when confronted with contrary evidence, the instinct is to entrench oneself further in defending the righteousness of the original statement. The *Ḥafetz Ḥayim* describes this phenomenon in detailing the unique egregiousness of this transgression.[50]

Kathryn Shulz, who discusses confirmation bias at length in her book *Being Wrong: Adventures in the Margins of Error*, notes elements of this tendency which may play a significant role in the theories of *lashon hara*. She writes,

> We are swayed by the conventions and prejudices of our communities, we draw swift and sweeping conclusions based on scanty evidence (there's an armada of psychological research showing that we form strong and often lasting impressions of other people within the first sixty seconds of meeting them – in fact, often within the first two seconds), and we are reluctant to change or revise those conclusions once we have formed them. As Thomas Gilovich has pointed out, this is particularly true of negative first impressions, since the negativity serves as a deterrent to seeking out additional evidence. If I think you are an inconsiderate

48. Brafman and Brafman, *Sway*, 97–100.
49. See Clay A. Johnson, *The Information Diet: A Case for Conscious Consumption* (Beijing: O'Reilly, 2012), pp. 45–47, and McRaney, *You Are Now Less Dumb*, ch. 9.
50. *Ḥafetz Ḥayim*, Introduction, prohibition 6, in *Be'er Mayim Ḥayim*.

blowhard, I'm likely to avoid your company, thereby limiting my chances of ever coming across any evidence to the contrary. None of this prevents us from thinking that we are keen observers of our fellow humans, of course. As the seventeenth-century French writer Francois de La Rochefocauld observed, "Everyone complains about their memory; no one complains about their judgment."[51]

PATTERN SEEKING AND ANCHORING

Further, the human mind has a tendency to seek out patterns, which is often very useful, except when those patterns do not actually exist.[52] In that case, information that is actually isolated will be used to string together a picture that is essentially a false one. Building on the work of Daniel Kahneman, Viktor Mayer-Schönberger writes in his book *Big Data,*[53]

> The fast-thinking side of our brain is hard-wired to jump quickly to whatever causal conclusions it can come up with. It thus often leads us to wrong decisions. Contrary to conventional wisdom, such human intuiting of causality does not deepen our understanding of the world. In many instances, it's little more than a cognitive shortcut that gives us the illusion of insight but in reality leaves us in the dark about the world around us. Just as sampling was a shortcut we used because we could not process all the data, the perception of causality is a shortcut our brain uses to avoid thinking hard and slow.[54]

Likewise, there is a concept known as "anchoring" or "priming," in which the mind, having been prepared to expect a particular impression, interprets all forthcoming information in the context of that impression.

51. Schulz, *Being Wrong,* 124–29.
52. See Gardner, *Future Babble,* 74–82
53. Viktor Mayer-Schönberger, *Big Data: A Revolution That Will Transform How We Live, Work, and Think* (Boston: Houghton Mifflin Harcourt, 2013), pp. 62–66.
54. See also Chabris and Simons, *Invisible Gorilla,* pp. 154–184.

This effect is blamed for all kinds of irrational impacts on thinking. For example, participants in a wine auction who were asked to write down the last two digits of their Social Security numbers before bidding were found to bid higher numbers if the Social Security numbers were higher.[55]

Studies have shown how priming in an unrelated judgment-neutral area can affect assessment of people to their detriment, a finding of particular importance to the realm of *lashon hara* and its impact. In his book *We Have Met the Enemy*, Daniel Akst describes a study by Yale psychologist John Bargh:

> One classic Bargh experiment involved having a research assistant greet participants while holding a beverage. The assistant casually asks each subject to hold the drink, ostensibly so that the assistant can have a free hand for writing. Some participants were handed a hot cup of coffee and others were given an iced version of the same drink. Then the subjects were given a packet of information on an individual and were asked to assess the individual's personality traits. Guess what? Those who had held the hot coffee rated the person as significantly warmer. Bargh has done a lot of this stuff and has reached a simple conclusion: "We have much less volition and autonomy than we think." What's at work here is a phenomenon called priming, whereby behavior is activated through the power of unconscious suggestion. In recent years the psychology literature has been flooded with priming studies, all of which suggest that we literally have no idea what we're doing, or at least no idea why we're doing it.[56]

---

55. See Watts, *Everything Is Obvious*, 39–40. See also Thaler and Sunstein, *Nudge*, 69–71; Marcus, *Kluge*, 46–48, 88–89; Dan Ariely, *Predictably Irrational: The Hidden Forces That Shape Our Decisions* (New York: HarperCollins, 2008), pp. 34–36; McRaney, *You Are Not So Smart*, ch. 39; and Dean Buonomano, *Brain Bugs*, pp. 147–152.
56. Daniel Akst, *We Have Met the Enemy: Self Control in an Age of Excess* (New York: Penguin, 2011), p. 162; and see pp. 162–67.

Solomon Asch conducted an experiment which demonstrated that anchoring can cause the order of words to influence how people are judged. As described by author Sam Gosling:

> Anchoring plays a big part in how we form impressions of other people. In an experiment... Solomon Asch, one of the pioneers of social psychology, gave participants six-word descriptions of target people – the words were intelligent, industrious, impulsive, critical, stubborn, and envious. He then asked the participants to generate a broader description of those people on the basis of the six words. As you can see, Asch included both negative and positive words. But for one group of participants he presented the positive words first; for the other, he reversed the order. For both groups, the words were exactly the same.
>
> Yet Asch found striking differences in how the participants characterized the target person, depending on whether the first words they encountered were positive or negative. Here are some excerpts from the responses of participants who were given the positive words first (that is, intelligent, industrious, impulsive, critical, stubborn, envious): "A person who knows what he wants and goes after it. He is impatient at people who are less gifted, and ambitious with those who stand in his way." "Is a forceful person, has his own convictions and is usually right about things." "Is self-centered and desires his own way." "The person is intelligent and fortunately he puts his intelligence to work. That he is stubborn and impulsive may be due to the fact that he knows what he is saying and what he means and will not therefore give in easily to someone else's idea which he disagrees with."
>
> The participants who heard the negative words before the positive terms had a significantly different take on the imagined person: "This person's good qualities such as industry and intelligence are bound to be restricted by jealousy and stubbornness. The person is emotional. He is unsuccessful because he is weak and allows his bad points to cover up his good ones." "This individual is probably maladjusted because he is envious and impulsive." Just changing the order of the words was enough to

> drastically alter the participants' final impression. The first word anchored the description and colored how they interpreted the rest of the words.[57]

Here again there is another unique role for negative attitudes, as described by Dr. Danielle Ofri in her book *What Doctors Feel,* which builds on the work of Dr. Jerome Groopman:

> In his insightful and practically titled book *How Doctors Think,* Jerome Groopman explored the various styles and strategies that doctors use to guide diagnosis and treatment, pointing out the flaws and strengths along the way. He studied the cognitive processes that doctors use and observed that emotions can strongly influence these thought patterns, sometimes in ways that gravely damage our patients. "Most [medical] errors are mistakes in thinking," Groopman writes. "And part of what causes these cognitive errors is our inner feelings, feelings we do not readily admit to and often don't even recognize." Research bears this out. Positive emotions tend to be associated with a more global view of a situation ("the forest") and more flexibility in problem solving. Negative emotions tend to diminish the importance of the bigger picture in favor of the smaller details ("the trees"). In cognitive psychology studies, subjects with negative emotions are more prone to anchoring bias – that is, latching on to a single detail at the expense of others. Anchoring bias is a potent source of diagnostic error, causing doctors to stick with an initial impression and avoid considering conflicting data.[58]

Further, as David Barash discusses in his book *Payback: Why We Retaliate, Redirect Aggression, and Take Revenge,* the priming of a negative

57. Sam Gosling, *Snoop: What Your Stuff Says About You* (New York: Basic Books, 2008), pp. 189–90.
58. Danielle Ofri, *What Doctors Feel: How Emotions Affect the Practice of Medicine* (Boston: Beacon, 2013), p. 2.

experience can make a subsequent interaction with someone else appear to be a part of a negative pattern when in fact it is isolated and possibly even innocent.[59]

GROUP POLARIZATION

The term "group polarization" describes the tendency of members of groups to make decisions that are more extreme than they would likely make on their own. The extent to which humans are influenced by the opinions of those they are friendly with, or simply those who surround them, is tremendous.

The best-known display of group effect upon individuals within it is a set of experiments that psychologist Solomon Asch conducted between 1951 and 1956. In his experiments, he asked students to compare the lengths of various lines. The images were clear and distinct, and when asked as individuals, 95 percent of his students answered each question correctly. However, when he added actors to the mix who intentionally gave the incorrect answer in a confident voice, the accuracy rate among the real students fell to 25 percent.

Gregory Berns, an Emory University neuroscientist, updated these experiments in 2005, with the benefit of an fMRI scanner, and confirmed the results, with an added insight. As Susan Cain describes it in *Quiet*:

> Peer pressure ... is not only unpleasant, but can actually change your view of a problem. These early findings suggest that groups are like mind-altering substances. If the group thinks the answer is A, you're much more likely to believe that A is correct, too. It's not that you're saying consciously, "Hmm, I'm not sure, but they all think the answer's A, so I'll go with that." Nor are you saying, "I want them to like me, so I'll just pretend that the answer's A." No, you are doing something much more unexpected – and dangerous. Most of Berns's volunteers reported having gone along with the group because "they thought that they had

59. David Barash, *Payback: Why We Retaliate, Redirect Aggression, and Take Revenge* (New York: Oxford University Press, 2011), p. 61.

> arrived serendipitously at the same correct answer." They were utterly blind, in other words, to how much their peers had influenced them.[60]

There are others aspects to this phenomenon as well. As Margaret Heffernan writes:

> Other insights emerged from this experiment. Knowledge of the group's decision seemed to reduce the mental load on the volunteers; less thinking took place when they knew what the others thought.... So instead of the group benefiting from the collective wisdom of many, in fact what it got was reduced thoughtfulness from each one. When asked in a debriefing questionnaire how they explained their conforming errors, the participants had no sense of having conformed; they believed that they had all reached the same decision purely serendipitously. They may have thought that they'd made a free choice where in fact, they had not.[61]

Further, the impact of group polarization is not only on the spread and acceptance of an opinion. Studies have also indicated that members of a group (who speak only with each other) not only accept each other's views but also tend to take on the most extreme versions of these views.[62]

---

60. Cain, *Quiet*, 91–92.
61. Margaret Heffernan, *Willful Blindness* (New York: Walker, 2011), p. 136.
62. See Weinberger, David, *Too Big to Know: Rethinking Knowledge Now That the Facts Aren't the Facts, Experts Are Everywhere, and the Smartest Person in the Room Is the Room* (New York: Basic Books, 2011), p. 82, citing Cass R. Sunstein, *Republic.com* (Princeton, NJ: Princeton University Press, 2001), p. 65ff. Sunstein discusses group polarization extensively as one of the major factors in the acceptance of false rumors in his *On Rumors* (New York: Farrar, Straus and Giroux, 2009), and in his article "Believing False Rumors" in Levmore and Nussbaum, *Offensive Internet*, pp. 91–106, and also (with Reid Hastie) in *Wiser: Getting Beyond Groupthink to Make Groups Smarter* (Boston: Harvard Business Review Press, 2015), in which many cognitive biases are discussed from the perspective of the particular vulnerability of groups. For further discussion of group polarization see Kida, *Don't Believe Everything*, ch. 12,

Worse yet, the impact of the group has a particularly nefarious effect in the area of disparaging others. David DiSalvo, in his book *What Makes Your Brain Happy and Why You Should Do the Opposite,* discusses "blame contagion," in which the fact of a group assigning blame to an individual causes other members of the group to share that opinion:

> A study conducted by researchers from the University of Southern California and Stanford University suggests that blaming someone in public is the psychological equivalent of coughing swine flu into a crowd. Over the course of multiple experiments, researchers showed that witnessing someone play the blame game significantly increased the chances of others' blaming someone else for their failures – even when those failures had nothing to do with what they witnessed. Blame contagion is essentially about self-image protection. The study authors believe that when someone watches another person level blame, the implicit takeaway is that self-image protection is a goal that she should also aspire to.

Interestingly, the suggestion made by the authors is evocative of the value contained in studying the topic of *lashon hara* as an antidote to the tendency to malign others. DeSalvo reports that the authors note, "In this study, blame became less contagious if people wrote down and affirmed their values before they witnessed someone attribute blame, which acted as a 'blame antidote.' The more self-affirmed people became (the more of the antidote they took), the less they felt the need to protect their image."[63]

There is an important distinction that must be made within this point. It is theoretically true that a position held by many people is more

---

and Solove, *Future of Reputation,* p. 101. See also Nassim Taleb, *Fooled by Randomness* (New York: Random House, 2005), p. 85 regarding "firemen effect," and see footnotes there. See also Gino, *Sidetracked,* 107–9 regarding the influence of social bonds.

63. DiSalvo, *What Makes Your Brain Happy,* 167–68, citing Nathanael J. Fast et al., "Blame Contagion: The Automatic Transmission of Self-Serving Attributions," *Journal of Experimental Social Psychology* 46 (January 2010): 97–106.

likely to be accurate than that held by fewer people. Indeed, James Surowiecki, in his well-known book *The Wisdom of Crowds,* argues for the increased accuracy that comes when the opinions or assessments of many individuals are aggregated into one.[64]

However, as Dylan Evans notes in *Risk Intelligence,* there is a vast difference between the combined opinions of many individuals, which may or may not prove to be wise, and the opinions shared by members of a group who influence one another, which could yield what Scottish journalist Charles McKay in an 1841 book called the "madness of crowds."[65] Evans writes, "the so-called wise crowds in these experiments are not really crowds but collections of individuals. The average estimate tends to be accurate only when all the people in the group figure out their personal estimates on their own.... As soon as the members of a group communicate, however, any signs of collective wisdom tend to evaporate as rumors spread and fashions develop."[66]

Further, the "group" doesn't even have to be made up of different people. Humans are susceptible to being misled by a false statement through the simple fact of the item being repeated many times. Familiarity can be interpreted by the brain as accuracy, and researchers have displayed that hearing an opinion expressed by one person ten times can have an impact on the brain equivalent to having heard ten people express the opinion once.[67] This tendency has been found to be particularly present when the listener is not paying close attention, in which case the repeated item subconsciously becomes taken as a given.[68]

---

64. James Surowiecki, *The Wisdom of Crowds: Why the Many Are Smarter Than the Few and How Collective Wisdom Shapes Business, Economies, Societies, and Nations* (New York: Doubleday, 2004).
65. Charles MacKay, *Extraordinary Popular Delusions and the Madness of Crowds* (New York: Harmony Books, 1980).
66. Evans, *Risk Intelligence,* 111–12. See also Pentland, *Social Physics,* 28.
67. Scott O. Lilienfeld, Stephen Jay Lynn, John Ruscio, and Barry L. Beyerstein, *50 Great Myths of Popular Psychology: Shattering Widespread Misconceptions About Human Behavior* (Malden, MA: Wiley-Blackwell, 2010), p. 10.
68. See DiSalvo, *What Makes Your Brain Happy,* 155.

As Nicholas DiFonzo discusses in his book *The Watercooler Effect*, there are various reasons why a rumor heard repeatedly is more likely to be believed. Some of these are reasonable; for example, it is logical to assume that if more people pass something on it is because more of them believe it to be true, and that may indeed be the case. However, he notes:

> A second reason that repeatedly hearing a rumor increases belief is more intriguing – and should give us pause. Repeated hearing leads listeners to feel familiar with the statement and that familiarity increases belief. This idea is based on what is known as the "illusory-truth effect": familiarity with the statement leads to greater belief in that statement.

DiFonzo then cites a study in which it was demonstrated that students remember familiar statements, even ones that had been identified as false, as truer than statements that were unfamiliar to them. He adds:

> The illusory-truth effect is counterintuitive; there is no logical reason that a statement with which we are more familiar should be invested with greater confidence. It may be that we use a simple heuristic in judging the truth of the statement – "that sounds like something I have heard before – it must be true!" The implication of all this is that if "everyone is saying it," then our belief in the hearsay rises. All other factors being the same, familiarity breeds confidence – not contempt.[69]

While any of these biases alone can be damaging enough to fair evaluations, they very rarely appear alone. Many of them are associated with each other and nourish each other. It is more likely that multiple biases are at play whenever information is being processed; especially negative information has the potential to disproportionately impact upon its subject.

69. DiFonzo, *Watercooler Effect*, 140–41. Regarding the halakhic status of a persistent rumor, see below pp. 155–156.

DISPROPORTIONATE IMPACT

Beyond these concerns, there is another major fear relevant to the processing of negative information. Even if the item itself is evaluated accurately by the listener, there is also the risk that the listener will take the information as a license not only to extrapolate beyond the scope of the information but also to act negatively towards the subject in a fashion that is not warranted by the report that was conveyed.[70]

This can happen on an individual level and on a group level as well. This risk represents one of the major harms caused by racism and by other forms of unjust discrimination. Not only is the prejudiced assessment false, an issue in and of itself, but the disparagement is often used as a pretext to impose mistreatment upon the subjects of the slurs.

Another concern related to disparate impact is the reality that hearing a rumor about someone activates its own particular effect on the listener. In *The Watercooler Effect*, the author discusses this "rumor effect":

> Hearing any idea, including a rumor, is like putting on a pair of colored glasses – it puts the scenery in a certain light. Hearing a rumor that someone has a particular personality trait, for example, makes us more likely to interpret what the person says in line with that trait. Rumor effects undoubtedly occur in part because they activate powerful mental frameworks that lead us to classify people in particular ways... hearing a negative remark can activate a generally negative framework – despite disbelief in the rumor. That is, a negative rumor can lead us to appraise the target of rumor more negatively – regardless of how believable we think the rumor is. "Mud sticks" as the old saying goes.... A second way that rumors accomplish their effects is to explain events using a cause that lasts over time; these explanations then affect our prediction of future events.... [Another] way that rumors bring about effects is that they simply teach us how we should feel about things. Psychologists have labeled this type of education social learning: We learn attitudes from others. Rumors may

70. See Solove, *Future of Reputation*, pp. 70–71.

> indeed be the main means by which we learn these attitudes.... Rumors support and legitimate [negative] attitudes.[71]

Disproportionate impact has at least two ramifications. One is that negative consequences in excess of what is appropriate will be directed toward the subject. Another is that the evaluation of the individual will ultimately be unfair, assessing too much discredit to the subject, and failing to account for, or even to be aware of, mitigating elements and the broader context of the act itself and of the subject as a whole. Indeed, the *Ḥafetz Ḥayim* says as much,[72] asserting that the prohibition of relaying true information is a function of the concern that the impact will essentially be false, leading one prominent student of his to assert based on his words that were it possible to correct for this, the prohibition would not apply.[73] However, such correction is often, if not always, beyond our ability to accomplish effectively.

BLINDNESS TO BIAS

Attempting to correct for these biases, while a necessary first step, is only helpful to a point. Another frailty of the human psyche is the lack of awareness as to when these biases are present, even those that are theoretically known. Our awareness is itself blinded by bias, known, appropriately, as "bias bias."[74] In the words of Dr. Robert A. Burton, "Our mental limitations prevent us from accepting our mental limitations."[75]

As Keith Stanovich writes in his book *What Intelligence Tests Miss*:

> Princeton psychologist Emily Pronin has surveyed research indicating that there is one additional domain in which people show biased self-assessments. That domain is in the assessment of their own biases. Pronin summarizes research

71. DiFonzo, *Watercooler Effect*, 28–36.
72. *Ḥafetz Ḥayim, Laws of Lashon HaRa, klal* 4, *Be'er Mayim Ḥayim* 33.
73. Rabbi Elḥanan Bunim Wasserman, *Kovetz He'arot, biurei aggadot* 8:9. See Rabbi Ḥayim Yudchik, *Shemuot Ḥayim*, Arakhin, ch. 3:24, for objections to his position.
74. See Gardner, *Future Babble*, 254; and see also Epley, *Mindwise*, 32–34.
75. Burton, *On Being Certain*, 159.

> in which subjects had to rate themselves and others on their susceptibility to a variety of cognitive and social psychology biases that have been identified in the literature, such as halo effects and self-serving attributional biases (taking credit for successes and avoiding responsibility for failures). Pronin and colleagues found that across eight such biases, people uniformly felt that they were less biased than their peers. In short, people acknowledge the truth of psychological findings about biased processing – with the exception that they believe it does not apply to them.
>
> In explaining why this so-called bias blind spot exists, Pronin speculated that when estimating the extent of bias in others, people relied on lay psychological theory. However, when evaluating their own bias, she posited, they fell back on an aspect of myside processing – monitoring their own conscious introspections. Modern lay psychological theory allows for biased processing, so biased processing is predicted for others. However, most social and cognitive biases that have been uncovered by research operate unconsciously. Thus, when we go on the introspective hunt for the processes operating to bias our own minds we find nothing. We attribute to ourselves via the introspective mechanism much less bias than we do when we extrapolate psychological theory to others.[76]

Accordingly, these biases operate in the background, while we are not always conscious of their presence. It is therefore not always possible to simply operate as if they are not impacting the thought process. For example, studies have shown that jurors who are told that evidence that they have heard is irrelevant and inadmissible are nonetheless unable to prevent that evidence from influencing their decision.[77]

---

76. Keith Stanovich, *What Intelligence Tests Miss: The Psychology of Rational Thought* (New Haven, CT: Yale University Press, 2009), pp. 109–10.
77. See Epley, *Mindwise,* 150, citing N. Steblay et al., "The Impact on Jury Verdicts of Traditional Instruction to Disregard Inadmissible Evidence: A Meta-Analysis, *Law and Human Behavior* 30 (2006): 469–92.

There are various factors that can exacerbate these tendencies. For example, the tiredness of the listener has an impact, as described by Margaret Heffernan in her book *Willful Blindness*:

> When we are tired or preoccupied – conditions psychologists call "resource-depleted" – we start to economize, to conserve those resources. Higher order thinking is more expensive. So too are doubt, skepticism, and argument. "Resource depletion specifically disables cognitive elaboration," wrote Harvard psychologist Daniel Gilbert. "Not only does doubt seem to be the last to emerge, but it also seems to be the first to disappear." Because it takes less brain power to believe than to doubt, we are, when tired, or distracted, gullible. Because we are all biased, and biases are quick and effortless, exhaustion makes us favor the information we know and are comfortable with. We're too tired to do the heavier lifting of examining new or contradictory information, so we fall back on our biases, the opinions and the people we already trust.[78]

Even in the absence of such complicating circumstances, our ability to account for biases is limited. Stanislas Dehaene, who wrote a book about the nature of consciousness entitled *Consciousness and the Brain*, writes as follows:

> We are conscious only of our conscious thoughts. Because our unconscious operations elude us, we constantly overestimate the role that consciousness plays in our physical lives. By forgetting the amazing power of the unconscious, we overattribute our actions to conscious decisions and therefore mischaracterize our consciousness as a major player in our daily lives. In the words of the Princeton psychologist Julian Jaynes, "Consciousness is a much smaller part of our mental life than we are conscious of, because we cannot be conscious of what we are not conscious of." Paraphrasing Douglas Hofstadter's whimsically circular

78. Heffernan, *Willful Blindness*, 78–79.

> law of programming ("A project always takes longer than you expect – even when you take into account Hofstadter's Law"), we might elevate this statement to the level of a universal law: We constantly overestimate our awareness – even when we are aware of the glaring gaps in our awareness. The corollary is that we dramatically underestimate how much vision, language, and attention can occur outside our awareness.[79]

If all or most of the above concerns are present and significant, we are left with the question: What can society then do in order to function effectively?

Are we doomed, as one contemporary writer put it, to be stuck in a "postmodern miasma"?[80] Our basic decision-making ability does not have to be paralyzed. As noted by many of those who write on the brain's cognitive tendencies,[81] there are a significant advantages towards our functionality that emanate from these tendencies, not least among them the possibility of optimism, resilience, focus, and efficiency of operation. Nonetheless, there are risks as well, and thus awareness of these tendencies can play a very constructive role in mitigating these risks.

When the reputation and associated well-being of another person is at stake, these risks attain an added significance. Accordingly, it is understandable that the dual considerations of accuracy and of necessity are of primary importance when considering relating negative information about someone, and Jewish law reflects that reality, demanding that such conversation be both necessary and true. When necessity has indeed been confirmed, the task remains to consider carefully how the biases and tendencies of cognition and human behavior affect the truth of the report and the justice of its impact.

From one perspective, it is certainly necessary to be aware of these issues and to correct for them to the greatest extent possible; as

79. Stanislas Dehaene, *Consciousness and the Brain: Deciphering How the Brain Codes Our Thoughts* (New York: Viking Adult, 2014), pp. 79–80.

80. DiFonzo, *Watercooler Effect*, 147.

81. See, for example, Mlodinow, *Subliminal*, ch. 10; Schacter, *Seven Sins of Memory*, ch. 8; Schulz, *Being Wrong*; and Pariser, *Filter Bubble*, 83–91.

Kahneman puts it, "decorrelate error." To focus on one example, in their book *Decisive* Chip Heath and Dan Heath devote a chapter to countering the confirmation bias, in which they suggest three strategies: making it easier for others to disagree; asking questions that are more likely to cause contrary information to surface; and checking the process by affirmatively considering the opposite possibility.[82] Touching on areas that are particularly relevant to *lashon hara,* they discuss the cycle of accumulated negative assumptions that sometimes develops, and note that some organizational leaders urge their employees to "assume positive intent, that is to imagine that the behavior or words of your colleagues are motivated by good intentions, even when their actions seem objectionable at first glance."

Nonetheless, as we have seen, for many reasons it is not always possible to correct for our biases, or to even be aware of them. Hence, it is understandable that if information, even if ostensibly true, can have unjust negative impact, it would be worthwhile to proceed with great caution in deciding if and how to disclose such information.

However, it must be strongly emphasized that there are many instances in which society needs such information to be disclosed in order to function properly, and therefore cannot simply maintain a policy of avoiding the disclosure of all negative information. However, a policy that gives strong weight to both necessity and the very significant efforts required in order to avoid inaccuracy, distortion, and outright falsity, is very much needed.

Further, there is another important lesson here. It emerges that due to the simple reality of human nature, many statements that are said about others turn out to be false, either in whole or in part. Nonetheless, the speakers of these statements are in no sense of the word lying; they are merely saying what they believe and perceive to be true. Appreciating this dichotomy is greatly significant towards improving human relations.

Similarly, Christopher Chabris and Daniel Simons urge a comparable attitude as the main lesson emanating from their important book *The Invisible Gorilla*:

82. Chip Heath and Dan Heath, *Decisive: How to Make Better Choices in Life and Work* (New York: Crown Business, 2013), ch. 5.

> When you think about the world with an awareness of everyday illusions, you won't be as sure of yourself as you used to be, but you will have new insights into how your mind works, and new ways of understanding why people act the way they do. Often, it's not because of stupidity, arrogance, ignorance, or lack of focus. It's because of the everyday illusions that affect us all. Our final hope is that you will always consider this possibility before you jump to a harsher conclusion.[83]

One of the most inflammatory accusations that enters all too frequently into modern discourse is the branding of an individual as a "liar." However, it is not at all difficult to see that an individual can be honest and yet his words may not be correct.[84] Acknowledging both halves of that sentence would go a great way toward understanding the prohibition of "true" *lashon hara,* and to improving the level of fairness, graciousness, and decency that are extended to speaker, listener, and their subjects.

---

83. Chabris and Simons, *Invisible Gorilla,* p. 242. See also Tavris and Aronson, *Mistakes Were Made,* 69.
84. Rabbi Yaakov Kaminetsky, in his *Emet LeYaakov* to Pirkei Avot, suggests a novel interpretation to the statement of the mishna (1:8) which advises rabbinical court judges to see both litigants as "evil" while they are in the court; however, when they leave after the judgment, they should both be seen as "innocent, as they have accepted the ruling." He understands this mishna as reflecting the fact that litigants might be speaking falsehoods without realizing it. Thus, if the judges are to reach the truth, they must view both testimonies as suspect, regardless of the reputations of the litigants. However, after the judgment has been rendered, they should both be viewed positively, as it is possible that they were both testifying in good faith, even if the facts were incorrect, and their honesty is confirmed by the fact that they have accepted the judgement.

Defining the Prohibition: A Forbidden Character Trait or Prohibited Behavior?

Having outlined some of the themes and elements present in the speech ethic, we can turn our attention to a more specific analysis of the prohibition of *lashon hara.* We can do so by drawing on two sets of tools, which, in this case, overlap. One set belongs to the philosopher; the other, the expert in talmudic analysis.

Philosophers have long considered the following question: What is the goal of moral instruction, of the ethical code, whatever it may be? Is it, on the one hand, to bring about just acts, to influence behavior toward that which is right and good? Or, rather, are we interested in creating good *people,* individuals of elevated character, whose souls are refined by moral influence, and whose personalities are the product of righteous training?

This question is not a new one, neither for philosophers nor for legal scholars. It has long been the subject of debate to what end should moral philosophy strive: toward the shaping of character, encouraging "virtue" and discouraging "vice," or toward the concrete influencing of behavior.[1] Additionally, law, which is more directed toward behavior, has its own debate regarding whether it should be comprised of rules, which are specific regulations as to what can and cannot be done (e.g., "do not drive more than fifty-five miles per hour"), or standards, which are more generalized principles as to the goals of the law (e.g., "do not drive dangerously").[2]

This is a broad question, prevalent in world philosophy, and addressed as well within the specific realm of Jewish religious thought. Does the Torah manifest itself as a book of laws, primarily conveying "do"s and "don't"s, independent of the character traits that lie beneath one's external behavior? To be sure, nobility of character is a fundamental interest in Judaism, but it may nonetheless be the case that this area is addressed indirectly rather than directly. This might be because of necessity; it might be understood that one cannot be instructed who to be, but only what to do and what not to do, with the hope that that will impact on character. In the words of the classic thirteenth-century discussion of the Torah's commandments, the *Sefer HaḤinnukh*, "the heart is directed by the actions."[3]

Our consideration of the question of the damage to the victims wrought by the speaking of *lashon hara*, as well as the effect on the character of the speaker, opens the door to a new stage in analyzing the prohibition. It seems clear that *lashon hara* represents at least two categories of evil: an act of damage, an offense against the subjects of the speech; and a base character trait, an aspect of the personality dangerous to the soul.[4] Interestingly, Maimonides, who is often associated with

---

1. For discussions of this, see the extensive listing at the online *Stanford Encyclopedia of Philosophy*, http://plato.stanford.edu/entries/ethics-virtue/; and also see Kwame Anthony Appiah's *Experiments in Ethics: What Is Good and Why* (Cambrige, MA: Harvard University Press, 2007), pp. 29–35, 191–196; and see as well Gerd Gigerenzer, *Gut Feelings* (New York: Viking, 2007), ch. 10.
2. For an extensive listing of some of the contemporary legal literature on this, see Jonathan Zittrain, *The Future of the Internet* (New Haven, CT: Yale University Press), ch. 6, p. 128n4.
3. *Sefer HaḤinnukh* 16.
4. The psychological makeup of the personality inclined toward gossip is discussed in Rosnow and Fine, *Rumor and Gossip*, 81–83.

an action-based understanding of the Torah's commandments,[5] does speak of character traits in his legal code, in which he notes that a Torah scholar "judges his fellow favorably, speaks in praise of his friend and never to his disparagement."[6] This latter element, the ideal personality, presents a question: Does a legal system, based on commandments of action, address this realm?

The very nature of the prohibition is subject to analysis in light of the above. Does *lashon hara* indeed represent the formal banning of what is essentially the character trait of mean-spiritedness? Such a notion would extend the range of legal authority beyond action into the realm of the personality. To some of the early authorities, such a notion may be entirely acceptable.

Others, however, may balk at such an extension. Undoubtedly, the Torah aims to transform the personality. However, that takes place at a remove; the Torah, as a book of laws, addresses itself directly to behavior, not to character traits. The latter is to be affected indirectly, through the practice of the former.

If the behavior-based view is dominant, then an alternative classification of *lashon hara* would be required. Instead of addressing a character trait, the prohibition would be directed at an identifiable action, with the indirect goal of impacting personality thematically crucial but practically irrelevant. The prohibition might then be formulated as the making of a statement that places another at risk of harm, without attention paid to the particular level of maliciousness. In this model, the nature of the offense would be indirectly harming another individual, or taking the risk of doing so. It is important to note that Jewish law normally exempts indirect causation of damages from compensation. However, this only refers to the ability of a court to extract payment after the fact; the a priori causation of harm to another, even indirectly, is certainly prohibited. Thus, even if it is not possible for a victim to

5. Regarding the technical formulation of the commandments, if not their purpose. In other words, even if the ultimate goal is an emotional or intellectual state, a mitzva would command an action as the means.
6. *Mishneh Torah, Laws of Personal Development* 5:7. See the discussion in *Emek HaLashon*, pp. 6–7.

collect damages for an act of *lashon hara* after the fact, this does not impact on its prohibition.[7]

These two possibilities in understanding the prohibition of *lashon hara,* as character trait- directed or as behavior-directed, thus provide somewhat of a framework to address the conceptual underpinnings of the precept. Further, it does not have to be one or the other; it is certainly possible that both elements are at play, and that the concept is directed both at behavior and at personality traits, or that it applies differently under different circumstances.

Similarly, the rules and standards debate is applicable to *lashon hara* as well, and has played a role in some of the controversy regarding the publication of halakhic works addressing *lashon hara* in a legalistic format. Even granted that the Torah bans *lashon hara* as prohibited behavior, how is this prohibition to be interpreted: Should it be read as a group of principles, general in formulation, and resistant to specific legislation? Or, should it be presented as actual rules and guidelines that identify the categories of speech that are prohibited, the categories that are allowed, and the categories that are obligatory?

The great medieval ethicist Rabbeinu Yonah of Gerona (1200–1263), in his major ethical tract *Shaarei Teshuva* (Gates of Repentance), identifies two elements in the transgression of *lashon hara:* first, the damage and embarrassment caused to one's fellow, and on top of that effect, the "decision to disparage one's fellow."[8] This formulation appears to isolate a corruption of character that infects the speaker, independent of the harm inflicted on the subject, and recognizes both as equal components.

Many authorities, including the *Ḥafetz Ḥayim,* have discerned this dual theme in the writings of Maimonides as well.[9] In the chapter of his legal code addressing the principles of *lashon hara,* Maimonides seems to define the prohibition twice.[10] First, he rules that one who disparages his fellow is in violation of this precept. In the following paragraph, he

7. This point is emphasized by the *Ḥafetz Ḥayim* in the introduction to his *Be'er Mayim Ḥayim* to the *Laws of Rekhilut.* Note also the distinction drawn on this point in *Zikhron David,* pp. 114–15.

8. *Shaarei Teshuva* 3:216.

9. *Ḥafetz Ḥayim, Laws of Lashon HaRa, klal* 3, in *Be'er Mayim Ḥayim* 7.

10. *Mishneh Torah, Laws of Personal Development* 7:2–4.

reintroduces the concept, now defining it as the relating of matter that, when passed from one person to another, will cause "harm to a man's person or to his property or will even [merely] anguish him or frighten him."[11] The implication here is that *lashon hara* incorporates two aspects: the general disparaging of others, indicative of a character defect of the speaker; and the actual harm inflicted upon others through derogatory speech, which manifests a flaw in the behavior of the speaker.

Some later scholars suggest that the multiplicity of sources in the Torah might correlate to varying elements of the prohibition and its effects. For example, the "peddler verse" (Lev. 19:16) might be addressing the general derogation of others, while the injunction against "bearing a false/unnecessary report" (Ex. 23:1) might address actual damage inflicted upon the subject.[12]

The notion that *lashon hara* manifests itself as a character flaw, independent of any potential or actual harm, has been associated with many biblical references. For example, the offense committed by the spies sent by Moses who disparaged the Land of Israel, and, as noted, has been identified by the Talmud as a form of *lashon hara,* may demonstrate that the attitude and proclivity of unjustified negativity is harmful and sinful, even without a human victim.[13] Similarly, Moses himself was the subject of negative conversation by his siblings Miriam and Aaron, for which Miriam was punished for her active role. However, the Torah in that context implies that Moses did not take any offense at what was being said, suggesting that the forgiveness of the victim does not mitigate the offense.[14] Accordingly, many commentators have understood the Torah's intent to be that *lashon hara* is condemned not

11. Ibid., 7:5.

12. See Rabbi Avraham Shmuel Papenheim, *Pinat Yakrat* to Bava Batra, sec. 133, and Rabbi Elyakim Shlesinger in *Ner LeEḥad, Parashat Kedoshim,* pp. 476–78. Compare, however, Rabbi Meir Yeḥiel Weinshtok, *Beit Shlomo* to Arakhin 14. A different theory regarding the two verses is advanced by Rabbi Natan Gestetner, *Natan Piryo* to Makkot, pp. 216–17.

13. See Rabbi Mordekhai Karlebakh, *Ḥavatzelet HaSharon al HaTorah,* Numbers, p. 437, as well as Rabbi Moshe Schwab, *Maarkhei Lev,* cited in *Ḥokhmat HaMatzpun,* Numbers, p. 367.

14. See *Birkat Reuven Shlomo,* Sota 30, *ot* 11.

only because of its effect on the victim, but equally because of its display of egregious character deficiencies, and is thus prohibited even in the absence of damage.[15]

This may also be read into the format of the Torah's core prohibition in this area. The impression created by a statement such as "You shall not go about as a *rakhil* [gossip, peddler]" rather than a more straightforward formulation such as "You shall not disparage" is that it is not an act that is being condemned, but rather a personality type; as if the instruction is not what not to *do*, but what not to *be*.

A further observation can be made from the fact that the Torah characterizes the act of gossip as "going about as a peddler." The *Ḥafetz Ḥayim* [16] offers the suggestion that the intent is to include not only the gossip itself but the prior acts leading up to it in the transgression.[17] If so, the message would seem to again be that *lashon hara* is damaging not only because of the effect on the subject, but that the entire process and mentality is corrosive to the speaker.

Along these lines, Nahmanides, in his commentary on this verse, notes that its grammatical construction is instructive as well. The actual word used (*rakhil*) is slightly different in form from the word that means literally "peddler" (*rokhel*). He suggests that *rakhil* is reflective of one who is engaged not merely in an activity but in a habit that defines his personality. Similarly, Maimonides, in his condemnation of the *baal lashon hara*, appears to delineate that beyond the prohibited act, there is a point at which the habitual offender becomes defined by this proclivity, and that that identity itself is prohibited by the Torah.[18]

---

15. See *Responsa VeDarashta VeḤakarta* 3, *Ḥoshen Mishpat* 20.
16. *Ḥafetz Ḥayim, Laws of Lashon HaRa, klal* 1, *Be'er Mayim Ḥayim* 4 and *klal* 2:12 in footnote, citing the *Shla*.
17. Although *Ḥelkat Binyamin*, p. 53, notes that the *Torat Kohanim* interprets the word differently. Compare also the comment of *Or HaḤayim* to Lev. 19:16, who suggests that the "walking" is a reference to the dissemination of the gossip by the listeners, to refute the perception that it may be safe to spread the gossip in a certain context where the subject would not seem to be affected. See also *Emek HaLashon*, pp. 7–10. For further exposition on this topic and alternative perspectives, see *VaYita Eshel* to Arakhin, 97.
18. See Rabbi Naḥum Brobovsky, *Shalmei Naḥum*, pp. 553–60. See also *Mishnat Yisrael* 7:18 in footnote, who finds a different emphasis in the words of Nahmanides, and

The recognition of these two constructs, the trait and the act, is an important step in understanding the prohibition of *lashon hara,* and in determining whether broad standards or more particular rules are best suited toward its application. As the practical realities of the speech ethic are debated, it often emerges that the most illuminating question is a basic one: Are we seeking to impact behavior, character, or some combination of both?

---

suggests that his reading renders *rokhel* as primarily a revealer of secrets (one who is introducing a new item on the market that would not be there without him), while Rashi in his commentary to that verse emphasizes the peddler's travels from place to place in search of gossip, a possible emphasis on disparaging speech.

Section Two:
The Application

Permitted Lashon HaRa: Purposeful and Beneficial Speech

DEFINING THE CONCEPT

One of the most consequential, controversial, and complex aspects of the laws of *lashon hara* is that known as *to'elet* or "purpose." Most importantly, this notion indicates that when the listener requires the information for his own protection, it is not only permissible to relate the information but obligatory. More broadly, a generally productive purpose, under certain circumstances, may also be considered justification for transmitting what otherwise could be termed *lashon hara*.

The concept of *to'elet* is consequential, then, in that an action flips from forbidden to mandatory. Controversial, not in its existence, which is undisputed, but in its application. The evaluation of *to'elet* is resistant to general legislation and is often dependent on painstakingly considered judgment. One of the rabbinical court judges in nineteenth-century Vilna, Rabbi Yisrael Isser Isserlein (1827–89), writes that while so many speak forcefully about the prohibition of *lashon hara*, an equally important issue is neglected:[1] the failure to speak when innocent people are at

1. *Pitḥei Teshuva, Oraḥ Ḥayim* 156.

risk of harm.[2] Similarly, a contemporary authority, Rabbi Moshe Sternbuch, expresses in forceful terms the pressing need to be well versed in the intricate details of *lashon hara* regulation. He observes that as severe a prohibition as *lashon hara* is, neglecting to inform when necessary can be a violation of equal or greater severity.[3] Thus, as well, the complexity.

Approaching the notion of *to'elet* at its roots may also call for a reflection upon the two previously mentioned perspectives: *lashon hara* viewed as a deficiency in character or *lashon hara* viewed as a flaw in behavior. If the prohibition of *lashon hara* is directed at the indulgence of a negative character trait, it might be explained that a statement for *to'elet* is simply not *lashon hara.*[4] As some have noted, such an understanding emerges from one of the scriptural instructions regarding *lashon hara,* "You shall not bear a false report" (Ex. 23:1). As already described, the word translated as false, *shav,* actually more often connotes "unnecessary," thus referring to derogatory information that cannot produce a benefit. By definition, then, if there is a benefit, the prohibition would appear to be inoperative. Motivated by the protection of another, the speaker lacks the malevolence that typifies the transgressor.[5]

---

2. Rabbi Shlomo Zalman Braun, in his commentary *She'arim Metzuyanim BeHalakha* to Rabbi Shlomo Gantzfried's *Kitzur Shulḥan Arukh* 30:2, places a citation of this comment at the beginning of the laws of *lashon hara,* apparently considering the warning a necessary introduction to the subject.
3. *Responsa Teshuvot VeHanhagot* I, 558. See also Rabbi Shraya Deblitsky, *Zeh HaShulḥan,* p. 62.
4. See Rabbi Yitzchak Hutner, *Paḥad Yitzḥak, Iggerot UKhtavim* 59. See also Rabbi Ariel Ḥiyun, in the journal *Torat HaAdam LeAdam* v, pp. 187–93.
5. Rabbi Asher Weiss (*Minḥat Asher al HaTorah,* Leviticus, p. 268) favors this understanding and considers it self-evident. This perspective is also taken in *Kodesh Yisrael* 15, who notes that the license of "purpose" is not discussed in the early codifications of *lashon hara,* with the *Ḥafetz Ḥayim* the first to write about it in detail and in specificity. He thus assumes that this can be attributed to such speech simply not being included in the definition of *lashon hara.* See also Rabbi Yehuda Herzl Henkin, *Responsa Benei Vanim* I, 42. Rabbi Elḥanan Bunim Wasserman (a prominent student of the *Ḥafetz Ḥayim*) asserts a broad formulation of *to'elet,* maintaining that it essentially justifies the overriding of any interpersonal commandment, in that they are all, in his understanding, defined by malicious intent, and thus permitted when the purpose is constructive (*Kovetz He'arot* to Yevamot 70.) Regarding this, see Rabbi David Ariav, *LeRe'akha Kamokha* 2, *biurim* 13.

Alternatively, if *lashon hara* is defined as an act of putting another at risk through speech, the exception of *to'elet* requires another explanation. The subject is still harmed, even if less so than the listener – or any potential victim – would have been. Thus, the transgression is not absent, only outweighed by a greater need. The Torah obligates protecting others from harm, as it is written, "you shall not stand idly by while your fellow's blood is shed" (Lev. 19:16). This reference to one's fellow's "blood" is understood to be not only to risk to his life, but to any type of harm.[6] Accordingly, *to'elet* would represent the danger to the listener overriding the harm to the subject.

This rationale is cited explicitly by the *Ḥafetz Ḥayim* as the motivation behind *to'elet*.[7] Indeed, this structure flows from a direct reading of another of the primary scriptural references to *lashon hara*, contained in the same verse: "You shall not go about as a *rakhil* (gossip) among your people; you shall not stand idly by while your fellow's blood is shed, I am God." The connotation is that while one is generally not to be a gossip, this ideal should not prevent one from acting to save one who is at risk.[8]

Thus, the license or mandate to speak "purposeful" negative speech about another has two possible models: either such speech is simply not included in the prohibition; or, alternatively, it is included, but the prohibition itself is overridden by the protection imperative.[9] There is a major difference between the two: In the second model, as an otherwise forbidden action is being advocated, the decision must rest upon a solid foundation of necessity. In other words, the threshold for justification is higher if one value, protection of the innocent, outweighs the other, the general abhorrence of negative speech. Alternatively, if

6. See Sanhedrin 73a, and *Sefer HaMitzvot* of Maimonides, negative commandment 297; *Responsa Radbaz* v, 218 (1582); Rabbi Yaakov Berukhin, *Responsa Mishkenot Yaakov, Ḥoshen Mishpat* 12; see also Rabbi Shmuel David Friedman, *Sedeh Tzofim* to Bava Kamma, p. 616. See also *Minḥat Ḥinnukh* 239:6, who applies this mandate to the prevention of spiritual harm as well.
7. *Ḥafetz Ḥayim, Laws of Rekhilut* 9:1.
8. As expressed by *Sefer Ḥaredim*, negative commandments, ch. 4, and others; see *Alei Be'er* 1. See also Rabbi Moshe Sternbuch, *Taam VeDaat* to Leviticus. Rabbi Ovadia Yosef, *Responsa Yeḥaveh Daat* iv:60, emphasizes this idea at length.
9. See also the extensive discussion in *Emek HaLashon* 8–9.

lashon hara is needless gossip, and "purposeful" speech is simply not in that category, a lower standard may suffice.

From the writings of the *Ḥafetz Ḥayim*, it seems that his premise is that "purposeful" speech is permitted because it justifies the offense being committed, not because it is outside of it. Accordingly, he refers, in his formulation of the protection mandate, to definite knowledge of potential harm.[10] It is specifically when the risk is definite that the dictum of "you shall not stand idly by" is understood as an obligation. When the harm is less apparent, "you shall not stand idly by" constitutes a praiseworthy ideal, rather than a mandatory directive that can outweigh conflicting values.[11]

Such an analysis might shed light on a surprising statement of the *Ḥafetz Ḥayim*. In a somewhat tentative comment regarding the consumer of a business, he suggests that although it is necessary to inform someone if they are potential victims of exploitative price-gouging, it may not be permissible to inform a customer that the merchandise is more expensive than the average, if the prices in that store are within the range of legitimacy.[12] Later authorities were astonished at this suggestion; surely, this type of "consumer report" should fall squarely within the realm of "purpose."[13] Addressing this question, some suggest that the *Ḥafetz Ḥayim* is not objecting to an effort to try to help another economize,[14] but rather to an attempt to disdainfully convey that the merchant is extravagantly expensive.[15]

10. See Rabbi Binyamin Kohen, *Ḥelkat Binyamin* 3 and 6.
11. See also Rabbi Yeruḥam Fishel Perlow, commentary to *Sefer HaMitzvot* of Rabbi Saadia Gaon, positive commandment 28. See also *Responsa LeḤafetz BaḤayim* III, 5, regarding the interaction of this mandate with the laws of *lashon hara*.
12. Printed as a footnote to *Ḥafetz Ḥayim, Laws of Rekhilut* 9:10, and expanded upon in *Be'er Mayim Ḥayim* 27.
13. See Rabbi Yisrael Pesaḥ Feinhandler, *Responsa Avnei Yashpeh* 1:26.
14. See Rabbi Moshe Kaufman, *Netiv Ḥayim* 8.
15. See further discussion of the issue in Rabbi Tzvi Shpitz, *Mishpetei HaTorah* III, 8:2 and n. 2, and extensively in *Kodesh Yisrael* 17, and in *Ohev Yamim, diyunim* 5. A lengthy and detailed treatment of this subject can be found in Rabbi Yehuda Itaḥ, *Netiv Yosher*, ch. 49, sections 3–19. See also *Tehor Sefatayim*, pp. 215–16. Rabbi Yehonatan Rozler, *He'arot Rigshei Ḥayim, miluim*, pp. 494–96, analyzes the issue under the premise that the shopper has already decided to purchase the item from the higher-priced seller, thus creating a potential "loss" for the seller.

The issue may hinge on the above consideration. If "purposeful" speech is by definition out of the realm of *lashon hara,* it may be that relaying beneficial information is simply permissible, without the need for an overwhelming urgency. By contrast, the *Ḥafetz Ḥayim* perceives the issue as one of a clash between the needs of the subject and that of a potential innocent victim. In such a case, it may be necessary to evaluate whether the "loss" to the third party justifies that of the subject.[16] If the situation is one of predator and victim, there is no question that the innocent must be protected. However, if there are simply opposing interests, it might be less certain that the desire of the customer to find the best possible deal is more compelling than the right of the vendor (who is in no way dishonest) not to be portrayed in a manner that may be ruinous to his livelihood, at least without other aggravating factors.[17]

THE CONDITIONS OF THE *ḤAFETZ ḤAYIM*

It is likely with this perspective in mind that the *Ḥafetz Ḥayim* proceeds to mandate specific conditions under which the relaying of derogatory information becomes permissible, even beyond the opening premise of "purpose," adding as many as six other conditions.[18]

Perhaps the primary condition, particularly in light of our premises regarding the core damage inflicted by *lashon hara,* is that the speaker know that the information is true. However, this condition, as important as it is, is not necessarily indisputable. It is possible that there may be some possible risk to another about which the speaker does not know with certainty, but the potential harm must be conveyed nonetheless to guarantee the protection of his fellows. Accordingly, it has been cogently asserted that this condition is adaptable through proper presentation. If the speaker is able to transmit the information in a fashion consistent

---

16. The nature and the elements of this evaluation are analyzed in detail in *Responsa LeḤafetz BaḤayim* 1:15.
17. See *Darkhei Ḥoshen,* pp. 421–22, and *Ḥelkat Binyamin* to *Ḥafetz Ḥayim, Laws of Rekhilut* 9:10.
18. *Ḥafetz Ḥayim, Laws of Lashon HaRa* 10:2 and *Laws of Rekhilut* 9:2. The lists are not exactly the same in the two locations, and there are more conditions regarding *lashon hara* than regarding *rekhilut.*

with his degree of certitude – in other words, to express that it is a concern rather than a certainty – this condition should be satisfied.[19]

Consistent with this concern for accuracy is another of the *Ḥafetz Ḥayim*'s conditions, that the information be presented in a completely straightforward manner, without any exaggeration or "spin."

Other conditions focus on the necessity of the revelation. Thus, the *Ḥafetz Ḥayim* requires that the misdeed under discussion be an actual, definable injustice that warrants such a step. Further, there must be no other way to address the situation, with all other methods – including speaking directly to the perpetrator – having been attempted to no avail. Presumably, speaking about the misdeed only when absolutely necessary would also include ascertaining that only those who are affected should be able to hear, and, for example, not relaying such information on the phone in a public place where uninvolved parties could eavesdrop.[20] Similarly, even once the decision is made to speak, an effort should be made, if possible, to limit the damage to the subject.[21]

This last consideration contains particularly interesting aspects. Making every effort to limit the damage to the subject would be a logical and understandable course of action if it were the speaker's aspiration to solve the problem without disparaging the subject. But, teaches the *Ḥafetz Ḥayim*, even if the speaker is compelled to paint a negative picture, it is preferable to do so indirectly and not via explicit statements.[22]

---

19. See *Responsa Avnei Yashpeh* I: 25.
20. See *Responsa LeḤafetz BaḤayim* 1:14, who reaches this conclusion for other reasons.
21. See ibid., II: 21.
22. See *Ḥafetz Ḥayim, Laws of Lashon HaRa* 10:2 condition 6 and *Laws of Rekhilut* 9:2 condition 4. From his language in the main text (*Mekor Ḥayim*), it is possible to read the *Ḥafetz Ḥayim* as advising achieving the necessary purpose without any revelation of negative information, if possible. However, from his *Be'er Mayim Ḥayim* (sections 11 and 35, respectively), it is clear that he includes in this recommendation revealing the information in a nonexplicit fashion. This can be discerned from a scriptural proof the *Ḥafetz Ḥayim* cites to buttress his point. In the book of Joshua (ch.7), God models the ideal of sensitivity to the laws of *lashon hara* by identifying a sinner whose transgressions register an impact on the rest of the population through a lottery, rather than direct identification. In the Talmud's telling, God explains the decision: "Am I to be a talebearer?"(Sanhedrin 11a). See *Shaarei Avraham*, pp. 245–46. See also commentary of *Or HaḤayim* to Gen. 27:46, and of

This is surprising, since the subject will suffer damage either way, despite the "clean hands" of the speaker. This requirement – to limit the damage caused to the subject – seems to be directed at the character component of the *lashon hara* prohibition rather than at its practical impact. It is indeed regrettable the statement necessarily causes damage, but at least the corruptive effect of engaging in negative speech can be limited.

The *Ḥafetz Ḥayim* also requires that the negative impact that will likely result from the report not be greater than justice dictates. However, this may not be possible to control while still adequately protecting others, and accordingly this factor is also assessed in light of the potential harm threatening others.[23]

One of the *Ḥafetz Ḥayim*'s criteria poses a particular challenge to the speaker. This condition mandates that the intent be purely to prevent harm, and not flow from any hatred of the subject. If indeed he is motivated by hatred, he nonetheless is not exempt from the obligation to prevent harm. Accordingly, rules the *Ḥafetz Ḥayim*, this standard obligates the speaker to relate the information, but only after performing the inner work necessary to dispose of his hatred.[24]

However, the very premise of the *Ḥafetz Ḥayim*, that a motive of "purpose" does not by itself justify the relating of information if it is tainted by an accompanying ulterior motive has been the subject of

---

Mahari Kara to I Sam. 20:38, and Rabbi Aharon Yehuda Grossman, *VeDarashta VeḤakarta al HaTorah* v, Part 2, p. 630, who cites the Gaon of Vilna as maintaining that *lashon hara* spoken for a necessary purpose is a deferred prohibition (*deḥuya*) rather than unequivocally permitted (*hutra*), and, accordingly, it is not permitted to speak explicitly when an implicit hint would suffice. It might be that such an indirect approach is valuable in emphasizing the need to ascertain that the negative speech is warranted in the first place, and correspondingly to avoid it if it is not; see the *Ḥafetz Ḥayim*'s comments in *Zekhor LeMiriam*, ch. 25, and see *Shemirat HaPeh KeHilkhato*, pp. 240–41.

See, however, Rabbi Shlomo Zalman Kook, *Bein Shenei Kohanim Gedolim*, pp. 148–49, who understands the talmudic passage differently, and suggests that the advantage of the lottery was that it would be public and therefore purposeful, as opposed to direct revelation to Joshua alone, which would have been private and therefore mere talebearing.

23. See also *Mishpetei HaShalom*, p. 234, no. 64, particularly regarding the necessity to attempt to first address the subject directly.

24. *Ḥafetz Ḥayim, Laws of Rekhilut, klal 9, Be'er Mayim Ḥayim.*

some debate. The ruling is based on statements of the great medieval authority Rabbeinu Yonah.[25] Once again, a serious objection can be raised from the need to protect the innocent; it may be that the only one in a position to provide this protection nonetheless bears a personal animus against the subject.

More conceptually, as many note, the premise can be challenged particularly when the question is abstracted to a broader issue in talmudic law: the role of intent or ulterior motive in undermining the legitimacy of suspending prohibitions under extenuating circumstances.[26] One might reach, for example, the obviously incorrect conclusion that one who is seriously ill may not eat on Yom Kippur on the grounds that he will enjoy the food, and thus his motive for eating is not purely to protect his health. The theoretical underpinnings of the issue are substantial enough that a later scholar, Rabbi Gershon Robinson, devoted an entire book to defending this premise of the *Ḥafetz Ḥayim*, particularly against the background of the broader talmudic issues.[27] The author notes that *lashon hara* may differ significantly from other areas of Jewish law in which mixed motivations are present. In the example of one who needs to eat on Yom Kippur for reasons of health, the fact that he may also enjoy the food does not affect the basics of the process. By contrast, if one has such an antipathy toward another that he is eager to speak negatively about him, that bias may fundamentally affect the content that he is relaying and indeed the decision to convey it in the first place.

Practically, the issue is complex and indeed the *Ḥafetz Ḥayim* himself emphasizes different elements of the equation at various points throughout his writings.[28] While the specifics of this consideration are

25. Rabbeinu Yonah ben Avraham of Gerona, *Shaarei Teshuva* 3: 216, 219, 228, and *Aliyot*, Bava Batra 39a, s.v *amar Rava*.
26. See Rabbi Shlomo Rozner, *Responsa LeḤafetz BaḤayim* 1: 44.
27. Rabbi Gershon Robinson, *Tokhaḥat Ḥayim*.
28. See *Ḥafetz Ḥayim, Laws of Lashon HaRa, klal* 10, paragraph 2, condition 5, and *Be'er Mayim Ḥayim* 10, and paragraph 14; *Laws of Rekhilut, klal* 9, paragraph 2, *Be'er Mayim Ḥayim* 3 and paragraph 12, where the emphasis is on intending for purpose and not for personal animus; however, in a footnote to ibid., *Be'er Mayim Ḥayim* 28, he cites a dispute in a different area of Jewish law (*Sefer Me'irat Einayim [Sma], Ḥoshen Mishpat* 421:28 and *Taz Ḥoshen Mishpat* 421:28 s.v. *kedei*), the analysis of which allows for two views on either extreme of this position: that intent is irrelevant, and necessary

controversial, it seems that two fundamental points emerge from the debate. First, one who is tainted by antipathy toward the subject is prone to the prevalent biases and prejudices that may skew the reliability and even the basic truth of the report, even if he believes he is motivated by the protection of another; thus, a more objective source, if available, is greatly preferable. Second, when there is no alternative, it is incumbent upon the speaker to take all steps possible to compensate for his predisposition and to present as untainted a report as is feasible.

Rabbi Shraya Deblitsky, a prominent rabbinic author from Benei Berak, Israel, notes that there is more latitude to account for this concern of mixed motivations when considering giving a negative report to protect oneself.[29] However, if another person is threatened, the protection imperative takes priority and the warning must be issued. In either case, he notes, the conditions of the *Ḥafetz Hayim* are difficult if not impossible to fulfill perfectly. Rather, they should be taken as important considerations that require a good-faith effort to address to the best of one's ability.[30]

The *Ḥafetz Ḥayim* also considers another factor, which he does not list as an absolute requirement. Addressing a situation where the listener is being advised against beginning a relationship with the subject, he recommends that careful attention be given to the risk that the listener will not believe the speaker, and will proceed to enter into a relationship with the subject despite the warning. Later, the truth of the allegations will become evident, and the listener will return to the speaker, and

---

speech is permitted regardless; and that not only ulterior intent but the mere presence of preexisting animus disqualifies (thus also rendering intent irrelevant, in the opposite way). The dispute between the *Sma* and the *Taz* is discussed at length in *Tokhaḥat Ḥayim*; see also Rabbi Moshe Samsonowitz, *Keriya BaKeriya* I, pp. 190–91; *Kodesh Yisrael* 15; and Rabbi Avraham Yitzḥak HaKohen Kook (of Rechovot) in the journal *Marpei Lashon* IV, pp. 6–12. See also the discussion of the topic by Rabbi Yehonatan Rozler, *He'arot Rigshei Ḥayim* to *Ḥafetz Ḥayim, miluim*, pp. 483–87.

29. Approbation to *Tokhaḥat Ḥayim.*

30. Note a similar approach, more tentatively, in *Mishpetei HaShalom*, pp. 262–63, where a distinction is drawn between purposeful speech that is of general benefit, which must pass a more rigorous test of purity of motive, and that which is urgently needed to protect someone from harm, in which the necessity may demand disclosure even when mixed motivations are present.

perhaps to others, to discuss the negative traits that were brought up earlier. Thus, the initial conversation will have been unsuccessful, and the later conversation will be too late to accomplish anything positive.

Rabbi Binyamin Kohen, the author of a contemporary commentary on the *Ḥafetz Ḥayim*, notes that the *Ḥafetz Ḥayim* appears on this last point to be more concerned about the eventual spread of useless *lashon hara* than he is about the initial conversation, despite the fact that that conversation was also fruitless (and predictably so). Rabbi Kohen suggests that this is reflective of the need to constantly evaluate the odds for benefit against the likelihood of harm, a point again consistent with the perspective of the *Ḥafetz Ḥayim* described above.

Aside from the *Ḥafetz Ḥayim*, other authors have also asserted parameters for what can credibly be maintained as "purposeful." A contemporary of the *Ḥafetz Ḥayim*, Rabbi Yeḥiel Michel Rabinowitz, delineated three criteria which he derived from a fascinating exercise in the analysis of biblical narrative. Before being sold into slavery by his brothers, Joseph is described by the Torah as having informed on them for their bad behavior: "And Joseph brought evil reports about them to their father" (Gen. 37:2). Rabbi Rabinowitz, assuming that the righteous Joseph would only engage in such reporting were it justified and permitted to do so, uses the passage to determine what conditions are necessary for such justification.[31]

First, there must be no other way to accomplish the desired corrective. Accordingly, one could ask why Joseph did not rebuke his brothers personally, rather than inform on them. The context reveals the answer; the previous verse identifies Joseph as a "lad" (*naar*) in the eyes of his brothers; clearly, he would not have been taken seriously

31. It should be noted that not all commentators considered Joseph to be completely blameless; see, for example, Rashi, Gen. 37:2 ; Rabbi Moshe Sofer, *Ḥiddushei Ḥatam Sofer* to *Parashat Vayeshev*, and *Tanḥuma* (Buber), *Vayeshev*. See also *Penei Yehoshua* to Shabbat 55b, s.v. *tanya;* and note, extensively, Rabbi Moshe Blau, *Mishnat Moshe* to Shabbat, pp. 74–75, concerning his comments, and see also Rabbi Yisrael Zissel Paltin, in the journal *Tevuna* 4, no. 62 (*Tevet* 5706). Also see the alternative explanation in Rabbi Avraham Y. Munseh, *Padeh et Avraham,* Genesis II, 37:1. The *Ḥafetz Ḥayim* is critical of Joseph in *Shemirat HaLashon* 2:14 and by implication in *Laws of Lashon HaRa* 8:25, in *Be'er Mayim Ḥayim*. See also *Emek HaLashon* 49.

by them. Second, the language of "bringing" reports is unusual; there are many words in Hebrew for "speaking" that would be more natural. Rabbi Rabinowitz suggests that the intent is to convey that the reports were brought just as a physical item is carried: it is the same item when picked up in the original location as it is when put down in the new one. So too, Joseph did not embellish his reports at all, nor did he offer his opinions; the facts that he reported were those that he witnessed.

Rabbi Rabinowitz's third condition parallels the *Ḥafetz Ḥayim*'s concern for the impact of an ulterior motive. He observes another irregularity of language, in that the Torah states that Joseph brought the reports to "their father," without mentioning the fact that Jacob was also Joseph's father. The intent, he maintains, is to emphasize that Joseph was thinking only about correcting the behavior of the brothers, and not at all of the fact that he might compare favorably to them in his own father's eyes. That possibility was irrelevant to his motivation, and thus instructive of the attitude necessary to justify such reporting.[32]

Still others dispute the need for criteria at all in establishing "purpose." The *Ḥazon Ish* maintains that there is essentially one simple determinant of permitted purposeful speech: that it have a purposeful intent.[33] As noted, the debate seems to center around the mechanism by which such speech is allowed, either as simply excluded from the *lashon hara* prohibition or as outweighing it through necessity.

With this background, we may consider some of the specific contexts in which the parameters of "purpose" have been evaluated. However, it must be emphasized that the core principle is not in question. Protection of the innocent is always the priority, and to knowingly allow harm or risk to come to another through the claim of *lashon hara* is a distortion of Jewish law. Despite the general care required not to violate Torah law, standing idly by while another suffers a risk of predatory behavior is not "erring on the side of caution" but a serious dereliction

32. *Afikei Yam*, preface to vol. II. See, similarly, Rabbi Aharon ben Samḥon, *Bigdei Yesha, maamar Sakhar VaOnesh*, p. 13.; and see also Nahmanides, Genesis, 37:2. For a similar grouping of the conditions into three items, see Rabbi Aryeh Katz, in the journal *Teḥumin* XXVII, pp. 180–84)

33. Cited in Rabbi Yehuda Silman, *Darkhei Ḥoshen* I, p. 300, and elsewhere.

of duty. The golden rule principle of "love your fellow as yourself" is an overarching foundational concept that of course includes a sensitivity to the needs of others not to be disparaged; however, it even more obviously extends to the rights of others not to be victimized. The responsibility is a heavy one, and many factors are relevant to making a proper and wise decision; but first and foremost, the priorities and the underlying values must be established.

THERAPY

"Purpose" may include not only the thwarting of a predator, but also necessary benefit to the speaker. In this vein, it is likely that to relate negative information in the process of confiding in a therapist, or other helpful individuals, is justified. This point is noted by the *Ḥafetz Ḥayim* and actually draws upon two distinct forms of benefit. [34]

Without a doubt, the crucial achievement of mental health is a self-evident priority that itself can justify many otherwise discouraged behaviors. More specifically, the benefit of talk therapy is mentioned in the Talmud (Yoma 75a). Interpreting Proverbs 12:25, the Talmud advises "one who finds worry in his heart should discuss the matter with others." According to the primary talmudic commentator Rashi, the benefit is that the listener may have some solution to the problem. Within that interpretation, the purpose of such conversation is functional in the practical sense.

However, it is also likely that the intent is that the very act of talking is productive as an emotional support. Accordingly, such unburdening of the mind should be permitted even if the listener is not likely to offer concrete advice. It seems that this justification is grounded not only in the productive benefit but also in that there is no intent to disparage the individual being discussed, but rather to provide therapeutic relief to the speaker.[35]

34. *Ḥafetz Ḥayim, Laws of Lashon HaRa* 10:14 in footnote, and see also 6:4. See *Birkat Yitzḥak*, pp. 310–11. See also Rabbi Yisrael Yaakov Fisher, *Respona Even Yisrael* IX, 164:5, and Rabbi Ḥayim Kanievsky, *Derekh Siḥa*, p. 429; and see also the comment of Rabbi Moshe Ḥayim Shaḥna in *Kovetz Simḥat Yeḥiel* to Kiddushin 33a.
35. See Rabbi Zevulun Shuv, *Shaarei Zevulun, Yoreh De'ah* 76.

The listener does not necessarily have to be a professional therapist if indeed the simple act of talking is deemed beneficial. Theoretically, such license could be extended to "venting," if that is productive; it should be noted, however, that there is some debate among experts in psychology as to the actual benefit of venting anger.[36]

Centuries earlier, the medieval pietist Rabbi Yehuda HeḤasid formulated this potential benefit, emphasizing also the perspective of the listener. He describes a situation in which an angry individual is on the verbal warpath, determined to share his fury with the world. In such a case, while listening to *lashon hara* is normally discouraged, it may make sense for one to decide that he will choose to provide an audience for this individual, under the assumption that by doing so, he can reduce the speaker's need to tell anyone else, while also playing a role in calming the speaker and trying to render his perspective more positive.[37]

The goal of reducing the number of listeners to the speaker is an important one. A "venting license" should not be taken as a free pass to widely disparage the source of one's anger. Emotional unburdening should be accomplished with a very limited number of people (preferably, one person) and should not involve the widespread dissemination of negativity.[38]

The therapeutic value of listening is significantly recognized in the halakhic literature; Rabbi Avraham Yaakov Pam, the revered Rosh Yeshiva of Yeshiva Torah Vodaath, emphasized in his lectures to his

---

36. See Robert Enright, *Forgiveness Is a Choice* (Washington, DC: American Psychological Association, 2001), pp. 54–55, and see McRaney, *You Are Not So Smart*, ch. 32, and the studies cited therein. Some studies indicate that "venting" either keeps initial anger running longer or causes an emotional dependency on the venting that otherwise would not be there. Note also that Rabbi Yaakov Kamenetsky, *Emet LeYaakov* to *Oraḥ Ḥayim* 156n182, distinguishes between one who is sharing his distress that an offender is going unpunished, which is permitted, and one who is using the publicizing of a misdeed as an expression of anger itself, which he maintains is prohibited. He compares such speech to the destructive behavior of one who smashes vessels in anger, implying that the speech is unproductive (or counterproductive) and thus not subject to a license of "purpose." Compare *Ḥelkat Binyamin, Laws of Lashon HaRa* 10:39 and *Netiv Ḥayim, Laws of Lashon HaRa* 1:12, with *Zera Ḥayim* p. 308.
37. *Sefer Ḥasidim* 64.
38. See *Responsa LeḤafetz BaḤayim* I:2, II:1.

students the often-overlooked possibilities to engage in acts of kindness even without leaving their study hall. Among his examples, he noted, citing the talmudic comment cited above, that the very act of listening to another, even when there is no practical advice to offer, is a fundamental act of kindness.[39]

A contemporary authority, Rabbi Yitzḥak Zilberstein, was asked a question by a woman whose mother was depressed and needed to discuss her problems with her daughter, including her grievances against various people.[40] The daughter was under the impression that she could listen, but that she must not believe the reports, and was concerned that such an approach would not allow her to be much help to her mother. Rabbi Zilberstein told her that she should indeed listen to her mother and she should believe her as well, while at the same time mitigate the effect through extending generosity of judgment to the subjects as far as their general character.[41]

The broader issue of "venting" and unburdening oneself to family members is a complex one. Generally speaking, there is no exclusion from the *lashon hara* injunction when speaking with close relatives; in fact, the highlighted episode in the Torah of *lashon hara* involves a sister talking to a brother about another brother, Miriam speaking to Aaron about Moses. In fact, the *Ḥafetz Ḥayim* asserts that *lashon hara* between spouses is actually a worse violation than other cases. This is because the natural sympathy the spouses have for each other will lead them to more readily accept the negative statements as true, and thus inflict even greater harm on the subject. Further, it is likely that the protective instinct one spouse has for another may provoke the receiving spouse to engage in unjustified fighting with the subject of the report.[42]

39. *Atara LaMelekh*, pp. 22–23.
40. In the journal *Kol HaTorah* LXI, pp. 180–82.
41. See also Rabbi Nachum Rabinovitch, *Responsa Siaḥ Naḥum* 91, regarding other issues relevant to the responsibilities of a therapist. Rabbi Zilberstein discusses the interaction of therapy and the prohibitions of *rekhilut* further in an article in *Assia*, XI, nos. 2–3, pp. 26–31; see also VIII, p. 205.
42. *Ḥafetz Ḥayim, Laws of Lashon HaRa* 8:10. See also *Avot DeRabbi Natan* 7:3 and *Responsa LeḤafetz BaHayim* 11:26.

However, there is another side to the equation. If there is any legitimacy to speaking for the purpose of mental relief, or for practical advice, it may be that a spouse is best positioned to play the role of listener. Further, if Rabbi Yehuda HeḤasid's point about one listener preventing the speaker from needing a greater audience is to be considered, once again the spouse may be the best choice. As with so many of the issues regarding *lashon hara*, there is weight to each of the opposing factors. As it is also so often the case, the resolution may lie in the details. For a husband to come home from work and share with his wife all the latest gossip, and to gleefully relate all the salacious details of his office life, may be an act even more harmful then general derogatory speech, and also may set a highly undesirable tone for a household. However, if that same husband is deeply distressed by a problem involving another individual, and is seeking a sympathetic ear and is desperate for useful advice, and further, if his mental stress is exacerbated by not being able to be fully open about his suffering with the one closest to him, unburdening himself to his wife may be the most advisable approach, and this position is endorsed by many major contemporary authorities.[43]

POTENTIAL MARRIAGE PARTNERS (*SHIDDUKHIM*)

The issue of "purpose" is particularly relevant when the question of a potential marriage partner, known as a *shiddukh* in traditional Hebrew/Yiddish usage, is raised. The stakes are unusually high: on the one hand,

43. See Rabbi Howard Jachter, "Is *Lashon Hara* Permitted Between Close Friends and Spouses," *Aḥrayut Ketuva* I, pp. 22–27, who cites Rabbi Hershel Schachter as endorsing the position that a spouse can be a primary example of an appropriate confidante when necessary. Rabbi Mordekhai Gros, *Om Ani Ḥoma* II, 87, pp. 300–301, cites Rabbi Shlomo Zalman Auerbach and the *Ḥazon Ish* as approving of this view, while also noting that such conversation does not require all of the conditions normally required for purposeful revelation, even according to the position of the *Ḥafetz Ḥayim*. Rabbi Yitzḥak Berkowitz. "Chofetz Chaim: A Lesson a Day," (New York: Artscroll Mesorah Publications, 2005) n. 113, quotes a similar position from Rabbi Yitzchak Hutner, noting that a husband has a spousal obligation to provide emotional comfort to his wife. See also Rabbi Yuval Cherlow, in the journal *Teḥumin* XXVII, pp. 168–79, and the discussion in *Tehor Sefatayim*, pp. 150–52. See as well *Shevilei Ḥayim* to *Ḥafetz Ḥayim*, *Laws of Lashon HaRa* 8:10 , 15; *Ḥelkat Binyamin*, *Laws of Lashon HaRa* 8:19 and 10:39; and *Shaarei Avraham*, pp. 381–82. Compare also *Responsa Teshuvot VeHanhagot* IV:312.

failing to disclose relevant information can wreak extreme and ongoing harm upon an unknowing marriage partner; on the other hand, inaccurate or irrelevant information can not only unnecessarily or unfairly derail the match currently under discussion, but all future possibilities for this individual.

Examining this question involves looking at two planes, which we will attempt to consider simultaneously, or at least in an overlapping fashion: (a) how much must one reveal to a potential spouse, not only at the phase when the couple is seriously contemplating marriage, but also at a relatively early stage in the dating process or even before the first date, and (b) how much relevant information must be revealed by a third party if it has not been divulged by the dating parties? (Such a question could arise either because the date has not revealed the information or simply because the third party was addressed first.)

There are no easy or absolute answers to these questions. While the principle of "purposeful" speech is indeed an undisputed one, one needs to use judgment to identify what information fits that category of speech, considering the risk of passing on information that is false, subjective, exaggerated, outdated, or irrelevant. Although the *to'elet* criterion applies in all instances, the dating process adds a new element: timing. While certain pieces of relevant information have to eventually be revealed to each of the dating partners, it is not always clear when the disclosure should take place. To do so too early may place undue emphasis on an issue, which, if considered within a broader perspective, would over time diminish in importance. In the language of many rabbinic authorities, premature revelation is dangerous because before the couple has had a chance to meet each other, *kol davar katan mekalkel* (any small matter will damage the prospect).[44] In other words, one party may ask, "Why should I go out with this 'flawed' person, when there are so many 'perfect' people out there awaiting me?" However, once there has been an opportunity for the two to see the appealing qualities of each other,

44. See *Kehillot Yaakov,* Yevamot 38; *Responsa Iggerot Moshe,* Oraḥ Ḥayim IV, 118, and Even HaEzer IV, 32:4. See also Rabbi Tzvi Shpitz, *Mishpetei HaTorah* 1:91, regarding further considerations of timing.

negative information can be evaluated in a wider context (whether or not that context is more "objective" is open to debate, but it is certainly different).[45]

This consideration is well established in the psychological literature as well. As Daniel Solove writes in *The Future of Reputation*:

> Revealing private facts when first getting to know a person can be…distorting. According to [sociologist Erving] Goffman, people need time to establish relationships before revealing secrets. Immediate honesty can be costly. When we first meet somebody, we have little invested in that person. We haven't built any bonds of friendship or developed any feelings for that person. So if we learn about a piece of that person's private life that seems bizarre or unpleasant, it's easy to just walk away. But we don't just walk away from people we know well. With time to gain familiarity with a person, we're better able to process information, see the whole person, and weigh secrets in context.[46]

Assessing the appropriate timing, which will also be affected greatly by variables such as the cultural norms for the pace of a relationship and the nuances of the individual *shiddukh*, is a highly complex endeavor. Of course, this timing consideration is only relevant if there is a possibility that it will make a difference; if the issue is one that will almost definitely interfere, then to delay the revelation will only cause pain to

45. Even the familiar yardstick of *ve'ahavta lere'akha kamokha* is difficult to apply in this regard (even if one considers only one of the parties involved). On the one hand, one might think, if it were me (or my daughter), I would demand that I have all the information in advance, so I can decide accordingly; thus, I owe that information to others. On the other hand, many happily married people (or parents of such people) are deeply grateful that certain facts were not relayed too early, because they would have interfered with a very successful *shiddukh* to the detriment of all involved. Thus, such people would argue that treating others as they would want to be treated would mean *not* revealing information too soon. See the discussion in Rabbi Mordekhai Menaḥem Veingurt, *BaYom SheYedubar*, pp. 41–43.

46. Solove, *Future of Reputation*, 69.

all involved and incur egregious violations of inflicting unnecessary emotional anguish (*onaat devarim*).[47]

There is an additional complexity to this time consideration. Clearly, the third party is obligated to speak up if one or both of the dating partners neglect to disclose something crucial. As mentioned, it is often legitimate to delay the revelation of relevant information until a later date. But the third party might assume that one of the partners is refusing to disclose relevant information when in fact he or she is merely delaying the disclosure; such a misreading of the situation could lead the third party to abruptly and unnecessarily interfere in a very damaging way.[48]

While the prevention of harm is certainly enough reason to mandate disclosure when appropriate, there is another consideration particular to the transactional nature of the marriage commitment. Failure to divulge relevant information could constitute a violation of misrepresentation (*genevat daat*), even if that information would not stop the *shiddukh* from going through. However, if the information is material to the point that one party would refuse the marriage were it known, in addition to the violation of fraud the marriage itself could possibly be considered an agreement under false or mistaken pretenses and therefore null and void.[49] Accordingly, the stakes involved in assessing what should or should not be discussed are raised even higher.

We may note some general principles that have been promulgated in this area. In determining the standards for purposeful speech, the *Ḥafetz Ḥayim* mentions some direct applications to considerations of *shiddukhim*.[50] Addressing a third party, he writes that if a couple is about to marry, it is appropriate to inform one of them of a major flaw in the other, including in this category issues such as heretical beliefs

47. Note the discussion of this in Rabbi Yitzḥak Eizik Silber, *Mishpetei HaShalom*, p. 251.
48. See *Zera Ḥayim*, p. 337. See also Rabbi Binyamin Cohen, *Ḥelkat Binyamin* to *Ḥafetz Ḥayim*, p. 364, who suggests a distinction between one who is asked and one who isn't.
49. See Kiddushin 50a; *Sefer Ḥasidim* 507, and note commentary of Rabbi Reuven Margoliyot, *Mekor Ḥesed;* and *Even HaEzer* 117:3–4. see also *Responsa Achiezer* 27:3.
50. *Ḥafetz Ḥayim, Laws of Rekhilut, klal* 9, *tziyur* 3.

and hidden illnesses.[51] However, he is quick to note that there are traits that are clearly outside of this grouping, offering as an example one who is naïve and unaware of the guile of others. Apparently, such a characteristic is not sufficiently objectively problematic to merit an unsolicited revelation. Further, asserts the *Ḥafetz Ḥayim*, it is wrong to relate that the young man is an inferior Torah scholar; it is the burden of the girl's family to research this area, to have the boy tested by competent scholars. If they fail to do so, they accept responsibility for the consequences.[52]

From the *Ḥafetz Ḥayim*'s specific examples some general guidelines emerge: (a) the awareness of information that could have a clear negative impact on an unwitting potential spouse mandates unsolicited intervention by a third party; (b) not all attributes that can be viewed negatively meet that threshold of "clear negative impact"; and (c) if an attribute can be investigated by the potential mate (or the advocates of that mate) and isn't, the responsibility falls on them and the third party need not volunteer involvement.[53]

---

51. The responsa literature regarding the disclosure of illnesses and other medical conditions is complex and detailed and will not be itemized here. See, for example, Rabbi Moshe Feinstein, *Responsa Iggerot Moshe, Even HaEzer* III:27 and, *Even HaEzer* IV 73:2 and *Oraḥ Ḥayim* V:118; Rabbi Eliezer Yehudah Waldenberg, *Responsa Tzitz Eliezer* XVI, 4 and XVII, 49:3; Rabbi Yaakov Breisch, *Responsa Ḥelkat Yaakov, Even HaEzer* 79; Rabbi Barukh Reuven Shlomo Shlesinger, *Responsa Birkat Reuven Shlomo* IV: 69; Rabbi Nissim Karelitz, *Ḥut Shani, Shemirat HaLashon* 7:1, p. 372; Rabbi Moshe Sternbuch, *Responsa Teshuvot VeHanhagot* I:879, II:624, 627; Rabbi Meir Brandesdorfer, *Responsa Keneh Bosem* I:121; Rabbi Shmuel Wosner, *Responsa Shevet HaLevi* IV:162 and VI:205; Rabbi Menashe Klein, *Responsa Mishneh Halakhot* V:254; Rabbi Yitzḥak Weiss, *Responsa Minḥat Yitzḥak* V:44; VI:139, VII:107; *Responsa Ḥavatzelet HaSharon* 63; *Responsa Maharsham* VII:152; Rabbi Meir Arik, *Responsa Imrei Yosher* 114:8; Rabbi Ḥanina Yisrael Rottenberg, *Diverei Ḥayil* 23:2, as well as Rabbi Ḥayim Kanievsky, quoted in *Maase Rav* I, ch. 7, sec. 12; and *Beit Ḥatanim*, p. 17n1; Drs. Yoel and Hanna Katan, in the journal *Teḥumin* XXV, pp. 47–58; *Mishpetei HaShalom*, p 251; Rabbi Yosef Aryeh Deutsch, *Divrei Yosef* 34; and *BaYom SheYedubar*, p. 109.
52. See, on this classification, Rabbi Moshe Kaufman, *Zera Ḥayim*, p. 436.
53. On that last point, it should also be noted that the *Ḥafetz Ḥayim*'s particular focus, the Torah scholarship of a potential groom, is subject to some adjustment in the modern context. On the one hand, if the girl is indeed concerned about this area,

With respect to the perspective of the one seeking information, the *Ḥafetz Ḥayim* confirms that it is his and her prerogative to ask questions, despite the fact that this may prompt the source to say negative things.[54] Further, he or she can ask about whatever they consider important, without limitations.[55] Similarly, they may ask many people, if doing so would contribute to clarity in the matter.[56] He also requires that the questioner make clear that his motives are for the justified purpose of a *shiddukh*, asserting that otherwise the justifiable intent may not attach to the third party, who may relay negative information without the validation of necessity and thus violate the prohibition of *lashon hara*.[57] This concern once again reflects the dual

it is not necessarily the case that she has the ability to have the boy "tested" as was once the practice, and thus the accuracy of the *Ḥafetz Ḥayim*'s premise may have changed. See *Zera Ḥayim*, p. 346, on this point, who also notes that it may be the case that the parents were charged with "research," and if they did so inadequately, it may not be fair to assign the responsibility for accepting the "loss" to the girl herself. Accordingly, the details of this particular consideration require further deliberation and application. See *Divrei Yosef*, 34.

Alternatively, as many authorities have perceived, it is important for one who is asked about this quality to understand what the girl or her family is genuinely concerned with; i.e., are they looking for a boy who is a future *posek* or Rosh Yeshiva; one who is respected by his peers; one who takes his religious obligations seriously; one who establishes time for Torah studies; one who is quick-witted or analytically gifted; or all of the above? If the question is properly understood (sometimes a daunting task), the one being asked can answer in an appropriate manner. See, for example, Rabbi Nissim Karelitz, *Ḥut Shani, Shemirat HaLashon* 7:1.

54. *Ḥafetz Ḥayim, Laws of Lashon HaRa, klal* 4:11, with *Be'er Mayim Ḥayim*.
55. From the perspective of the answerer, Rabbi Ovadia Yosef (cited in *Yalkut Yosef, Laws of Respect for Parents*, p. 495; and see also his introduction to *Laws of Prayer*, p. 17) asserts that if the inquiry is not about an issue of consequence, the talmudic license to alter the truth for the sake of peace (Yevamot 65b) would apply. However, it needs to be determined if, apart from the halakhic issue, such an approach is wise; further, as some have noted (see also *Mishpetei Shalom*, p. 249), such an approach may risk a violation of *genevat daat*. On the importance of honesty in these matters (even on secondary issues), see also *Sefer Ḥasidim* 388.
56. See *Zera Ḥayim*, pp. 442.
57. See *Responsa LeḤafetz BaḤayim* 11:3. The *Ḥafetz Ḥayim*'s assumption, that conveying objectively necessary data is not justified if the speaker is unaware of the necessity, is questioned by Rabbi Moshe Sternbuch, *Responsa Teshuvot VeHanhagot* 111:479. See also *Tokhaḥat Ḥayim* pp. 81–89.

nature of *lashon hara;* it is conceivable that the spoken report may be permissible and necessary, while the speaker, unaware of the necessity, may nonetheless be corrupting his character by indulging in what he thinks is mere gossip.

Again, setting down absolute guidelines in what is a situation of clear negative impact is difficult and subjective.[58] However, we can glean insight from moving from the general principles to surveying some of the specific cases that have been addressed in the responsa literature. It is noteworthy that in many of these cases, there is a distinction drawn between whether or not the third party is asked about the particular issue. If the justification to reveal such information is premised on the mandate to protect the innocent from harm, it would seem to be irrelevant whether or not the question was asked; the information is either necessary for protection or it is not.

One approach to this question is to assume there are objective problems, which require proactive revelation, and subjective problems, which need to first be defined as problems before justifying discussion. Thus, the inquiry expressed by one side defines the subjective issue as relevant. To some extent, focusing on the concerns expressed by the questioner is particularly important, as subjective assessments by the responder can inject unwarranted negativity into the response, whether it is regarding the assessment of the importance of a particular detail, or, even more subjectively, the responder's opinion of whether the suggested couple has compatible personalities.[59]

Some advance a different but related approach: As long as the subjective issue is not brought up, its damaging impact remains uncertain (*safek heizek*), and thus discussion of the issue is not justified in light of the definite damage it will wreak upon the subject.[60] Alternatively, others suggest, in interpretation of the *Ḥafetz Ḥayim,* that it is only definite harm that falls under the mandatory rubric of the protection imperative (Lev. 19:16), *lo taamod al dam re'ekha* (you shall not stand idly by

58. For a discussion of these issues in a different context, see Rabbi Yitzḥak Zilberstein, *Responsa Avnei Ḥoshen* III, pp. 546–49.
59. See the discussion in *BaYom SheYedubar,* pp. 60–62.
60. See Rabbi Shlomo Rozner, *Responsa LeḤafetz BaḤayim* 1:19.

while your fellow's blood is shed).[61] Issues that are more subjective are revealed due to a different mandate, that of the requirement of providing good advice and avoiding bad advice, which are only triggered by a direct inquiry.[62]

Alternatively, it could be maintained that the information that is covered by the protection mandate must indeed be provided even without a direct inquiry. The information that is provided only upon request is that which is justified because it is productive for the potential relationship, and is thus considered purposeful, rather than specifically protective. It becomes understood as such when the inquiring party asks about it.

FURTHER CONSIDERATIONS OF *LASHON HARA* AND *SHIDDUKHIM*

In addition to the specific disclosure considerations, there are a number of other relevant issues in considering *lashon hara* and *shiddukhim*. We will briefly note a few of them.

Among the *Ḥafetz Ḥayim*'s criteria to justify a conversation under the heading of "purposeful speech" is that the one speaking not be a "hater," someone with a bias against the subject of the conversation.[63] In addition to concerns for the speaker's transgression, there is the serious worry that the listener will receive flawed or skewed reports. In the environment of dating, it is not uncommon to encounter people who, even thought they cannot be labeled "haters," have reason to be biased against an individual who is proposed as a *shiddukh*. For example, the speaker himself or herself might be interested in dating the individual under discussion, or be an embittered ex-date of that person. It is incumbent on the one making the inquiries, both for halakhic reasons and for functional personal ones, to ensure that the people he or she turns to for information do not have any alternative agendas, which could affect their assessment, even subconsciously.

---

61. See Rabbi Nissim Karelitz, *Ḥut Shani, Shemirat HaLashon* 7:1.

62. See also Rabbi Moshe Faniri, *Beit Ḥatanim*, p. 16.

63. See the distinction suggested in *Responsa LeḤafetz BaḤayim* 11:13.

In fact, as some authors note, the concern about a "hater" is more relevant in the area of inquiring regarding a possible mate than it is in general questions of purposeful *lashon hara*.[64] This is because the investigation of a potential date is a search for positive qualities of compatibility, and there is a concern that the conflict of interest will lead the responder to omit or downplay these positive qualities. By contrast, when an inquiry is made regarding a possible threat, and the assumption is that negative traits are present, the conflicted responder may have ulterior motives, but will at least be able to fulfill the role of providing the necessary cautionary information.

Similarly, a less blatant but equally relevant concern is that the responder might not have a bias against the individual under discussion, but also might not genuinely know the person well. Often, families inquire of the one person they know with any connection to the potential date, regardless of how strong that connection is. As this person is their only source of information, they accord this person more authority than deserved, and form misimpressions, again contrary both to their personal interests and to halakha.

Further, it is crucially important that the inquirer and the responder speak the same "language." It is often the case that the questions or answers are imparted in vague generalities or idioms that miscommunicate either what the inquirer wants to know about, or what the responder wishes to say. In either event, the goal that justifies the conversation can be missed.[65] It is also possible, when parents are doing the inquiring, that the parents and the child might not be completely in agreement as to what is desired, and this poses a responsibility on the responder to evaluate what kind of answer is truly considered a benefit.[66]

Another point about which it is especially important to be sensitive to concerns of *lashon hara* is when a relationship doesn't work out. At that time, there is often a tendency to discuss why the *shiddukh*

64. See *Kodesh Yisrael* 15.

65. For several examples of this, see *Mishpetei HaShalom*, p. 246, and see also *Zera Ḥayim*, p. 445.

66. See *Ḥut HaShani* 7:1; *Zera Ḥayim*, pp. 446–47; and Rabbi David Ariav, *LeRe'akha Kamokha* VII, p. 302.

failed, but doing so is fraught with risk. Unless the former date poses a danger to others, it is generally wrong to relate to uninvolved parties what was undesirable about the individual.[67] This concern applies even when talking with parents or with a matchmaker. While those individuals are tasked with finding an appropriate match for the one speaking, and thus could benefit from constructive feedback that sharpens the picture of "the right one," it is crucial that the conversation be limited to that constructive content, preferably in general terms, and not needlessly disparage the former date.[68]

Conversely, there is also a serious risk of damaging *lashon hara* in the opposite situation, when a relationship does work out, or has reached the point where it seems unlikely to be derailed by any further information. At that stage, sharing negative information may be counterproductive; it will not deter the parties from getting married, but it may nonetheless have an effect on their respect for each other. Consequently, the individuals will indeed marry, but at moments of tension down the line will see their relationship suffer as they recall disparaging items they were told.[69] In this vein, it is worth remembering the opinion of Hillel (Ketubot 17a), who advised praising a bride even in an exaggerated manner, once the relationship is already a committed one.[70]

As a closing note on this subject, it is instructive to return to one of the issues referenced above. An overwhelming concern in this area is avoiding a *mekaḥ ta'ut*, a mistaken transaction wherein one party enters a commitment unaware of information that would have terminated the deal had he had advance notice of the information. It is universally agreed that any information of such a nature must be revealed, either by the

67. See the discussion of this (and other issues of ended relationships) in *Responsa LeḤafetz BaḤayim* 1, 31.

68. See *Yalkut Yosef, Laws of Respect for Parents*, p. 495; *Ḥut Shani* 7:1, p. 371; and Rabbi Shlomo Zalman Auerbach, cited in the journal *Mevakshei Torah*.

See also Rabbi Yosef Yitzḥak Pinter, *Ohev Yamim, diyunim*, sec. 6, who considers an unusual question of "purposeful" speech in this instance: Is it permissible to tell a disappointed suitor that the desired date, who is uninterested in continuing the relationship, is in some way flawed, in order to assuage the disappointment? He considers both sides of the issue before concluding with an inclination to prohibit.

69. See *Ḥut Shani* 7:1, p. 372.

70. See *Mishpetei HaTorah*, 1:91.

principals themselves, or by a third party, prior to marriage. However, there is a secondary issue that is harder to avoid: misrepresentation (*genevat daat*). This addresses information which, while not crucial to the decision to proceed with the marriage, creates by its nondisclosure a false impression. The result is that the party marries someone whom they would have married regardless, but does so thinking the spouse is more "perfect" than he or she actually is.

The parallel in the business world would be as follows. If one sells an item under false pretenses, such that the buyer would not have made the purchase had he known the truth, such a transaction creates a *mekaḥ ta'ut* and voids the sale, and, if the sale is not voided, constitutes price fraud (*onaa*) and monetary theft. If, however, the purchaser would have bought the item anyway, and at the same price, but the seller conveyed the misimpression that the item was worth more, the seller violates *genevat daat.*

This second scenario, if transferred to the world of *shiddukhim*, seems impossible to avoid. Granted, any issue that might have invalidated the marriage is usually disclosed. But it is not necessarily the case that every lesser "flaw" is disclosed. No person will reveal every imperfection, no matter how minor, before marriage, and one who did so would never get married. How, then, can any marriage take place without a serious violation of *genevat daat*?[71]

One approach to this question was suggested by Rabbi Yisrael Yaakov Kanievsky, known as the Steipler Gaon.[72] He explains that the comparison of marriage to the business world is an imprecise one. When dealing with merchandise, the purchaser has no attachment to the individual unit that he purchases. Thus, if the unit he buys is flawed in some way, while he may not regret the purchase, he would happily agree to trade his item in for a perfect version, if given the opportunity to do so.

This has no parallel in marriage or in human relationships in general. Any happily married person – meaning, one who does not regret

71. For an extremely thorough analysis of this issue, see Rabbi Yisrael Weinman, *Mishnat Yisrael,* ch. 21, pp. 359–83.

72. *Kehillot Yaakov,* Yevamot 38. See also Rabbi Naphtali Nussbaum, in the journal *HaYashar VeHaTov* VIII, p. 46–47.

marrying their spouse – would not seek to trade that spouse in for a "perfect version." There is no such thing; every human being is unique, and being happy with one's mate means accepting them in totality, the pluses and the minuses. Accordingly, the merchandise model of marriage falls seriously short.

A different approach can be seen from the writings of the Klausenberger Rebbe, Rabbi Yekutiel Yehuda Halberstam.[73] He notes a statement of the Rema that in later generations, the custom had been to not be too exacting (*medakdek*) in matters of *shiddukhim*, as long as there is no halakhic impediment to the couple marrying.[74] He interprets this to mean that there is a custom to "look the other way" from certain "imperfections" when looking to marry, and, following the merchandise model, compares this to a trade policy enacted for the betterment of the community. In other words, while strictly speaking, there may be potential issues of *genevat daat*, those who enter the *shiddukh* "market" agree to suspend their right to demand full disclosure, in the interest of allowing for harmonious marriages to take place.[75]

Both approaches are helpful in gaining perspective on this issue. True, marriage is a deeply serious commitment with lifetime consequences. As such, no material information should be concealed when it is necessary to make a responsible decision, or certainly when necessary to protect an innocent party from one who may cause them harm or misery. However, in the course of investigating the other party, it is often too easy to get lost in the details, and to approach marriage like a business investment, assessed in terms of objective profits and losses. It is necessary sometimes to be reminded that we are dealing with unique human beings, who are not interchangeable, and cannot be reduced to numbers and value assessments. Further, failing to deviate from a "merchandise" approach will often affect one's perspective to such an extent that they cannot see beyond the details to what could be a wonderful lifelong marriage. In a broad sense, the laws of *lashon hara* serve to protect the individual from losing his or her uniqueness

73. *Responsa Divrei Yatziv, Even HaEzer* 15.
74. *Even HaEzer* 1:3, citing Rivash.
75. See also Rabbi Yitzḥak Shmuel Shechter, *Responsa Yashiv Yitzḥak* XXV:44.

in a blur of gossip and disconnected detail. It is hoped that the proper appreciation of these laws, and their careful application, will go hand in hand with the mutual respect and esteem that allow two individuals to truly come together as one.

EDUCATIONAL ISSUES

One of the debated points in the realm of "purposeful speech" is the permissibility of informing one's rabbi or teacher of issues with a congregant or student so that they can rebuke or correct the individual. The *Ḥafetz Ḥayim* permits this only when attempting to directly address that guilty party is impossible or has proven unsuccessful.[76] Some later scholars consider it self-evident that license would be granted even to one who could successfully issue rebuke himself, if the authority figure could do so more effectively or more expeditiously.[77] Furthermore, even if the victim can speak directly to the perpetrator, the authority figure should issue the rebuke if he can do so more effectively and expeditiously than anyone else. Even though normally one should speak to the perpetrator directly rather than involve someone else, the *Ḥafetz Ḥayim* acknowledges that such direct communication is not always productive, given that human habits and tendencies are not likely to change and if that appears to be the case speaking to the subject first might not be worthwhile or necessary.[78]

The issue of informing educational authority figures, and its effect on the educational process, is another arena in which the variety of views on this subject is displayed. In an oft-quoted responsum from 1966, Rabbi Moshe Feinstein, the most prominent American rabbinic authority of the twentieth century, recommends against teachers asking children to identify a student who has behaved improperly, out of concern that such a practice in an educational setting will train children

76. *Ḥafetz Ḥayim, Laws of Lashon HaRa* 8:11. See also *Responsa LeḤafetz BaḤayim* 1:30.

77. See for example, Rabbi Moshe Kaufman, in his *Netiv* Ḥayim, *Laws of Lashon HaRa* 8:11, and Rabbi Yisrael Pesaḥ Feinhandler, *Responsa Avnei Yashpeh* III:13. Rabbi Shlomo Rozner, *Responsa LeḤafetz BaḤayim* 1:23, however, questions the accuracy of such an assumption within the formulation of the *Ḥafetz Ḥayim*, while at the same time asking several textual questions on the premises of the *Ḥafetz Ḥayim*.

78. *Ḥafetz Ḥayim, Laws of Rekhilut, klal* 9, *Be'er Mayim Ḥayim* 14.

to be habituated to *lashon hara.*[79] While he acknowledges a talmudic source (Arakhin 16b) that an individual can report on a student to his teacher, Rabbi Feinstein maintains that this is only permissible if the reporter does so on his own initiative. However, for a teacher to instruct a student to do so is a very different situation. As it is, adults who engage in such reporting often do so based on ulterior motives; a child who is pressured to inform will be even less likely to be purely motivated.[80]

Despite the prominence of its author, Rabbi Feinstein's ruling was very controversial. Among the concerns expressed were the issues of necessary purposeful speech. Is it not possible, his detractors countered, that such an attitude might result in bad behavior going unpunished? In a subsequent responsum, Rabbi Feinstein stands his ground.[81] Responding to Rabbi Meir Munk, he argues that even if indeed bad behavior would ensue, it is unclear that this is a greater concern than training children in a mindset of *lashon hara.*

Rabbi Yeḥiel Michel Stern, who interprets Rabbi Feinstein's ruling to apply regardless of the circumstances, argues against the assumption that the children will not be honorably motivated.[82] Further, he maintains that even if there is a mixture of motivations, it would still seem necessary for the well-being of others.

The debate continued into the rabbinical journals. In one such journal, the author also takes issue with Rabbi Feinstein's assumption that motivation will differ profoundly in correlation with whether one is coming forward on their own or being pressured to do so.[83] He further asserts that the entire mission of the educator is to teach the difference between right and wrong, and that conveying a nuanced message shouldn't be impossible in such a situation. He concludes with a distinction between a situation in which the student under discussion is simply underperforming or otherwise harming only himself, and one in which

---

79. *Responsa Iggerot Moshe, Yoreh De'ah* II:103.
80. This point is discussed at length in *Tokhaḥat Ḥayim,* pp. 106–12.
81. *Responsa Iggerot Moshe, Yoreh De'ah* VIII:30.
82. *Imrei Yaakov, Yoreh De'ah, Laws of Teachers* 245:10, sec. *habiurim.*
83. *Kovetz Shaarei Horaa* V, 5765, pp. 154–56.

the student is influencing others, and thus must be stopped presumably even at the expense of extracting the information from other students.

In another journal, Rabbi Ḥayim Yehuda Kohen defends Rabbi Feinstein's ruling, stressing that he is focused not on incidental adult behavior but on educational training and habituation.[84] It is for this reason that his distinction between self-motivation and external pressure from the teacher is significant. He concludes that Rabbi Feinstein's approach is an important one to consider practically. Perhaps our current issues with *lashon hara* would be less severe, he suggests, if more such sensitivity were incorporated into the educational process.[85]

A well-known contemporary authority, Rabbi Asher Weiss, takes issue with Rabbi Feinstein's assessment, and asserts that Rabbi Feinstein's recommendation is only appropriate for very young children, who are completely incapable of distinguishing between differing situations.[86] However, for older children it is equally beneficial for them to learn the value of benefiting society as a whole by protecting their interests from malefactors. Similarly, Rabbi Moshe Sternbuch maintains that it should be possible to extract the necessary information while simultaneously conveying the message of the general severity of *lashon hara*.[87]

This entire debate appears to revolve around the fundamental question of the nature of the *lashon hara* prohibition. Focusing on the issue as one of character may lead to an emphasis on the educational message and its impact on the cultivation of a personality sensitive to its core ethos. Alternatively, directing attention to *lashon hara* as a practical matter, defined as inflicting damage upon others, may lead to a more detail-oriented perspective. In that vein, "purposeful" speech that is beneficial only as an enhancement, rather than as a protective necessity, might be less of a priority than the broader educational message. However, negative speech that is needed to prevent harm to others would continue to be necessary even when the information must be solicited by the teacher (and presumably Rabbi Feinstein would agree).

84. *Kol Torah* LIV, pp. 59–61.

85. See also *Responsa LeḤafetz BaḤayim* III:4.

86. *Minḥat Asher al HaTorah*, Leviticus, 41:4.

87. *Responsa Teshuvot VeHanhagot* I:839.

It should also be noted that there are other instances in Jewish law where nuanced and complex principles are adjusted when children are involved. The Talmud (Sukka 46b) warns that one should not speak falsely to a child, for fear of teaching him dishonesty. The question is obvious: Isn't it prohibited to lie to anyone, adults included? As many explain, there are circumstances when it is permissible to speak falsely: for example, for the preservation of harmony (Yevamot 65b). However, even in such circumstances, if children are involved, a different policy is called for; otherwise, the child will simply come away with the lesson that it is acceptable to lie.

The renowned business ethicist Rabbi Dr. Aaron Levine illustrates this distinction with an example. Often, one receives phone calls that he doesn't have the time (or the inclination) to take. Not wishing to offend the caller, he asks his wife to say that he is not home. Under the harmony principle, that is acceptable.[88] What may not be acceptable is instructing his five-year-old son to say the same thing.[89] Too young to appreciate the circumstances, the child will only see it as a lie. In both this case and the *lashon hara* question, an assessment must be made as to the developmental stage of the child, whether he is able to appreciate nuance and distinction, or whether it is a higher priority to focus on the core value in an uncomplicated way.

Interestingly, the inverse consideration was addressed by one of the rabbinical court judges of the Belzer Hasidim, Rabbi Shammai Gross. In his responsa, he discusses the question of whether the notion of *lashon hara* should be taught to children at all.[90] Perhaps, he relates, we should be concerned that their educational development will be inhibited if they are taught that there are things they cannot say. Adducing talmudic support, he reiterates the priority of careful instruction of this value at the earliest stage of a child's cognitive development.[91]

---

88. However, note Sanhedrin 97a where it is implied that such falsehoods are unacceptable, at least in the ideal. Nonetheless, Rabbi Yaakov Yeḥizkiah Fish, *Titten Emet LeYaakov* 5:24 cites Rabbi Shlomo Zalman Auerbach as permitting.
89. See Rabbi Naḥum Yavrov, *Niv Sefatayim* 3:32, *ḥiddushim*, pp. 57–58.
90. *Responsa Shevet HaKehati* VI:469.
91. See also Rabbi Barukh Rakovsky, *Sefer HaKatan VeHilkhotav* 78:3, with footnote; and *Tehor Sefatayim*, pp. 137–38.

Another issue related to education involves a teacher or other such figure who wishes to inspire, or perhaps to warn his audience, by invoking the story of a figure whose past or present is less than noble. On the one hand, the educationally beneficial remark may nonetheless harm the reputation of the subject; if the prohibition is defined as harming another through speech, the inspirational impact may not be sufficient justification.[92] If, however, malicious intent is the focus, it might be fairly argued that such is absent in this case.[93]

A further complication of the issue emerges from the general assumption in the halakhic texts that to reveal that someone is a repentant transgressor is considered *lashon hara.* However, in modern usage, the term referred to, *baal teshuva,* also identifies one who came to religious observance despite not being provided in youth with an observant upbringing. In either connotation of the term, identifying someone as a *baal teshuva* can be meant to credit and inspire just as likely, if not more so, as it would be meant to derogate. As such, some contemporary authorities[94] assume that the operative issue is the subject's willingness to be identified in that manner.[95]

To return to the issue of informing a teacher or a parent so that they can correct the child's behavior, one may draw the impression that such discipline is the only justifiable reason to pass on negative information to an authority figure. However, Rabbi Moshe Kaufman, in his commentary to the *Ḥafetz Ḥayim,* argues strongly that this is not the case.[96] When a parent asks about the welfare or the activities of a child, even if he is not in a position to influence that child's behavior, the question is legitimate and appropriate as an expression of love for

---

92. See *Shaarei Avraham,* pp. 383–84.

93. See *Ḥafetz Ḥayim, Laws of Lashon HaRa, klal* 1, *Be'er Mayim Ḥayim* 13; note, however, *Tehor Sefatayim,* pp. 161–63. For an extensive discussion of this issue see *Zera Ḥayim* 4:10, pp. 330–40.

94. See, for example, *Responsa Shevet HaKehati* II:321, and, at length, Rabbi Nissim Karelitz, *Ḥut Shani: Shemirat HaLashon,* pp. 337–38.

95. See *Responsa LeḤafetz BaḤayim* I:16; *Responsa Rivevot Ephraim* III:405; Rabbi Shlomo Zalman Kook, in *Bein Shenei Kohanim Gedolim,* p. 146; *BaYom SheYedubar,* pp. 79–81; and *Shemirat HaPeh KeHilkhato,* pp. 90–91.

96. *Zera Ḥayim* I, 4:11.

the child.[97] This concern is what it means to be a parent, an involved relative who by definition is affected by the welfare of the child. By extension, this would be true of anyone in a comparable position, including a teacher who is striving to maintain a relationship with a student. Rabbi Kaufman acknowledges that this logic can be misused, and offered as a pretext by one merely curious and intrusive; nonetheless, he feels the principle is not only true but important enough to emphasize in his work.

BUSINESS ISSUES

As noted above, the *Ḥafetz Ḥayim* has some ambivalence about informing a consumer that a specific vendor (legitimately) charges more than others, while other authorities are quite confident that such information is well within the realm of permissible purposeful speech. If the vendor is actually defrauding or otherwise unjustly depriving his customers, there would be no controversy; all authorities would agree to the necessity of informing the potential victims of this threat to their resources.

Slightly more complicated are cases that fall in the middle: business practices that are improper, but do not actually inflict losses upon others. The Talmud discusses various instances of this behavior; for, example, the case of an employer or employee who reneges on an agreement to work with the other, but before the other has incurred any costs such as investing time or money or missing alternative opportunities. In these cases, the Talmud says the other party has a "grievance" (*taromet*).

There are a range of interpretations of the practical significance of a "grievance" if there is no ability to collect damages. Some suggest that that is the whole point: it is a negative declaration, stating that the other side has only his dissatisfaction and no monetary compensation. Similarly, some suggest that it is a condemnation of the bad actor: a way of declaring that such behavior is immoral or improper, even if the court is unable to impose a penalty.

Others suggest that the term comes to allow interpersonal behavior that is otherwise prohibited or discouraged, such as treating the

97. Note, however, *Tehor Sefatayim*, p. 207.

offending party with anger, or bearing a grudge against him. Rashi, in his talmudic commentary, implies that one with a "grievance" is permitted to speak badly about the source of his grievance.[98] Rabbi Yehuda Silman, a prominent rabbinical court judge in Israel, endorses the position that a technical "grievance" is a license to speak to others about what was done.[99]

There are a few ways to understand this dispensation. The *Ḥafetz Ḥayim* explains the general value of speaking about bad behavior as being multifaceted.[100] One purpose is to protect victims from such acts. Another purpose is to discredit the bad behavior itself, and to thereby set a social standard. In this case, it may be that relating the actions of the other party will serve as a deterrent, both proactively and after the fact, and will as well incentivize the other party to correct his actions. Such a perspective may serve as a model to legitimize the contemporary practice of consumers publishing, online and elsewhere, reviews of the service they have received from businesses and other professional services. Some authorities maintain that the license is solely for the purpose of encouraging the offender to correct his behavior, and thus the publicity must only be in a context and to a degree that is consistent with that possibility.[101]

Alternatively, the purpose of such public declarations might be directed to the benefits of the consuming public, under the premise that they are entitled not only to be protected from corruption and theft, but also to have all information relevant to decisions involving the spending of their money and their time. In that sense, purposeful speech includes not only that which prevents them from being victimized but also that which provides any data that may affect these decisions. It is with this attitude that reviews of books and other consumable media are countenanced.[102] Of course, recognizing the practice as legitimate does not excuse the reviewer from responsibility and care in ensuring that the reviews posted be fair, honest, and unbiased.

98. Bava Metzia 52b, s.v. *im leḥasid.*

99. *Darkhei Ḥoshen* I, pp. 299–303. See also Rabbi Betzalel Stern, *Responsa BeTzel HaḤokhma* V:159 and *Responsa LeḤafetz BaḤayim* I:2.

100. *Ḥafetz Ḥayim, Laws of Lashon HaRa, klal* 10:4.

101. See *Responsa Teshuvot VeHanhagot* V:374.

102. However, see *Responsa Az Nidberu* XIV:67:12, who is inclined to prohibit.

A related area is the question of employers and managers compiling evaluations of their workers. As contemporary authorities have noted, this should be considered purposeful as it allows the company to run more efficiently. However, judgment should be exercised to ensure that the evaluations are actually for the purpose of creating a more productive work environment and not merely to create the impression that management is doing its job.[103]

Similarly, the question of compiling archives and formal records, with information of a mixed nature relating to business, legal, and medical matters, is generally perceived as within the realm of purposeful communication.[104] However, a more complicated question concerns communications between an authority figure and an individual that are meant to remain confidential. Is it appropriate for the authority figure to use a secretary for these communications, thus exposing a third party to information that is private, and possibly negative as well? One great contemporary authority, Rabbi Eliezer Yehuda Waldenberg, allows this, for a combination of reasons: such mechanisms are necessary for the system to work efficiently; the administration and staff are considered, for all intents and purposes, one body; and those who interact with the system know that is how it operates and agree to it.[105] Nonetheless, there were those who disagreed, including the highly influential authority Rabbi Yosef Shalom Elyashiv.[106] Once again, various factors and rationales compete within this complex balance.

---

103. See *Responsa Even Pina* II:180, and also *Shoshanat HaAmakim: BiInyanei Halakha (Kollel Halakha URfua)*, p. 136n73.

104. See Rabbi Aryeh Katz, in the journal *Teḥumin* XXVII, pp. 180–84; Rabbi Yitzḥak Zilberstein in the journal *HaBe'er* (Sanz) XXIV, pp. 63–64; and *Responsa BeMareh HaBazak* VI:96.

105. *Responsa Tzitz Eliezer* XX, 52:1.

106. See *Aleinu Leshabeaḥ* V, pp. 568–69, where Rabbi Yitzḥak Zilberstein quotes Rabbi Eliashiv as forbidding even a system where the assistant works on forms with the names omitted, out of concern he will figure out the identities. By contrast, Rabbi Yitzchak Hutner, *Iggerot Paḥad Yitzḥak* 119, appears to understand a talmudic passage (Moed Katan 16a) as permission for all disclosure necessary for procedural matters. See also *Shaarei Avraham*, p. 279, and see the position of Rabbi Shlomo Zalman Auerbach and others as quoted in Rabbi Avraham S. Avraham, *Nishmat Avraham* IV, pp. 130–31.

CONTENTIOUS PEOPLE (*BAALEI MAḤALOKET*)

There is a striking sentence in the Talmud (Y. Pe'ah 1:1) apparently allowing *lashon hara* against a certain category of people. The Hebrew term for this group is *baalei maḥaloket,* which is difficult to translate but may be understood as "contentious people" (or, perhaps more colloquially, "troublemakers").[107]

However, major authorities maintain that this is not a blanket dispensation; this negative speech is only allowed for the purposes of quieting the dispute.[108] When this is not possible, the laws of *lashon hara* are unchanged.[109] The *Ḥafetz Ḥayim* rules that even when leniencies are operative, strict guidelines still govern their employment.[110] These conditions include the speaker must know the information personally, and not be relying on another; the intent must be pure; there must be no other feasible method of bringing peace; and all of the above must be carefully evaluated. He emphasizes that this title should not be conferred upon people lightly, and if there is some doubt, this license should not be implemented. Conversely, some have suggested that while the goal must be the quieting of the disruptive behavior, the license differs from that of general "purposeful" speech in that it is permitted not only to identify the behavior, but to actively disparage it.[111]

---

107. This is based on the verse in 1 Kings 1:14. On this derivation, see Rabbi Avraham Price, *Mishnat Avraham* to *Semag* 10:9:4, and *Ḥelkat Binyamin* 8:17. Several authorities codify this principle; see *Sefer Mitzvot Gadol,* negative commandment 10; *Sefer Mitzvot Katan* 8; *Sefer Ḥasidim,* 631; *Hagahot Maimoniyot, Laws of Personal Development* 7:3; *Shaarei Teshuva* 3:58; and *Magen Avraham, Oraḥ Ḥayim* 156. See also Rabbi Shimshon Ḥayim Naḥmani, *Zera Shimshon, Parashat Koraḥ* 9. Note as well the comments of Rabbi Elḥanan Bunim Wasserman in his *Kovetz He'arot* (Yevamot 70).

108. See *Gilyon HaShas* to the Jerusalem Talmud.

109. See also *Maḥatzit HaShekel, Oraḥ Ḥayim* 156; Rabbi Yonatan Shteif, *Mitzvot Hashem,* vol. 2, p. 30; Rabbi Mordekhai Lichtenstein, *Mitzvot HaLevavot* 2:21; Rabbi Meir Dan Plotzki, *Keli Ḥemda, Parashat Metzora* 1; and Rabbi Deror Binyamin Sandler, in the journal *Torat HaAdam LeAdam* 4, pp. 194–95. Note the additional limitations recorded by Rabbi Avraham David Wahrman, *Milei DeḤasiduta,* p. 36, and see *Imrei Yehosef* to *Sefer Mitzvot Katan.* See, however, *Maor HaShaar,* p. 130.

110. *Ḥafetz Ḥayim, Laws of Lashon HaRa* 8:8; he also notes that this dispensation is not found in the codes of Maimonides, the Rosh, or the Rif. An extensive analysis of the concept can be found in Rabbi Ḥayim Shlomo Abrahams, *Birkhat Shlomo* 21.

111. See Rabbi Shlomo Rozner, *Responsa LeḤafetz BaḤayim* 11: 5, 11.

The imposition of these conditions may reflect a position on this license that is subject to debate, thus possibly putting the conditions themselves in question. Many scholars understand the permissibility of speaking negatively about contentious individuals as a function of those individuals forfeiting their protection through the harmful and sinful act of provoking dissension.[112] The *Ḥafetz Ḥayim* himself, however, is hesitant to label these people as wantonly sinful; he notes the fact that while provoking strife is indeed prohibited, it differs from more standard transgressions which manifest themselves in an objective fashion.[113] In a dispute, each party believes himself justified and the other to be malevolent. It is logical to assume that it is this perspective that prompts the *Ḥafetz Ḥayim* to rule that any act of harmful speech be undertaken with caution, reflective of the tentative character of the allegedly sinful act.[114] By contrast, those who advocate a more expansive understanding of the license may feel that this is specifically the lesson the Talmud is conveying: despite the self-justification of the provocateurs, their behavior is sinful nonetheless.[115]

One of the great rabbinic leaders of the eighteenth century, Rabbi Moshe Sofer, known as the *Ḥatam Sofer*, has a different understanding of the Hebrew term, to which he adds a possessive adjective.[116] Thus, in his rendering, the reference seems to be not to a person who is generally contentious, but rather someone who is specifically in a conflict with the speaker. Accordingly, it is permitted to say something one time, only to the extent necessary to identify the subject as someone in opposition to the speaker; beyond that, no negative speech about him is permitted.

---

112. See Rabbi Naphtali Tzvi Yehuda Berlin, *Haamek She'ela* 28:1, *Brit Moshe* to *Semag*, negative commandment 10; *Arukh HaShulḥan, Oraḥ Ḥayim* 156:13; Rabbi Ḥayim Shaul Kaufman, *Mishḥat Shemen* 179, pp. 333–36; and *Shemuot Ḥayim*, Arakhin, ch. 3, sec. 19. See also the analysis of the two possibilities in Rabbi Avraham Yitzḥak Toker, *Bikkurei Aretz*, Berakhot 29.
113. *Be'er Mayim Ḥayim, Laws of Lashon HaRa* 8:17, and see *Ḥafetz Ḥayim, Laws of Lashon HaRa* 10, *Be'er Mayim Ḥayim* 30.
114. See *Ḥelkat Binyamin* 19; *Netiv Ḥayim* 7; and *Alei Be'er.*
115. See also *Ohev Yamim* to *Ḥafetz Ḥayim*, and *Tehor Sefatayim*, pp. 156–59.
116. *Ḥiddushim* to Moed Katan 15b, p. 59.

It seems that the Ḥatam Sofer understands this concept differently than others. It is sometimes necessary for an individual to inform others that someone bears animus toward him, and that actions or statements he produces should be seen in that context.[117]

Other commentaries glean further details of this lesson through talmudic analysis.[118] Among these is a position similar to the point of the Ḥatam Sofer but with the more general application: negative declarations

---

117. See also at great length Rabbi Yitzḥak Ratzabi, *Einei Yitzḥak, Shulḥan Arukh HaMekutzar* 141n17, pp. 337–41; and note the comments of Rabbi Naphtali Katz in *VeTziva HaKohen* 19. This topic is addressed in great detail in *Shemirat HaPeh KeHilkhato*, pp. 197–203.

118. The Talmud (Moed Katan 16a) derives from a verse (Num. 16:14) that an agent of the rabbinic court may relate to the court the disrespectful behavior of one who is summoned to the court and refuses to come. The context is refusal of Datan and Aviram to cooperate with the summons of Moses during the rebellion of Korah (see Rashi and *Torah Temima* (Num. 16:14, and Rema, *Ḥoshen Mishpat* 8:5, with *Sma*; see also Rabbi Avraham Yeshayahu Turtzin, in the journal *Otzerot Yerushalayim* LXIV, pp. 663–64). The commentators (see *Ḥokhmat Shlomo* to *Ḥoshen Mishpat*; *Gilyon HaShas*, Pe'ah 1:1, citing *Ḥatam Sofer*, and *Tal Ḥayim*, citing *Kevod Ḥakhamim*) question this derivation: Datan and Aviram were well known as contentious individuals, and if *lashon hara* is indeed permitted against contentious individuals, *lashon hara* against Datan and Aviram would be permitted even without any special dispensation for the agent of the rabbinic court. In response, some commentators suggest that the two principles are actually the same (see *Torah Temima*, Num. 16:14), while others suggest that the exclusion for contentious individuals is more limited, as discussed above, for example only being permitted to calm the conflict. In addition, other suggested resolutions focus on unique aspects of the Datan and Aviram case, such as: noting that the report was likely to provoke further conflict, while the general license is only when it would reduce conflict (Rabbi Yosef Jolofsky, *Yad Yosef* to Moed Katan); or, even though they were known rebels, Moses refused to label them as such and thus did not assume accordingly. (See Rabbi Natan Gesteteiner, *Lehorot Natan* to Numbers, and Rabbi Moshe Sofer, *Torat Moshe* to Numbers). See also the journal *Kol Torah*, LVI, pp. 18–19; Rabbi Shmuel Rothschild, *Peirot Te'ena* to Moed Katan 16a; Rabbi Yaakov Meskin, *Mishpat LeYaakov*, p. 11; Rabbi Raphael ben Mordekhai Ankiva, *Paamonei Zahav* to *Ḥoshen Mishpat*; *Ḥavatzelet HaSharon al HaTorah*, Numbers, p. 539; and Rabbi Eliyahu Shick, *Ein Eliyahu*, Pe'ah, p. 281. Rabbi Yosef Shaul Nathanson, *Responsa Shoel UMeshiv* III, 1:80, among other suggestions, offers the possibility that in the case of Datan and Aviram, the messenger went further in not only relating their response but in interpreting it as well.

are permitted only on a one-time basis, to identify the individuals as contentious; and they are limited only to the contentious behavior itself, and not other criticisms.[119]

ADDITIONAL ISSUES OF "PURPOSE" AND SELF-DEFENSE

The parameters of the balance between *lashon hara* and necessary or beneficial, purposeful speech are the subject of much analytical literature. In addition to the above topics, some queries posed include the following: Person A tells a secret to Person B, who breaks Person A's confidence and tells Person C. Can Person C tell Person A his secret has been breached? Is that necessary for his protection, or will it simply anger him and thus constitute forbidden *rekhilut?*[120] Does the license to speak negatively for a beneficial purpose apply also when the subject is one's parents, or does the special deference due to them change the equation?[121]

One frequently discussed scenario does not involve the mandate to protect others but rather the purposeful speech necessary to defend one's own reputation, when accused of a misdeed. Rabbi Yisrael of Beruna required that one only state his own innocence when defending himself, without naming others as guilty,[122] and this appears to be the position adopted by the *Ḥafetz Ḥayim.*[123] Later authorities considered the matter of identifying a guilty party and noted proof

119. See Rabbi Eliezer Zev Devoretz, in the journal *Tevuna* IX, p. 85.

120. See Rabbi Avraham Genichovsky in the journal *HaBe'er* (Sanz), vol. 24, pp. 45–46.

121. This is a topic of dispute; see Rabbi Nisan Kaplan, in the journal *Kol HaTorah* L, p. 25, and in LIV; Rabbi Yitzḥak Zilberstein, p. 172, and Rabbi Moshe Tzimerman, p. 3, and see also *Beyad HaLashon*, pp. 352–54. Note also *Rishumei Aharon* I, *Yoreh De'ah* 240:3, citing Rabbi Moshe Feinstein.

122. *Responsa Mahari Beruna* 38.

123. *Ḥafetz Ḥayim, Laws of Lashon HaRa, klal* 10, 17, and *Be'er Mayim Ḥayim* 43. In fact, he goes further, recommending that one who is particularly pious voluntarily take the blame to spare the guilty party. However, this is assuming it is a minor matter, in which the only consequence would be embarrassment; see below.

texts in both directions.[124] Contemporary commentaries generally assume that one may identify the guilty culprit if there is no other way to clear one's own name, especially if it is a matter of seriousness (even with no punishment involved). In that case, the right to reputational self-defense combines with the mandate to avoid suspicion (an obligation emphasized by Rabbi Yisrael as well) to indicate that the accused must assert his innocence and allow the chips to fall where they may.[125] Of course, if the actual offender poses any kind of a risk, that fact itself would obligate his exposure to those affected. Similarly, if the questioner has a legitimate claim of action against the unknown offender, there would again be an obligation to reveal who it is.[126]

In recognition of the need to be able to defend one's reputation, Rabbi Shlomo Rozner, a present-day commentator on the *Ḥafetz Ḥayim* as well as author of a work of responsa devoted to *lashon hara,* allows the relaying of slanderous statements to the subject so that he may refute them.[127] This is significant, as it indicates a limitation on the prohibition of *rekhilut,* which normally prohibits informing the subject of gossip, out of concern that conflicts will result. Nonetheless, if there is concrete benefit to the subject, such as the ability to defend himself, this benefit outweighs the fear of strife.[128]

---

124. See Rabbi Ḥayim Shlomo Avraham, writing in the journal *Or Yisrael* 30:1 pp. 254–55 and in his *Devar Torah,* Genesis, pp. 213–214. See also Rabbi Ḥayim Kaufman in the journal *Kol Torah* XL, p. 119.

125. See *Shevilei Ḥayim* (3), *Alei Be'er* and *Ohev Yamim,* all to *Ḥafetz Ḥayim, Laws of Lashon HaRa, klal* 10, 17, #3; *Birkat Yitzḥak,* pp. 313–14, and *Responsa LeḤafetz BaḤayim* I:17. See also Rabbi Elḥanan Bunim Wasserman, *Kovetz Shiurim* to Bava Batra, 595.

126. A detailed analysis of the whole topic (include a consideration of a number of other issues regarding *lashon hara*) can be found in Rabbi Yaakov Zide, *Responsa Bo Tashiv,* 6.

127. *Responsa LeḤafetz BaḤayim* II:4. The *Ḥafetz Ḥayim, Laws of Lashon HaRa* 10:5, appears to prohibit informing the subject, even indirectly; however, Rabbi Rozner suggests this is only true when the purpose is a general critique of the original speaker's engaging in *lashon hara*; however, when the purpose is to provide an opportunity for defense, such informing is necessary, as explained below. Compare also *Responsa LeḤafetz BaḤayim,* I, 38. See also *Shaarei Avraham,* pp. 422–27.

128. See also *Shemirat HaPeh KeHilkhato,* p. 249.

Questions such as these display the careful balance struck between on the one hand the prohibition of disparaging others and the recognition of the risk inherent even with factual negative information, and on the other hand the various ways in which such speech is sometimes necessary and beneficial and thus must be allowed. A careful cost-benefit analysis, premised on sensitivity and awareness of the factors on both sides of the equation, is always called for. The harm caused by a mistake in either direction can be significant, and the task of understanding the elements is the first step towards responsibility.[129]

129. For further discussions regarding purposeful speech, see Rabbi Ephraim Natan Rothchild, in the journal *Kol HaTorah* LXIV, p. 164; *Responsa Ohalei Yehuda,* pp. 153–58; Rabbi Yitzḥak Zilberstein, in the journal *Marpei Lashon* IV, pp. 46–48.

"Accepting" Lashon HaRa

DEFINING THE PROHIBITION

One of the most difficult, and at the same time, most illuminating, areas of study and practice in the realm of *lashon hara* is the unique prohibition of "receiving" (*kabbalat*) *lashon hara*. The prohibition of malicious speech is extended not only to the speaker, but to the listener as well; the listener is identified by the Talmud (Arakhin 15b) as one of three victims of *lashon hara*'s destructive impact, together with the speaker and the subject. In fact, as will be detailed below, receiving *lashon hara* is condemned with a force equal or possibly even greater than that of the initial act of speaking.

It is here, then, that we find both the difficulty and the illumination. First, the difficulty: How can one be prohibited from "receiving," a role that is essentially a passive one, and a generally involuntary one at that? And, perhaps even more challenging: even if it is granted that one can control what he "receives," is it truly desirable to do so? As we have established, *lashon hara* includes the relating of true information that is disparaging. As such, would refusing to "receive" such information not constitute willful self-deception, an act essentially both dishonest and irrational in nature? Understanding the Torah's directive in this case requires both a careful analysis of earlier and later sources, and a considered and balanced investigation as to how integrity and intellect can coexist with the injunction.

It is in this process that the illumination is brought forth as well. The parsing of the aspect of "receiving" goes to the core of understanding the entire concept of *lashon hara.* This is particularly so in light of the fact that receiving *lashon hara* is not considered a secondary or subsidiary violation, but a sin equal to that committed by the speaker, and possibly the primary locus of the *lashon hara* interdict itself. If so, to understand the concept of "receiving *lashon hara*" is to better understand the foundation of *lashon hara* in its totality.

That said, it makes sense to begin the journey with the key talmudic passage introducing the prohibition. In that passage, R. Sheshet, on the authority of R. Elazar ben Azaria, issues a harsh condemnation of three apparently equal and connected offenses: speaking *lashon hara,* receiving *lashon hara,* and bearing false witness.[1] All three are attached to one biblical verse (Ex. 23:1), "You shall not accept (*tissa*) a false (*shav*) report." This represents a tentative translation of some Hebrew words that will be seen to be ambiguous (earlier we rendered *tissa* as "bear").

There are a number of striking aspects to this scriptural derivation. One is that the connotation of the verse appears to be passive ("shall not accept"); as such, it would be satisfactory as a source for the prohibition of receiving *lashon hara,* but less obviously so for the proscription of speaking *lashon hara.* The Talmud addresses this apparent incongruity by advocating an alternate reading of the word *tissa.* Instead of "accept," the Talmud suggests *tassi,* a word with a similar spelling but different pronunciation connoting "inducing or misleading"; the sense of the verse would therefore be, "You shall not mislead with a false report." Then again, some commentaries do not relate to the Talmud's elucidation, and understand the verse according to its simple meaning ("shall not accept").[2]

According to either understanding of the word *tissa,* the basic prohibition against speaking *lashon hara* is being sourced by this passage in the context of receiving *lashon hara.* This is not the expected hierarchy; one would think that speaking *lashon hara* is the primary sin, deserving the most attention from Scripture, with receiving merely an ancillary

1. Pesaḥim 118a. See also *Mishneh Torah, Laws of the Sanhedrin* 21:7.
2. See, for example, Rashbam, Pesaḥim 118a.

activity that deserves secondary mention.[3] R. Sheshet's formulation inverts that expectation: "receiving" is the primary subject of the verse, and "speaking" is derived from it. This could potentially redefine our conceptualization of *lashon hara*: the main crime is perpetrated by the listener, who is enabled by the speaker, and not the other way around.[4]

In that light, it is noteworthy that Maimonides, in his code, identifies receiving *lashon hara* as not merely equal to, but actually worse than, speaking *lashon hara*.[5] This is a surprising formulation, as it exceeds what the Talmud says. Accordingly, much has been written in explanation of Maimonides's statement.[6] Most simply, it may be that if the controlling source indeed focuses on the aspect of receiving, it follows logically that this act is an even greater transgression than speaking.[7]

---

3. As to whether and under what circumstances accepting *lashon hara* is a violation of the halakhic prohibition of enabling sin (*lifnei iver lo titten mikhshol),* see *Ḥafetz Ḥayim, Introduction,* prohibition 4; and commentaries there: *Alei Be'er; Shevilei Ḥayim* 12; *Ohev Yamim* 4–6; *Birkat Yitzḥak,* pp. 14–19; Rabbi Reuven Grozovsky in the journal *Kol Torah* LV, pp. 54–55; and see also *Ḥut Shani, Shemirat HaLashon* 1:1, and Rabbi Yehonatan Rozler, *He'arot Rigshei Ḥayim,* p. 20.
4. One interesting question to consider is to what extent the prohibition of *kabbala* is a direct correlate of the prohibition of speaking, and to what extent it is an independent concept. In other words, is there a prohibition of accepting any and every time the speaker is subject to a prohibition? Conversely, is there ever a prohibition of accepting even if the speaker is permitted to say what he is saying? See *Ḥafetz Ḥayim, Laws of Lashon HaRa* 6:9, and *Ḥelkat Binyamin,* loc cit.; *Birkat Yitzḥak,* pp. 14–15; Rabbi Yosef Aharon Openheimer, in the journal *Kol HaTorah* LX, p. 97; *LeRe'akha Kamokha,* p. 153, in *Nir LeDavid* 2; see also *Ḥafetz Ḥayim* 6:3, in note.
5. *Mishneh Torah, Laws of Personal Development* 7:3.
6. See *Avodat Melekh* and *Ḥelkat Binyamin, lashon hara* 6:3. See also *Minḥat Yitzḥak* to *Minḥat Ḥinnukh* 236: 3 who suggests an explanation based on the notion that without acceptance the transgression is incomplete; see also Rabbi Shmuel Aryeh Leib of Bialya, *Rimza DeḤakhmata,* p. 137, writing from a kabbalistic perspective. *Netiv Ḥayim* 6:3 suggests that the accepter transgresses more seriously than the speaker because the latter's unjustified reliance on the report may indicate greater irresponsibility than that of the speaker; see also see *Daat UMaḥashava* to *Mishneh Torah, Laws of Personal Development.* For further suggestions, see Rabbi Menaḥem Troyesh, *Oraḥ Meisharim* 8:23, and also *Shaarei Avraham,* p. 376.
7. See also *Ḥafetz Ḥayim,* Introduction, prohibitions, *Be'er Mayim Ḥayim* 3, as to whether the recipient is equally susceptible to the affliction of *tzaraat.* See *Zikhron David,* pp. 27–28.

The second, equally striking aspect of R. Sheshet's statement centers on the word *shav*, rendered above as "false". If, as we have repeatedly seen, the transgression of speaking *lashon hara* includes the relating of true information, why would the verse refer to a "false" report? Such language would seem to fall short of the mark, as it would fail to address the receiving of true disparaging reports.[8]

Indeed, the proper translation of the word *shav* is the topic of debate. The term "false" is consistent with the understanding of many major commentaries, who equate it with the word *sheker*, the general term for falsehood.[9] Nonetheless, there are other possible translations of the term; one possibility, which we discussed above in the context of necessary permitted speech, is that it connotes "useless," meaning that *lashon hara* may be accepted when there is a pressing purpose, but not otherwise. Others define the word as "hated" or "despised," referring to the prohibited and malicious nature of the speech, and not necessarily indicating that the content is factually false.[10]

If, however, the word is indeed translated as "false," the initial question remains as to how this is consistent with the factual nature of *lashon hara*. One approach, adopted by Rabbeinu Yonah of Gerona, is to insert the modifier "possibly" before "false report." Thus, the verse exhorts us not to accept as definitely true a report that *might not* be true. As some have observed, this might be the only tenable explanation; no one needs to be instructed not to accept a report that they know is false.[11] Rather, the verse warns against accepting as true a report that might not be true. It emerges, then, that to accept a report as possibly true rather than definitely true might not be a violation of accepting a "*shav* report."

---

8. See Rabbi Yaakov Zvi Meklenberg, *HaKetav VeHaKabbala* to Exodus.
9. See Rashi and Onkelos to Ex. 23:1.
10. See *Yad HaKettana, Laws of Personal Development* 9; as well as Rabbi Aharon HaKohen, *Imrei Aharon, Parashat Mishpatim*, p. 62; and Rabbi Shlomo Wolbe, *Alei Shur* II, p. 534. See also Rabbi Aryeh Lubetsky, *Naḥal Kedumim* to Exodus, pp. 32–33; Rabbi Moshe David Valley, *Brit Olam* to Exodus, pp. 360–61; and Rabbi Tzvi Shlav, *Niflaot MiTorat Hashem Yitbaraḥ*, ch. 56, pp. 241–43.
11. See Rabbi Avraham Yitzḥak Brazil, *Iyyunei Rashi* (Exodus: *Parashot Mishpatim–Pekudei*, pp. 176–78).

Similarly, the *Sefer HaḤinnukh* places this prohibition within the context of the Torah's broad aversion to dishonesty.[12] Since falsehood is not only prohibited, but condemned with a more sweeping exhortation to "keep far away [from it]" (Ex. 23:7), included in this avoidance is a sensitivity to falsehood in the speech of others, and a refusal to participate in the slander even in a passive role.[13] Further, the effect of the Torah's commandment to judge others favorably may add to the need to thoroughly consider the possibility that the negative report is false.[14]

Other possible interpretations are consistent with our earlier discussions about the complex nature of *lashon hara*, which can be factually accurate and yet false at the same time. Accordingly, the *Ḥafetz Ḥayim* is concerned that even if the core item is true, false details will be woven in.[15] In addition, even if all the facts mentioned in a statement are true, it is still possible to emerge with a false picture of the subject, as we have seen.[16] Further still, the issue might not be the facts themselves, but rather the assessment: even if the item is true, the result that the subject will be diminished in the eyes of the listener, due to some insignificant flaw, is an injustice that is in essence false.[17]

In this vein, we can examine how some of the translations of the word *shav* (Ex. 23:1) relate to each other, particularly the notions of "false" and "useless." It is instructive that the same verse is cited by the Talmud and Maimonides also as a prohibition for a rabbinic court judge to listen to ex parte testimony.[18] In that context, both translations are equally compatible with the intent of the prohibition. It can be understood that listening to one party outside the presence of the other yields "false" results, as the speaking party is able to express its views without the benefits of opposition and correction from the other party. The translation "useless" is equally appropriate, in that such testimony,

12. Commandment 74.
13. However, note the comment of *Zera Ḥayim*, p. 360.
14. See *Ḥelkat Binyamin*, *klal* 7, 3, and Rabbi Tzvi Hertzka, *Ateret Tzvi*, to Exodus.
15. Introduction, positive commandments, in *Be'er Mayim Ḥayim* 2; see also *Shemirat HaLashon*, ch. 12. See also *Oraḥ Meisharim* 8:26.
16. See *Shaarei Avraham*, p. 235n147.
17. See *Ḥelkat Binyamin*, beginning of *klal* 7, and *Zera Ḥayim*, p. 362–64.
18. Shavuot 31a and *Mishneh Torah, Laws of the Sanhedrin* 21:7.

lacking the elements of necessary balance, is worthless in a courtroom setting, and thus contributes nothing to the judicial process. As such, it constitutes both a breach of judicial integrity and a violation of *lashon hara.* In that sense, the falsity and the uselessness of the reports are essentially products of each other.

We can suggest, then, that this application to listening to ex parte testimony is quite instructive in its location in the same verse as general acceptance of *lashon hara.* It sheds light on the concept of *lashon hara* as a whole, and the nature of factually true statements conveying false impressions. Negative speech that is protected from corrective opposition from the subject is by its nature susceptible to distortion and false impacts, and thus is useless for any constructive purpose. In that sense, the judicial application is reflective of the general application of *lashon hara* and the inherent relationship between unwarranted gossip and falsity.[19]

All of these factors were relevant considerations discussed earlier as to why a speaker should choose not to share information that he would consider to be true. However, it is possible that there is an even greater concern regarding the listener of such information, and thus there might be particular relevance to the prohibition of *kabbalat lashon hara.* In his book *The Watercooler Effect,* Nicholas DiFonzo describes a study entitled "Why Listeners Hear Less Than They Are Told," conducted by social psychologist Robert S. Barron and his team, which was undertaken in an effort to understand why people who listen to a story of someone's misdeeds rate that person more negatively than people telling the story do.

As the author puts it:

> This is known as the teller-listener extremity effect – the listener's rating of the person is more extreme than the teller's. Barron's study makes a convincing case that the culprit behind

19. A suggestion along these lines is asserted by Rabbi Eliyahu Bakshi-Doron in *Responsa Binyan Av* III:66. This notion may also be relevant to understanding the position of some authorities that statements made in the presence of the subjects are by definition not *lashon hara,* even if they constitute other offenses; see pp. 167–172.

> this effect has to do with the limits of human attention while attending to a disjointed message. The details that people tell one another are often so hard to follow that listeners are only able to process the main storyline; the finer points and subplots are simply missed.

He further cites other studies which indicate that listeners, in order to make a story they are hearing simpler and more comprehensible, tend to adapt and conflate details, a behavior pattern known as "leveling" and "sharpening."[20]

WHAT DOES IT MEAN "TO ACCEPT"?

Defining this prohibition in a practical sense is somewhat complex. "Receiving" or "accepting" indicates more than mere "listening" (which will be discussed below), while still referring to something that is essentially passive, and perhaps even involuntary. Accordingly, pinning down the scope of this prohibition has been a matter of considerable debate.

Some explain the prohibition as an injunction against believing the report to be true. This interpretation is rooted in the early talmudic commentaries,[21] and is adopted by the *Ḥafetz Ḥayim.*[22] Strikingly, he maintains that this prohibition remains in effect even when the information is necessary for the protection of oneself or others. It is granted and indisputable that one may protect himself and others by taking into consideration the possibility that the information is true. Beyond the needs of protection, though, the listener must remain internally convinced that the information is false. This approach is based on a statement of the Talmud (Nidda 61a), regarding *lashon hara,* that "*af al pi dilkabulei lo miba'ei. meiḥush lei miba'ei*": one is required to account for the possibility [that the item is true], but not to accept it." In other words, there is a distinction between taking protective measures, which

20. DiFonzo, *Watercooler Effect,* pp. 154–63.

21. See Rashbam, Pesaḥim 118a, s.v. *hamekabel;* see also *Be'er Mayim Ḥayim, Lashon HaRa* 6:1.

22. *Ḥafetz Ḥayim, Laws of Lashon HaRa* 6:1.

are not predicated on accepting the information as definitely true, and actually believing the report.[23]

The Rosh asserts that even this limited license is based on the risk of harm.[24] Interestingly, he starts from the premise that one is obligated to protect oneself, and includes in that requirement the protection of others. Rabbi Yom Tov Lipman Heller, in his commentary to the Rosh's code, assumes this to be a function of the mandate of "love your fellow as yourself."[25] This approach adds a broader element to the mandate of "you shall not stand idly by," invoked in the context of speaking *lashon hara* for a necessary purpose.

Rabbi Yitzchak Hutner explains the mechanics of this process.[26] Normally, a mere "concern" about another's behavior would be insufficient to deprive that person of any preexisting benefit. However, when that concern affects another person, it becomes appropriate for that affected person to take that factor into account when making decisions necessary for his own protection (and, by extension, that of others). This emerges from the fact that the general concern about accepting *lashon hara* and *rekhilut* is premised upon the report being both unnecessary and an intrusion into the affairs of others. However, under the circumstances in question, the revelation is not unnecessary, nor is it exclusively the business of the subject; because it affects the listener, incorporating the concern is not a violation of accepting *lashon hara.*

Some contemporary authors question the feasibility of the above position forbidding believing.[27] Believing or not believing, according to this formulation, is not a voluntary act. The Torah has been placed

---

23. See also Rabbi Yitzḥak Sorotzkin, *Rinat Yitzḥak* to Jer. 41:9. Note, however, that the *Tosafot Ḥakhmei Anglia,* Nidda 61a, does include "believing" (*lehaamin*) in the category of *limeiḥush.* Similarly, this word appears in *Tosafot* on the page (s.v. *atmirinkhu*), but it may be read in that context as meaning "it may be believed as far as it is relevant to protection, but not for other purposes." See also Maharsha to Nidda 61a, who distinguishes between protective measures and punishment, as well as *Responsa Shoel UMeshiv* 1, 1:185. See *Shaarei Avraham,* pp. 405–6 and *Responsa Ohalei Yehuda,* pp. 153–58.
24. Nidda 9:5, and *Tosfei HaRosh,* Nidda 61a, s.v *atmirinkhu.*
25. *Maadanei Yom Tov,* to Rosh, Nidda 9:5.
26. *Iggerot Paḥad Yitzḥak* 59.
27. See *Responsa Teshuvot VeHanhagot* 1, 555, and *Zera Ḥayim,* pp. 368–70.

in the realm of human beings, not angels; it is unlikely that mortals can exert such active control over their recognition of a well-known associate's credibility.[28] If a trustworthy individual conveys an item of news, the listener knows with near certainty that the item is genuine. Similarly, the *Ḥazon Ish* found the *Ḥafetz Ḥayim*'s position on this matter practically unfeasible, and relevant only on an academic plane ("*lomdus*").[29]

Rather, suggest the advocates of this approach, it must be assumed that the prohibition of *kabbalat lashon hara* is relevant not to internal perceptions, but to actions.[30] The imperative would be to guarantee that one's behavior toward the subject not change as a consequence of the shared information. The mental acceptance, though, would be understood to be unavoidable and forgivable.

---

28. Presumably, according to the *Ḥafetz Ḥayim,* even a verbal declaration that one is "not accepting" the *lashon hara* would not be helpful if his mental state is otherwise; this position is taken in an analysis by Rabbi Reuven Grozovsky in the journal *Kol Torah* LV, pp. 53–54.
29. Rabbi S. D. Munk, *Responsa Pe'at Sadekha* 1:29. Part of the *Ḥazon Ish*'s objection has to do with an additional technical difficulty imposed by the *Ḥafetz Ḥayim.* One might have thought that while one is constrained from accepting the item as true, it should be considered as a possibility (*safek*). However, the *Ḥafetz Ḥayim* asserts that one should account for the risk reflected in the item without even considering it a *safek.* The *Ḥazon Ish* felt this distinction was impossible to translate from concept to practice. See *Zekher Shmuel,* Shabbat 31, who suggests that the notion that it cannot even be considered a *safek* is a consequence of the additional imperative to judge favorably, beyond the requirements of *kabbalat lashon hara.* Some contemporary authors maintain that the intent of the *Ḥafetz Ḥayim* is that the subject should not be stigmatized as a *safek* offender with attendant consequences, but not to prohibit precautions taken out of the concern that he might indeed be an offender. (See *Responsa LeḤafetz BaḤayim* II:15 and IV:9, and *Zera Ḥayim,* p. 367.) They also suggest that the *Ḥazon Ish* does not disagree with the *Ḥafetz Ḥayim*'s position, but just emphasizes the practical difficulty. See the entire essay of *Zera Ḥayim,* pp. 367–73. See also *Shaarei Avraham,* pp. 405–6, who endorses the position of the *Ḥafetz Ḥayim* while noting the practical difficulty, which he asserts will serve as a defense and a source of heavenly assistance for one who makes a good faith effort to comply. Alternatively, see *Zikhron David,* pp. 84–85, who notes various indications that it is permitted to believe *lashon hara* as long as one does not accept the item definitively, and accordingly the *Ḥafetz Ḥayim* is referring to an additional, rabbinic prohibition of believing as a *safek.*
30. This approach has a strong basis in the words of Rabbi Aḥai Gaon, *She'iltot* 28 and 129.

Again, the two previously discussed possibilities regarding the definition of *lashon hara* present themselves. The *Ḥafetz Ḥayim* seems to be reasoning from the perspective of character traits. The vice of gossip is a shared experience; the listener and the speaker play equal roles. That granted, if the prohibition of *kabbalat lashon hara* teaches that *lashon hara* must not be allowed to "succeed," responsibility calls for halting the process in its tracks. Thus, even on a mental level, the gossip must not be accepted at all.[31]

The second view interprets the prohibition as action focused, forbidding harmful speech. Thus, the responsibility not to receive *lashon hara* would translate into the listener ensuring that no damage ensue as a result of hearing the information.

An interesting hypothetical posited by the early-twentieth-century Polish authority, Rabbi Yeḥezkel Michaelson (1863–1942), may also be indicative of the above analysis.[32] What reaction would be required, he asks, of someone approached with an offer of gossip, when the prospective listener, unbeknown to the speaker, is actually the subject of the gossip? Rabbi Michaelson apparently assumes that the subject is too gentle to inform the speaker of this fact, and thus allots two options to the subject. One approach would be to treat the offer like any other invitation to *lashon hara*, and firmly decline to participate.

The other possibility would be to assume that the potential for harm in the case is limited, as the listener is also the subject. Thus, it might be advantageous to listen silently to the information, and thus acquire the heavenly praise the Talmud ascribes to those who "are insulted and do not insult in return, who hear their disgrace and do not respond" (Gittin 36b). The two possibilities are dependent on the above explanation: if *lashon hara* is primarily about character traits, it should be protested, even if it has no capacity to harm; while if it is about the infliction of damage, this case may constitute an exception.

Even if this second position on this matter, that receiving *lashon hara* is about action, rather than belief, is to be accepted – the concession

31. The two possibilities are applied to the definition of *kabbalat lashon hara* differently in *Emek HaLashon* 25.
32. *Responsa Tirosh VeYitzhar* 57.

to the reality of human limitations in this area may indeed be compelling – we can glean a few relevant lessons from the position of the *Ḥafetz Ḥayim.*

First, it should be pointed out that not believing the information is by no means the same thing as considering the speaker to be a liar. As we have seen, there are myriad reasons why even resolutely honest people say things that are false or at least inaccurate. Further, even if the facts are true, the main concern is that the subject not be disparaged in the eyes of the listener. Thus, the mission of the listener may not necessarily be to believe that the report is factually false, but to assume there is a broader context.[33] We can reconcile the two views about accepting *lashon hara* by invoking the formulation, "do not believe the information in a way that disparages the subject."[34]

Second, the distinction made between believing and acting upon for protection is worth considering and has broad implications. Intellectually, the distinction is hard to process, as once someone is suspected of an offense, there is a significant social stigma, and his reputation suffers.[35] Thus, it seems nearly impossible to factor in a risk posed by an individual without simultaneously tainting that individual.

The question, then, is whether the Torah is promoting, to the extent possible, a different mental attitude. This new attitude would put a premium on protection of the innocent, while acknowledging that this caution does not reflect upon the status of the individual under question (even though it may thereby deprive him of opportunities, which admittedly constitutes a loss). The fact that the human mind finds such a bifurcation challenging does not necessarily mean that it should not be an ideal.

The *Ḥafetz Ḥayim*'s formulation, based on the Talmud, of "taking into account without believing" is striking in its implications in two directions – not only in preserving the reputation of the subject, but also in its emphasis on the importance of protective measures. The initial impression it makes regards the former – it seems surprising that even

---

33. See *Ḥafetz Ḥayim, Laws of Lashon HaRa, klal* 6, in *Be'er Mayim Ḥayim* 1.
34. See *Kodesh Yisrael* 11.
35. See Yoma 19b.

when taking steps for protection, there continues to be a prohibition to "accept" the information. But its true innovation may be in the other direction. There are individuals who are known to be predatory, who have provided solid basis for their suspicion, and in that case, there is no prohibition to "accept" derogatory information about them. Thus, the statement here is an expansion of the protection mandate: even when an individual has not earned the condemnation of the community through evident, harmful behavior, if some credible risk still exists, it is necessary to account for that risk and to take steps to counter it.[36]

As noted, even such intermediate steps do have a negative impact on the subject, possibly resulting in a loss of a professional position or similar deprivation. Thus, this step is not taken frivolously; it is undertaken when there is significant basis for concern (in Hebrew, *raglayim ladavar*; translated both literally and colloquially, "the matter has legs"). Yet, it neither requires the subject to have been previously stigmatized with guilt, nor imposes that effect at the time of the speaker's statement.

To illustrate the point, imagine you are considering going into business with someone, and you subsequently learn that there is a one-third chance that the individual is a thief and a con man. You would

36. It is possible that there is a difference of opinion among the medieval authorities as to the threshold of risk necessary for this category. The Talmud, in this passage, tells the story of R. Tarfon, who declined to provide sanctuary to a group of accused murderers, citing the obligation to account for the possible truth of *lashon hara,* even if full acceptance is not warranted. The *Piskei HaRashbetz* (cited in *Shitot Kamai* to Nidda) quotes Rabbeinu Tam as emphasizing that he took this stance in order to protect himself from possible danger; however had there been no danger to himself, he would have protected them. Rashi, by contrast, implies that simply protecting them would have been wrong in and of itself, despite both the unsubstantiated nature of the allegations and the lack of danger to another party. Similarly, *Tosafot* (Nidda 61a, s.v. *atmirinkhu*) records the position of Rabbi Aḥai Gaon, also in apparent contrast with Rashi, that the license is so as to "not come to loss for himself or for others." See R. Aḥai Gaon's *She'iltot* 129, where he refers to "causing anguish." Examples of protective measures taken by major decisors of Jewish law in actual cases include the removal of a teacher of children suspected of dangerous behavior, even in the absence of actual testimony, sanctioned by Rabbi Yosef Shaul Nathanson, *Responsa Shoel UMeshiv* 1, 1:185; and the allowing of the relaying of negative information about a ritual slaughterer, with the knowledge that it would endanger his livelihood, by Rabbi Naphtali Tzvi Yehuda Berlin, the Netziv.

likely consider the risk too great, and would decline to take him as a partner. However, what if the question were posed as follows: Is it more likely that this man is or is not a thief? Statistically, the answer would be that there is a two-thirds likelihood that he is *not* a thief. Thus, we make one decision when seeking to best insulate ourselves and others from harm, and a different decision when evaluating the personal status of the individual in question.[37]

To reiterate, the thrust of this distinction then is not to diminish the steps taken toward protection, but to emphasize them, to extend them even when the subject's reputation has not reached the threshold of a clear and present danger. At that stage, we are encouraged, as difficult as it may be, to accommodate both protective measures and presumption of innocence simultaneously. When that guilt standard has been reached, and there is no longer a presumption of innocence, then protection becomes the singular priority.

Third, it is also valuable to consider the objection raised against the *Ḥafetz Ḥayim* that human beings are unable to control what they believe, and thus that cannot be the intent of the prohibition of "accepting" *lashon hara*. Upon reflection, there are several ways in which one plays an active role in processing information that is received. As the philosopher Ludwig Wittgenstein put it, "Knowledge is in the end based on acknowledgement."[38]

One such way is to arm oneself with the simple awareness that, as we have seen, even honest people can be wrong, for manifold reasons. Another way is to reach an internal decision on how much significance to give to the information. One commentator notes that the verb used in the verse prohibiting accepting *lashon hara* is "*tissa*," which also translates as "lift." Thus, the intent would be, do not "elevate" the report, do not give it more significance than it deserves.[39]

37. For further illustration, see *Big Data*, 162, where Viktor Mayer-Schönberger discusses the distinction that must be drawn between the information gleaned by data regarding a large population and the value therein, and the judgment of any single individual within that population, which is not decided by that data.
38. Ludwig Wittgenstein, *On Certainty* (New York: Harper, 1969), p. 378.
39. See Rabbi Avraham Ḥayim of Zlotov, *Oraḥ LeḤayim*, Exodus, p. 175.

Further, the listener has the ability to consider mitigating context. As has been noted, this ability is always present when one is confronted with criticism about oneself; there is always a justification or explanation as to why the criticism is unwarranted. Accordingly, one who truly loves his fellow "as himself" should be able to extend that attitude to others as well. This is not to say that such an attitude comes easily; much mental training is required to attain this perspective.[40]

In considering the mental processes involved in accepting information, it is illuminating to consider a study performed by Harvard psychologist Daniel Gilbert and his team. Their study indicates that the brain first automatically believes what it hears, and then has to perform an active process in order to "un-believe" it. They demonstrated that the sooner a distraction takes place after the information is transmitted, the greater is the likelihood that the listener will believe information he would otherwise (for good reason) discount, due to his inability to go through the "un-believing" process.[41] If this is true, it has implications in two directions: one, in the degree to which the mind is actively and passively involved in evaluating what to believe; and two, regarding the risks involved in even listening to information that may be slanderous, a topic to which we will now turn.

A PROHIBITION TO LISTEN?

As we have seen, opinions vary as to what constitutes "accepting" *lashon hara*; however, there seems to be agreement that it is more than simply hearing the information itself. Thus, we can ask: Is there anything wrong with listening to *lashon hara*, if one can prevent it from being "accepted."

On the one hand, it seems highly advisable to avoid listening, as there is a very short jump from listening to "accepting," whatever the definition of that term might be. One who chooses to listen is setting up quite a

---

40. See Rabbi Eliezer Piltz, in *BeYad HaLashon*, p. 299, and *Netiv Ḥayim* 6:1.
41. Daniel T. Gilbert, Daniel T. Romin, W. Tafarodi, and Patrick S. Malone, "You Can't Unbelieve Everything You Read," *Journal of Personality and Social Psychology* 65(2) (1993): 221–33, discussed in Kahneman, *Thinking Fast and Slow,* 81–82; and Kevin Dutton, *Split Second Persuasion: The Ancient Art and New Science of Changing Minds* (Boston: Houghton Mifflin Harcourt, 2011), p. 234. See also Tammet, *Embracing,* pp. 200–201.

difficult challenge.[42] This is particularly true considering what we have seen in terms of the power of cognitive biases to influence perception in ways that are hard to remedy, if we are even aware of the biases in the first place.

Indeed, the *Ḥafetz Ḥayim* assumes that there is a prohibition of listening, if not included in the biblical prohibition of accepting *lashon hara,* then at least as a ban enacted by the Rabbis to prevent the inadvertent violation of the Torah prohibition.[43] However, the *Ḥafetz Ḥayim* also believes that the biblical prohibition itself includes listening, a point he derives from the source verse, which bans the "bearing of a false/unnecessary report" (Ex. 23:1). As noted above, the Talmud associates another prohibition with this verse: a rabbinical court judge may not listen to one litigant outside the presence of the other. In that case, the prohibition must refer not only to "accepting," but even to just listening. Since both prohibitions are covered by the same words in the same verse, it would then follow that accepting *lashon hara* is also defined as including the simple act of listening.[44]

---

42. For an ethical discourse on the spiritual impact of even passive acts of listening, see Rabbi Natan Tzvi Finkel, *Koaḥ HaShmia, Or HaTzafun,* pp. 23–27.
43. The Talmud (Ketubot 5a) in interpreting Deut. 23:14 implies there is an obligation to cover one's ears to avoid hearing *lashon hara* (and other inappropriate material). See *Ḥiddushei Ḥatam Sofer* to Ketubot; Maharal, *Netivot Olam, Netiv HaTzniut,* ch. 2; Rabbi Yosef Engel, *Gilyonei HaShas,* Shabbat 108b; and Rabbi David Mandelbaum, *Pardes Yosef HaḤadash* to Deuteronomy. The *Ḥafetz Ḥayim, Laws of Lashon HaRa* 6, *Be'er Mayim Ḥayim* 2, understands this to reflect a rabbinic prohibition; see also Rabbi Yitzḥak Abuhav, *Menorat HaMaor, ner* 2, 53, and *Oraḥ Meisharim* 8:28. See also *Mishpetei HaShalom,* p. 221n27. The *Sefer Ḥaredim,* however, lists this under the heading of *Mitzvot Aseh Min HaTorah HaTluyot BeOzen* (3:3). See *Alei Be'er,* pp. 155–56.
44. *Ḥafetz Ḥayim, Laws of Lashon HaRa* 6:2. Interestingly, Rabbi Yisrael Moshe Fishelder, *Mivtzar Yisrael,* p. 275, interprets the verse to actively exclude a prohibition on listening; since the emphasis is on accepting a report that is *shav,* it may follow that one must first listen to ascertain that the report is indeed in that category, and then disregard the report if it is. By contrast, an opposite interpretation is suggested by Rabbi Zalman Sorotzkin in his *Oznayim LaTorah.* Commenting on the verse in Exodus, he notes that the word *shav* can mean falsehood, but in contrast to the word *sheker,* connotes a blatant, obvious falsity. Accordingly, the listener may feel that since he knows the statement is false, there is no danger in listening. This is the attitude the Torah is warning against: do not take in a slanderous report, even when you are aware of its falsity; the act of listening will encourage the speaker, and generate more conversation of a harmful nature.

As many note, and the *Ḥafetz Ḥayim* himself acknowledges, it is possible to question this derivation.[45] The verse might be interpreted in a general way as not allowing truth to be compromised as a recipient of information. For a judge, who has the responsibility to be completely neutral, mere ex parte listening would skew his perspective and might lead to a false verdict.[46] By contrast, a private citizen might not incur the same risks just by listening, and might only be barred from "accepting."[47]

Building on his premise, the *Ḥafetz Ḥayim* assumes a general prohibition, at least on some level, of listening to gossip and thus advises avoiding situations in which such conversation is likely to occur.[48] However, he also acknowledges that there are circumstances that cannot be predicted in advance. Further, once entrenched in such a context it may be very difficult for a listener to either influence the environment positively or to extricate himself from the

---

45. See *Mo'adim UZmanim* VII:204; *Ḥelkat Binyamin, Biurim* 7:6 and *Shevilei Ḥayim* there, and see also Rabbi Hillel Zaks, in the journal *Marpei Lashon* 1, pp. 9–11. See also the questions raised in *Netivot Ḥayim, netiv* 4, and *Shevilei Ḥayim,* 4 (*aleph*) and see *Zera Ḥayim* at length; see also the discussion of *Kodesh Yisrael* 10.
46. See also *Responsa Maharil* 195, for limitations on the prohibition regarding the judge, which affect the comparison; see *Shemirat HaPeh KeHilkhato,* p. 135–36.
47. It should be noted that Maimonides refers to a prohibition of listening in writing (*Laws of Personal Development* 7:6) regarding *baalei lashon hara* that "it is prohibited to live in their neighborhood, and all the more so to live among them and to listen to their words." See *Emek HaLashon* 47 who considers whether this is a specific prohibition regarding the *baal lashon hara,* or, alternatively, if it is a general prohibition, what reason is there to mention it specifically in the context of the *baal lashon hara.*
48. See *Ḥafetz Ḥayim, Laws of Lashon HaRa* 9:4, and see his footnote there regarding sitting in synagogue near those with a proclivity to gossip. See also *Birkat Yitzḥak,* p. 276. As to the possibility of an independent prohibition to live among gossipers, see *Alei Be'er,* p. 236 and *Shaarei Avraham,* pp. 334–39. Regarding continued employment at a workplace where *lashon hara* is rampant, see *Ḥafetz Ḥayim, Laws of Lashon HaRa* 1:6 and *Responsa LeḤafetz BaḤayim* III, 2.

    See the journal *Beit Aharon VeYisrael,* vol. 108, 18:3 (110), p. 163 (comments of Rabbi Ḥenoch Eizenberg) regarding the role of Aharon in the *lashon hara* spoken by Miriam.

situation.[49] Accordingly, he issues guidelines for those who might find themselves in such a context and consider it impractical to leave or to avoid the physical act of listening.[50]

First, these individuals should not say anything or make any gesture that indicates support or agreement with the negative information being spoken (in fact, the body language should indicate disapproval). Second, they should endeavor not to cross over into "acceptance." Third, in a condition perhaps closely connected to the second, they should mentally commit not to derive any enjoyment from that which is being said.[51]

---

49. To rebuke the speakers for engaging in *lashon hara,* while apparently indicated by the Torah's mandate to rebuke the wrongdoer (Lev. 19:17; see Shabbat 54b), is a risky endeavor, as the likelihood is great that the speakers will react by committing further to the gossip rather than refraining, and thus requires a careful analysis as to whether silence is preferable. (See Yevamot 65b, and *Ḥafetz Ḥayim, Laws of Lashon HaRa* 6:9 and 9:4, and *Responsa. LeḤafetz BaḤayim* 1, 40.)

    However, if objecting will not be effective but will also not exacerbate the problem, it still may be called for to do so as not to give the impression of acquiescence; see *Shevilei Ḥayim,* pp. 23–24 and *Alei Be'er,* pp. 164–67.

50. *Ḥafetz Ḥayim, Laws of Lashon HaRa* 6:5.

51. This last condition is based on a technical principle that exists in Jewish law, most often applied, but not exclusively so, to the laws of Shabbat. The rule is that while an individual is not necessarily held responsible for an action performed without intent (*davar she'eino mitkaven*), he is liable if the result was certain to occur (*pesik reishei*). However, this liability is only imposed when the result is desirable to the actor (*niḥa lei*); if it is undesirable, the exemption remains in place. Thus, the *Ḥafetz Ḥayim* states that one is not to be held accountable for conversation that he cannot help but overhear, but only as long as he does not "enjoy" what is being related. As noted above, this may actually be to some extent the definition of accepting *lashon hara,* thus making the second and third conditions closely related. See Rabbi Gedalya Finkel, *Imrei Gedalya,* Ketubot 6b (pp. 106–9), for an extensive analysis of whether the concepts of *pesik reishei* and *niḥa lei* apply to this case; he notes that *kabbalat lashon hara* is different from other Torah prohibitions, as it does not in any event involve an action, but is wholly defined by the acceptance; accordingly, without intent, the violation may not exist. See similarly *Netiv Ḥayim* 10. See also Rabbi Zevulun Shuv, *Shaarei Zevulun, Yoreh De'ah* 77; Rabbi Uriel Eisenthal, *Megillat Sefer,* Shabbat 88 and Rabbi Yeḥiel Rothstein, in the journal *Kovetz Shiurei Torah* v, pp. 158–65. See also the explanation of the *niḥa lei* principle as relates to *lashon hara* in *Responsa LeḤafetz BaḤayim* 1:4 (and see also sec. 1), who discusses overhearing conversation in a restroom.

WHEN LISTENING IS NECESSARY

However, even if we grant that there is a prohibition of listening to *lashon hara* and not just of actually accepting it, there are still important distinctions to be drawn between the two. Consequently, there may be circumstances in which, even if the negative information should not be accepted, it might still be permissible, and sometimes necessary, to listen to it. This is most important when there is a possibility of harm to the listener or to others, in which case the speech would correspond to the concept of necessary or purposeful information. As noted above, this factor may be relevant even in circumstances in which the information itself is not grounded enough to be uncritically accepted. Thus, we find that there are certainly contexts in which it is necessary to listen to what is being alleged, even if it is not currently justified to consider the information as true.

This might be all the more the case when considering certain realities of modern life. The author of a major commentary on the *Ḥafetz Ḥayim*, Rabbi Moshe Kaufman, asserts at length in his work that contemporary society involves an interdependence on others that makes it even more necessary to be aware of possible concerns regarding the character of one's associates. Thus, he advises emphasizing the purposeful element in such listening, rather than avoiding listening altogether (a position he acknowledges is somewhat at variance with that of the *Ḥafetz Ḥayim*).[52]

Further, those in leadership positions and with responsibility for the care of others bear an even greater obligation to be aware of the importance of purposeful listening. Rabbi Ḥayim Ozer Grodzinski (1863–1940), a towering Lithuanian rabbinic authority, asserts that anyone who is in a position of communal leadership, entrusted with the care of a community, school, or the like, is obligated to know and to listen to that being said which may affect those under his care. To refuse to do so out of concern for receiving *lashon hara,* he maintains, is a misguided abdication of responsibility.[53] Obtaining this awareness certainly does

52. *Netiv Ḥayim* 6:4, with *Zera Ḥayim*, p. 365.

53. The statements of Rabbi Grodzinski, and others like it, are cited by Rabbi Moshe Sternbuch, *Responsa Teshuvot VeHanhagot* V:398, who strongly emphasizes that message.

not constitute a transgression of *lashon hara,* since the need to protect students and other dependents is a clear priority. Similarly, the responsibility inherent in the position unequivocally establishes such awareness as "purposeful" and not gossip.

As the *Ḥafetz Ḥayim* himself notes, there are other times as well that it is appropriate to listen to *lashon hara* and *rekhilut.*[54] For example, if one is in a position to effectively defend the subject, or to make peace among quarreling parties, there may be a constructive role to play by partaking in such a conversation. If one can be successful in changing the direction of the talk, a case could be made that this is the preferable approach even if it would have been possible to stop the speech from happening in the first place. At times, it is counterproductive to engage the speaker, but it may still be beneficial to address the other listeners afterward.[55]

Accordingly, maintaining a balance between the prohibition of accepting *lashon hara* and carrying out one's responsibility towards others, may actually entail creating a greater mental space between the act of listening and the act of accepting, however the latter term is defined. Alternatively, if the information being related is unlikely to be of any consequence for the listener or for those to whom he could extend protection, and is seemingly of an inconsequential, salacious nature, then avoiding hearing it in the first place is likely the most appropriate policy.

CREDIBILITY FACTORS

An important topic to consider is whether there are factors or circumstances that make it more appropriate to accept negative information, independent of the concern of protection. Are there, for example, elements that make an item more credible, and therefore make it unreasonable not to accept it?

Some possible factors that could enhance credibility are nonetheless dismissed by authorities such as the *Ḥafetz Ḥayim.* For example, the fact that many people are present when the negative information is related does not render the statements more acceptable than they

54. *Ḥafetz Ḥayim, Laws of Lashon HaRa, klal* 6:4.

55. See *Netiv Ḥayim, Laws of Lashon HaRa, klal* 6:4, 7.

would be were the audience small in number.[56] Even if the subject himself were present in the large crowd,[57] the *Ḥafetz Ḥayim* maintains that we should not assume that if the statements made were false, the subject would have protested; either he might have been intimidated or he might be an individual who feels that he does not need to respond to insults (a quality that the Talmud [Yoma 23b; Gittin 36b] considers extremely praiseworthy).

The Talmud (Pesaḥim 113b) does acknowledge the possible existence of an unusually trustworthy individual, who is believed as if he were two witnesses. However, the *Ḥafetz Ḥayim*[58] asserts that this category is no longer practically applicable.[59] In explaining his position, he notes that there is empirically no indication that there is anyone who can relay a story with precise accuracy, without adding or subtracting details of significance.[60] This assessment is in line with what we have seen; even the most honest among us are not immune from conveying falsehood, despite the best of intentions.

In certain circumstances, Jewish law grants credibility to one who is discussing a matter in which the truth will ultimately be known one way or another (Rosh HaShana 22b; Bekhorot 36a); in such a case, it is assumed that the speaker would not lie, for his fault soon would eventually be discovered. However, transferring such an approach to the laws of *lashon hara* is a delicate process. As we have discussed, we are concerned not only that the speaker might be lying, but that for many other reasons he might be saying something that is wholly or partially false. In such a case, he would not be deterred by the fear of exposure, as he himself does not fully appreciate the inaccuracy of

56. *Ḥafetz Ḥayim, Laws of Lashon HaRa* 7:1.

57. Ibid. 7:2.

58. *Ḥafetz Ḥayim, Laws of Rekhilut* 6:7. See also Rabbi Meir Menaḥem Maggid in the journal *Kol Torah* LV, pp. 66–68.

59. See however *Shevilei Ḥayim, klal* 7 and elsewhere, who argues that there is limited applicability to the concept. See also Rabbi Moshe Feinstein, *Responsa Iggerot Moshe, Oraḥ Ḥayim* 1:53, regarding a student who relies completely on the teachings of his *rebbe.* Inversely, Rabbi Feinstein discusses a *rebbe* relying on reports of a trusted student in *Yoreh De'ah* II, 103.

60. *Ḥafetz Ḥayim, Laws of Rekhilut* 6:7, *Be'er Mayim Ḥayim* 16.

his remarks.[61] This would apply even when one is quoting a source such as a newspaper, which could easily be checked. It is not at all uncommon for a reader, especially a casual reader of headlines who may or may not skim the story itself, to come away with a lack of appreciation for the details of the story or even its main points.[62]

Similarly, sometimes we consider the casual mention of a matter – made in the course of talking about other things (*mesiaḥ lefi tumo*) – more credible than actual testimony in court. The assumption is that one would not lie if he is unaware that what he is saying is even significant to begin with. However, once again it would seem that this is not a safeguard against simple error or inaccuracy, and the *Ḥafetz Ḥayim* is disinclined to make an exception for this circumstance.[63]

However, the considerations may be different if the matter itself has inherent credibility. The Talmud (Shabbat 56a) discusses a standard of believability referred to in Hebrew as *devarim hanikarim*, which may be understood as supporting evidence. In the reading of one medieval authority, this standard refers to the factors and elements that make it seem that the story is true. Apparently, the reference is to supporting

---

61. This concern is implied, in slightly different form, by the *Ḥafetz Ḥayim* in *Laws of Rekhilut, klal* 9, *Be'er Mayim Ḥayim* 36. In *Laws of Lashon HaRa, klal* 7, *Be'er Mayim Ḥayim* 8, he does acknowledge this factor as a basis for belief (when purposeful); see *Ḥelkat Binyamin, Laws of Lashon HaRa, klal* 7, *Be'er Mayim Ḥayim* 8, for an analysis of the parameters.
62. Compare however, the opposite ruling in *Ḥelkat Binyamin, Laws of Lashon HaRa, klal* 7, *Be'er Mayim Ḥayim* 8, and in *LeRe'akha Kamokha*, p. 207. See also the discussion in *Responsa LeḤafetz BaḤayim* IV:17 for further analysis regarding the relevance of the principle that one is not suspected of lying regarding a matter in which the truth will ultimately emerge. *Shemirat HaPeh KeHilkhato*, p. 168, quotes Rabbi Yosef Shalom Elyashiv as maintaining that this principle is no longer applicable, as people in the modern era are more arrogant and brazen and would lie even if they know they will ultimately be exposed.
63. *Ḥafetz Ḥayim* 7, *Be'er Mayim Ḥayim* 14; see also Rashi to Moed Katan 16a, s.v *amar lei* and *Sedeh Tzofim* to Moed Katan 16a, and *Responsa LeḤafetz BaḤayim* I:3. Note, however, *Kodesh Yisrael* 13, who distinguishes between one who does not intend to testify and one who does but does not realize the negative implications of what he is saying. For parameters of this concept in practice see *Shemirat HaPeh KeHilkhato*, pp. 178–81.

indications that constitute more than an unsubstantiated rumor,[64] but are not conclusive and absolute proof.[65]

The Second Book of Samuel (chs. 9, 16, and 19) relates that King David received a negative report about Mephiboshet, the son of Saul, and his plans to rebel against him.[66] The Talmud records a debate as to whether David sinned in accepting the report, and violated thereby the prohibition of *kabbalat lashon hara*.[67] According to one opinion, King David did not commit any sin in this episode, because there were supporting indications that the report was true.

Based on this discussion, the literature addresses the question of whether or not supporting evidence justifies acceptance of a derogatory report. The *Ḥafetz Ḥayim* allows acceptance,[68] but only with several conditions in place.[69] He and other major commentators emphasize that the listener must have seen the evidence himself, and not merely have heard from others of its existence.[70] The *Ḥafetz Ḥayim* further stresses that the supporting evidence must be directly relevant to the alleged action, that the listener must be careful and unbiased in assessing its validity, and that the listener is still not exempt from his obligation to judge favorably when possible and reasonable. Ultimately, the *Ḥafetz Ḥayim* understands that this category is only applicable when the supporting evidence is such that it does not allow for any alternative explanation.[71] Further, this does not constitute a license for the listener to spread the information to others.

---

64. *Sefer Mitzvot Gadol*, negative commandment 10: "*tzedadim ve'inyanim shenira hadavar emet*."
65. See *Responsa LeḤafetz BaḤayim* 111:13.
66. Concerning this story, see Rabbi Menaḥem HaKohen Rizkov, *Torat HaKohanim VeAvodat HaBeit HaMikdash VeHaKarbanot* 90:2.
67. Shabbat 56a–b. See the analysis of this debate in *Kodesh Yisrael* 12.
68. *Ḥafetz Ḥayim, Laws of Lashon HaRa, klal* 7:10–11.
69. See also *Shulḥan Arukh HaRav, Oraḥ Ḥayim* 156:10, who allows acceptance when such indications are present; however, his brother, in *Responsa She'erit Yehuda, hosafot* 19, cites him as ruling in his *Responsa* (no. 17) that only a king such as David is permitted (as per the talmudic discussion) as a function of his broad judicial authority.
70. See Maharsha and Maharshal to Shabbat, and *Ḥafetz Ḥayim* in *Be'er Mayim Ḥayim* 7:26.
71. *Ḥafetz Ḥayim, Laws of Rekhilut* 6:9 and *Be'er Mayim Ḥayim* 20.

The *Ḥafetz Ḥayim* also notes that additional care must be taken in assessing this supporting evidence, because of the human tendency to be influenced by internal bias and the misinterpretation that can result.[72] Rabbi Moshe Kaufman, in his commentary to the *Ḥafetz Ḥayim*,[73] expands on this point, asserting that we no longer possess the soundness of judgment to reliably assess such evidence, noting that Maimonides[74] and the *Shulḥan Arukh*[75] have already ruled that evidence of this type is insufficient for use in a rabbinic court for the purposes of compelling payment.

Some later authorities explain this license as somewhat of an excuse: since the listener is influenced by the supporting evidence, it is too difficult for him to disbelieve the report, and thus he cannot be blamed for doing so.[76] The implication is that even if it is permitted to accept such information as true, doing so may still not be in the interest of fairness or social harmony. Indeed, it is instructive that the talmudic discussion concludes by noting that King David's acceptance of the report, justified or not, led to the ultimate division of his kingdom.

The halakha recognizes that the persistence of a rumor has the potential to boost the perceived credibility of the negative statement.[77] Indeed, Jewish law characterizes a widely known and disseminated report as equivalent to the testimony of witnesses.[78] It is important to acknowledge, however, that there are significant limitations to this concept. The *Ḥafetz Ḥayim* notes the possibility that one person alone can spread

72. *Laws of Rekhilut* 6:9, in footnote.
73. *Netiv Ḥayim, Laws of Rekhilut* 6:9,15.
74. *Mishneh Torah, Laws of the Sanhedrin* 24:2.
75. *Ḥoshen Mishpat* 15.
76. *Responsa Pe'at Sadekha* 1:29. See also *Responsa Mahari Beruna* 38, who rules that one is not obligated to extend favorable judgment in circumstances of *devarim hanikarim*. The *Arukh HaShulḥan, Oraḥ Ḥayim* 156:14, writes that if there are *devarim hanikarim*, it is appropriate to be concerned the item might be true (*ra'ui laḥush*), essentially equating the matter to the Talmud's recommendation when the information may be necessary for protection. The reference there identifies the *Hagahot Maimoniyot* as the source; however, the language there (*Laws of Personal Development* 7:4) is actually *ra'ui lehaamin ulkabel*, "it is appropriate to believe and accept."
77. See Megilla 25b and Rashi, s.v. *desani shomanei* and Kiddushin 81a.
78. See Rema, *Ḥoshen Mishpat* 79:9.

a rumor far and wide, which enjoins us to carefully ascertain that the prevalence of such a rumor is not due to the efforts of one malevolent individual,[79] and that the reiterated and persistent statements are genuine.[80] Accordingly, if the source is one who bears an antipathy toward the subject, the rumor is likely attributable to a slanderous campaign. Furthermore, the *Ḥafetz Ḥayim* asserts that in such an instance, the item is not to be accepted as definitely true, but rather as a concern to be taken into account.[81]

It is noteworthy that despite the detailed treatment of the laws of *lashon hara* in his *Mishneh Torah*, Maimonides does not mention any limitations on the prohibition of receiving *lashon hara*. He also does not explicitly state that prohibition in the first place (in this section; he does record it elsewhere), in fact only mentioning it almost incidentally in the context of noting that the recipient is one of those "killed" by *lashon hara*, and then asserting, as mentioned above, that the recipient is worse (literally, "more") than the speaker.

In addressing this lacuna, one may take one of two opposite approaches. Perhaps Maimonides understands the mindset, the unjustified disdain of others, of *lashon hara* as the actual offense, and speaking as merely the vehicle for conveying that sinful attitude to others.[82] If so, we would understand that receiving *lashon hara* does not merit a specific

---

79. See *Responsa Maharik* 188, and *Be'er Mayim Ḥayim* 7:10 in footnote.

80. *Ḥafetz Ḥayim, Laws of Lashon HaRa, Be'er Mayim Ḥayim* 7:8.

81. Ibid. 6:25, from Ketubot 36b. There are two situations in which the *Ḥafetz Ḥayim* allows action to be taken based on a *kol* (persistent rumor). One is when the subject is a communal prayer leader suspected persistently of serious sin; he may be removed from his position, apparently because the nature of the position includes a unique burden on the bearer to remain free of all suspicion (*Mishna Berura* 53:15, and *Biur Halakha* 25, s.v. *im.*). The second situation is when the subject has already been confirmed as a sinful individual; in that case he lacks a *ḥezkat kashrut* (presumption of righteousness) and the *kol* is sufficient to assume continued guilt (*Be'er Mayim Ḥayim* 7:10). See *Shaarei Avraham*, pp. 415–17. For further parameters of acting based on a *kol*, see *Shemirat HaPeh KeHilkhato*, p. 172.

82. This explanation would not address what Maimonides discusses in the following paragraph, the disclosure of harmful information, independent of intent to disparage. It is possible that Maimonides discusses here two different forms or aspects of *lashon hara*. On *lashon hara* as primarily a corruption of perspective on the part of the speaker, see Rabbi Avigdor Nebenzahl, in *BeYad HaLashon*, pp. 296–97.

direct mention, as it is the context for the entire prohibition, including the speaking. Further, there would be no need to mention any exceptions or justifications, as those would simply be excluded from the mindset of unjustified condemnation that typifies *lashon hara.*[83]

Alternatively, we might suggest that Maimonides recognizes only speaking as a prohibition, and does not see receiving in and of itself as a prohibition. This would not be due to a lack of concern for the damage inflicted through receiving; quite the contrary, he acknowledges the talmudic condemnation of this, and makes reference to it in this statement in *Mishneh Torah*. Rather, this may reflect a general approach in his legal code to focus legislation on actions only, and not on emotions or mindsets. This would emanate from a premise that only actions can be dictated, but attitudes, as important as they are, cannot be directly commanded, but only indirectly influenced through the mandated actions or prohibitions. If so, it could be understood why Maimonides neither addresses receiving as a prohibited action, nor discusses exceptions or justifications. He instead notes the tremendous harm that results when *lashon hara* is accepted internally, and allows that to serve as a cautionary message to encourage us to do whatever is indeed possible to prevent either the spread or the acceptance of *lashon hara.*[84]

---

83. A similar but significantly different approach can be found in *Emek HaLashon* 25–26. For a wholly different approach, see Rabbi Hillel Zaks, in *BeYad HaLashon,* pp. 329–32.

84. It is also noteworthy that Maimonides's language that describes greater severity to the recipient than to the speaker may not necessarily be meant to be translated as "he is committing a greater sin" (although note the language of *Sefer Mitzvot Gadol,* prohibition 9, and *Magen Avraham, Oraḥ Ḥayim* 156 where that connotation is found more clearly). Following the statement of the damage that *lashon hara* inflicts, Maimonides writes *vehamekablo yoter min haomro,* which may equally be translated as "the recipient is damaged by the transgression even more than the speaker" (The language of the *Sefer HaḤinnukh* 236 is more compatible with this interpretation). See also *Shemuot Ḥayim,* Arakhin, ch. 3, no. 18.

The fact that Maimonides does record the prohibition elsewhere (*Mishneh Torah, Laws of the Sanhedrin* 21:7) may actually support this theory. In that context, he records the related prohibition of a judge listening to one side of a dispute not in the presence of the other. In that circumstance, there is an overt and identifiable act that is taking place, and accordingly that is a context in which acceptance can more readily be legislated as a prohibition.

The complex issue of "accepting" *lashon hara* is representative of the broad themes of the general concept of *lashon hara*. It demands a careful balance of sensitivity, generosity of judgment, discretion, awareness of risk, readiness to take protective action when necessary, healthy skepticism, and appreciation for the strengths and weaknesses of human cognition and expression. To successfully incorporate all of these elements into a unified approach toward interpersonal interactions is challenging to say the least; nonetheless, it might simply be what fair, compassionate, and responsible coexistence requires.

Lashon HaRa that Is Public Knowledge, in the Subject's Presence, and Indirect

"IN THE PRESENCE OF THREE" (*APEI TELATA*)

Introducing the factor of publicity into the discussion of *lashon hara* has a multidirectional effect. From the perspective of the speaker, it seems undeniable that the greater the number of listeners, the greater the offense: if it is bad to speak gossip or slander to one person, it is far worse to do so to many people. However, when considering the "item," publicity has an opposite effect: the more well-known the information, the less harm involved in repeating it. Taken together, these two factors create somewhat of a paradox. The larger the audience of listeners, the greater the transgression; but as the news spreads, further offenses seem to lose their sting.

As a question of Jewish law, both directions must be considered: what effect is there on the transgression of *lashon hara* when it takes place in front of a larger audience? And, conversely, what mitigation, if any, comes from the fact that the news is far from a secret?

Both or either of these questions are addressed by a single enigmatic statement that appears twice in the Talmud (Bava Batra 39a–b; Arakhin 16a). Brief in its formulation, it has inspired much analysis and debate as to its interpretation and its impact. The commentaries of the medieval era take radically different stances in its translation, and thus provoke somewhat of a question as to what legal conclusions can be drawn.

Some sages, such as the *Ḥafetz Ḥayim*, maintain that the range of interpretations itself guides the legal conclusion, forcing a broad one that can accommodate all the interpretations.[1] This is not a simple stringent approach, "hedging" by taking into account all possible options; rather, the multifaceted approach stems from the recognition that all the interpretations reflect realities of human nature, whether or not they are the basis for the relevant principle of Jewish law. As such, they present genuine concerns in this realm that are best acknowledged in practice, and the *Ḥafetz Ḥayim* asserts that the license is almost inapplicable in a practical sense.

The enigmatic statement of the Talmud asserts that "anything that is said in the presence of three (*apei telata*) people [or more], there is no [prohibition of] lashon hara involved." "In the presence of three" is an indication that the item is either publicly known or soon to be publicly known. Since "your friend has a friend, and the friend's friend has a friend," we can assume that that which is known to three people will inevitably become public knowledge. Somehow, this fact mitigates or eliminates the prohibition; the question, however, is how. Intuitively, one would have thought the polar opposite: if it is an offense to speak *lashon hara* to one person, that offense would be magnified exponentially with an increase in the number of listeners. This is explicitly stated by the *Ḥafetz Ḥayim.*[2]

There are essentially four different positions among the classical authorities as to how to understand the talmudic statement and the accompanying concept in and of itself, and the circumstances in which it applies.[3]

---

1. *Ḥafetz Ḥayim, Laws of Lashon HaRa* 2:10.
2. Ibid., 2:1. Concerning the technical question of whether additional listeners constitute additional prohibitions for the speaker, see also the observation of Rabbi Yitzḥak Yosef Zilberberg, in the journal *Kovetz Torani Merkazi* (Gur) IV (Adar 5745), pp. 193–94.
3. For further analysis of these positions see Rabbi Binyamin Friedman, in the journal *Beit Aharon VeYisrael* XIV, 3 (81) pp. 49–51; Rabbi Avraham Ḥaputa, *Reshit Hashlama* to Bava Batra, pp. 55–57; Rabbi Avraham Toledanu, *Zaharei Shmuel,* Bava Batra 38; Rabbi Yinon Shmueli, *Orḥot Yom Tov,* pp. 97–100; *Kodesh Yisrael* 6. A particularly extensive and thorough analysis can be found in *Mishnat Yisrael* 7.

The first two positions both assume that *apei telata* applies to the listeners of the information, while the latter two assume that it applies to the speaker.

The first position, advanced by Maimonides[4] and Rabbi Shmuel ben Meir (ca. 1085–1158), known as Rashbam, holds that the meaning of the talmudic passage is that the members of the public, the "three" who stand in for the general population, are permitted to repeat what they have heard.[5] This poses a fundamental problem, presenting the question of how the information was conveyed in the first place; further, it creates the unusual and surprising conclusion that the commission of a transgression, once it has happened, allows the damage to continue.

Moreover, this appears to be a license to spread negative information simply because it will eventually be spread anyway. Is that not comparable to allowing one to steal property that is left unguarded, since it will eventually be stolen? How does the fact that an offense will eventually be committed make it permissible?

Further, as we have seen, *lashon hara* involves a negativity of character in addition to the damage it inflicts on the subject. Even if it could be accepted that relating this information would not increase the damage, wouldn't the additional speaker still be indulging an unsavory character trait? How is that element mitigated by the inevitable spread of the information? (In addition, the people who heard the item might be observant of the *lashon hara* prohibition, in which case the information might not spread;[6] in fact, the *Ḥafetz Ḥayim* rules that this license is not operative when the listeners are "God-fearing," or are otherwise unlikely to spread the information, for example, if they are

4. *Mishneh Torah, Laws of Personal Development* 7:7.

5. There is a difference between the formulations of Maimonides and the Rashbam: according to Maimonides, the subject is *lashon hara*; while according to the Rashbam, the subject is *rekhilut*. This difference is significant in that *rekhilut* is only meaningful in its revelation, and thus it is more understandable that independent publicity negates its damage. In the case of *lashon hara*, where the speech itself is corrupting and harmful, this point is less obvious, and thus Maimonides's version of this position is more innovative. See also *Kodesh Yisrael* 6.

6. See Rashash to Arakhin 16a.

close relatives.[7]) Another objection could be raised from the rule against "accepting" *lashon hara*: Would not spreading the information be a form of acceptance, and worse?[8]

To some extent, these questions are addressed by Maimonides's formulation. When he codifies this principle, he adds a clause not found in the Talmud: "as long as he does not intend to spread the matter further."[9] Maimonides apparently assumes that this permission is only for an incidental reference in the context of a general discussion, that is not specifically geared toward the item of the *lashon hara*. With this brief addition, Maimonides makes several points. One is that he does not allow committing an offense that has not yet taken place; he only allows discussing the matter when it comes up, without intentional dissemination, thus presumably not adding at all to the degree to which it is spread.[10] This might also lead to the conclusion that if public discussion of the matter has subsided, any permission to revive the topic also must cease.[11]

Further, his condition also addresses the character issue. By allowing only incidental discussion and prohibiting intentional dissemination, Maimonides is ensuring, in effect, that no malicious motivation will be present. It is possible that his premise is, as discussed earlier, that

---

7. *Ḥafetz Ḥayim, Laws of Lashon HaRa* 2:5, based on Sanhedrin 29a. See Rabbi Shemaryahu Yosef Berman, *Birkat Shai* to Sanhedrin, who asks a number of questions on the *Ḥafetz Ḥayim*'s proofs, as does *Birkhat Yitzḥak*, pp. 115–19, who concludes against his position.

   Such distinctions prompt further questions, such as whether the assumption of publicity accompanying three people is that all three are liable to disclose, or that when three are in involved, at least one is liable to disclose; see *Ḥafetz Ḥayim* in *Be'er Mayim Ḥayim* 15, and *Birkat Shalom* to Bava Batra 83, at length, and see also the journal *Ḥokhma VeDaat* to Bava Batra, pp. 217–18, no. 18.
8. This objection is raised by the *Avodat Melekh*, who does not resolve it.
9. The *Ḥafetz Ḥayim, Laws of Lashon HaRa, klal* 2, *Be'er Mayim Ḥayim* 3 suggests a source for this clause in a different talmudic passage, Sanhedrin 31a. However, note *Hagahot Maimoniyot* to *Laws of Personal Development*, ch. 7 no. 7, and see Rabbi Ḥayim Dov Altusky, in the journal *Marpei Lashon* 1, pp. 12–14. See also Rabbi Yaakov Rosenthal, *Mishnat Yaakov* to *Laws of Personal Development*.
10. See *Kesef Mishneh, Laws of Personal Development* 7:7, and see also Rabbi Yitzḥak Berakha, *Birkat Yitzḥak* to *Ḥafetz Ḥayim*, p. 113 and *Beit Leḥem Yehuda* to *Bava Batra*.
11. See *Ḥelkat Binyamin, biurim* 17.

there are two distinct elements inherent in the prohibition of *lashon hara.* One is the character trait, and it is that to which he refers in his opening comments in the laws of *lashon hara.* When malice is present, no amount of preexisting publicity will mitigate the transgression. However, he adds a second element to the prohibition, the exposure of material that could be harmful or aggravating to the subject. This act might be done without malice aforethought, yet might be harmful nonetheless, and is thus prohibited. However, if the information is already public or will inevitably become public, it is possible that neither harm nor negative character traits are being indulged, and it is only in that circumstance that Maimonides would permit speaking "in the presence of three."[12]

The *Ḥafetz Ḥayim* suggests that Maimonides might be basing his position on scriptural interpretation.[13] When the Torah uses the imagery of a peddler (*rokhel*) to present the speaker of *lashon hara,* the connotation is one who brings items from one place to another, a metaphor for revelation – making something present in a context where it was not previously. Perhaps this imagery is invoked, says the *Ḥaftez Ḥayim,* to

12. This does not appear to be the understanding of the *Ḥafetz Ḥayim,* (although he does make the distinction elsewhere, and see also *Mishnat Yisrael* 7:21) but is suggested by many others; see, for example, *Birkat Shalom* to Bava Batra, 83; *Responsa Az Nidberu* II:74 (note the exchange between the questioner and responder); Rabbi Yitzchak Hutner, *Sefer Zikaron LeMaran Baal HaPaḥad Yitzḥak,* p. 331–33; Rabbi Zevulun Shuv, *Shaarei Zevulun, Yoreh De'ah* 78:3; Rabbi Shmuel Greineman, *Zekher Shmuel,* Shabbat 31:2; Rabbi Shlomo Rozner, *Alei Be'er,* pp. 97–98; Rabbi Avraham Shmuel Papenheim, *Pinat Yakrat,* Bava Batra 133; (see also *Ḥelkat Binyamin* 3; *Avodat Melekh* to *Laws of Personal Development; Zera Ḥayim* pp. 310–11; Rabbi Shlomo Goldstein, in the journal *Marpei Lashon* VII, pp. 9–11; and *Ḥut Shani* 1:6, based on Shabbat 33b). Compare also Rabbi Moshe Schapiro, in *BeYad HaLashon,* pp. 378–79, and *Emek HaLashon* 42, 43. The *Ḥafetz Ḥayim, Laws of Lashon HaRa, Be'er Mayim Ḥayim* 2:3 assumes that Maimonides is terming only subsequent revelations as not constituting *lashon hara* after the fact, but not as actually permitted; however, Rabbi Ovadia Yosef, *Yalkut Yosef, Kibbud Av VeEim,* p. 535, is inclined to disagree. See also Rabbi Yitzḥak Meir Patziner, *Parashat HaMelekh* III, to *Laws of Personal Development* and Rabbi Yeshayahu Pineḥas Rottenberg, *Responsa Minḥat Peri* IV:65.
13. *Ḥafetz Ḥayim. Laws of Lashon HaRa, Be'er Mayim Ḥayim* 2:4. Concerning Maimonides's source here in general, see *Sedei Ḥemed, Maarekhet HaLamed* 63. For more regarding Maimonides's position, see also Shmuel K. Mirsky, ed., commentary of Rabbi Yitzḥak Eizik Stein to *Semag,* in the journal *Talpiyot* VII, 1, pp. 53–54.

teach that *lashon hara* is primarily an act of exposure. When the item is already public, the relevance of *lashon hara* recedes.

Within this view of Maimonides, the situation is one in which the content of the speech is actual *lashon hara,* and permitted only because it does not increase the damage anyway being inflicted on the victim. If that is the case, it is understandable that there would be certain limitations on the license, as the *Ḥafetz Ḥayim* indeed assumes. For example, there would continue to be a prohibition of "accepting" the report, with all the accompanying restrictions;[14] and the license would apply only in the area in which the information is likely to spread, and not beyond.[15]

One of the issues raised in application of the *apei telata* principle is the question of whether it applies to a gathering such as a teachers' meeting. Presumably, more than three individuals would be present at such gatherings, where sensitive conversation regarding confidential matters often takes place. In analyzing this issue, Rabbi Shlomo Rozner notes at least three relevant considerations:[16] (a) a talmudic passage (Sanhedrin 29a) prohibiting a rabbinical court judge from revealing which judges voted for which litigant, presumably because of the harmful effects of such disclosure; (b) the understanding of that passage of the *Ḥafetz Ḥayim,* that the rule of *apei telata* would not apply in a setting in which the participants are God-fearing individuals who would not be expected to disseminate the information; and (c) the general prohibition

14. *Ḥafetz Ḥayim, Laws of Lashon HaRa* 2:10.

15. Ibid., 2:6. It is noteworthy that this last point, that disclosure within a specific circle may not equal disclosure to the wider population, is currently being addressed in the sphere of secular civil law. University of Chicago Prof. Lior Strahilowitz has written extensively about "social network theory," which analyzes, among other things, the flow of information from one circle to another, and the resulting implications for assessing when private information has genuinely become public (Lior Jacob Strahilevitz, "A Social Network Theory of Privacy," 72 *University of Chicago Law Review* 919 [2005]). The argument has been made by him and others (for example, Saul Levmore and Martha C. Nussbaum in *Offensive Internet,* p. 28, and n. 26, and Daniel J. Solove in *Future of Reputation,* pp. 178–81) that such analysis must be factored in for purposes of civil tort legislation and related issues.

16. *Responsa LeḤafetz BaḤayim* 1:20.

of "revealing secrets," which would bind participants to honor the confidentiality of a closed meeting.[17]

The second position regarding *apei telata,* put forth by Rashi in his talmudic commentary, also applies the statement to the listeners, but with a different focus.[18] Rashi holds that since the speaker revealed the information in front of three or more listeners, an act that guarantees publicity, it can be safely assumed that the speaker approves of the information being spread.[19]

If this is the basis for permission, it is clearly a very narrow license. The approval of the speaker does not help for conventional *lashon hara;* the speaker is in the wrong for saying it in the first place, and his agreement that it may be spread further is useless in mitigating the violation. Quite the contrary: the illicit gossip is usually interested in having his reports spread, which certainly does not justify listening by those present. The only possible understanding of Rashi's interpretation is that the reference is extremely limited, involving one of the few situations in which the speaker's acquiescence would make a difference. For example, the information might be a personal revelation by the speaker, which would normally demand confidentiality on the part of the listeners; however, if the revelation took place in public, it can be assumed that the speaker does not object to its exposure.[20] Alternatively, the statement might be a type of *rekhilut,* with the speaker commenting about a third party; the concern would be that transmitting the information to that third party would provoke a conflict. However, that it was said in public indicates that it is expected that the subject will hear about it, and it is not inflammatory in nature.[21]

---

17. For further regarding Maimonides' position, see *Netivot Ḥayim,* pp. 309–14 and *Alei Be'er,* pp. 53–54.
18. Arakhin, 16a.
19. This is also the implication of *She'iltot DeRav Aḥai Gaon* 28.
20. See also *Sefer HaHashlama* and Ritva to Bava Batra, and *Beit Leḥem Yehuda.*
21. The *Ḥafetz Ḥayim, Laws of Lashon HaRa, Be'er Mayim Ḥayim* 3, asserts that Rashi is not referring to *rekhilut;* see, however, *Zera Ḥayim,* citing the *She'iltot.* See also *Ḥelkat Binyamin, biurim* 21, and also 22, where he raises the objection that the additional prohibition of contentious behavior, which is a result of *rekhilut,* should not be subject to the consent of the parties.

This narrower context provokes a further question as to the mechanics of the license: is it permissible because the speaker approves of its dissemination,[22] or because, following Maimonides's interpretation, the information will inevitably emerge?[23] That question could affect other questions, such as the rule in a situation where the speaker does not desire that the information spread, but it becomes public without his knowledge,[24] or without his full consent (such as when compelled to speak in court[25]).

The third position regarding *apei telata* is most surprising: there are views among the early authorities that the license of "in the presence of three" is applicable not to the listeners, but actually to the speaker, justifying his speech when a larger audience is present. One authority to maintain an interpretation in this vein was Rabbeinu Yonah of Gerona.[26] He asserts that the context is one who is speaking negatively about another for a necessary purpose. Even if that motivation is present, the speaker is still required to ensure that his words are actually justified, and do not constitute unproductive *lashon hara*. Accordingly, if the premise is that the negative speech is necessary to accomplish some purpose, then it must be stated in a way that the public, possibly including the subject, will hear what is being said. If the comments would be whispered to one or two individuals, without likelihood of wider dissemination, it would probably indicate that the speech is mere gossip and not focused on actual improvement of society or an individual.

There is a fourth understanding of the concept of "in the presence of three," one that also maintains that the license for the rule is

---

22. See *Yad HaKettana, Laws of Personal Development* 9:2 and *Avodat Melekh, Laws of Personal Development* 7:5, citing Rabbeinu Gershom.

23. See *Ḥafetz Ḥayim, Laws of Lashon HaRa* 2:8.

24. See Rabbi Yom Tov ben Moshe Tzahalon, *Responsa Maharitatz* 132; and *Mishnat Yisrael* 7:15.

25. This point was a debate between the *Yad HaKettana* (*Laws of Personal Development*, ch. 9, nos. 19–21), who felt this license only applied when the speaker was divulging openly of his own free will, and the *Ḥafetz Ḥayim*. See the extensive discussion in *Birkat Yitzḥak*, p. 123.

26. *Aliyot* to Bava Batra; see also *Shaarei Teshuva* 3:228, where it is expressed somewhat differently. For an additional perspective on the various views, see Rabbi Yisrael Yaakov Fisher, *Responsa Even Yisrael* VI, *Ḥiddushim* to Bava Batra 39b.

applicable to the speaker.[27] However, in order to fully understand this concept, we must consider another related comment also found the Talmud, one perhaps even more surprising than *apei telata.*

IN THE PRESENCE OF THE SUBJECT

There is another enigmatic statement in the Talmud that closely parallels the statement highlighted in the previous section. One would think that while it is prohibited to speak badly of another who is not present – to speak "behind his back" – to do so in his presence would compound the offense. Not only is the subject being disparaged, but he is being humiliated as well, which itself is an egregious transgression, subject to severe condemnation in the Talmud (Bava Metzia 58b).

Accordingly, the *Ḥafetz Ḥayim* rules that while speaking *lashon hara* about another is a transgression, doing so in the presence of the subject is a significantly worse transgression.[28]

As such, it is a surprise to find a statement in the Talmud (Arakhin 15b) that asserts that "anything that is said in the presence of the subject involves no [prohibition] on account of *lashon hara.*" As this appears to contradict the above assumptions, the statement is the topic of considerable analysis. In fact, there are some authorities, including apparently Maimonides, who assume that this is merely a minority view and is not the accepted legal conclusion.[29]

27. Focusing the license on the speaker then presents an additional question. Does the permission granted to the speaker extend to permitting the listeners to "accept" the information"? See *Responsa LeḤafetz BaḤayim* 1:18 who assumes that there must be a parallel license; and see *Birkat Yitzḥak*, pp. 120–21, who inclines in an opposite direction. See also *Kodesh Yisrael* 7:5.

28. *Ḥafetz Ḥayim, Laws of Lashon HaRa* 3:1.

29. *Mishneh Torah, Laws of Personal Development* 7:5; see *Kesef Mishneh,* and see also the analysis of *Emek HaLashon* 40, and Rabbi Meshulam David Soloveichik, *Shiurei Rabbeinu Meshulam David HaLevi,* Arakhin 15b. *Mahari Beruna* 38 asserts that the view is disputed and not accepted as practical halakha. See also Rabbi Shmuel ben Elkana of Altuna, *Responsa Mekom Shmuel* 1:91, and see as well Rabbi Yaakov Ettlinger, *Arukh LaNer,* Yevamot 105b, s.v *biota,* and Rabbi Ḥayim Yosef David Azulai, *Responsa Ḥayim She'al* 11, 43:6, and *Kodesh Yisrael* 7. Note also Rabbi Avraham Toker, in the journal *Knesset Yisrael Zikhron Mordekhai* 1, pp. 46–49.

Others interpret the statement in the Talmud in light of theories of *lashon hara* that narrowly focus on it as the abuse of the tool of communication to others. According to these views, it would have to be assumed that speaking badly in the presence of the subject is certainly an offense, and an egregious one at that. However, it would not be classified as *lashon hara,* which has a specific meaning that is not applicable under these circumstances; rather, it is an act of humiliating the other, and likely several other offenses.

For example, the great medieval authority Rabbi Eliezer of Metz suggests that the concept of the "peddler" can be instructive in this case, and particularly by considering an additional scriptural reference.[30] Citing the passage "going about with slanders (*holkhei rakhil*), they are bronze and iron" (Jer. 6:28), he explains that a peddler has two facades: one which is "bronze," glimmering and pleasant, and one which is "iron," the deadly material of the sword.[31] In other words, the symbolic reference is to a speaker who is two-faced; while in the presence of the subject he is friendly, but absent the subject, he bares his weapons. Thus, the speaker who openly disparages the subject to his face, while guilty of many things, it is nonetheless not engaged in *lashon hara.*

The famed rabbinic philosopher Rabbi Yehuda Loew (1520–1609), known as the Maharal of Prague, also posits a theory that excludes negative speech in the presence of the subject from the definition of *lashon hara.*[32] While his language is somewhat difficult, he appears to maintain the following: the term "*lashon hara*" refers specifically to speech as a unique tool of harm that can be perpetrated from a distance. When one's target is present, there are other ways in which one can directly engage him; the role that speech plays is less important. Also of significance is the fact that a statement made in the presence of the target enables him to respond to the allegations.

Many comment on the Maharal's formulation, which essentially is an extension of the talmudic opinion that derogatory speech in the presence of the subject is not termed *lashon hara.* One present-day

30. *Sefer Yere'im* 191 (41).
31. See *Toafot Re'em* to *Sefer Yere'im.*
32. Maharal, *Netivot Olam 2, Netiv HaLashon,* ch. 7.

commentator on the *Ḥafetz Ḥayim* suggests that the issue hinges on the primary biblical source for the prohibition: if the "peddler verse" (Lev. 19:16) is the main source, the thrust is the taking of information from one place and bringing it to another. Thus, speech in the subject's presence may not technically be included in the prohibition, as it does not involve the transmitting of the information to a new location. By contrast, if one of the other verses is the main source, then damage to the victim may be the emphasis, and his presence would not seem to be a significant factor.[33]

From a textual narrative perspective, the *Ḥafetz Ḥayim* and others challenge the Maharal's position by noting the story of Miriam's *lashon hara* against Moses.[34] According to at least one midrashic opinion, Moses was present at the time. Apparently, this does not change the classification of the conversation as *lashon hara.*

In response to that objection, a number of authors, including some modern intellectual descendants of the Maharal's general philosophical approach, advance a distinction to support his position. They maintain that there are two scenarios under discussion. In the first, there are objective negative facts that do not involve assessments or judgment, and the statement is a direct factual allegation. In such a case, the presence of the subject would negate the classification of that revelation as *lashon hara.* In the second, there is a negative judgment of the subject and a failure to fulfill the obligation to judge favorably. In this case, the speech is considered *lashon hara* even if the victim is present. That was the case with Miriam and Moses: no information was being conveyed, rather, Miriam was negatively assessing Moses's undisputed behavior.[35]

33. See *Ḥelkat Binyamin, lashon hara klal* 2, *biurim,* p. 53.

34. *Ḥafetz Ḥayim, Laws of Lashon HaRa Klal* 2, in n. 2.

35. See Rabbi Yitzchak Hutner, *Paḥad Yitzḥak, Shavuot, maamar* 3, as well as *Iggerot,* p. 268, and *Sefer Zikkaron LeMaran Baal HaPaḥad Yitzḥak,* pp. 333–34; Rabbi Moshe Miernik, in *Torat HaAdam LeAdam* V, pp 178–86 (and see as well his essay in Rabbi Chaim Yaakov Goldvicht, *Asufat Maarakhot, Bemidbar,* pp. 169–79); Rabbi Moshe Schapiro, in *BeYad HaLashon,* pp. 373–79. A similar approach can be found in *Zera Ḥayim,* pp. 318–19, distinguishing between truth and falsehood. A more expansive version of this approach, in the context of a broader analysis of the *lashon hara* prohibition, authored by Rabbi Ephraim Natan Rothschild, appeared in the journal *Kol HaTorah* LXIV, pp. 157–64. A critique of this approach, and an alternative, can

Others suggest that the story of Moses and Miriam is actually a proof to the Maharal's position. Their assumption is that the main factor that determines the status of speech "in the presence of the subject" is the ability of the victim to respond; if the subject can do so, the words of the speaker would not constitute *lashon hara.* However, since Moses is described by the Torah in this context as exceedingly humble, the implication is that this constitutes a unique situation where the victim would not respond, and therefore his presence renders Miriam's words as *lashon hara,* an exception to the general rule.[36]

The point, however, is mostly theoretical, as it is universally agreed that speaking negatively in the presence of the subject at the very least constitutes the transgression of a different prohibition, one that is very serious in its own right. Further, as we have seen, many authorities, including Maimonides and the *Ḥafetz Ḥayim,* do not acknowledge any distinction in practice regarding the presence or absence of the subject as far as the prohibition of *lashon hara* is concerned, and one midrashic opinion asserts that the story of Miriam includes a lesson as to how the transgression of *lashon hara* is intensified if the subject is present.[37]

Nonetheless, the conceptual implications are illuminating, and this returns us to our earlier discussion concerning *lashon hara* and public dissemination, the concept of "in the presence of three."

There is another interpretation of that passage which addresses both passages together, the statements excluding remarks said in public, and those said in front of the subject, from *lashon hara.* The major medieval authorities known as the authors of the Tosafot assert that both passages are referring to a very narrow situation, one that has very limited practical application but may be more significant for its underlying presumptions.[38]

---

be found in Rabbi Avraham Gurewitz, *Or Avraham* to *Laws of Fasts, Kuntres Seder HaKinot* 2.

36. Rabbi Dovid Kohn, *Harḥavat Gevul Yaavetz,* pp. 92–93.

37. *Yalkut Shimoni* 1:565.

38. *Tosafot,* Bava Batra 39b, s.v. *leit* (2nd) and Arakhin 15b, s.v. *kol milta.* The *Ḥatam Sofer, ḥiddushim* to Bava Batra, asserts that the Tosafists had a text of the talmudic passage in Arakhin that connects the two passages; note also the alternative interpretation in Rabbi Yisrael Beruna, *Responsa Mahari Beruna* 38. See also the analysis

The Tosafists maintain that the context of both categories of statements is not the conveying of actual disparaging information.[39] Rather, the context is one of a speaker who wishes to make a statement that is somewhat ambiguous, and could be interpreted by the listeners as either negative or positive. The speaker intends that the words be accepted as positive; otherwise, the statements would be clearly forbidden. However, we are still concerned that the listeners will not grasp this fact and will take the statements as negative. Accordingly, it might be maintained that the speaker should not utter his words.

It is here that the presence or lack of presence of the public or of the subject is significant. If the statement is made in private, the listener indeed might be unsure as to how to interpret the message. However, if the speaker knows that his words will be spread publicly, and particularly that the subject himself now hears or will later hear them, the listener can conclude that the message is a positive one.[40]

The *Ḥafetz Ḥayim* poses two models to understand the nature of this license. In the first model, the atmosphere – the presence of three and/or the subject – serves as a "check" on the speaker, who will limit himself to a positive message because of who is listening.[41] According to this understanding, the concern is not so much the manner in which

---

of Rabbi Yitzḥak Eizik of Shavel, *Responsa Ateret Yitzḥak* 47. (Rabbeinu Yonah, in *Shaarei Teshuva* 3:228, also connects the two passages, in a manner consistent with his interpretation mentioned above.)

39. This is the understanding of *Ḥafetz Ḥayim, Laws of Lashon HaRa, Be'er Mayim Ḥayim* 2, 1–2. Compare, however commentary of Maharsha to Bava Batra; see also the analysis of this position in *Mishnat Yisrael* 7:24.

40. However, there remains some risk that the listener may be ungenerous in interpretation, and thus some feel this license is difficult to apply with full confidence; see Rabbi Yeḥiel Michel Lubetzky, in the journal *Otzerot Yerushalayim,* vol. 64, pp. 348–49. Further, there may still be a prohibition on the listeners to relay the information to additional parties; see Maharshal, *Ammudei Shlomo* to *Semag,* negative commandment 9, s.v *vihu.*

41. This is the assumption of the *Ḥafetz Ḥayim* in *Laws of Lashon HaRa* 2:2; compare *Laws of Rekhilut, klal* 2, footnote, s.v *vi'im.* See also *Mishnat Yisrael* 7:11, who notes conflicting implications in the passages in Bava Batra and Arakhin. See also *Haflaat Arakhin,* 16. See *Tohar HaLashon,* pp. 181–83, for a discussion about the differences between the presence of the subject and of three strangers in effecting the same atmosphere.

the listeners will interpret the message but rather the possibility that the ambiguous nature of the content will allow the speaker, consciously or subconsciously, to insert negativity into the presentation. In the second model, the license is based on the premise that the presence of the others serves as a clarification of the speaker's intent. Accordingly, the listeners will understand the message to be a positive one and accept it in that manner.

The premise of the Tosafists, that the presence of the public or of the subject will create an environment where speech is more likely to be positive, is illuminating and will be further explored later.[42] First, we will turn our attention to one aspect of the scenario described by the Tosafists, situations which may indirectly or inadvertently yield negative effects.

THE "DUST" OF *LASHON HARA*

There is an additional category of *lashon hara* described in the Talmud, known in Hebrew as *avak lashon hara,* translated literally as "dust of *lashon hara,*" or legally as "second degree *lashon hara.*"[43] This category comprises speech or even actions that result in an effect of *lashon hara,* even if either the form or intent differs from that of standard *lashon hara.* This broader definition of *lashon hara* ultimately creates a category that imposes great vigilance on the speaker. Indeed, the Talmud (Bava Batra 165a) states that everyone is guilty of *avak lashon hara.* The classic talmudic commentator Rabbi Shmuel Eidels, known as the Maharsha,[44] understands this statement to mean that if human nature is left alone

42. See *Zera Ḥayim,* pp 319–20.
43. See also Rashi to Sukka 40b, s.v. *kama kasheh.* It is unclear whether *avak lashon hara* is a biblical or rabbinic prohibition; see *Responsa Az Nidberu* XIV:62, who assumes that *avak lashon hara* is prohibited on a rabbinic level. See also *Responsa Az Nidberu* XIV:, 63. Note *Kiryat Sefer, Laws of Personal Development* 7:4, and *Ḥafetz Ḥayim, Laws of Lashon HaRa,* 3, *Be'er Mayim Ḥayim* 5 in footnote, and see at length, *Emek HaLashon* 32.
44. *Ḥiddushei Aggadot LeMaharsha,* Bava Batra 165a. See also *Sefer Kovetz al Yad HaḤazaka* to *Laws of Personal Development* 7:4, and note the comment of the *Ḥafetz Ḥayim* in the second footnote in his introduction, and in *Shemirat HaLashon, shaar hatvuna,* ch. 15.

without careful moral direction, it is inevitable that such transgressions will result.

The Talmud (Arakhin 16a; Bava Batra 164b) conveys this concept through a surprising ruling. It is well understood that the prohibition of *lashon hara* proscribes negative speech about others. However, apparently positive speech can also be prohibited, under the category of *avak lashon hara*.[45]

Some of the early authorities understand the rubric *avak lashon hara* to apply only when the statement is said in the presence of detractors of the subject, or when they might be present.[46] Such a limitation relates to the nature of this unusual prohibition. Others understand the concept to relate to limited positive statements that may leave the impression that what is left unsaid is not positive, thereby creating a negative impact.[47] It is for this reason that Rabbi Avraham Yaakov Pam advocates giving evasive answers if asked by unrelated parties about the quality of a specific student even if the student in question is excellent; his concern is that inquiries will be made about other students, and they would look bad if no glowing report is given about them.[48] If this

45. This is identified as *avak lashon hara* in the *Tosefta,* Avoda Zara, ch. 1.

46. *Yad Rama,* Bava Batra 164b, 51; see also *Mishneh Torah, Laws of Personal Development* 7:4, with *Kesef Mishneh* and *Hagahot Maimoniyot*; see also *Divrei Yirmiyahu; Yad Eitan; Maase Rokeaḥ;* and *Ḥukkei Ḥayim,* to *Mishneh Torah,* and, extensively, *Mesharet Moshe.* Many commentaries note that the qualifier is particularly necessary for Maimonides's position, in that he has asserted elsewhere that it is a desirable quality of Torah scholars to speak in praise of others (*Laws of Personal Development* 5:7). See also Rabbi Ḥayim Yosef David Azulai, *Responsa Tov Ayin* 18:49; Rabbi Shmuel Yitzḥak Hillman, *Or HaYashar,* Avot 2:8; Rabbi Shmuel Yitzḥak Gad HaKohen Yudaikin, *Divrei Shalom* 111:30; and Rabbi Yitzḥak Meir Patziner, *Parashat HaMelekh* 111, to *Laws of Personal Development.*

47. Rashi to Arakhin 16a understands that the issue is that either the speaker himself will come to mention the negative qualities as well (see also Rashbam to Bava Batra 164b), or the listeners will interpret the positive qualities mentioned as exclusive of others. See also Rabbi Kalonimos Kalman Steinberg, *Divrei Meḥokek* to Arakhin. However, see Rabbi Nissim Karelitz, *Ḥut Shani, Shemirat HaLashon* 1, 6, pp. 337–38, who does allow praising members of a group who act properly, even when the inference will be clear that others are not acting properly. See also Rabbi Peretz Steinberg, *Peri Etz Ḥayim* to *Laws of Personal Development.*

48. *Moreh Tzedek,* p. 153.

and similar considerations are the issue, it would seem to be irrelevant who the listeners are.

Others are concerned that when positive statements are made about someone, the listeners may be provoked to express their disagreement. Thus, this risk correlates with the presence of listeners likely to object to the praise. The *Sefer Ḥasidim* notes that an enemy is "unable" to hear the praise of his opponent;[49] similarly, to praise a professional in front of others of that profession is likely to arouse the disapproval of his competitors.[50]

These differences in application flow from another conceptual difference in understanding the concept itself as interpreted by various medieval authorities. In his commentary to the Mishna (Avot 1:16), Maimonides understands "dust of *lashon hara*" to be disparagement that is implicit rather than explicit. Accordingly, he prohibits statements along the lines of "who would ever have thought he would have turned out so well" or "don't get me started on that person – you don't want to know what he has done!"[51] Some commentaries emphasize that such phrases constitute actual *lashon hara* if they convey a specific criticism, even through implication; the characterization here as *avak lashon hara* is due to the undefined nature of the comments, which cast a vague negativity over the subject without providing any detail.[52] Maimonides also notes that the nonexplicit nature of the speech allows the speaker to deny that he meant what was implied, or to disavow any actual knowledge of the subject (ibid.).

Rabbeinu Yonah understands the term *avak lashon hara* to mean statements that will lead to disparagement, even if the sentences themselves are neutral.[53] Thus, he rules that positive statements are permitted when the audience is a small one made of individuals who are not

---

49. *Sefer Ḥasidim* 64.
50. It similarly follows that it would be inadvisable to speak at all about someone in the presence of listeners who would be inclined to disparage the subject as soon as his name is mentioned, regardless of the content; see *Alei Be'er* 1, 9:4.
51. *Mishneh Torah, Laws of Personal Development* 7:4.
52. See *Daat UMaḥashava* and *Avodat Melekh* to *Mishneh Torah.*
53. *Shaarei Teshuva* 3:226. *Emek HaLashon,* 33, suggests that the issue revolves around whether *lashon hara* is primarily about the character trait, and thus implicit speech

antagonistic to the subject, or, conversely, if the setting is such that a detractor would be inhibited from expressing his disapproval.

This concern also appears in Maimonides's rulings,[54] and is based on the language of the Talmud, but there is a textual issue to note. Rabbeinu Yonah expresses concern that positive speech will lead to *genuto*, the subject's disparagement. The Talmud's language in that context is actually *raato*, the subject's disadvantage, or misfortune, and both terms appear in Maimonides's formulation.[55] The two terms might mean the same thing, that the disadvantage to the subject will be that he will be disparaged. Indeed, this is Rashi's interpretation;[56] he also understands that the praise is excessive, and thus either will provoke a rebuttal or will result in the original speaker mentioning the deficiencies together with the praise.[57] This concern is relevant even in instances when disproportionate praise is the norm, such as at a testimonial dinner or other event focused on a specific individual at which this protocol is often breached.[58]

However, *raato* could also simply connote that the subject will endure difficulties, rather than disparagement.[59] This nuance is relevant to understanding a statement that the Talmud includes in its discussion

is a secondary form, or is primarily about damage, and thus indirect causation of damage is the secondary form.

54. *Mishneh Torah, ibid.*
55. See also *Oraḥ Meisharim* 8:13 and *Sefer Zikkaron LeMaran Baal HaPaḥad Yitzḥak*, pp. 332–33.
56. Arakhin 16a, s.v. *ba lidei raato.*
57. The *Sefer Yere'im* 191 (41) asserts that the only prohibition is when the praise is excessive (he uses the term *toledot* [derivatives of] *lashon hara*, rather than *avak*). See also *Divrei Shalom* III: 29. However, the implication of Bava Batra 164b is that even praise that is not excessive is problematic; see Rashbam, Bava Batra 164b, and *Ben Yedid* and *Benei Binyamin* to *Mishneh Torah*, and *Magen Avraham, Oraḥ Ḥayim* 156. See also *Responsa Rabbeinu Avraham ben Rav Yitzḥak Av Beit Din* 56; *Toafot Re'em* to *Sefer Yere'im*; and Rabbi Moshe Maimon, *Lev Tov*, pp. 42–43.
58. See Rabbi Yitzḥak ben Shoshan, *Daltei Teshuva* to *Shaarei Teshuva*, 3:226. However, *Ḥatam Sofer* (*Responsa* VI:59, s.v. *vehineh, Torat Moshe* to Deut. 24:9) asserts that there is so no concern for this issue when the praise is a fulfillment of a mitzva; *Shaarei Avraham*, pp. 318–320, applies this to instances such as the praise of a bride and groom.
59. See *Otzar HaMelekh* to *Laws of Personal Development.*

of possibly prohibited speech. It is apparently problematic to say that an individual's kitchen always has an oven running.[60] One understanding of the problem with this statement is that it is a subtle criticism of the resident, implying that he is gluttonous and constantly indulging in the food and drink, or that he is stingy despite his wealth.[61] However, it may be understood differently: the statement may actually be a positive one, indicating that the resident is generous and hospitable. Nonetheless, calling attention to this fact indiscriminately could result in a besieging of the host by greedy individuals and a depleting of his resources. Thus, the statement is a form of *lashon hara* not because it is disparaging but rather because it is harmful speech, in that it places the subject at a form of risk.[62]

PURIM PLAYS

Some of what we have discussed regarding *avak lashon hara,* and the impact of the environment on the status of what is being said, is instructive in considering the phenomenon of *shpiels*, plays and skits performed on the festival of Purim (or similar events at any other time), in which specific individuals are often portrayed in a humorous light. The early authorities discuss a relaxed attitude toward demanding compensation for damages incurred in the context of Purim celebrations, an implicit agreement in order to facilitate exuberant merriment.[63] In later generations, the controversial practice of the "Purim *shpiel*" took shape, in which humorous skits would be performed, often incorporating the

60. Arakhin 15b and Rashbam, Bava Batra 165a, s.v. *avak.*
61. See Rashi and Maharsha to Arakhin.
62. See commentary of the Vilna Gaon to Prov. 27:14, and *Iggerot Moshe, Yoreh De'ah* III:95. See also Rabbi Elḥanan Bunim Wasserman, *Kovetz He'arot, biurei aggadot* 8:9, who in discussing actual *lashon hara,* notes that unjustified praise can bring harm upon the subject in various ways, such as leading to an appointment to a position that he is unqualified for, and ensuing embarrassment or related problems. See also *Shemuot Ḥayim,* Arakhin, ch. 3, no. 25, who takes issue with this.
63. See *Mordekhai,* Sukka 2:742; *Tosafot,* Rosh, *Aguda,* Sukka 45a; Rema, *Ḥoshen Mishpat* 378:9, and *Oraḥ Ḥayim* 695:2. Rabbi Yisrael Grossman, *Responsa Netzaḥ Yisrael* 15; Rabbi Binyamin Yehoshua Zilber, *Responsa Az Nidberu* IX:49. Note also the discussion of Rabbi David Shperber, *Responsa Afarkasta DeAnya* 1:148; and of Rabbi Alter Gelernter, in the journal *HaEmek* 64, pp. 16–20.

lampooning of individuals, including respected figures such as rabbis and Rashei Yeshiva.[64]

Regarding the *shpiel*, different yeshivas developed different approaches. Many distinguished yeshivas allow and support *shpiels* on Purim, as have many in the past, most notably the "mother of yeshivas," the Volozhin Yeshiva. Rabbi Moshe Zvi Neriah describes the experience of Rabbi Avraham Yitzḥak HaKohen Kook in Volozhin on Purim, in a manner starkly reminiscent of the contemporary Purim *shpiel*:

> In delivering his Purim compositions, the Rav [Rabbi Kook] imitated the Netziv's [Rabbi Naphtali Tzvi Yehuda Berlin, the Rosh Yeshiva] manner of speech and enunciation. But he was repaid in kind many years later by the great-grandson of the Netziv, Rabbi Yitzḥak Ḥarif, who was chosen to be "Purim Rav" in Yeshivat Merkaz HaRav. Rabbi Yitzḥak, having internalized every word that he'd heard the Rav speak, proceeded to make a Purim speech in precise imitation of the Rav's style and cadence. He analyzed his position of "Purim rav": did it encompass only the rabbinate of Jerusalem, or did his nomination entitle him to officiate as the chief rabbi of Eretz Yisrael? The scholarship and mental agility which he brought to his speech amazed all those present. The Rav was also impressed by Rabbi Yitzḥak's address. He admitted that he had been unaware of the rabbi's greatness in Torah and added, "Now I am getting my due. The great-grandson is repaying me here in Jerusalem for that which I said to his great-grandfather in Volozhin."[65]

However, this practice has also been subject to strong opposition from halakhic authorities. As would be expected, these authorities have worried about issues such as detraction from the honor of Torah and

64. See the brief survey of the history of this practice by Zohar HaNegby in Rabbi Daniel Sperber, ed. *Minhagei Yisrael* v I, pp. 201–2.

65. Rabbi Moshe Zvi Neriah, *Mo'adei HaRe'iya*, translated by Pesach Jaffe as *Celebration of the Soul: The Holidays in the Life and Thought of Rabbi Avraham Yitzchak Kook*, Genesis Jerusalem Press, 1992, p. 124.

Torah scholars, and the humiliation of any individual portrayed in the performances.[66]

While it is clear that many great rabbinic authorities have developed a different and more accepting attitude toward this innovation, it is equally clear that the objections raised by the detractors represent very real concerns of tremendous spiritual import. Thus, it must be assumed that the pro-*shpiel* camp is equally concerned with these risks, and incorporate into their support mandated safeguards and controls to protect against abuse. As such, these objections must be carefully studied and valued in order to guarantee that that mandate is met.

These performances often entail implicit or explicit statements about individuals which in another context might be termed *lashon hara*. It is not immediately clear what justifies such theatrical productions. The defense that "it is just a joke" is not a sustainable one;[67] both Maimonides[68] and the *Ḥafetz Ḥayim*[69] assert clearly that *lashon hara* "in a manner of joking" (*derekh seḥok*) is prohibited. According to the

66. Among others, see Rabbi Avraham David Horowitz, *Responsa Kinyan Torah BeHalakha* II, 125:2; Rabbi Yosef Tzvi Dushinsky, *Responsa Maharitz*, I, 56; Rabbi Avraham Yaakov Pam, *Atara LaMelekh*, pp. 193–94; Rabbi Moshe Sternbuch, *Mo'adim UZmanim* II:191, n. 2; Rabbi Shlomo Zalman Auerbach, *Halikhot Shlomo, Mo'adim* II, ch. 19, n. 77; and Rabbi Ovadia Yosef, *Responsa Yeḥaveh Daat* V, 50. See also *Tehor Sefatayim*, pp. 139–40, who assumes the subject is always unwilling to be portrayed, even if he outwardly participates; but note also the exceptions he details on p. 227.

67. It is important to address as well the general misuse of this defense to justify other acts of malfeasance. In the context of *lashon hara*, this defense is inadequate but at least has some merit; the fact that a statement is not meant seriously does somewhat mitigate its potentially negative impact. However, this statement is sometimes invoked by those who harass others, such as bullies who inflict suffering upon innocent victims, and then argue that "it was just a joke." In this case, the joke is one-sided; the victim is certainly not amused, and the fact that the perpetrator took pleasure in the harassment makes him sadistic rather than innocent. The stated excuse obscures the fact that nothing within it alleviates at all the suffering of the victim. "Practical jokes" may be justifiable in a setting in which both parties enjoy the experience, at least after the fact, and are understood as such; but in the one-sided fashion in which they are generally perpetrated, they are squarely within the scope of the egregious prohibition of *onaat devarim*. See *Responsa Ḥatam Sofer, Ḥoshen Mishpat* 176.

68. *Mishneh Torah, Laws of Personal Development* 7:4.

69. *Ḥafetz Ḥayim, Laws of Lashon HaRa, klal* 3, 3. See Rabbi Moshe Kaufman, *Zera Ḥayim* pp. 321–22.

latter, such presentations involve *lashon hara,* while according to Maimonides, it is unclear as to whether such shows involve *lashon hara* or actually *avak lashon hara.*[70] In interpreting this language, Rabbi Binyamin Yehoshua Zilber, a great twentieth-century halakhic authority and ethicist, suggests there are two types of *avak lashon hara.* The first, as discussed above, is that which causes others to engage in disparaging talk. The second, which is relevant here, emerges when one says disparaging things about another, but is not motivated by genuine negativity. This latter category, he asserts, may be included in the Torah's core prohibition of *lashon hara.*[71]

A second effort at justification – to maintain that the subjects are *moḥel,* or waive their rights to protection – is only slightly more successful. While it is certainly the case that at least implicit *meḥila* (pardon, forgiveness) is a prerequisite for such involvement, it might not be enough. Some authorities maintain that such *meḥila* is only effective for monetary rights (i.e., the victim can forgo restitution) but not to allow the infliction of personal suffering.[72]

It seems, rather, that the firmest ground on which to permit this activity is based on the creation of an atmosphere and a context in which it is abundantly clear that the *shpiel* is affectionate rather than malicious. This notion can be based on the perspective we have seen in the Tosafists' words, that statements of ambiguous impact, when said in public or in the subject's presence, can be assumed (presuming the decency of the speaker) to evoke a positive interpretation. Similarly, in the case of an appropriately executed Purim *shpiel,* with those portrayed often in (hopefully genuine) cheerful participation, it might be fair to trust that the intent is innocent, loving, and playful rather than nasty and malicious. Writ large, this notion has implications for humorous statements year-round; it is necessary to create, through one's personality, a context in which these statements will enlighten rather than demean.

---

70. As the *Ḥafetz Ḥayim* notes, the implication of Nahmanides to Deut. 24:9 is that a Torah commandment is violated by harmful speech, even when the speaker has no intent to harm or cause embarrassment.

71. *Responsa Az Nidberu* XIV, 63. See also *Daat UMaḥashava* to *Mishneh Torah* for a different distinction. See also *Emek HaLashon* 35.

72. See *Zera Ḥayim,* pp. 324–25.

(Of course, it is also crucial that the intent correspond to this attitude, and not actually be malice concealed by Purim celebration.)

WIDELY SPREAD PUBLIC KNOWLEDGE

It should be noted that "in the presence of three" is not the only possible category of public knowledge. There is another category, alluded to by the *Ḥafetz Ḥayim* and others, called "known to all" (*mefursam lakol*).[73] In contrast to the former category, which refers to information that will ultimately become known within a certain context and to which the speaker is not significantly adding to the damage by speaking about it, this additional classification addresses information that is already widely known. For example, an incident extensively discussed in widely read newspapers, a matter of well-known public record, may constitute a subject which is saturated and not affected at all by additional conversation on the individual level.

In such a case, there may be, strictly speaking, no relevant prohibition of *lashon hara*, at least as far as an assessment of the damage inflicted is concerned. However, there are additional factors to consider, such as negative character trait reinforcement, unwarranted acceptance, expression of hatred, issues of honesty and accuracy, and instances in which there actually would be an extension of the harm to the subject.[74] Further, the designation of an item as "known to all" is a subjective one, and not necessarily a permanent one; an item that is prominently in the news may become forgotten, and revert to a status where basic prohibitions of *lashon hara* apply.[75]

---

73. See *Ḥafetz Ḥayim* in *Be'er Mayim Ḥayim* 4:41.
74. See also *Ḥelkat Binyamin, Laws of Lashon HaRa* 2:4; *Responsa LeḤafetz BaḤayim* I, 27, Rabbi Yitzḥak Eizik Zilber, *Mishpetei HaShalom* 19:74; *LeRe'akha Kamokha* VII, ch. 2, n. 149; *Shaarei Avraham*, pp. 290–91; *Kodesh Yisrael* 4; see however *Birkat Yitzḥak*, pp. 121–22. See also *Responsa Az Nidberu* XI, 40, 41, and *Tehor Sefatayim*, p. 140. For a discussion of practical applications of this principle, see Rabbi Gil Student, "Lashon HaRa, Democracy, and Social Media," in *Morasha Kehillat Yaakov: Essays in Honour of Chief Rabbi Lord Jonathan Sacks* (Jerusalem: Maggid, 2014), pp. 163–70.
75. Rabbi Azriel Ariel (*Tzohar* V, p. 42) cites Rabbi Avraham Schapiro and Rabbi Dov Lior as assessing the time period of a news item remaining in the public awareness as one year.

Privacy and Confidentiality

One major area of contemporary concern that is associated with the talebearing prohibition is that of privacy and confidentiality. Invasion of privacy – whether defined as obtaining personal information or the public dissemination of personal information – is addressed by the "peddler verse" (Lev. 19:16) both on a textual and conceptual level.

On a textual level, the key word *rakhil* is identified elsewhere in Scripture with breaches of confidentiality. The verse in Proverbs declares, "He who reveals secrets is a talebearer (*rakhil*), but he who is of a faithful spirit conceals the matter."[1] Thus, it should be assumed by definition that the talebearing prohibited by the verse includes not only negative information but anything which is private, of any nature.

In fact, the Talmud issues a sweeping assertion that anything one is told by another person may not be related to any other without the explicit permission of the original speaker.[2] However, some later authorities understand this as recommended behavior, rather than an

1. Prov. 11:13; see similarly 20:19. It should be noted that some, such as Rabbeinu Yonah and the Vilna Gaon, interpret the intent as saying that a *rokhel* is likely to reveal secrets, but not necessarily that revealing secrets is an act of *rekhilut;* that is, however, the interpretation of Ibn Ezra and others.
2. Yoma 4b, per Lev. 1:1.

absolute prohibition.[3] Nonetheless, if the statement is clearly of a confidential nature, whether because the content or the context indicates as such or the speaker identifies it as such, a clear prohibition applies.[4]

On the conceptual level, it is also clear that breaches of confidentiality and malicious gossip are equally prohibited. As we have noted, in one of his definitions of *lashon hara* Maimonides includes the revelation of any information that would be a harmful to the subject. Included in his delineations of harm is anguish, which certainly includes the emotional suffering felt when one's privacy is breached.[5]

This categorization would clearly apply to one who reveals private information to others, regardless of whether he obtained this information legitimately or illegitimately. Further, it would also address the obtaining in and of itself of others' private information, even if it is not disseminated to any third party. As some formulate, there is no reason why the talebearer cannot play two roles in the process, acting both as the speaker and as the listener, and communicating this information to himself.[6] This was similarly phrased by an earlier authority, Rabbi Yaakov Ḥagiz (1620–74), who posed the rhetorical question: "What difference does it make if one peddles tales to another, or to oneself?"[7] In other words, it should not be assumed that *lashon hara* is only violated when one is communicating with another person.

---

3. See *Ḥafetz Ḥayim, Laws of Lashon HaRa* 2:13, and Rabbi Betzalel Stern, *Responsa BeTzel HaḤokhma* IV, 84, based on *Dina DeḤayyei* to *Semag*, negative commandment 9, and *Meiri* to Yoma. Maimonides does not record a prohibition; see also the explanation of Rabbi Yehuda Assad, *Responsa Yehuda Yaaleh* 19. The commentary of *Or HaḤayim* to Ex. 7:8–9 and 25:2 implies that there is an actual prohibition involved. This is also the implication of the language of *She'iltot DeRav Aḥai Gaon* 28, although Rabbi Stern interprets this as nonliteral. The *Semag* (negative commandment 9) quotes the statement of the Talmud verbatim, leading some to the conclusion that he perceives there to be a biblical prohibition; the *Torah Temima* to Lev. 1:1 interprets the *Semag* as such, but he himself maintains the talmudic association is an *asmakhta* and thus constitutes a rabbinic prohibition.
4. The prohibition of repeating a statement without express permission is recorded in *Magen Avraham, Oraḥ Ḥayim* 156, who then adds that if there is an explicit directive not to repeat the information, doing so would constitute *lashon hara*.
5. *Mishneh Torah, Laws of Personal Development* 7:5.
6. See Rabbi Rephael Stern, *Nizkei Shekhenim*, p. 179
7. *Responsa Halakhot Kettanot* 1:276.

Some commentaries also maintain that Maimonides, in his formulation of *rekhilut,* includes a prohibition of revealing secrets. While it is commonly understood that that transgression is committed when one relates a private conversation to the subject of the conversation, and thus likely provokes his anger against the speaker, Maimonides's formulation does not explicitly state that that is the case. Thus, it is possible to understand that his model of *rekhilut* is actually the general exposure of secrets, which inflicts tremendous harm on society through the erosion of trust. Early commentators, such as the *Kesef Mishneh,* who add the detail that the listener is the subject, would not necessarily differ from this interpretation. The point is simply that a secret will only be of interest to parties who are directly affected, and thus the risk of causing damage through revelation is greater in that context.[8]

There are other precepts that are relevant as well to the invasion of privacy. The famed commandment to love one's fellow as oneself (Lev. 19:18), while phrased as a positive obligation, has been interpreted by many authorities as a prohibition. It is impossible, practically, to provide care for others, in the form of attention and service, to the same degree as one does for oneself. However, it is possible to apply "as yourself" to the negative: one should not do to others what one would not want done to himself. Accordingly, the verse prohibits any type of behavior that can be reasonably interpreted as universally undesirable. In line with this approach, many have explicitly included breaches of confidentiality and privacy within this directive as well.

It is important to point out that the mandates relating to privacy are not purely victim based, and therefore do not necessarily disappear if the subject is not opposed to the revelations. The Torah describes how the Jewish people were praised by Balaam, an archenemy who had come with intent to curse them. "How goodly are your tents, O [People of] Jacob" (Num. 24:5). The Talmud (Bava Batra 60a) explains what it was that had impressed him: he saw that the people lived with modesty and privacy, in dwellings that did not have doors that opened opposite each other, allowing their neighbors full view of the interior.

8. This interpretation is advanced in *Kodesh Yisrael* 2:1.

The implication is that it is irrelevant whether or not their neighbors wanted to be seen; modesty is a communal standard and value to uphold. This standard draws from many principles of Jewish law and philosophy, but among them is a strong basis in the precepts of *lashon hara.*

The Talmud (Bava Batra 2a–3a, 59a–b) considers the question of damage inflicted upon a person who has his privacy violated through being seen against his will, what is known as "damage through seeing." Much like damage inflicted through malicious speech, there are no monetary penalties imposed for such a violation, but it is nonetheless recognized as an offense, resulting both in a codified prohibition and the possibility of injunctive relief when applicable.[9]

The commentaries analyze the nature of this offense.[10] To some, the focus is the emotional and psychic suffering people undergo when they are violated on a personal level. Although such anguish may not result in the collection of monetary damages, it is understood as genuine and harmful. Alternatively, or perhaps additionally, some see the issue as essentially a monetary tort. By compromising the privacy of another, one restricts that person's ability to use their property as desired. This may result in reduced productivity of business endeavors, or simply an obstruction to the subject's obtaining the full value of his property. Thus, the unwanted visibility imposes a monetary loss, albeit indirectly. Again, such indirect economic harm is not actionable as far as collecting penalties, but is nonetheless prohibited.

Particularly noteworthy is a third perspective, to which Nahmanides alludes in his talmudic commentary.[11] He connects the issue of "damage by seeing" to an unspecified concern of *lashon hara.* His intent might be to assert that *lashon hara,* as a general concern, is breached when boundaries of privacy are lowered, and neighbors are unnecessarily intertwined in each other's affairs. This is true even before one word of the gossip is spoken; the mere exposure of what should otherwise

9. See Rema, *Ḥoshen Mishpat* 154:3 and 7; and *Sefer Me'irat Einayim* 14, and *Netivot HaMishpat* 18. See also Rabbi Yitzḥak Zilberstein, *Torat HaYoledet,* p. 168.

10. See the discussions in Rabbi Yisrael Yaakov Kanievsky, *Kehillot Yaakov,* Bava Batra 1, and Rabbi Asher Weiss, *Minḥat Asher,* Bava Batra 2.

11. *Ḥiddushim* to Bava Batra, 59b, s.v. *ha detenan.*

be personal is laying the foundation of the mentality that is a fundamental part of "talebearing."[12]

Some interpret Nahmanides's comments in a victim-based fashion, suggesting that he is alluding to that which is expressed more explicitly by later authorities: accessing the private information of another, even without revealing it to a third party, constitutes a violation of *lashon hara.* This may also find a precedent in an earlier source, in the Jerusalem Talmud (Pe'ah 1:1), where a listing of offenses and offenders included in *lashon hara* includes "he who knows it." This condemnation of a seemingly passive state may actually refer to one who actively seeks to learn information that is meant to be confidential.[13]

Some of the early commentators note that the Talmud's concern for "damage by seeing" is not paralleled with any expressed concern for "damage through hearing."[14] Later authorities, however, are quick to point out that this should not be understood as permission for eavesdropping. Rather, the context in the Talmud is that of building construction, and limitations placed upon structures regarding visibility of neighboring structures. A neighbor's exposure to unwanted visibility can interfere with construction plans that pose that risk. By contrast, if a neighbor is worried that another's house will be placed in earshot, allowing him to overhear private conversations, this is not sufficient to prevent the construction; rather, the responsibility is on the speaker to adjust his volume to avoid being overheard. However, intentional eavesdropping on the personal conversations of others is certainly prohibited.[15]

There are a number of elements to this prohibition. As we have seen, the mandate of "love your fellow" and the prohibition of talebearing are involved. Further, the Talmud is unequivocal in prohibiting *genevat daat,* which is generally understood as deceptive behavior, but

12. See *Shaarei Avraham,* pp. 308–9.
13. *Responsa VeDarashta VeḤakarta* 111, *Ḥoshen Mishpat* 7 (the commentary *Penei Moshe* to the Jerusalem Talmud interprets the passage differently).
14. See Meiri to Bava Batra 2a and *Responsa Rabbi Eliyahu Mizraḥi (Re'em)* 8. *Shaarei Avraham,* pp. 312–13, suggests that the distinction is due to the fact that overhearing requires no effort, while seeing into another's property takes intent.
15. See *Emek HaMishpat, Laws of Neighbors* 26 and Rabbi Shlomo Deichovsky, in the journal *Teḥumin* XI, pp. 299–312.

literally translates as "stealing knowledge." As such, some have associated this prohibition with the unjustified appropriation of information, whether classified as intellectual property theft or the invasion of privacy.[16]

The great medieval authority Rabbeinu Gershom (960–1040) imposed a communal sanction (*ḥerem*) against one who would read someone else's mail.[17] This has also been taken to prohibit the recipient of mail from disclosing the contents to a third party.[18] Some later authors understand this sanction to include eavesdropping, while others forcefully argue that such behavior is already prohibited by the Torah itself.[19] The two positions do not necessarily create a practical or even a theoretical difference; the behavior may be prohibited on a biblical level and reinforced by the later communal sanction.

Nonetheless, there may be factors, such as self-protection, which can justify overriding these prohibitions, as the contemporary halakhic authority Rabbi Yitzḥak Zilberstein mentions in separate discussions prohibiting eavesdropping[20] and the recording of conversations without the other party's knowledge.[21] It can be presumed that the threshold for such evaluation varies in correlation with the severity of the infringement, with eavesdropping considered a greater violation than second-party recording, a distinction reflected in American law, which requires a warrant in the first instance and, in many states, not in the second instance.

Similarly, doctors and other similar professionals are bound to confidentiality regarding their services, both by the dictates of *lashon hara* and related precepts, and by professional ethical standards, sometimes emphasized through an oath (which might be considered halakhically significant). Nonetheless, there are circumstances when disclosure

16. See *Responsa Ḥikekei Lev* 1, *Yoreh De'ah* 49.
17. See *Responsa Maharam MiRottenberg,* Prague edition, IV, 1022; *Shiltei Gibborim, Shavuot* ch. 5, 17a in pages of the Rif; *Knessset HaGdola/Be'er Heitev, Yoreh De'ah,* 334, glosses to *Tur* 5; *Kol Bo,* 116; and *Responsa Maharam Mintz* 102:73.
18. See *Ḥikekei Lev,* 1, *Yoreh De'ah* 49.
19. See the debate between Rabbi Tzvi Shpitz, *Responsa Mishpetei HaTorah* 1:92, and *Responsa VeDarashta VeḤakarta* 1, *Yoreh De'ah* 46.
20. *Ḥashukei Ḥemed,* Bava Batra 4a, p. 46, s.v. *of hashamayim.*
21. *Ḥashukei Ḥemed,* Bava Batra 39a, pp. 217–18, s.v. *lo timru.* See also *Ḥikekei Lev,* 1, *Yoreh De'ah* 49. for an earlier version of this approach.

may be required, either for the protection of the patient or client or for the protection of others. In these cases, halakhic authorities often mandate disclosure, while some also give weight to considerations of the deleterious effect this may have on other patients, and the related fear of loss of a professional license.[22]

22. See Rabbi Ovadia Yosef, *Responsa Yeḥaveh Daat* IV:60; Rabbi Nachum Rabinovitch, *Responsa Siaḥ Naḥum* 117; Rabbi Yaakov Ariel, *Responsa BeOhala shel Torah* 1:83; Rabbi Yitzḥak Zilberstein, in the journal *HaBe'er* (Sanz) XXIV, pp. 63–69; and *Ohev Yamim, diyunim* 4.

Contemporary Culture: Journalism, the Internet, and Politics

JOURNALISM

For society to function effectively and responsibly, it is necessary to have citizens who are informed and aware of the issues that affect them, and even more so, of those issues upon which they are empowered to have an impact. Accordingly, to become informed and to inform others regarding these areas, especially in a democratic society, seems to be well within the bounds of purposeful and necessary speech. However, this justification does not detract from the vigilance and sensitivity required by the precepts involving *lashon hara;* quite the opposite, it raises the stakes and makes these considerations all the more relevant.

In this vein, the *Ḥazon Ish* asserts that we are permitted and in fact required to be aware of the character and behavior of communal leaders, as such involvement by the populace is necessary to ensure an appropriate level of leadership. Nonetheless, in the same breath he warns that extreme care must be taken to not deviate from the truth and fairness, and not go beyond what is relevant and necessary even to the smallest degree, lest one finds himself slandering a scholar.[1]

1. *Iggerot Ḥazon Ish,* vol. II, *iggeret* 133b.

Likewise, Rabbi Nissim Karelitz, the *Ḥazon Ish*'s nephew, in his work on the laws of *lashon hara,* gives an illustration of the balance that we need to maintain. He notes that if one is removed for cause from a public position, it is permissible and sometimes necessary for the members of the community to be informed of the reason for the removal. However, to discuss it excessively and without purpose, or to take that as an excuse to disparage the individual in unrelated areas, would constitute *lashon hara.*[2] Of course, as with all other such matters, it takes careful judgment to know what is considered excessive and unnecessary; at times, public protection will require more than removing the individual from a current position, and such an action must be weighed with utmost seriousness.

In light of these concerns, the field of journalism is positioned to perform an important role within society, a role that was alluded to by the seventeenth-century Galician authority Rabbi Yaakov Reischer in his responsa, in which he allowed the reading of newspapers on Shabbat.[3] He notes that in contrast to historical texts, journals that address current events can inform their readers about existing human needs, which they may be in a position to address. Newspapers are uniquely positioned to influence society both positively and negatively. Rabbi Avraham Yitzḥak HaKohen Kook, in one of his letters, asserts that a newspaper must aim to elevate the community; thus, in its focus and presentation it should aim to be one level above its readership: above, rather than catering to base interests and prurient tastes; but only one level above, so that its words and message should be accessible to its readers and can set a tone that is noble and idealistic.[4]

Clearly, the valuable role newspapers can play does not eliminate the concern of *lashon hara,* and in fact journalism is confronted with challenges that are unique or intensified regarding the precepts involving *lashon hara.* It is therefore important to identify factors and elements that

2. *Ḥut Shani* 1:5.
3. *Responsa Shevut Yaakov* III:23. See also Rabbi Yuval Cherlow, in the journal *Teḥumin* XXVII, p. 175.
4. Quoted in *Tehor Sefatayim,* p. 240. See also pp. 258–65.

differentiate journalism from everyday conversation so that concerns can be addressed and benefits can be maximized.

It should first be noted that there is no reason to assume that the act of *lashon hara* is limited to the spoken word; the offense is one of communication, not "speaking."[5] Quite the contrary, not only is the written word equally subject to its regulations, there are aspects of writing and printing that intensify the damage that can be inflicted. In fact even before the advent of the Internet, the written word made a longer

5. *Ḥafetz Ḥayim, Laws of Lashon HaRa* 1:8. See also Rabbi Tziyon Shimon Bognim, *Responsa Shivat Tziyon* I, 29. For a discussion of the relationship of this point to the notion that *lashon hara* is particularly egregious because of its misuse of the unique power of speech, see *Emek HaLashon* 4.

There is an extensive literature on the question of the equation, for purposes of Jewish law, of writing to speech (*ketiva kedibbur*); see Rabbi Akiva Eiger, *Responsa* 29–32; Rabbi Moshe Sofer, *Responsa Ḥatam Sofer* VI, 19; Rabbi Avraham Shmuel Binyamin Sofer, *Responsa Ketav Sofer, Yoreh De'ah* 106, 136; Rabbi Shimon (Eiger) Sofer, *Responsa Hitorerut Teshuva,* in several places; Rabbi Shmuel Engel, *Responsa Maharash Engel,* vol. I, *Yoreh De'ah* 61; *Responsa Divrei Malkiel* VI:60; Rabbi Avraham Yehuda Schwartz, *Responsa Kol Aryeh, Oraḥ Ḥayim* 11; Rabbi Barukh Epstein, *Torah Temima,* Exodus 18:7, Numbers 5:121, Deuteronomy 21:144 and 25:135; Rabbi Yo'av Yehoshua Weingarten, *Responsa Ḥelkat Yoav,* vol. I, *Mahadura Tinyana* 19; Rabbi Shlomo Heiman, *Ḥiddushim, Hosafot Ḥadashot* 2; Rabbi David Sikili, *Responsa Kiryat Ḥanna David,* vol. I; Rabbi Ḥayim Mordekhai Yaakov Gottleib, *Responsa Yagel Yaakov, Oraḥ Ḥayim* 10; Rabbi Yosef Chaim Sonnenfeld, *Responsa Salmat Ḥayim* 49; Rabbi Natan Gestetner, *Responsa Lehorot Natan* VII:77; Rabbi Shlomo Gross, *Responsa Mishna Shelema* 560; *Responsa Halakha LeMoshe* II, 106; Rabbi Yosef Neḥemia Kornitzer, *Ḥiddushei Rabbi Yosef Neḥemia* 70; Rabbi Yeḥiel Michel Leiter, *Responsa Darkhei Shalom* 19; Rabbi Menaḥem Mendel Schneebalg, *Responsa Siftei Ani* I, 115; Rabbi Moshe Natan Nota Lemberger, *Responsa Ateret Moshe* 204; Rabbi Yeruḥam Ciecanowicz, *Responsa Torat Yeruḥam* I:15; Rabbi Simḥa Elberg, *Shalmei Simḥa* I, 61; Rabbi Shraga Feivel Shneebalg, *Responsa Shraga HaMeir* VIII, 20:3; Rabbi Moshe Sternbuch, *Responsa Teshuvot VeHanhagot* II:40; Rabbi Avraham Yafe-Shlesinger, *Responsa Be'er Sarim* 252:1; Rabbi Shmuel Greenberger, *Responsa Merkaḥat Besamim* 17; Rabbi Avraham Binyamin Silverberg, *Responsa Mishnat Binyamin* 58; Rabbi Shammai Kehat Gross, *Responsa Shevet HaKehati,* vol. I, and III:248; and Rabbi Menaḥem Genack, in the journal *Or HaMizraḥ* 48:1–2, pp. 28–31. Nonetheless, regarding the prohibition of *lashon hara,* it would seem that the violation is incurred either way. See also Rabbi Yitzḥak Yaakov Wachtfogel, in the journal *Nitei Ne'emanim* I, p. 207.

lasting impression than its spoken counterpart and had a far greater potential to inflict unjustifiable damage.[6]

Ideally, news publications are staffed by professionals who are careful to ascertain that their stories are both true and balanced, as well as necessary or at least beneficial to society. Nonetheless, reality is not always ideal, and a burden is placed on the consumer to be sensitive to the possibility that any of these factors may be compromised in practice, and to exercise discretion and judgment in evaluating the reported information.[7] Newspapers are often granted automatic credibility, thereby requiring, paradoxically, the reader to approach the contents with a greater degree of vigilance to confirm that such credibility is deserved. Further, for reasons both financial and fundamental, newspapers focus on the unusual and noteworthy, which is by definition atypical, and thus may at times fail to paint a complete picture of an individual or a situation.

Subject matter deemed to be in violation of the precepts of *lashon hara* places obligations and prohibitions on the reader in terms of "accepting." As we have noted, accepting is not the same as merely listening, and while there are dangers and prohibitions associated with listening as well, at times it is necessary to be aware of what is being claimed even if full acceptance is not justified. This might lead to the conclusion that reading certain publications may be justified or necessary even if full acceptance of their contents is not. However, this can be a complex issue because the prohibition of accepting extends to activities that support the actions of the speaker. Accordingly, we would need to evaluate whether purchasing a news publication (or, alternatively, clicking on a website) provides support that is unwarranted. This question is a particularly complicated one in that it is nearly impossible for a publication to be perfect in its output; thus,

---

6. See *Responsa Rema* 10, and also *Responsa Maharsham* VII, 92 and *Responsa Ḥayim She'al* II:13. As to the question of whether the violation is incurred by the writer, or also by those involved in the distribution, see *Responsa Az Nidberu* XIV:64, whose inclination is that the distributors are not responsible for *lashon hara* contained within the newspapers (note as well the contrasting position taken by his questioner.)
7. See, for example, Freedman, *Wrong*, 166.

the evaluation would involve weighing the benefits of the publication and its consumption against the damage being inflicted by items that do not meet the standard.[8]

THE INTERNET AND SOCIAL MEDIA

Moving within and beyond journalism, we find the wide world of the Internet. One of the most passionately analyzed aspects of contemporary culture, the Internet simultaneously brings to the world phenomenal benefits and serious risks. Fantastic things have become possible through the Internet. Whether it is the spread of Torah study and other valuable knowledge, the ease with which important functions can now be accomplished, or the extension of kindness and service to others made possible by the global interconnectedness of the system; the Internet is a tool that can bring great good to the world.

Further, the benefits of the Internet do not relate only to "nice" things. Some roles played by the web are not pleasant but are nonetheless necessary. As we have seen, there are times when it is crucially important that negative information be transmitted, whether for the protection of the innocent or for the alleviation of social problems. In this context, the broad reach of the Internet is sometimes vitally important in accomplishing these difficult but vital tasks.

Nonetheless, as we have also seen, there are critically significant considerations that apply to these missions, and the possibility of mistakes and misjudgments in this area is a very real one. Accordingly, just as it is always necessary to exercise great care and sensitive discretion in attempting these tasks, it is important to investigate how the culture and context of the Internet affect the equation.

It is abundantly clear that despite the great benefits afforded by the Internet, there are significant risks involved as well. These risks are present in many areas, and have been extensively

8. It is also a significant technical question to consider whether publication in a newspaper automatically invokes the standard of "in the presence of three"; see *LeRe'akha Kamokha*, p. 171, and *Nir LeDavid* 47. See also the discussion regarding the role of journalism and the issue of *lashon hara* by Rabbi Aryeh Klapper in the journal *Aḥrayut Ketuva* 1, pp. 121–36.

documented. In the context of the careful balance necessitated by the laws of *lashon hara* and purposeful speech, it is instructive to become aware of both positive and negative ways in which the differences between online and direct personal interaction register an impact. The point is not necessarily to discourage or prohibit use of the Internet, but to understand how its environment creates a different set of responsibilities so that the correct decisions can be made, the innocent can be protected, and the values of the Jewish speech ethic can be properly upheld.[9]

CHECKING OF INFORMATION

If central to concerns of *lashon hara* is that damaging and potentially misleading information not be spread, the unprecedented speed at which information travels on the Internet, as well as its equally unprecedented reach, presents a clear and present risk. The question is, though, does the problem come with a parallel solution? Perhaps the speed and scope of the Internet can be equally harnessed toward the correcting of errors, and, further, perhaps the diversity of perspectives now available can contribute to a more accurate overall picture.

In his *The Future of Reputation*, Daniel Solove notes the advantages and disadvantages inherent in the Internet regarding the correction of errors:

> In the past, rumors and falsehoods would readily spread around the small village, but the Internet lacks the village's corrective of familiarity. In the small village, people had a long history together and knew the whole story about an individual. But now someone reading an online report about some faraway stranger rarely knows the whole story – the reader has only fragments

9. See Westacott, *Virtues of Our Vices*, 69–70, for a discussion as to how even a pro-gossip perspective is altered by the Internet in the direction of greater caution. It should also be noted that, while the Internet and its technology have radically altered the nature of communications, some components of the Internet culture, such as social interactivity and anonymity, have been elements of discourse for centuries, as documented in great detail by Tom Standage in his book *Writing on the Wall: Social Media, The First 2000 Years* (New York: Bloomsbury, 2013).

> of information, and when little is invested in a personal relationship, even information that is incomplete and of dubious veracity might be enough to precipitate ridicule, shunning, and reproach.
>
> The rapid information-spreading power of the Internet can be a virtue too. Judge Richard Posner points out: "The blogosphere as a whole has a better error-correction machinery than the conventional media do. The rapidity with which vast masses of information are pooled and sifted leaves the conventional media in the dust. Not only are there millions of blogs, and thousands of bloggers who specialize, but, what is more, readers post comments that augment the blogs, and the information in those comments, as in the blogs themselves, zips around blogland at the speed of electronic transmission."[10]

However, as Solove points out, this favorable aspect to error correction on the Internet is not absolute, and various factors can contribute to the full truth either not making it to the screen, or making it too slowly to offset the damage. Further, if a premise of *lashon hara* is that even factually true information can present an incomplete or unjustly harmful picture, we have more reason to be concerned. It is extremely unlikely that factually accurate items will be challenged, at least not to the degree that the risks of *lashon hara* will be mitigated.

In his book *The Watercooler Effect*, Nicholas DiFonzo argues that the tendency of online users to interact primarily with those with whom they identify outweighs the potential benefit of diversity that the World Wide Web otherwise offers. He advises,

> For the rumor consumer then, one question is, Has this rumor been checked or independently verified? And to what extent is the group able to check, given its motivational inclinations, sources of insider information, expertise on issues pertinent to the hearsay, group standards for evidence, diversity of opinions,

10. Solove, *Future of Reputation*, 37–38.

> and discussion activity? By estimating the group's capacity to check a particular rumor, one can get a rough sense of the accuracy base rate.[11]

These guidelines are emblematic of some of the mental safeguards that are wise to implement when engaging with the content on the Internet and in similar contexts. Awareness of the impact that the environment may have on truth is crucial for taking that which is valuable and leaving behind that which is not.[12]

GROUP POLARIZATION

Another element that is exacerbated by certain aspects of the Internet is the group polarization effect. As discussed earlier, there is a tendency for like-minded people who associate with each other to intensify their beliefs in one direction and to emerge more convinced and more extreme in their views. This tendency can again detract from the likelihood of accuracy emerging.

As William H. Davidow puts it in his book, *Overconnected: The Promise And Threat of the Internet*:

> Contagions, as we know, are spread through interconnections. And there is no medium for interconnection quite like the Internet for helping them flourish. It is inexpensive and fast. And unlike conventional media, it enables participants to listen and speak, making them feel more a part of things.... Thought contagions are driven by positive feedback processes. The key to initiating and sustaining them is the ability to recruit new participants. For contagion to exist, at least one new member must be added for everyone lost. The Internet is an ideal vehicle for supporting this positive feedback. Since the Internet's reach is

---

11. DiFonzo, *Watercooler Effect*, 184–85.
12. For a book length treatment of how the elements of the Internet facilitate falsehood to previously unheard of levels, see Charles Seife, *Virtual Unreality: Just Because the Internet Told You, How Do You Know It's True?* (New York: Viking, 2014). The issue is considered from a different angle in Eli Pariser, *Filter Bubble*.

> global, the number of people an idea can reach for a minimal cost is very large. For one thing, potential believers can find like-minded groups just by doing a simple Internet search. For another, once people meet in virtual space, the Internet provides valuable data, in the form of text and images that can reinforce the idea. Finally, the Internet can be used to organize remote groups to recruit new believers.

Further, Davidow quotes technology writer Nicholas G. Carr who notes in his discussion of the tendency for slight biases to lead to segregation:

> In the real world, with its mortgages and schools and jobs and moving vans, the "mechanical forces" of segregation move fairly slowly; there are brakes on the speed with which we pull up stakes and change where we live. In Internet communities, there are no such constraints. Making a community defining decision is as simple as clicking on a link – adding the feed to your blog reader, say, or a friend to your social network. Given the presence of a slight bias to be connected to people similar to ourselves, the segregation effect would thus tend to happen much faster – and with even more extreme consequences – on the Internet.[13]

THE COST OF SPEED

The pace of discussion on the Internet, whether on news sites, opinion sites, or blogs, can also work against accuracy. In contrast with traditional news outlets in earlier generations, when the news was delivered at regular, spaced-out intervals, the current climate places no limitation on how quickly information can be disseminated, resulting in pressure to do so at the earliest possible opportunity, for a variety of reasons.[14]

---

13. William H. Davidow, *Overconnected: The Promise and Threat of the Internet* (Harrison, NY: Delphinium Books, 2011), pp. 156–159.
14. See Howard Rosenberg and Charles S. Feldman, *No Time to Think: The Menace of Media Speed and the 24-Hour News Cycle* (New York: Continuum, 2008), p. 84, 107n, and throughout.

As Bill Kovach and Tom Rosensteil note in their book *Blur: How to Know What's True in the Age of Information Overload,* it is often no longer the case that the process of journalism has the time necessary to analyze, interpret, and assess the "ingredients" of the news and thus develop a fully formed product. This reality, which intensified in earlier years with the advent of twenty-four-hour news channels, often means that the "raw ingredients of journalism – the rumor, innuendo, allegation, accusation, charge, supposition, and hypothesis – get passed on to the audience directly. The ingredients become the product."[15]

In his book *Too Big to Know,* David Weinberger elaborates on this aspect of the Internet as follows:

> It's hard to tell exactly how much stupider we are as a culture thanks to the Net because the previous media tended to make hard-won truths globally available while keeping ignorance local: What got published generally was what made it through careful, albeit imperfect, filters, whereas the niggling falsehoods flourished outside the broadcast towers. Nevertheless, it seems undeniable that falsehoods now find a wider audience and lodge themselves in that audience more firmly than ever.[16]

THE ONLINE DISINHIBITION EFFECT

A major environmental shift engendered by the Internet is what has been labeled by psychologists as the online disinhibition effect. This refers to the reality that one who is operating behind the protection of a computer screen often discards proper inhibitions such as moral standards, sensitivity, and empathy towards others, and becomes capable of egregious interpersonal behavior that they would otherwise abhor.

This disinhibition stems from a number of factors. On the one hand, being physically disconnected from the subject of one's comments decreases the ability to empathize with that person.

However, there is another element here as well, which was documented long before the advance of the Internet. When one is placed

---

15. Kovach and Rosenstiel, *Blur,* 41.

16. Weinberger, *Too Big to Know,* 156.

in a context which deemphasizes his personal identity and assimilates him into a larger population, he becomes less grounded in his personal standards and more susceptible to the pressures of the many, even if that involves the behaviors which he would otherwise consider objectionable. This is referred to as "deindividuation," and was displayed by psychologist Philip Zimbardo (who also conducted the well-known Stanford prison experiment) in 1969, and has wide ranging effects.[17]

Certainly, all these negative consequences are exacerbated significantly when anonymity is added into the mix. Anonymity has the effect not only of deindividuating the people involved but also insulating them from the consequences of their actions, not only those externally imposed but even those stemming from their own internal recognition of the ramifications of their actions.

We noted earlier the exchange in Plato's *Republic* concerning whether one could be expected to remain moral if one was invisible. If we assume that there are offenses that can be committed in the realm of speech, it then follows that such offenses will be more rampant when the offenders cannot be seen or identified by others.

However, while anonymity contributes significantly to the online disinhibition effect, it is not the only element, or even a necessary one. As Dr. Elias Aboujaoude writes in his book *Virtually You: The Dangerous Powers of the E-Personality*:

> Anonymity can make it possible for people to "convince themselves that those online behaviors 'aren't me at all,'" writes [Rider University psychologist Dr. John] Suhler. If they "aren't me," it follows that they don't reflect on me and that I'm not responsible for their consequences. This gives us carte blanche to engage in them with more abandon. As we will see, however, and as anyone who has ever sent an impulsive e-mail or text to a boss, colleague, or friends will agree, lack of anonymity hardly protects us from disinhibited actions. Some of our most regrettable online gaffes carry our proud signatures at the bottom of the message.

17. See Philip Zimbardo, *The Lucifer Effect* (New York: Random House, 2007), and McRaney, *You Are Now Less Dumb*, ch. 14.

> Like anonymity, being invisible also encourages online disinhibition.... Being out of sight facilitates problematic actions, not to mention all sorts of outpourings over e-mail, on blogs, and text messages, and in chat rooms.... As Suhler reminds us, people in real life will avert their eyes and look away when discussing something personal or embarrassing.... Not seeing who we are interacting with increases the chance of a heart-to-heart and of unrestrained effusions of the very personal kind. Depending on what it is that gets shared and whom we are sharing it with, that is not necessarily a good thing.

Dr. Aboujaoude also identifies some other elements of this phenomenon:

> The absence of the face-to-face cues that normally guide our offline interactions can erase boundaries among people in cyberspace, also contributing to disinhibition in the virtual world.... Finally, the lack of true status differential in cyberspace also encourages disinhibition. Typically, authority figures, such as parents, teachers, and police officers, announce and assert themselves through various visible trappings of strength and influence that arrived with them. Online, however, people are separated from the real-life markers of their authority. On the Internet's level playing field, everyone is equal and equal to the megabytes per second speed of his connection. We are all peers in cyberspace, and what's a little disinhibition among friends?[18]

Of course, disinhibition has an impact on a wide range of transgressions, not only that of *lashon hara*. The Torah and the Talmud strongly prohibit

18. Elias Aboujaoude, *Virtually You: The Dangerous Powers of the E-Personality* (New York: W. W. Norton, 2011), pp. 40–42, and see also pp. 98–102 (and throughout, as this is essentially the theme of the entire book). See also John Freeman, *The Tyranny of E-mail* (New York: Scribner, 2009), p. 5 and pp. 152–53; Robin M. Kowalski, Sue P. Limber, and Patricia W. Agatston, *Cyberbullying: Bullying in the Digital Age* (Malden, MA: Wiley-Blackwell, 2012), pp. 86–88; and Larry D. Rosen, Nancy A. Cheever, and L. Mark Carrier, *IDisorder: Understanding Our Obsession with Technology and Overcoming Its Hold on Us* (New York: Palgrave Macmillan, 2012), pp. 10–11.

inflicting emotional anguish on others unnecessarily. However, empirical evidence will clearly display that the sensitivity that routinely exists in personal interactions is often absent online. One need only look at the comments on the news sites when a tragedy is reported. The commenters are aware that the family members will usually see these comments, and yet allow themselves to write things that they would never express verbally to a mourner.

Broadly speaking, empathy suffers when the subjects are invisible. As Adam Smith put it 250 years ago, "if [a man] were to lose his little finger tomorrow, he would not sleep tonight; but provided he never see them, he would snore with the most profound security over the ruin of a hundred million of his brethren."[19] Theoretically and often practically, the Internet can serve as a corrective to such loss of empathy, allowing a more direct exposure to the suffering of others who may be thousands of miles away. However, as often or perhaps more often, the nature of the interactions is such that the default mode of discourse is one in which the other is hidden from sight. In her book *Quiet*, Susan Cain quotes a 2010 University of Michigan study that maintained that college students are 40 percent less empathetic than thirty years prior, a finding that the authors speculate is related to prevalence of social media, in addition to reality TV, and "hyper-competitiveness."[20]

As Paul J. Zak puts it in his book *The Moral Molecule*:

> No one has proven it, but there's also the worry that lack of immediate feedback, as well as anonymity, may in some cases diminish empathy, which might account for the kind of cyberbullying that's already become a serious problem in teenage culture online.... Simply put, while technology creates new opportunities for connection, it can sometimes provide new opportunities for neglect.[21]

---

19. "The Theory of Moral Sentiments" (1750), quoted in Davidow, *Overconnected,* p. 184.
20. Cain, *Quiet,* p. 141. See also Susan Greenfield, *Mindchange: How Digital Technologies Are Leaving Their Marks on our Brains* (New York: Random House, 2015), pp. 36–37.
21. Zak, *Moral Molecule,* 195. See also, on this topic, William Powers, *Hamlet's Blackberry: A Practical Philosophy for Building a Good Life in the Digital Age* (New York, Harper, 2010).

On the other end of the experience, the necessary and religiously obligatory process of apology and reconciliation after an offense can also be undermined by the cultural changes generated by the Internet. As Sherry Turkle puts it in her book *Alone Together*:

> Technology makes it easy to blur the line between confession and apology, easy to lose sight of what an apology is, not only because online spaces offer themselves as "cheap" alternatives to confronting other people but because we may come to the challenge of an apology already feeling disconnected from other people. In that state, we forget that what we do affects others. Young people, bruised by online skirmishes, can be the most articulate about looking back to the best practices of the past in the pursuit of a classic apology. Two sophomore girls at Silver Academy make the point that there is too much online apology going around. For one, "Texting an apology is really impersonal. You can't hear their voice. They could be sarcastic, and you wouldn't know." The other agrees: "It's harder to say 'Sorry' than text it, and if you're the one receiving the apology, you know it's hard for the person to say 'Sorry.' But that is what helps you forgive the person – that they're saying it in person, that they actually have the guts to actually want to apologize." In essence, both young women are saying that forgiveness follows from the experience of empathy. You see someone is unhappy for having hurt you. You feel sure that you are standing together with them. When we live a large part of our personal lives online, these complex empathetic transactions become more elusive. We get used to getting less.[22]

It is thus unsurprising that anonymity has been shown to play a major role in what has been termed "cyberbullying." As related by the authors of *Cyberbullying: Bullying in the Digital Age*:

> The anonymity afforded by electronic communications is a much bigger factor than one might think at first blush, and may be

22. Sherry Turkle, *Alone Together: Why We Expect More from Technology and Less from Each Other* (New York: Basic Books, 2010), pp. 233–34.

> responsible for cyberbullying having such a strong intimidation factor associated with it. In a survey that we conducted examining the incidence of cyberbullying among over 3,700 middle school children, close to 50% of the individuals did not know the identity of the perpetrator (Kowalski & Limber, 2007). Among college students, this statistic jumped to 60% (Kowalski et al., 2012). [Researcher F.] Mishna and her colleagues (2009) found that many youth do not find out who cyberbullied them until much later, only to then determine that it was someone known to them, such as a classmate.[23]

FURTHER ASPECTS OF ANONYMITY

Continuing on the subject of anonymity, there is much to consider about its effects, which go beyond the sense (and reality) of the impunity it bestows. This is not to assert that there is never a need or a value to anonymity; there are certainly instances where grave injustices persist because those who would call attention to them are intimidated or, worse, prevented from objecting due to fear that their names be disclosed. There are entire societies where tyranny prevails and thrives on the ability to squelch all dissent, and the only hope that exists is protest by individuals or groups that are beyond the sphere of retaliation by the authorities.[24]

Very importantly, there are offenses that are so personal that victims may never come forward if they had to do so openly and publicly; indeed, much deep and lasting trauma has been caused or intensified as a result. On a more basic level, there are matters of importance and significance that cannot benefit fully from discussion and analysis if the discussion participants cannot engage without identifying themselves.[25]

Nonetheless, these very real factors must be weighed against and analyzed in light of the many complications imposed by anonymity. If the

---

23. Kowalski, Limber, and Agatston, *Cyberbullying*, p. 86.
24. Although it should be noted that the properties of the Internet can also work to strengthen tyranny and limit liberties, as argued by Evgeny Morozov in his book *The Net Delusion: The Dark Side of Internet Freedom (How Not to Liberate the World)* (New York: Public Affairs, 2011).
25. For an argument in favor of anonymity on the Internet, see Cole Stryker, *Hacking the Future: Privacy, Identity, and Anonymity on the Web* (New York: Overlook Duckworth, 2012).

advantages are to be realized, these issues must be accounted for, most prominently the possibility that the speaker is saying something false, or otherwise subject to justified societal sanction, and is more able to do so because of the lack of accountability that accompanies anonymity. Similarly, other effects of anonymity can either diminish its benefits or create offenses so egregious that they cannot be dismissed.

Since the Internet provides an unprecedented vehicle for anonymous interaction, any assessment of its impact must consider both the serious positive and negative elements of anonymity.[26] This need is intensified by the view held by some that anonymity is not only a feature of the Internet, but a defining element. As Lee Seigel puts it in the epilogue to his book *Against the Machine: Being Human in the Age of the Electronic Mob*:

> Such absolute liberation from constraints is why anonymity is so widespread on the Internet, and why everything on the Internet tends toward anonymity: the hidden solitude of sitting before the screen; the spectral half-person presence of being online: the sense of yourself and of other people as having no boundaries. After expertise, authority, and merit have fallen away as obstacles, identity remains the last barrier to the vicarious, acquisitive, totally accessing, fully participating Internet will. Anonymity, you might say, is the Internet's ultimate identity. If you are not who you are, you can be anyone you wish to be. The husband and father can be a fleet-footed single man; the political operative can assume an innocent nonpartisan voice; the blogger can throw his mediocrity into a tantrum of entitlement and tower over the famous novelist. Identity is the last inhibitor to "previously managed drives and desires." Once you can shift in and out of different lives, you can shift in and out of different markets.[27]

---

26. For further discussion of the positives and negatives of Internet anonymity, see Scott Rosenberg, *Say Everything: How Blogging Began, What It's Becoming, and Why It Matters* (New York: Crown, 2009), chs. 6, 10; Andrews, *I Know Who You Are*, 72–73; and Turkle, *Alone Together*, ch. 12. For further discussion about the negative effects of anonymity, see Fertik and Thompson, *Wild West*, ch. 5.
27. Lee Siegel, *Against the Machine: Being Human in the Age of the Electronic Mob* (New York: Spiegel and Grau, 2008), pp. 175–76.

The experience of anonymity seems to have an impact upon personality beyond simply concealing one's identity and protecting one from repercussions. It loosens inhibitions on a more subconscious level. In her book *Sidetracked,* Francisca Gino relates a study she conducted in which participants who were being paid to solve problems on a test were found to cheat more frequently when they were in a darkly lit room. The important element of the experiment is that this finding emerged even though the participants could not be seen by others regardless of the degree of lighting; all the darkness did was increase the feeling of anonymity on the part of the actor. As she puts it:

> We reasoned that, beyond simply producing conditions of actual anonymity, darkness may create a sense of what we referred to as illusory anonymity. This type of anonymity is likely to loosen inhibitions surrounding dishonest behaviors such as lying and cheating. People in a room with a slightly different lighting, we reasoned, may feel anonymous not because the relative darkness has reduced others' ability to see or identify them (which it hasn't), but because they are anchored in their own experience of darkness. When people experience impaired vision as a result of darkness, they might unconsciously generalize that experience and expect that others will conversely find it difficult to perceive or see them, even when these others are sitting in a different location (such as another room). Just as small children close their eyes and believe that others can't see them, the experience of darkness, we theorized, would trigger the belief that we are warded from others' attentions and inspections.... Although darkness had no bearing on actual anonymity, it still increased morally questionable behaviors.[28]

In what might be termed a vicious paradox, anonymity on the Internet can actually make items more credible, rather than less credible.

28. Gino, *Sidetracked,* 199–203.

Dr. Robert Goldberg, writing out of concern for the effect of the Internet on reliable medical information, describes the process as follows:

> This situation is constructed to be self-reinforcing through links to other sites offering the same information and beliefs. An accusation made by one person can quickly get picked up by dozens more and repeated over and over. For those who believe it, the reality does not matter. The charge is simply accepted as truth and then repeated, spread onward from one site in articles, post, comments, and e-mails. Rendered anonymous by the web, contributors are no longer constrained by the mores that hold in face-to-face conversations; their criticisms grow ever larger, their language ever more hyperbolic, and their positions ever more radical and hardened. Over time, it becomes difficult to trace the original source of a claim, so the allegation acquires a patina of respectability, no matter its reliability. After enough repetition, a newcomer stumbling on such information on this or that website has no way of knowing that the indictment is even debatable. Because society has already gone a long way down the road of eroding trust in the scientific and medical communities, conflict-of-interest accusations often feel plausible, and that is enough for them to be taken unquestioningly. Even those who are skeptical will find that checking the veracity of such charges is difficult or impossible with the resources available. This leaves those who doubt the truth of the claim on the defensive, caught up in a "he said, she said situation" where the outcome rests not on evidence, but on who can tap into the emotions and biases of the onlookers more effectively. It isn't about science; it's about solidarity — about keeping, and energizing followers.[29]

These effects of anonymity pose genuine concerns relating to *lashon hara* as well as to general civility and decency. These factors must be given considerable weight when evaluating whether or not the allowance of

29. Robert Goldberg, *Tabloid Medicine: How the Internet Is Being Used to Hijack Medical Science for Fear and Profits* (New York: Kaplan, 2010), pp. 95–96.

anonymity is an appropriate policy for those controlling a given Internet context, and also how the presence of anonymity should be entered into the consumer's assessment of the contents in front of him. It is unsurprising that major newspapers have reportedly been regretting and reevaluating policies to allow anonymous commenting, and the attitude is certainly understandable, considering the effects in evidence.[30]

TONE MISREADING

In light of the concerns that the laws of *lashon hara* place on accuracy of detail and intent, correct interpretation of the tone of the statement is crucially necessary. As we have seen, it is possible to disparage another by conveying a demeaning message through tone and implication, even without any negative speech. As such, appropriate communication through e-mail and the Internet requires an awareness of how tone in discourse over the electronic media is perceived and assessed.

Indeed, the absence of face-to-face interaction and other visual cues, or audible indications, does often result in serious misinterpretation. In his book *The Tyranny of E-mail,* John Freeman quotes a survey in the *Journal of Personality and Social Psychology* that readers misunderstand the tone of an e-mail 50 percent of the time.[31]

In his book *Mindwise,* Nicholas Epley describes a study he performed with a collaborator in which he similarly found that communications through text messages were correctly understood only about 50 percent of the time, in contrast with the same messages transmitted over the phone. (The test subjects were asked to assess whether a statement was sincere or sarcastic.) What was particularly disturbing, though, is that regardless of the error rate the speaker consistently felt that he was

30. George Brock, *Out of Print: Newspapers, Journalism and the Business of News in the Digital Age* (London: Kogan Page, 2013), p. 116.

31. Freeman, *Tyranny of E-mail,* pp. 5ff. Shlomo Breznitz, in his *Maximum Brainpower: Challenging the Brain for Health and Wisdom* (New York: Ballantine Books, 2012), p. 222, associates this statistic with teenagers, as opposed to adults, and adds, "If they are seldom face-to-face, how will young people improve their ability to gauge one another's psychological state?" See also the studies discussed and the personal experiences related by Giles Slade in his *The Big Disconnect: The Story of Technology and Loneliness* (Amherst, NY: Prometheus Books, 2012), pp. 237–38.

transmitting the message clearly, and what's more, the listener equally frequently believed he was interpreting the message correctly. As the author puts it, "People using ambiguous mediums think they are communicating clearly because they know what they *mean* to say, receivers are unable to get this meaning accurately but are certain that they have *interpreted* the message accurately, and both are amazed that the other side can be so stupid."[32]

This phenomenon can also play a significant role in exacerbating cyberbullying as well. As noted by the authors of *Cyberbullying: Bullying in the Digital Age*:

> The inability to read the emotional reaction of the other also extends from victim to perpetrator. There are no contextual cues for the victim to use to interpret the messages that they receive. In face-to-face interactions, victims can scan the faces of potential bullies or individuals they perceive to be hurting their feelings for signs that a tease is really just a tease. Teases that are accompanied by winks, smiles, or the like may convey information to the target regarding the prosocial nature of a tease (Campos, Keltner, Beck, Gonzaga, & John, 2007). When communicating electronically, however, targets cannot see the faces of the perpetrator. Thus, they have no means of "reading" the intentions of the perpetrator through nonverbal behaviors.... When we communicate sarcasm, for example, over e-mail, we can "hear" the sarcasm in the sentences as we type them. However, the same sarcastic tone is not being played for the receiver. Thus, what may begin as "innocent" teasing over e-mail or instant messaging may be taken for something other than what was intended. The result could be a flaming war or some other type of cyberbullying.[33]

ADJUSTMENT OF EXPECTATIONS

The laws of *lashon hara* are particularly sensitive to context and to a balance of all relevant factors in the creation of a complete picture. As

32. Epley, *Mindwise*, 108–9.
33. Kowalski, Limber, and Agatston, *Cyberbullying*, pp. 87–88.

such, it is also significant to consider how the Internet might create a distorted image, as certain facts are likely to be more prominent in that arena while others might be less so or absent, resulting in a disproportionate presentation that is at odds with the actuality of real life. Accordingly, allowing a search engine, however powerful, to dictate what should be the most important facts (true or false) about a person's life may be terribly unfair. As Siva Vaidhyanathan puts it in his book, *The Googlization of Everything*, "Faith in Google is dangerous not because of anything specific that Google does. It's dangerous because of how we allow it to affect our expectations and information about the world. Using Google habitually raises our expectations about matters both deep and shallow."[34]

Similarly, the authors of *Wild West 2.0* term the skewed reality that can emerge from building a picture based only on that which is prominently available on the Internet as the "Google Truth." This is defined as "Not the actual truth. Instead ... the stylized caricature version of reality that appears in a Google search for your name or the name of your business ... [it] may appear superficially accurate, but it is often incomplete and sometimes flat wrong."[35]

More pointedly, technology critic Evgeny Morozov argues that efforts to catalogue information on the Internet are hampered by "information reductionism," essentially the belief that ideas exist autonomously and independent of the context of their original form. As he puts it, "the quest to organize the world's knowledge cannot proceed without doing at least some violence to the knowledge it seeks to organize."[36]

"ACCEPTANCE" ISSUES

Concerns such as those mentioned above highlight some of the unique challenges the Internet poses not only to the risk of disseminating *lashon hara*, but also to the prohibition of accepting *lashon hara*. As we have seen,

34. Vaidhyanathan, Siva, *The Googlization of Everything* (Berkeley: University of California Press, 2010), p. 80.
35. Fertik and Thompson, *Wild West 2.0*, throughout.
36. Morozov, Evgeny, *To Save Everything, Click Here: Smart Machines, Dumb Humans, and the Myth of Technological Perfectionism* (New York: Perseus, 2013), pp. 85–89.

there are a number of components to this precept, and correspondingly there are a number of areas that require particular attention.

First, we have seen that one who is on the receiving end of *lashon hara* must be careful not to act in a way that endorses or supports the offending speech. As such, we must evaluate to what degree clicking on websites, and all the more so linking to a website or distributing a link, acts as an extension and facilitation of the original message. Of course, these acts are sometimes necessary in order to counter a false or unjust message, and thus a careful cost-benefit analysis is sometimes called for.

Beyond this, there is the issue of the internal relationship to the information being presented. As we have seen, being a responsible, informed citizen often requires listening or reading certain otherwise objectionable material, while at the same time creating a greater space between that basic intake and full-blown accepting. The Internet allows more of that possibly necessary information to get to more people faster than ever before, while at the same time presenting greater risks of false or distorted information disseminating with equal efficiency.

Achieving this balance requires creating a space between intake and acceptance that allows for an evaluation of the credibility and the value of the information being presented. Such a process involves being sensitized to all the ways that the Internet can affect the message that it conveys, and indeed all the manners in which any news source might transmit a false or incomplete picture. Bill Kovach and Tom Rosensteil, in their book *Blur*, advocate what they call "the way of skeptical knowing" which involves six evaluative steps: (1) identifying what kind of content is being encountered, and questioning: (2) if a news account is complete; (3) how sources are assessed; (4) how evidence is assessed; (5) how the evidence is being used; and (6) if the news source is providing what the consumers need to know.[37]

37. Kovach and Rosenstiel, *Blur*, throughout. Lee Rainie and Barry Wellman, in their book *Networked*, refer to this awareness as "skepticism literacy" (pp. 273–74), and Clay Johnson's entire book *The Information Diet* is devoted to concepts such as this.

There is another aspect of the Internet that poses a challenge in this area. Ironically, hyperaccurate factual recording might ultimately be at odds with truth, in the sense of the complete picture that requires a balancing of all relevant details, including those that are not as meticulously recorded on the web. Evgeny Morozov discusses this issue at length in his *To Save Everything Click Here*. Challenging those who believe that extensive and detailed archiving is an unmitigated public good, he writes:

> We might very well ask for the truth in court – but why assume that the entire field of social interactions is like our legal system?... And does our legal system function [that way]? As information scholar Jean-Francois Blanchette points out, "court proceedings are ruled by elaborate rules governing the admissibility and evaluation of evidence, and the most cursory examination of these rules cannot fail to point to the fact the courts have, thanks to the adversarial process, a sophisticated understanding of the technological mediation of evidence." Evidence might be "true" – whatever that means – but it may still be disregarded.

Morozov continues by noting the complexity of the issue:

> The idea that we somehow have a duty to always remember the wrongdoing and the suffering we have endured rests on dubious moral foundations. Theologian Miroslav Volf attacks it head-on in *The End of Memory*. Volf argues that we need not presume that remembering will always yield morally superior results than forgetting. He writes, "Instead of simply protecting a person, memory may wound another. Instead of generating solidarity with victims, it may breed indifference and reinforce cycles of violence. Instead of truthfully acknowledging wrongdoings, it may bolster a victim's false self-perceptions and unjust demands. Instead of healing wounds, it may simply reinjure." Or it may do none of those things – a possibility of which Volf is acutely aware. The point is that...we should not presume that remembering is the right thing to do in each and every case. [Technological] solutionism

> cannot replace moral reasoning; we should not let it dictate solutions presumed to be right only by virtue of being easy.[38]

It is important to reemphasize that this argument is not advocating the automatic erasure of misdeeds, nor denying that at times the preservation of such memories is a crucial and necessary part of healing, progressing, obtaining justice, or protecting the innocent. The point is merely that the existence of technology that can archive in greater and greater detail certain aspects of the history, while omitting others, is not automatically in the interest of any of these important goals; an independent moral analysis must take place, and that analysis must correct for the influence of such technology and assign it its proper place.

OTHER ISSUES OF *LASHON HARA* AND THE INTERNET

Some of the themes that emerge from the conceptual underpinnings of the laws of *lashon hara* find particular relevance in the world of the Internet. To give one example, we noted earlier the understanding of the authors of Tosafot regarding the talmudic exclusions from the classification of *lashon hara* of speech said in public or in the presence of the subject. According to this understanding, the exclusions reflect the assumption that a speaker who is making statements in such settings could be safely assumed to be expressing only positive or neutral sentiments. However, it is hard to argue that this assumption applies in the modern era. Items are placed on the World Wide Web, not merely in the presence of three people but before several billion, which more often than not will be seen by the subject as well. Nonetheless, this degree of exposure does nothing to temper the negativity that is expressed in this venue. Clearly, the assumption of the Tosafists in their interpretation of the Talmud must be adjusted to fit the contemporary context. If it is indeed true that our online interactions have fundamentally altered the nature of our discourse, the impact that has on the civility of that

38. Morozov, *Click Here*, pp. 270–80. At some points in his analysis, Morozov advocates the value of "deception," although such endorsement is not necessary to recognize the value of his argument that archiving does not always convey a complete truth for all moral purposes.

discourse, and the moral and religious implications associated with that, must be carefully considered.[39]

In addition, we have seen that the concept of *avak lashon hara* teaches that not only is one responsible for the words he actually says but also for the statements he evokes from others. From the perspective of Jewish law, this places a responsibility on an individual far beyond that which he writes on the Internet, to include that which one elicits and hosts, for example in an open comments section.

The risk of transgressing the laws of *avak lashon hara* is further exacerbated by the significantly broader audience on the web. In face-to-face conversation, it is possible for one to realistically assume that no one present bears animosity towards the subject of conversation and thus to rely on that assessment to speak positively about someone without fear of evoking a rebuttal from the audience. However, on the World Wide Web it is increasingly difficult to find any subject or individual, no matter how seemingly uncontroversial, that does not have passionate opponents who will argue with any positive assessments. While it is difficult to conclude practically that this reality means nothing positive can be said about anyone, it does place a greater responsibility on one who writes on the Internet to act carefully, at least in regard to the hosting of comments and reactions and their potential for *lashon hara*.

On this subject, the words of Rabbeinu Yonah, discussed earlier, both illuminate the problem and point in the direction of a solution.[40] He asserts that the concern about evoking criticism while praising someone is particularly applicable when the audience is a large one, the factor that is exacerbated in the case of information disseminated on the World Wide Web. However, he also notes that it is possible to create a context in which even a large audience would not foster inappropriate disparagement. This environment, in his formulation, is one in which an attacker would be exposed for his injustice and would feel that his negativity is unwelcome. Applied in the modern context of the

39. For a technical discussion of the positions of *Tosafot* and the contrasting position of Maimonides, and the implications for dissemination via the Internet, see Rabbi Avraham Maimon HaLevi, *Derekh HaAtarim,* ch. 53.

40. *Shaarei Teshuva* 3:226.

Internet, this would discourage anonymity and encourage a controlled and fair atmosphere.[41]

An additional concern regarding Internet usage and *lashon hara* involves linking and forwarding. Earlier, we noted that those actions may at times constitute an act of acceptance of *lashon hara*. A different violation could occur if the linking or forwarding is carried out with the intent of displaying the inadequacy or ineptitude of someone else's writing. The *Ḥafetz Ḥayim* explicitly forbids showing someone a letter that another has written from which it is clear that the writer is lacking in wisdom or intelligence or the like, even if no explicit disparaging commentary is provided.[42] The ease with which one can forward an e-mail or a link has made this concern an even more real one, and thus it is important to become sensitized to the damage that can be caused.

PRIVACY ISSUES

We have also seen that the conceptual basis of the laws of *lashon hara* places importance upon the values of modesty and privacy, even when the subjects themselves do not fully appreciate such values. Accordingly, if the online culture to any extent detracts from these values, it is important to be aware of that reality and to make the required corrections.

Andrew Potter, in his book the *Authenticity Hoax: How We Get Lost Finding Ourselves*, laments the confusion of authenticity with self-revelation:

> Perhaps there is a flaw in the ideal of authenticity as complete disclosure. To see what it might be, let's think back to why transparency was ever seen as a virtue in the first place. Remember that for Rousseau, the aspiration was to bring your deepest thoughts, feelings, and aspirations into line with how others perceive you. That is, the authentic project is to bring the outer appearance

41. The word he uses is for the speech that is to be discouraged is *shav*, which, as we have seen, can refer either to falsehood or nonpurposeful speech.

42. *Ḥafetz Ḥayim, Laws of Lashon HaRa, klal* 1, *Be'er Mayim Ḥayim* 14, See also *Ḥelkat Binyamin, Laws of Lashon HaRa, klal* 1, 13; *Ali Be'er* pp. 45–46; *Zera Ḥayim*, 1, 1:5; *He'arot Rigshei Ḥayim*, pp. 76–77; and Rabbi Yitzḥak Sorotzkin, *Rinat Yitzḥak*, Kings, p. 34.

> and inner sentiment into alignment, to become who you feel yourself to be, and have others recognize you as that person. But this project was never about merely telling facts about yourself. More than that, it was seen as a moral achievement, the result of a long, arduous, and artistic process of self-creation. That is why the Facebook-style habit of promiscuous disclosure very much misses the point, because what makes transparency and openness valuable is that there is a voluntary and somewhat discretionary aspect to it.... Honesty, trust, intimacy, discretion: these are ... the public virtues of a liberal democracy, founded on the promise that there is a distinct, if constantly evolving, line between matters that are in the public interest and those that are, and ought to remain, private.[43]

Similarly, as Lori Andrews puts it in *I Know Who You Are and I Saw What You Did*:

> Control over private information is essential to respect, friendship, love, trust, and personal liberty, according to privacy scholar Charles Fried. We achieve intimacy with other people by parceling out information about ourselves bit by bit. Each new revelation demonstrates additional trust. It's healthy to be able to show different aspects of ourselves in different settings. We need to explore or grow without our former digital lives coming back to haunt us. Disclosure of private posts and e-mails can be emotionally devastating. In fact, psychiatrists and philosophers disagree completely with the Facebook founder's notion that all information about a person should be "transparent." Philosopher Sissela Bok says, "Control over secrecy provides a safety valve for individuals in the midst of communal life.... Psychosis has been described as the breaking down of the delineation between the self and the outside world: the person going mad "flows out onto the world as through a broken dam." Privacy is also the way we maintain civility and dignity in the larger society. Robert Post,

43. Potter, *Authenticity Hoax*, 166–69.

> the dean of Yale Law School, says, "'privacy' is simply a label we use to identify one aspect of the many forms of respect by which we maintain a community. It is less important that the purity of the label be maintained, than that the forms of community life of which it is a part be preserved."[44]

Andrew Keen, in his book *Digital Vertigo: How Today's Online Social Revolution Is Dividing, Diminishing, and Disorienting Us,* argues against the perspective that "social utopians" who maintain that the culture of public exposure will create a more understanding and sympathetic society. Citing multiple contrary anecdotes, he asserts:

> There is little evidence that networks like Facebook, Skype and Twitter are making us any more forgiving or tolerant. Indeed, if anything, these viral tools of mass exposure seem to be making society not only more prurient and voyeuristic, but also fueling a mob culture of intolerance, schadenfreude and revengefulness.[45]

It is important to emphasize that many of these points are arguable, and are not meant to suggest that the Internet is exclusively and inherently harmful. The main message of our observations about the electronic media is that the technology introduces certain ethical and moral challenges into the environment that a responsible user needs to be aware of in order to respond correctly to those challenges. Nicholas Carr, who warns strongly against cognitive effects of the Internet, writes in his book *The Shallows,* "It's possible to think deeply while surfing the Net, just as it's possible to think shallowly while reading a book, but that's not the type of thinking the technology encourages and rewards."[46] We need not go even that far in merely asserting that the Internet generates its effects,

---

44. Andrews, *I Know Who You Are,* p. 133.
45. Andrew Keen, *Digital Vertigo: How Today's Online Social Revolution Is Dividing, Diminishing, and Disorienting Us* (New York: St. Martin's, 2012), pp. 52–56.
46. Nicholas G. Carr, *The Shallows: What the Internet Is Doing to Our Brains* (New York: W. W. Norton, 2010), p. 116.

and those effects should be considered carefully and understood to the greatest extent possible so that the advantages of utilizing the Internet can be maximized while risks can be accounted for.

THE POLITICAL CULTURE AND NEGATIVE CAMPAIGNING

Technically speaking, the prohibition of *lashon hara* likely doesn't apply to a presidential campaign, or in any situation where the information can be crucial to making a decision on an important matter. It might be necessary, as some have noted, to allow the candidates to go at each other mercilessly in order to guarantee that any potentially relevant information will come out. However, that doesn't change the fact what emerges can be misleading, and that voters ignore that fact at their own risk. It is important for voters to be fully informed as to the positives and negatives of the individuals who seek to lead them. It is thus equally important to correct for factors that may detract from the accuracy of what is presented to voters, who eventually come to feel that they are drowning in a sea of slung mud.

Negativity gets an additional edge from the natural inclination to enhance one's self-image at the expense of others. Consequently, the desire to see larger-than-life political figures "cut down to size," coupled with the necessarily zero-sum nature of a competitive election that can have only one winner, further distorts the picture, skewing in a decidedly negative direction.

Add partisan politics into the mix, and a few other factors also come into play. A preexisting political view risks confirmation bias, the tendency to interpret all information through the prism of what you already believe. (This bias is clearly on display after each debate, when Democrats overwhelmingly assign victory to the Democratic candidate, and Republicans to the Republican candidate.) And the habit of fraternizing with others of like political views gives rise to a polarization effect, the likelihood of members of a group to hold views more extreme than they would if they were alone.

This issue is exacerbated by the fact that politics is about winning elections, and negative advertising is simply considered more effective than positive advertising. Negative publicity is far more likely to catch the attention of the voter, and consequentially more likely to motivate action on his part. Further, as Andrew Potter notes, in contrast with the commercial realm, politics is a zero-sum game. In business, purely negative advertising is less prevalent, as it is less likely to be beneficial to a company or a product to simply smear one's competitor. In politics, however, demolishing one's opponent can often produce a direct gain for the attacking candidate.[47]

Clearly, these factors, while possibly very real for the candidates themselves, do nothing to guarantee the accuracy or the fairness of the attacks, and are thus relevant to the laws of *lashon hara*. Even if this is of no concern to the candidates, from an "acceptance" perspective, it should be the concern of the voters.

It is problematic enough that those predisposed to dislike one candidate will be skewed further in that direction by attack politics. What is even more disturbing is a finding described by Dr. Marco Iacoboni in his book *Mirroring People*. In an experiment conducted during the 2004 US presidential campaign, advocates of either John Kerry or George W. Bush registered positive emotions (as measured by neural testing) when shown pictures of their preferred candidates. Several months later, however, after extensive negative campaigning, even supporters failed to display positive emotions in connection with their own presidential preferences.

Dr. Iacoboni, a neurologist at the University of California at Los Angeles, theorizes that "the campaign had tainted all of the candidates, even for their partisan supporters.... Negative ads can create a dangerous emotional disconnect between voters and the leaders who should represent them." He further opines:

> A healthy democracy... needs mechanisms of empathy and identification between the people and their political representatives. Without these unifying emotions, we run the risk of an ever-growing disenchantment with the political system that may make

47. See Potter, *Authenticity Hoax*, 192–99.

> people more receptive to other forms of government... [which] have proved to be much worse than what we have now.[48]

Journalism, the Internet, social media, and political campaigning are all important parts of contemporary society, and they have brought many benefits and made possible many of the basic functions and improvements of modern life. To fully realize their benefits, however, we must be aware of the unique components of all of these arenas and understand the effects they foster. The practical and conceptual principles of the laws of *lashon hara* not only regulate these realms but simultaneously bring important perspectives and correctives to allow the full value of these principles to emerge.

48. See Marco Iacoboni, *Mirroring People: The New Science of How We Connect with Others* (New York: Farrar, Straus and Giroux, 2008), chs. 9–10. See also Stephen Ansolabehere and Shanto Iyengar, *Going Negative: How Political Advertisements Shrink & Polarize the Electorate* (New York: Free Press, 1995). For more about the advantages and disadvantages of negative campaigning, see Emmett H. Buell and Lee Sigelman, *Attack Politics: Negatvity in Presidential Campaigns Since 1960* (Lawrence: University Press of Kansas, 2008).

Further Aspects of the Dual Nature of Lashon HaRa

In an addition to the broader principles we have so far discussed, there are many other more localized and detailed issues within the realm of *lashon hara*. In many cases, the dual nature of *lashon hara*, as speech that is practically harmful and that corrupts character, is relevant in assessing the permissibility or prohibition of each scenario.

NO NAMES

It is popularly assumed that it is permissible to relay derogatory information as long as no names are used. However, some halakhic authorities wonder if this is indeed the case, and some, in fact, conclude that such conversation is forbidden,[1] while others allow if it is clear there will be no harm caused.[2] It should be emphasized that the discussion here is relevant only to a situation where the identity is actually concealed; if

1. See, for example, Rabbi Shimon Eiger-Sofer, *Responsa Hitorerut Teshuva,* vols. I–II, 270. See Rabbi Shabbetai Sofer, *Shaarei De'ah,* to *Mishneh Torah, Laws of Personal Development* 7, who understands such to be the position of Maimonides.
2. See Rabbi Ḥayim Kanievsky, in *She'elat Rav* I, ch. 7, no. 9.

it is at all possible the identity could be discerned, all agree that the law of *lashon hara* is violated.[3]

Those who are stringent in this situation apparently assume that the concealment of the identities to protect the guilty does not eliminate the prohibited nature of the conversation. Indeed, just as a gossip column might relay salacious information without specifying the subject, merely stating that "a well-known politician" has been implicated in some scandal, readers have a prurient interest in such stories even without knowing the identities of the protagonists. This interest can nurture the negative character traits associated with *lashon hara,* and thus pose a problem even when damage is not being inflicted on the subject.[4]

Rabbi Shmuel Hominer, the author of a summary adaptation of the *Ḥafetz Ḥayim*'s writings, asserts that relating *lashon hara* without revealing the name of the subject might not be an act of "talebearing," but is nonetheless a violation of character, and that by reinforcing the perception of the subject in his mind, the speaker himself commits an act of "acceptance" of *lashon hara.*[5] He maintains that such gossip is addressed by the scriptural verses, "let none of you plot evil against his brother in your hearts" (Zech. 7:10) and "And let none of you plot evil in your hearts against his fellow."[6]

However, such conversation might be permitted according to all views if the intent is not to gossip but rather to convey an educational message or cautionary exhortation. In that case, since there is neither harm to the subjects nor a salacious motive, both elements of *lashon hara* appear to be mitigated. Rabbi Hominer acknowledges this as well, but warns that it is necessary to ascertain that all listeners are

3. See *Ikvei Sofer,* to *Responsa Hitorerut Teshuva,* vols. I–II, 270. *Responsa LeḤafetz BaḤayim* II:19, asserts that there is no violation if the identity is incidentally revealed afterward despite the concealment of the speaker. See also III:12.
4. See also Rabbi Aharon Roth, in the journal *Marpei Lashon* II, pp. 16–19.
5. *Ikkarei Dinim, klal* 3, in footnote.
6. Zech. 8:17. See also *Responsa Minḥat Peri,* IV:65. Rabbi Yisrael Pesaḥ Feinhandler, in the journal *Bikkurim* II, pp. 802–4, asserts that if the identity is concealed, there is no violation of the specific prohibition of *lashon hara,* but there are many other prohibitions that may be transgressed, which he proceeds to enumerate.

aware of the motivation, so as to prevent any misunderstanding that would result in the perception of an endorsement of gossip.

WHEN THE SUBJECT DOESN'T CARE

Viewing *lashon hara* as corrupting even when it does not harm the subject poses other questions as well. Included in this list would be a situation in which the subject is unconcerned about what is said about him and permits the disparaging remarks to be said. It might be argued that the victim's acquiescence is only partially helpful; if malicious speech erodes the character, it does so even when the subject does not object.

The *Ḥafetz Ḥayim* appears to allow such conversation when the subject has indicated that he has no objection, although the context of his ruling is the more benign one of a subject who openly discusses his business details, despite the concern that such exposure might be against his interests.[7] Accordingly, he distinguishes between discussions of topics with which the subject has indicated comfort and the speaker intends no harm, which are permitted; and comments with which the speaker intends to disparage the subject, which are prohibited even if the subject has indicated he does not object.[8] What emerges is that speech that demeans, whether in intent or in effect, is prohibited even with the subject's permission; however, the subject does have the latitude to determine that he does not consider certain content to be damaging.[9]

---

7. *Ḥafetz Ḥayim, Laws of Lashon HaRa, klal* 2, 13.
8. *Laws of Lashon HaRa, klal* 2, *Be'er Mayim Ḥayim,* 28.
9. See also *Shaarei Avraham,* pp. 277–83, 286–87; Rabbi Ḥayim Shaul Kaufman, *Mishḥat Shemen* I, p. 335, and *Iyyunim BaParasha,* Numbers, pp. 88–91. Rabbi Moshe David Shapiro argues at length that the subject is entitled to waive objections to speech about him in the journal *Kol Torah* XLII, pp. 391–93. See also *Shemirat HaPeh KeHilkhato,* pp. 84–85, who argues against the possibility of permitting *lashon hara* through the subject's consent, while Rabbi Avraham Yitzḥak HaKohen Kook (*Orot HaRambam, Laws of Personal Development* 5:7, in *Bein Shenei Kohanim Gedolim,* p. 138) maintains that in any event a Torah scholar would not engage in such speech even if it were technically permissible. See also *Tehor Sefatayim,* p. 141. See also *Responsa Minḥat Peri* IV:65, who discusses as well the relaying of information that is disparaging in the eyes of the speaker but not according to the subject. See also *Zeh HaShulḥan,* p. 66.

LASHON HARA ABOUT ONESELF

Similarly, a related question might be whether it is permissible for one to speak disparagingly about oneself. Intuitively, it might be assumed that since, by definition, the speaker does not object or feel he is undergoing any harm, therefore no transgression is taking place. However, negativity in and of itself is harmful, and allowing an individual to be demeaned, even if that individual is the speaker himself, might be problematic.

In *Ḥafetz Ḥayim,* the author appears to permit such speech about oneself,[10] but a story that is told about him, if true, calls into question whether that is indeed his final conclusion. The story, found in several later works and in many different versions, involves something along the following lines: The *Ḥafetz Ḥayim* was traveling to a town in order to lecture on the dangers of *lashon hara.* The driver of his wagon, not recognizing his distinguished passenger, told him that he was fortunate to be traveling to that town on that day, as he would have an opportunity to hear the great *Ḥafetz Ḥayim* speak. Wishing to act modestly, the *Ḥafetz Ḥayim* did not identify himself, but claimed that the *Ḥafetz Ḥayim* was actually not as great as the driver believed. The driver immediately became extremely upset at a disparagement of such a beloved figure, and ejected his passenger from the wagon, not aware that he had just ordered away the subject of his reverence. Reflecting upon the incident, the *Ḥafetz Ḥayim* was heard to remark, "I now realize that it is even wrong to speak *lashon hara* about oneself!"[11]

There is significant discussion in the later literature as to whether the story, true or not, reflects an actual halakhic premise. Rabbi Joseph B. Soloveitchik[12] notes that the Torah indeed commands, "and you shall be guiltless (clean) before God and Israel" (Num. 32:22), which translates practically into an obligation to preserve and maintain a positive

10. *Ḥafetz Ḥayim, Laws of Lashon HaRa, klal* 1, in *Be'er Mayim Ḥayim* 15.
11. Among the works in which versions of the story can be found are Rabbi Dov Katz, *Tenuat HaMusar* IV, p. 90; *Kol Yehuda, mahadura ḥadasha, Parashat Metzora;* Rabbi Avraham Tobolsky, *KeTzet HaShemesh BiGevurato,* p. 198 and in the journal *Tevuna* I:114, p. 136.
12. Quoted in *Nefesh HaRav,* p. 150.

reputation, either so others are not misled into imitating seemingly inappropriate behavior, or, more relevant to this point, because one is not permitted to allow oneself to become the subject of disrepute. Similarly, the Talmud (Bava Kamma 90b) prohibits the infliction of a physical wound not only upon others but even upon oneself, a model that may be relevant here. Further, if negativity of thought and speech are considered corrosive, that might be true regardless of the subject, and such speech might be discouraged either because of its direct effects or because of its harmful habituation.[13]

Focusing narrowly on this particular story may also yield a more specific conclusion. In this case, the listener did not know that the speaker was the *Ḥafetz Ḥayim* himself, thus creating an environment in which at least from the speaker's perspective *lashon hara* was being transmitted. This might be a situation more problematic than one in which a speaker is openly self-deprecating, and the listener appreciates it as such.[14]

The last scenario is significant, making this more than a standard case of the attribute of *lashon hara* without the substance of the damage. In such an instance, the listener believes he is participating in gossip, even though in reality the speaker is the subject. This may also be a case of *avak lashon hara,* since the *Ḥafetz Ḥayim* includes in this category one who creates the impression that he is speaking *lashon hara,* even if in reality the speech is actually permissible.[15] Apparently,

---

13. See the extensive discussion in *Responsa Ateret Paz,* (I part 3, cm 7, in footnote) and Shagiv Amit, *Rav Lehoshia,* p. 353.
14. This distinction is noted by Rabbi Ḥayim Kanievsky, *She'elat Rav* I, ch. 7:8. *Responsa LeḤafetz BaḤayim* I, 24 also adopts this understanding in coming to the conclusion that there is no prohibition to speak disparagingly about oneself. Rabbi Avraham Duri, in his *Zekhut Avot, Parashat Metzora,* pp. 144–49, concludes similarly, noting as well that if the speaker is recognized as the subject, it is permitted to minimize one's stature for reasons of modesty, but it is not appropriate to publicize one's sins; see also his *Responsa Aderet Tiferet* IV, 64. See also *Shaarei Avraham,* pp. 284–87; *He'arot Rigshei Ḥayim* p 78; *Emek HaLashon* 5, and the footnotes of Rabbi Aharon Joffen to *Ḥiddushei HaRitva,* Yevamot 49b, s.v. *mishum,* n. 382.
15. *Ḥafetz Ḥayim, Laws of Lashon HaRa* 9:3, following Rabbeinu Yonah, *Shaarei Teshuva* 3:228.

this is because such behavior weakens the stigma against *lashon hara* by making it seem more common, and thus indirectly leads to more *lashon hara* being spoken.[16]

"HARMLESS" *LASHON HARA* AND UNKNOWN BENEFIT

The focus on personality corrosion independent of harm gives rise to a number of other issues. For example, *lashon hara* would be prohibited even if we could envision a situation in which the speaker could credibly maintain that the subject would not be harmed.[17]

Conversely, if a speaker speaks with malice, but the matter is afterwards determined to be important and justified, that result would not mitigate the original offense, and the speaker would still have to undergo an internal process of repentance.[18]

SPEECH ABOUT GROUPS

A common misconception is that while speaking against an individual can be harmful, speaking against a group of people does not inflict any actual harm. However, the halakhic literature vigorously opposes this premise, stressing that speaking against a group is the greater offense.[19]

---

16. See *Shaarei Avraham,* p. 403. Rabbi Moshe Feinstein is quoted in *Mesorat Moshe, inyanim shonim* 11, as prohibiting both *lashon hara* about oneself and about one who has granted permission.
17. *Ḥafetz Ḥayim, Laws of Lashon HaRa, klal* 3, 6. See also *Tehor Sefatayim,* pp. 140–41, who understands the issue to be a dispute between Maimonides and Rabbeinu Yonah. Note *Responsa Az Nidberu* XIV:59, who assumes that this prohibition would not include incidental discussion of information already known to the listener. Other than that category, however, he maintains in a later responsum (XIV:65) that there is no *lashon hara* that can actually be characterized reliably as harmless. See also *Emek HaLashon* 15, regarding this and related issues, and also *Responsa VeDarashta VeḤakarta* III, *Ḥoshen Mishpat* 20, and *Responsa Minḥat Peri* IV: 65. See also, at length, Rabbi Shlomo Arieli's introduction to his expanded edition of *Ḥiddushei Rabbi Akiva Eiger* to Pesaḥim.
18. *Ḥafetz Ḥayim, Laws of Lashon HaRa* 4:11. See Rabbi Mordekhai Karlebakh, *Ḥavatzelet HaSharon,* Numbers, pp. 338–39 and *Ḥut Shani, Shemirat HaLashon* 1:6.
19. *Ḥafetz Ḥayim, Laws of Lashon HaRa* 10:12. See also *Sefer Ḥasidim* 482, and Radak to II Chr. 13:20, and see also *Mordekhai,* Yoma, no. 724, citing a comment from the *Tanḥuma* that Moses was criticized for his statement, "And behold you have risen in your fathers' stead, an increase of sinful men, to increase still more the fierce anger

This is not to say that there is never a need or a justification to do so; rather, the general considerations and warnings regarding *lashon hara* are in effect in this situation as well, possibly with even greater severity.[20] Similarly, it is important not to allow justified criticism of individuals to broaden into unwarranted attacks on a group.

It would seem that this additional severity is not only a factor of multiplication, but also emerges from the likelihood that completely innocent individuals would be smeared by a blanket criticism against their relevant group, under the veneer of justification that the statements are not targeted at them.[21] This is a strong element of the dangers associated with racism and prejudice, and is worthy of careful attention.

Further, there is additional harm inflicted by such generalized derogation. For example, Claude Steele, in his book *Whistling Vivaldi*, describes what he terms "stereotype threat," the phenomenon in which one who feels labeled by a group criticism becomes inhibited from rising above that designation, creating essentially a self-fulfilling prophecy.[22] Similarly, contemporary authorities point out that just as it is wrong to disparage a group, it is equally damaging and prohibited to use that group identity as a term of criticism for others ("you're acting like a ...").

Clearly, the corrosive effects of negativity and cynicism are at play when malicious group condemnations are expressed. However, the damage is not limited to that arena; the impact such speech has on the subjects is greater than is sometimes assumed, and is intensified by the mistaken perception that such comments are harmless.

---

of the Lord towards Israel" (Num. 32:14) because the term "fathers" appeared to unfairly include Abraham, Isaac and Jacob. The Vilna Gaon, *Biur HaGra, Oraḥ Ḥayim* 606:3, also cites this midrash, for the purpose of illustrating that one should not disparage the deceased (see below). (The *Mordekhai* also brings it in this context, but includes the explanatory phrase that indicates that unfair generalization was involved.) See Rabbi Shmuel DeModena, *Responsa Maharshdam* 100, *Responsa LeḤafetz BaḤayim* 1:1; and Rabbi Yosef Lieberman, *Responsa Mishnat Yosef* XI:209.

20. Rabbi Eliezer Papo, *Peleh Yoetz, erekh lashon hara,* expands on this at length.

21. See also Rabbi Shraya Deblitsky, in the journal *Marpei Lashon* 11, pp. 12–14 and *Tehor Sefatayim,* pp. 42–45, and also *Netiv Ḥayim* 10:17.

22. Claude Steele, *Whistling Vivaldi* (New York: W. W. Norton, 2010).

SPEECH ABOUT THINGS

It would seem, though, that the applicability of the laws of *lashon hara* should be limited to speech against human beings, and not extend to statements against inanimate objects. However, even this is not such a simple assumption, a message that may emerge from the condemnation of the spies and their slander of the Land of Israel.[23] Indeed, the *Ḥafetz Ḥayim* and others do record a prohibition of slander against objects.[24] From one perspective, this may stem from the association certain objects have with specific human beings, particularly if the object in question is merchandise used in business.[25] However, this concern may also emerge from the corrosive effects of negativity and cynicism, even without a human target.[26]

SPEAKING ILL OF THE DEAD

Even those who are merciless in their treatment of people around them often change their behavior when speaking of the deceased, assuming the existence of a new obligation of "respect for the dead." While it is certainly true that those no longer living should be treated respectfully, the obligation toward those who are alive and aware is certainly more crucial. Nonetheless, there is a prohibition of speaking badly of the departed.

---

23. See *Mishpetei HaShalom,* p. 232, no. 23, with n. 28. For an analysis of the prohibition of disparaging the Land of Israel, and its relevance as a source for a general prohibition of speaking badly about inanimate objects, see Rabbi David Yitzḥak Mann, *Be'er Miriam* to *Laws of Kings* II, pp. 91–92. Concerning the nature of the disparagement against the land, see Rabbi Meshulam David Soloveichik, *Shiurei Rabbeinu Meshulam David HaLevi,* Arakhin 15a, and see also *Ḥelkat Yehoshua,* Arakhin 15a, no. 19.
24. *Sefer Yere'im* 191, (41), quoted by *Ḥafetz Ḥayim, Laws of Lashon HaRa* 5:7. See also Rabbi Avraham Yisrael Moshe Solomon, *Netivot HaKodesh* to Arakhin, who notes further questions on this passage. See also *Zera Ḥayim,* pp. 356–58, and Rabbi Mordekhai Karlebakh, *Ḥavatzelet HaSharon,* Numbers pp. 436–38.
25. See Rabbi Yehuda Itaḥ, *Netiv Yosher,* ch. 49 n. 1. Note, however, the surprising suggestion on this point of Rabbi Uri Jungreiss, in the journal *Ateret Shlomo* 5762, pp. 264–66. As noted by Rabbi Shlomo Zalman Kook, *Bein Shenei Kohanim Gedolim,* p. 147, if the merchant is present, the speaker is also in violation of the transgression of verbal oppression.
26. See *Responsa Az Nidberu* XIV, 66:13; Rabbi Shalom Yuchik, *VaYita Eshel* to Arakhin, no. 93; and *Emek HaLashon,* addendum to no. 18.

However, it is not clear that this is included in the general concept of *lashon hara.*[27] In the early halakhic sources, this prohibition is cited as an injunction of the earlier authorities,[28] which may create the impression it is not included in the Torah's prohibition of *lashon hara.* However, it might be understood that this injunction is merely an added method of enforcement and communal condemnation of what was already prohibited;[29] this position is expressed by the eminent contemporary authority Rabbi Yosef Shalom Elyashiv.[30] By contrast, the prominent twentieth-century Rosh Yeshiva, Rabbi Yaakov Kaminetsky, asserts a different approach, maintaining that the Torah does not refrain from reporting negative behavior about biblical figures because the deceased are not included in the prohibition of *lashon hara*[31] (and, presumably, the instructional value justifies the disclosure).[32]

Practically speaking, there are authorities who maintain that if the injunction is indeed a new enactment, it relates only to slander and not to factual information, as the language used in some of the sources

27. Note the language of Rabbi Yitzhak Zahler, *Yalkut Yitzḥak, mitzva* 237, no. 4.

28. *Mordekhai,* Bava Kamma 8:82, *Shulḥan Arukh, Oraḥ Ḥayim* 606:3 and Rema, *Ḥoshen Mishpat* 420:38, where the requirements for repentance are noted, and see also Rabbi Yekutiel Yehuda Greenwald, *Kol Bo* to *aveilut* 3:1.

29. See the discussion of Prof. Naḥum Rackover in the journal *Sinai* XXVI, 51.

30. *Shiurei Maran HaGrish Elyashiv,* Berakhot 19a, with nn. 53–54.

31. *Emet LeYaakov* to Gen. 37:18, p. 194. It should be noted that an exchange recorded in the Talmud (Shabbat 96b–97a) suggests that (at least according to the opinion of R. Yehuda ben Beteira) there is a prohibition regarding disparaging the dead, whether the statement is false or true.

32. The question of whether negative disclosures about biblical figures are justified by dint of purposeful instructional value is considered by *Zikhron David,* pp. 99–100. He poses the question as to whether it is the purposeful nature that is the justification, or whether it is perhaps a distinct license connected to the eternal value that is unique to the Torah and Scripture. In the context of this question, he speculates as to whether purpose is indeed a license in disparaging the dead, and inclines to assume that it is, in light of the fact that this license exists by the biblically prohibition of *lashon hara* and thus should certainly apply here. However, it might be that if this is indeed an additional rabbinic prohibition, it could be applied more broadly, perhaps not to exclude a justification of purpose but to limit it, or perhaps because of the particular disadvantage of the subject who is unable to defend himself.

indeed indicates.[33] As some explain, it is the slanderous aspect that requires the special enactment: the concern is that the speaker is exploiting the fact that he cannot be contradicted to fabricate information in a way that would be impossible were the subject alive to defend himself.[34]

This last point presents a fundamental question. If indeed the prohibition of *lashon hara* does not apply to speech about the deceased, what is the nature of a separate rabbinic ban on such speech? One perspective might be that it is a specific protection for the honor of the deceased, and, particularly as the deceased can no longer defend himself, is focused on falsehood. Alternatively, this ban may reflect the negative character traits associated with gossip, which are invoked here as well, even if there is no actual victimization.[35]

Nonetheless, the concerns we have discussed regarding the often misleading nature of seemingly factual accounts, combined with the broader concern of the impact of negativity, would seem to be relevant and to dictate caution in this area as well.[36] Furthermore, there is the potential of actual harm, emotional or otherwise, to relatives of the subject that must also be considered.

33. See *Emet LeYaakov* to Gen. 37:18, p. 194 and *Sinai* XXVI, 51. However, as discussed earlier, it is possible that the term *motzi shem ra* does not always indicate falsehood. *Responsa Az Nidberu* XIV:68 concludes that speaking ill of the dead, whether a true or false statement, is a Torah prohibition, while the communal ban that reinforces the principle is specifically directed towards slander. See also *Oraḥ Meisharim* 8:3, and *Shemirat HaPeh KeHilkhato,* pp. 203–4.
34. See Rabbi Hayim Elazar Schapiro, *Nimukei Oraḥ Ḥayim, Oraḥ Ḥayim* 606:3.
35. See *Ohev Yamim, diyunim* 1.
36. See also the discussion of Rabbi Menaḥem Long, in the journal *Marpei Lashon* IV, p. 25, as to whether the concern of *avak lashon hara* involved in speaking praise applies if the subject is deceased.

Fixing It: Reparations, Repentance, and Redemption

FINANCIAL RESTITUTION

An oft-told story involves a man who came to his rabbi to seek advice on how to repent for the offense of speaking *lashon hara*. The rabbi advised him that it is indeed possible to repent, albeit complicated. He instructed him to take a pillow – the old-fashioned kind, with feathers inside – and to cut a hole in it and then walk around his town, allowing the feathers to escape from the pillow. Having done that, he returned to the rabbi and asked him for the next instruction. The second step was significantly harder than the first: "Now pick up all the feathers."

The message is, clearly, that repentance for speaking *lashon hara* is uniquely challenging for the penitent. As has been noted, one explanation for the particular severity attributed to *lashon hara* has to do with the impediments to repentance, restitution and repair.[1] Indeed, much

1. The early literature extensively refers to *lashon hara* as a transgression that is resistant to repentance; see Rif to Yoma 6a with Ran; *Maḥzor Vitri* 531; *Sefer HaḤinnukh* 364; *Mishneh Torah, Laws of Repentance* 4:1, 5, with *Kesef Mishneh* to 4:1; *Responsa Rambam* 121; Rosh, Yoma 8:18; *Shaarei Teshuva* 1:52.

literature is devoted to assessing what can be done after the offense of *lashon hara* has been committed.

One question is whether any restitution is due to the victim. On this front, there is not much to be done, as this offense is generally not enforceable by a rabbinic court through the collection of damages. As noted earlier, damages that are inflicted indirectly are generally not actionable, and *lashon hara,* even when it has a significant negative impact, causes its harm indirectly.

However, this does not mean that a rabbinic court must ignore an act of *lashon hara,* and particularly an egregious one. The medieval authorities agree that even if the letter of the law does not provide for restitution, extralegal methods exist in order to discourage such behavior and to address to some extent the rift and the harm that has been created. For example, Rabbeinu Asher asserts that due to the great severity of the sin and the emotional pain imposed by the act, the court should excommunicate the offender until he appeases the victim in accordance with his personal honor,[2] and in his responsa, he notes that it is the custom of "all Israel" to enact safeguards and penalties in this matter.[3] Similarly, Maimonides notes that while the letter of the law does exempt the offender from restitution, it is appropriate for a rabbinic court to establish protective measures and penalties, "in every time and every place as they see fit," although he does not mention excommunication.[4] The later codifier Rabbi Yaakov, author of the *Tur* and son of Rabbeinu Asher, combines in his rulings his father's view with that of Maimonides.[5] The code of Jewish law, the *Shulḥan Arukh,* rules that one who embarrasses another with words should be excommunicated until he appeases the victim,[6] and Rabbi Moshe Isserles, in his glosses, emphasizes that slander is included in this category.[7] Despite the basic exemption from monetary damages, the victim may legitimately condition his forgiveness on some

2. Bava Kamma 8, 2 in the Rosh.
3. *Responsa* of Rosh 101:1.
4. *Mishneh Torah, Laws of Injury and Damage* 3:5.
5. *Tur, Ḥoshen Mishpat,* 1, 420. See Rabbi Tzvi Lifshitz in the journal *Teḥumin* XVI, pp. 381–91.
6. *Ḥoshen Mishpat* 1:6.
7. *Ḥoshen Mishpat* 420:38; see *Sefer Me'irat Einayim* 49.

kind of restitution.[8] Indeed, throughout the generations, rabbinic courts and individual authorities have considered the question of what actions should be taken against specific perpetrators of disparagement and slander, and have acted accordingly.[9] In 1965 (with later emendations), the Israeli government, basing itself of the values of Jewish tradition, passed a law that imposes penalties, including imprisonment, for acts of *lashon hara* against another.[10]

However, the question of monetary compensation is actually the less vexing part of the equation; it is the appeasement that is significantly more challenging. As noted, the effects of *lashon hara* are far ranging and often irreparable. As such, it is often not possible for the offender to come to the victim and claim he has resolved the issue and rectified the problems he has caused, and consequentially, it is understandable that the victim is hesitant to forgive what is essentially an ongoing offense.

Indeed, there is a view in the Talmud and brought in the later codes, that while it is considered "cruel" or even sinful not to forgive someone who is truly penitent, it may be acceptable not to forgive a slanderer.[11] As the commentaries explain, attempts at rectification are unreliable; too many people may have heard the slanderous accusations but not the correction and apology.[12] Regardless, it is still laudable and

---

8. See *LeRe'akha Kamokha* VII, pp. 317–19.
9. Prof. Naḥum Rackover thoroughly reviews the history and substance of these rulings in the journal *Sinai* vol. XXVI, 51, pp. 197–209 and pp. 326–45 and in the journal *Shaarei Tzedek* X, pp. 282–94. Much of the literature builds on analysis of a talmudic passage (Pesaḥim 113b) in which an individual brings testimony against another in rabbinic court, but because he does so without another witness as required for any action to be taken, his testimony is considered unproductive disparagement, and the court flogs him. Regarding the question of whether a wife who engages in *lashon hara* forfeits her *ketuba*, see Rabbi Eliyahu bar Shalom in the journal *Beit Hillel*, p. 63. Concerning the disqualification of one who speaks *lashon hara* from testimony, see Rabbi Kalfun Moshe HaKohen, *Responsa Shoel VeNishal* II, *Yoreh De'ah* 52. See also *Responsa Ohalei Yehuda*, pp. 153–58.
10. Rabbi Ratzon Arusi considers the implications of this law from the perspective of Jewish law and rabbinic responsibility in the journal *Shaarei Tzedek* X, pp. 267–81.
11. Y. Bava Kamma 8:7; *Mordekhai* to Yoma 723; *Sefer Ḥasidim* 613, 631; *Sefer Mitzvot Gadol*, positive commandment 16; *Hagahot Maimoniyot*, *Laws of Repentance* 2:10; *Responsa Terumat HaDeshen* 307 and *pesakim* 212, and Rema, *Oraḥ Ḥayim* 606:1
12. *Magen Avraham*, *Oraḥ Ḥayim* 606:5.

recommended to forgive nonetheless, but the justification of the hesitancy is instructive.[13] (Presumably, these considerations are not limited to slander, but apply to any of the set of interpersonal offenses that have irreparable consequences.) Some authorities assert that if the speaker has made a sincere effort to correct his slander in the eyes of the listeners to the greatest extent possible, he indeed has a right to be forgiven.[14]

It should also be noted that if forgiveness from the victim is needed following an act of *lashon hara*, an additional factor is then present when a group of people, rather than an individual, is disparaged. In that case, obtaining forgiveness from all the victims is likely impossible, if it is even feasible to identify all of them.[15]

ASKING FORGIVENESS: THE CONTROVERSY

However, there is another factor that is very significant in obstructing reconciliation in many cases of *lashon hara*, and this factor sits at the center of a major dispute between two giants of Jewish ethical leadership.

One of the primary advocates of the movement calling for an active focus on character development, known as *Musar* movement, was Rabbi Yisrael Salanter (1810–83). Given this focus, it is to be expected that he would have strongly supported the efforts of the *Ḥafetz Ḥayim* in his writings. Nonetheless, according to several reports, he declined to give a written endorsement to the book. Apparently, while he agreed with the work's general message, there was one ruling in it that he felt he could not associate himself with, and that the risk was too great that his endorsement would be seen as concurrence with this ruling.[16]

---

13. *Magen Avraham, Oraḥ Ḥayim* 606:5. Note however *Penei Moshe* to the Jerusalem Talmud. See also *Matteh Ephraim* 606:3; *Responsa Ḥayim She'al* II:13; and Rabbi David Eikhenstein, *Responsa Devar Tov* 6. See as well the discussion in Rabbi Aharon Kahn, *Yismaḥ Avikha* II, pp. 50–57.
14. See *Arukh HaShulḥan* 606:2.
15. See *Birkat Yitzḥak*, p. 182.
16. See Rabbi Eliyahu Lopian, *Lev Eliyahu*, vol. 1, p. 108, and *Meorot HaGedolim* 141; *Mishnat Yisrael*, p. 337 in foonote; and Rabbi Ahron Soloveichik, *Paraḥ Matteh Aharon, madda*, pp. 186–89. See also Rabbi Yom Tov Zanger, *Maadanei Yom Tov* III:10. However, it is noteworthy that Rabbi Yitzḥak Blazer, perhaps the most prominent student of Rabbi Yisrael Salanter, writes in the introduction to his *Responsa Peri*

This single controversial ruling concerns the question of apology and reconciliation following an offense of *lashon hara*. The Talmud teaches that repentance for offenses committed against another person is ineffective unless the offender apologizes to the victim and obtains his forgiveness (Yoma 85b). As a general rule, at least the first part, the apology, is in the hands of the offender. However, the issue of *lashon hara* presents a unique challenge. It is usually expected that in apologizing, one is required to specify the offenses of which one is aware, rather than mouthing a general confession lacking any recognition of the particular manner in which harm has been done to the other.[17] Often, the hurtful comments have been made outside the presence of the subject, who is blissfully ignorant. To apologize under such circumstances would mean the infliction of emotional pain on one who has already been the victim of malicious gossip. Is that warranted?

To Rabbi Yisrael Salanter, the answer is clear. The Torah's strong prohibition against causing emotional suffering is the priority. The offender has to find some other way to assuage his conscience and set things right; but to do so at the expense of his victim is not acceptable. However, to the *Ḥafetz Ḥayim*, the issue is somewhat more complicated.

If the gossip was ineffectual, causing no apparent damage to the subject, the *Ḥafetz Ḥayim* agrees that there is little to be gained by informing the subject in order to obtain his forgiveness. However, if indeed harm was inflicted by the speech, it is then necessary to tell the subject what had been done and to apologize.[18] Reportedly, Rabbi Yisrael found this ruling so objectionable that he refused to associate his name with the entire book, despite its immense overall value.

The ruling of the *Ḥafetz Ḥayim* has a strong foundation, apparently based on an earlier statement of the great medieval ethicist Rabbeinu Yonah of Gerona.[19] Nonetheless, many later authorities seem to be in

Yitzḥak that he does not have an approbation from Rabbi Yisrael, as it was his general practice not to provide them.

17. See *Bayit Ḥadash, Oraḥ Ḥayim* 606:2.

18. *Ḥafetz Ḥayim*, part 1, *klal* 4:12.

19. *Shaarei Teshuva, shaar* 3:207.

agreement with Rabbi Yisrael.[20] It is reported that the famed Rabbi Aharon Kotler, who founded and led the Lakewood yeshiva, asserts that Rabbi Yisrael was qualified to argue with the rulings of the great medieval authorities due to his phenomenal expertise and prominence in these matters. Others endorse Rabbi Yisrael's position while interpreting the view of Rabbi Yonah as being in agreement as well (and in some cases also interpreting differently the view of the *Ḥafetz Ḥayim*).[21]

If seeking *meḥila* (pardon, forgiveness) and specifying the offense is indeed contraindicated, other options might still exist. The first is to ask for a general forgiveness, without identifying a particular wrongdoing. This tends to arouse suspicion, and in this vein some note that this may be a situation in which a less-than-ideal social phenomenon may be utilized. As Yom Kippur draws near, many approach

20. See Rabbi Moshe Mordekhai Karp, *Hilkhot Ḥag BaḤag, Laws of the High Holy* Days, ch. 21, no. 111, and Rabbi Shlomo Zalman Auerbach in *Halikhot Shlomo, mo'adim* 3:6. See, though, *Aleinu Leshabeaḥ*, Deuteronomy I, *response* 138, where Rabbi Yosef Shalom Elyashiv is quoted as emphasizing the spiritual benefits accruing to the victim who is told about the offense, as he can be gracious and forgiving and earn great merit through his suffering for the sake of a sinner's forgiveness. However, this seems more of a consolation after the fact rather than a recommended approach; this is also implied in the presentation of Rabbi Yisrael Veinman, *Mishnat Yisrael*, p. 241, who extensively surveys practical approaches to the issue (pp. 233–42). A different approach can be found in Rabbi Elimelekh Winter, *Minḥat Elimelekh* II, pp. 366–369. Rabbi Moshe Sternbuch, in *Responsa Teshuvot VeHanhagot* V:397, quotes Rabbi Eliyahu Dessler as endorsing the approach of Rabbi Yisrael Salanter, while ultimately recommending a dual approach of omitting the painful revelations while emphasizing overtures necessary for reconciliation.
21. See, for example, Rabbi Binyamin Yehoshua Zilber, *Responsa Az Nidberu* VIII:68 who is of the opinion that the *Ḥafetz Ḥayim* would certainly agree that the victim should not be informed of negative talk against him of which he is unaware; it is only when he knows of the gossip but not the source that he would advocate confession. A similar suggestion is made by Rabbi Yisrael Isser Hertzog in the journal *HaDarom* LII, 62–67 as well as by Rabbi Tzvi Hirsch Scheinberger in the journal *Beit Aharon VeYisrael* XVIII, 1 (103), p. 84. See also *Responsa LeḤafetz BaḤayim* I:5. See also *She'elat Shmuel*, in *Orḥot Ḥayim* to *Shulḥan Arukh*, and Rabbi Yoḥanan Segal Vosner, *Responsa Ḥayyei HaLevi* III:100, who suggests that the *Ḥafetz Ḥayim* is referring to a situation in which the offense would have eventually become known to the victim, and thus it is better heard from the antagonist than from anyone else. (Note *Ḥafetz Ḥayim, Be'er Mayim Ḥayim* 48.) See also *Ḥut Shani*, p. 335, and Rabbi David Binyamin Brezakher in the journal *Kol Torah*, XX, pp. 67–68.

all of their friends and associates and ask for forgiveness practically by rote, without identifying (usually even in their own minds) any specific offense. While this actually falls short of the standard normally required of such apologies, in this case it may be preferable.[22] Some argue, however, that this might be effective only when the gossip is routine. If, however, the *lashon hara* is extensive and egregious, it is harder to assume the subject would be able to express any kind of meaningful forgiveness.

Interestingly, some of the students of Rabbi Yisrael might also have endorsed such an approach. One of his most prominent disciples, Rabbi Yitzḥak Blazer (1837–1907), corresponded with another, Rabbi Naphtali Amsterdam, when the former was leaving a rabbinical position and was concerned that he may have spoken badly about some of his congregants and now needed their forgiveness. The latter advised him to apologize in a general way, noting that this transition provided a good opportunity to ask for a broad forgiveness for any offenses during his tenure, without provoking focus on any specific deed.[23]

Rabbi Ahron Soloveichik suggests that in the instance of *lashon hara*, in place of begging absolution, it is appropriate to spread information that will counteract the negative effects of the gossip;[24] in this case, such action is more consistent with increasing harmony than seeking

22. See Rabbi Shlomo Wahrman, *Orot Yemei HaRaḥamim* 37, and Rabbi Moshe Sternbuch, *Mo'adim UZmanim* 1:54. However, in *Responsa Teshuvot VeHanhagot* V:397, he writes that a completely nonspecific request is insufficient; it should rather be a request along the lines of "perhaps I spoke some *lashon hara* about you, I don't remember exactly…" without providing the full details. See also the discussion of this in Rabbi Mordekhai Babad, *Minḥat Maḥavat* II:132 and *Maor HaShaar* to *Shaarei Teshuva*. See also *Yalkut Yosef, Kitzur Shulḥan Arukh* 2, 606:16, and *Nitei Gavriel, Laws of Yom HaKippurim*, ch. 17 n. 2, and see also Rabbi Yosef Lieberman, *Responsa Mishnat Yosef* IV:44.
23. Published in Rabbi Avraham Rosenberg, *Tenuvot Sadai*, p. 354; note footnote on p. 355; also, *Kokhvei Or, mikhtavim* 11, p. 225. See *Mishnat Yisrael*, p. 240.
24. *Paraḥ Matteh Aharon, madda*, pp. 186–89. The dispute between Rabbi Kagan and Rabbi Salanter is recounted in detail here; see also, pp. 86–88. This is part of a longer discussion as to the function and mechanism of *teshuva* and *meḥila*. Rabbi Soloveichik suggests a similar notion in a different context as well, that of when the precise victim is unknown (p. 197).

the victim's pardon.[25] However, this advice is easier said than said; as we have seen, successfully countering the effects of the initial negative speech can be, more often than not, a very daunting task.[26]

To respond to the question of whether the ruling of the *Ḥafetz Ḥayim* has been accepted in practice, we could start with the opinion of the *Ḥafetz Ḥayim* himself. The *Ḥafetz Ḥayim* was also the author of an extremely authoritative commentary on the code to Jewish law (which was published after the book *Ḥafetz Ḥayim*) known as the *Mishna Berura*. In that work, in the section of laws of asking for forgiveness prior to Yom Kippur, the author approvingly quotes a view of the seventeenth-century authority *Magen Avraham* that appears at odds with his position in the book *Ḥafetz Ḥayim*. In the *Mishna Berura*, the ruling is that if a request for forgiveness will embarrass the victim, the offender should not specify his wrongdoings. Thus, he appears in this work to favor the view of Rabbi Yisrael Salanter, against his own position in his book *Ḥafetz Ḥayim*.[27]

A number of suggestions in the later literature are advanced to reconcile the two statements, although the basis for any of the distinctions is hard to find in the original sources. One suggestion is that in *Ḥafetz Ḥayim*, the author refers to a situation where the request will cause anguish to the victim, a result he apparently considers necessary. In the *Mishna Berura*, he refers to actual embarrassment, which indeed makes apologizing counterproductive.[28] However, this distinction is not only hard to assess, it is also not mentioned in the original source material. Furthermore, the infliction of anguish and embarrassment

25. Similarly, see Rabbi Re'em HaKohen, *Responsa Badei HaAron, Oraḥ Ḥayim* 19, who asserts that if damage was done to the subject on a public level, then repentance would require addressing that damage, but not necessarily telling the victim, as this would inflict unjustified pain.

26. Rabbi David Ariav, *LeRe'akha Kamokha* VII, 7:3 in *Nir LeDavid*, asserts that one would not have to adhere to strict honesty in attempting to "undo" *lashon hara*, as this would be included in the talmudic license of dishonesty in the service of harmony.

27. *Oraḥ Ḥayim* 606:3. See also *Shalmei Toda*, High Holy Days, p. 200.

28. See *Halikhot Shlomo* in *Orḥot Halakha*, ch. 3, no. 24, and *Mo'adim UZmanim* 1:54, n. 1 (who rules against the position of the *Ḥafetz Ḥayim*).

are both included in the same Torah prohibition, making it difficult to distinguish between them in practice.[29]

Another suggested distinction, somewhat related to the first, is that the situation described in the *Mishna Berura* is one in which the victim knows about what happened, but would endure embarrassment to hear it revisited. Whereas Rabbi Yisrael is referring to more than that, where in the first place the victim does not know about what happened, and in that case Rabbi Yisrael rules that he may not be told.[30]

A third distinction is that in the *Mishna Berura* the ruling is that one need not go into detail that would increase a sense of embarrassment to the victim, but to simply inform him that something was said is still necessary. If this is indeed the position, one can understand the objection of Rabbi Yisrael, who presumably would be concerned that informing the subject of the fact of negative speech without detailing its contents is likely to cause him equal if not greater anguish.[31]

It is important to note that Rabbi Yisrael's position is not a leniency, exempting the offender from the necessity of apologizing. Rather, it is a stringency; the need for reconciliation and forgiveness for damages inflicted is still present (and in this sense, perhaps Rabbi Yisrael is actually in theoretical agreement with the earlier ruling of Rabbeinu Yonah), but the offender is precluded from achieving atonement because of the cost to the victim.

Thus, we see that *lashon hara* is a transgression that poses a unique challenge to repentance, for many reasons, including the one just mentioned, and an ounce of prevention is worth a pound of cure. Some suggest that the purpose of offering apology is to express concern and

---

29. See *Mishnat Yisrael*, p. 238.
30. See *Mo'adim UZmanim* 1:54, n. 1, and *LiTeshuvat HaShana* 2, s.v. *vekhol hamitga'eh* no. 3. See *Mishnat Yisrael*, p. 238., who again notes the absence of support in the text, and also the position of Rabbi Naphtali Amsterdam in the above-cited letter who disputes this interpretation of the position of the *Magen Avraham*.
31. See *Mishnat Yisrael,* and *Maḥatzit HaShekel* to *Magen Avraham*. See also *Shaarei Avraham*, pp. 439–40, in footnote, who assumes there is no contradiction between what is written in *Ḥafetz Ḥayim* and in the *Mishna Berura,* nor with the position of Rabbi Yisrael Salanter; the ruling in *Mishna Berura* is authoritative, and he merely did not record the point in *Ḥafetz Ḥayim*.

sympathy for the victim and a concern for his well-being; in that case, refraining from asking for forgiveness, when doing so would inflict pain, is actually the more compassionate and thus more appropriate choice. Thus, the inaction is in place of, and preferable to, the action of informing the victim.[32]

This controversy, the dispute between the two titans, the *Ḥafetz Ḥayim* and Rabbi Yisrael Salanter, might revolve around differing conceptual understandings of the main principles involved. For example, it could be that they disagree as to the underlying concepts of *lashon hara*. Perhaps, at least as far as repentance is concerned, the *Ḥafetz Ḥayim* focuses on *lashon hara* as a negative character trait; thus, attempting to reconcile with the victim, even if it is a difficult conversation for him, may still be an attempt to reverse the taint of character. Conversely, Rabbi Yisrael might understand the offense as inflicting harm through speech; thus, to inflict even more harm, by anguishing the victim through informing him, would be blatantly counterproductive.

Alternatively, the debate might center on the true purpose of seeking forgiveness, with Rabbi Yisrael understanding that the purpose is a removal of tension between the parties; thus to create tension would certainly be ill advised. Conversely, the *Ḥafetz Ḥayim* might see a waiver of claims for damages as a primary focus; thus, it would be necessary to inform the victim so that he is able to release the claims.

It is similarly illuminating to consider the *Ḥafetz Ḥayim*'s distinction on the matter, in which he maintains that one need apologize only if the *lashon hara* was "successful," but not if it did no damage.[33] This lays the foundation for a number of questions. First, it is worth noting that the *Ḥafetz Ḥayim* distinguishes on this point between *lashon hara* and *rekhilut*. In the case of *lashon hara*, it is possible that the speech made no impact, as the listener might not have really been interested in the subject or paying any attention. However, in the case of *rekhilut*, the listener is the subject, and therefore by its very nature there will be

32. See Rabbi Shmuel Azriel, *Ḥazon Shmuel*, pp. 250–51, and Rabbi Yitzchak Hutner, *Paḥad Yitzḥak, Yom HaKippurim* 2:8.

33. See also Rabbi Shlomo Aviner, *Am KeLavi* 1:181, and Rabbi Yitzḥak ben Shoshan, *Responsa Toledot Yitzḥak* 1:29.

some negative impact. Accordingly, the *Ḥafetz Ḥayim* rules in the latter instance that his premise that an apology is necessary is applicable in all cases.

This distinction emerges from a context in which the *Ḥafetz Ḥayim* poses a question on his own position.[34] What if the gossip does not appear to have inflicted any damage yet, but there is reason to believe that it will in the future? Certainly, the ideal would be to stop the process in its tracks. However, considering that that is often not possible, should the apology requirements correlate to the current extent of damage or anticipated future damage? In presenting this question, the *Ḥafetz Ḥayim* distinguishes between *lashon hara,* which might not impose significant damage if the listener is disinterested, and *rekhilut,* in which can be assumed that there is always some degree of damage.[35]

The *Ḥafetz Ḥayim*'s position is also noteworthy in view of his assumption that it is possible to speak *lashon hara* which does not inflict damage. In such a situation, the *Ḥafetz Ḥayim* asserts that there is no interpersonal impact, although there is certainly a sin involved, and the indulgence of a negative character trait. Thus, the offender must repent, but this penitence is between him and God and need not involve the subject. This distinction reflects the dual nature of the transgression of *lashon hara* that we have already explicated.

However, there are those who challenge the claim that there can ever be a situation of *lashon hara* that does not cause damage. Rabbi Yitzchak Hutner, who in practice endorses the position of Rabbi Yisrael Salanter that one should not inform the victim for the sake of seeking apology, nonetheless addresses the *Ḥafetz Ḥayim*'s assumption on this point. Rabbi Hutner asserts that every act of derogatory speech has a negative impact, regardless of the acceptance of the listener. This is due to the mandate to "love your fellow as yourself." To express negative sentiments about the other, even if they are not accepted by another party, is to detract from the feelings of love due to

34. See *Ḥafetz Ḥayim, Ḥafetz Ḥayim,* part 1, *klal* 4, in *Be'er Mayim Ḥayim* 48, and in *Laws of Rekhilut* 4:3, in *Be'er Mayim Ḥayim* 4.

35. This explanation is expressed in *Mishnat Yisrael,* p. 236. See also *Rokeaḥ,* no. 28.

that subject.[36] He supports this point by noting Maimonides's position that one who curses his fellow, also the transgression of a Torah prohibition, must seek forgiveness from the target of the curse,[37] despite the fact that Maimonides does not ascribe any actual practical impact to the curse itself.[38]

The distinction of the *Ḥafetz Ḥayim* also gives rise to the question as to what meets the threshold for damage. Does this refer to actual material harm, or would the "acceptance" on the part of the listener itself constitute damage?[39] As we have seen, acceptance in its own right is a transgression of a prohibition, also presenting the question as to what penitence is necessary for the receiver. To this, the *Ḥafetz Ḥayim* asserts that an apology is not called for, but instead, the receiver is required to "remove the matter from his heart."[40]

Clearly, that is also a task that can be far more daunting then the words might imply. However, it may go to the essence of the question of repentance for the transgression of *lashon hara*. If, as was discussed earlier, the acceptance of *lashon hara* is actually the primary offense, with the speaker the facilitator rather than the main protagonist, then the internal work necessary to correct the effects of *lashon hara* on the personality and the mental framework may actually be the question of central importance, and deserving of attention on its own.

---

36. *Sefer Zikkaron LeMaran Baal HaPaḥad Yitzḥak*, p. 335, no. 8.

37. *Mishneh Torah, Laws of Repentance* 2:9.

38. This is in distinction to the position of the *Sefer HaḤinnukh* 231; see also *Ḥelkat Binyamin* to *Ḥafetz Ḥayim* part 1, *klal* 4, 45, and *Mishnat Yisrael*, p. 236. Note also the understanding of Rabbi Yonatan Eibshutz, *Tumim* 27:4, of the prohibition of cursing others. See also *Shalmei Toda, Laws of the High Holy Days*, pp. 199–200, and Rabbi Barukh Rakovsky, *Birkat Avot* 42:2.

39. For varying perspectives on this issue, see *Shevilei Ḥayim* 20; *Responsa LeḤafetz BaḤayim* 1, 5; and see also *Birkat Yitzḥak* pp. 181–182.

40. *Ḥafetz Ḥayim, Laws of Lashon HaRa* 6:4, in note; see *Ḥelkat Binyamin*, 6, and see also *Responsa LeḤafetz BaḤayim* I, no. 5. Apparently, this is actually more than repentance, in that it eliminates the transgression retroactively and completely; see *Netiv Ḥayim, Laws of Lashon HaRa* 6:4, 9 and *Ohev Yamim, Laws of Lashon HaRa* 6:4 51. Regarding mere listening to *lashon hara*, which, as discussed above, the *Ḥafetz Ḥayim* maintains is independently prohibited, see *Responsa Az Nidberu* XI:40, 41, who asserts that the transgression is interpersonal in nature, but not one that calls for asking forgiveness from the subject.

PERSONAL REPENTANCE FOR *LASHON HARA*

Apart from the issues of apology and reconciliation, *lashon hara* is a transgression like any other, and leaves an impact on the soul of the offender in addition to any harm it inflicts upon others. In fact, as we have seen, *lashon hara* causes greater spiritual corruption to the offender than a standard transgression causes; furthermore, *lashon hara* registers a dual effect, harming the subject and the speaker at once. As such, in addition to the appeal for forgiveness from the victim, the basic steps of general repentance are called for: confession, regret, and commitment to better behavior in the future. However, there are additional themes that are particularly relevant to *lashon hara*.

The Torah prescribes that one who has been afflicted with *tzaraat*, and is thus assumed to have been guilty of speaking *lashon hara*, be separated from the Jewish encampment. The Talmud explains the appropriateness of this measure, by noting that the gossiper separated people from each other through his harmful speech, and thus it is fitting that he should be separated from the community as a whole.[41]

The Talmud (Arakhin 16a; Zevaḥim 88b) also identifies another atoning element for *lashon hara*: the special coat (*me'il*) that was worn by the Priests serving in the temple. The coat, which was fitted with bells, made sounds; thus, an item which makes sounds and is utilized in the service of God is invoked to atone for a transgression that involved sound. The Talmud states that the affliction and the priestly coats correspond to two different types of *lashon hara*. The affliction is visited upon one who has inflicted damage through his negative speech. If, however, no harm has actually taken place, then the speech is atoned for by the coat.[42]

---

41. See also Rabbi Moshe Sternbuch, *Taam VeDaat*, who suggests, in a homiletic vein, symbolism in the *tzaraat* afflictions regarding the internal attributes that lead to indulgence in *lashon hara*. For one, the Torah uses the word *se'et*, which is related to the word meaning "to lift;" this represents an arrogant individual, who sits in judgment of others and thus derogates them. Another term the Torah uses is *baheret*; this is related to the word meaning "clear," and represents one who finds matters to be so simple and obvious that he can assess their worthiness without consideration of additional factors or broader context.
42. The Talmud also mentions another source of atonement for *lashon hara*, the incense, and suggests that the coat atones for *lashon hara* spoken in public, and the incense for that spoken in private. Regarding that distinction, see *Torat HaOla* of the Rema,

This distinction is not a quantitative one, but a qualitative one. One who has not actually inflicted harm through his negative speech has committed a transgression that is primarily a corruption of his own personality. Thus, the symbolism expressed through the coat is an appropriate tool to address the mental attitude required for internal change. One who has actually injected divisiveness into the community, however, is in need of the more functionally oriented exile that is provoked by the affliction of *tzaraat*.[43]

Rabbi Shneur Kotler notes an additional symbolism inherent in the coat.[44] The coat incorporates the *tekhelet*, the particular shade of blue that is also included in the Torah's commandment of tzitzit, the fringes attached to four-cornered garments. The Talmud describes the significance of *tekhelet* as being representative of the ocean, which reflects the sky, which in turn reflects the heavenly throne. The imagery is that of being directed to an ever-broadening picture that moves farther and farther back in its perspective. Thus, the message is to take in as broad a picture as possible, with as many details and as long-ranged a perspective as possible. The flaw of one who indulges in *lashon hara* is shortsightedness and narrowness of vision; thus, the coat, with the *tekhelet* within it, is an appropriate corrective.[45]

3:7, and *Shemirat HaLashon* II, 20:9. For a discussion of the symbolism of the incense as an atonement for *lashon hara*, see Rabbi Avigdor Nebenzahl, *Siḥot LeSefer Shemot*, pp. 325–28 and *Siḥot LeSefer Bemidbar*, pp. 156–58; *BeYad HaLashon*, pp. 153–54 and pp. 367–70 (by Rabbi Michel Zilber); Rabbi David Kronglass, *Siḥot Ḥokhma UMusar* 20; and *Shemuot Ḥayim*, Arakhin, ch. 3, no. 28. For further observations regarding both the coat and the incense, see *VaYita Eshel* to Arakhin, 100, and, at length, *Emek HaLashon, Kuntres Keter HaMe'il*, pp. 170–90. Note also the implication of Y. Yoma 5:3 is that the coat atones for all types of *lashon hara*; see *Emek HaLashon* 17 for an analysis of the difference between the two formulations.

See also Rabbi Yehuda Aryeh Leib Choshki, *Lev Aryeh*, Genesis, p. 109, who suggests that Joseph was given a coat as a gift by his father Jacob in order to offset the negative speech he relayed concerning his brothers.

43. See *Divrei Yaakov* to Arakhin.
44. In the journal *Kol HaTorah* 61, p. 47.
45. For further comments on the symbolism of the coat, see Rabbi Mordekhai Benedict, *She'arim Metzuyanim al HaTorah*, pp. 458–59.

However, in the modern era, in which we have neither priestly vestments[46] nor instances of the *tzaraat* affliction,[47] there is still another specific remedy for *lashon hara* expressed by the Talmud, in addition to a general effort to increase one's sense of humility. There is one activity, we are told, which is able to accomplish that which other methods cannot in fixing the internal flaws associated with *lashon hara,* and that is the study of Torah.[48]

---

46. Although some understand that the priestly vestments continue to atone today, per Yoma 72b.
47. The *Ḥafetz Ḥayim* (*Shemirat HaLashon,* ch. 7) expounds the absence of *tzaraat* in modern times as due to the lack of a purification process, explaining that the affliction was not meant to be punitive, but corrective; see also *Shemuot Ḥayim,* Arakhin 15b. Other perspectives are surveyed in *VaYita Eshel* to Arakhin 99.
48. Arakhin 15b, based on Prov. 15:4. The Talmud has two versions of this suggestion; in one version, Torah study and humility are effective for repenting from *lashon hara;* the other version maintains that no remedy is possible after the fact, but that these are effective in preventing *lashon hara* in the first place. This second view is addressed by the *Ḥafetz Ḥayim* in his *Shemirat HaLashon, shaar HaTorah,* in a footnote, in which he offers two interpretations. One is that the Talmud is identifying the two aspects present in *lashon hara,* the interpersonal aspect which cannot be addressed without the forgiveness of the victim, and the corruption of the speaker, which is addressed through Torah study. A second distinction is cited from the *Menorat HaMaor, ner 2, klal* 4, who asserts that the view that there is no remedy is referring only to one who is habituated to *lashon hara* and continues to engage in it, not to one who has stumbled on occasion; see *Oraḥ Meisharim,* 8:31. Note also *Be'er Mayim Ḥayim, Laws of Lashon HaRa* 4:49. Alternatively, Rabbi Raphael of Hamburg, in his *Marpei Lashon,* takes the Talmud's statement at face value, and assumes that Torah study and humility are only effective in preventing *lashon hara* in the first place; after it has been spoken, the only option is absolute repentance.

    See also *Lev Aryeh,* pp. 323–24; *Erekh HaḤayim,* Arakhin 16b; *Shemuot Ḥayim,* Arakhin, ch. 3, no. 20; and *Ḥelkat Yehoshua,* Arakhin 15b, no. 22. For another talmudic statement regarding the role of Torah study as a corrective for *lashon hara,* see Y. Taanit 1:1. For further comments regarding Torah study as an atonement for *lashon hara,* see Rabbi Eliezer Geldzehler, *Torat Eliezer,* letter 6, p. 205, n. 18, and see, at length, *Emek HaLashon,* pp. 228–36.

    The Vilna Gaon, in his commentary to Proverbs, asserts that Torah study is only effective when it is constant; an explanation for the source of this idea (as well as one for another author's assertion that the motivation for the study must be pure) is suggested in *Responsa Birkat Reuven Shlomo* IV:49. See also *Shemuot Ḥayim,* Arakhin, ch. 3, no. 21.

However, many who were themselves great scholars found this suggestion difficult. The tendency toward *lashon hara* is broad and pervasive, and appears to exist even among those very well versed in the Torah and the Talmud (Sota 21a). This concept requires some explanation, and to seek a greater understanding we turn now to our final chapter.

Epilogue: Remembering Miriam

The biblical Miriam, one of the great heroines of Jewish history, is ironically associated in a formal way with one regrettable episode of her noble and distinguished life. Speaking to her brother Aaron, she says something regarding their brother Moses and his relationship with his wife, although the Torah does not explicitly detail the words that she uttered.[1] Following this act, she was afflicted with *tzaraat,* and healed after Moses prayed on her behalf (Num. 12:1–15).[2]

1. There is much discussion as to how Miriam's comments constituted *lashon hara,* especially as they are considered a cautionary model for all of us. Many maintain that her offense was an assessment of Moses as comparable to others, without regard for his unique status. If so, such diminishment is relevant to the general *lashon hara* concern when it is categorized as any comment that reduces the status of the subject in the eyes of the listeners (see *Netiv Ḥayim* 8:2). Others note that Miriam failed to extend the benefit of the doubt to Moses, and that is an aspect of *lashon hara.* (See *Ḥafetz Ḥayim, Laws of Lashon HaRa, klal* 8, *Be'er Mayim Ḥayim* 1, and *Paḥad Yitzḥak, Shavuot* 3.) Rabbi Shlomo Zalman Kook assumes the commandment to remember Miriam is focused on *lashon hara* that is false; see *Bein Shenei Kohanim Gedolim,* p. 143. See also *Emek HaLashon* 48.
2. There is some discussion as to why Miriam was so afflicted when the Talmud says this is only a consequence for "successful" *lashon hara,* which was presumably not present here. See commentary of Rabbi Yeshaya Pik to *She'iltot* of Rabbi Aḥai Gaon

The incident with Miriam is central to an unusual commandment in the Torah. The verse states "Remember what the Lord your God did to Miriam on the way, when you were leaving Egypt" (Deut. 24:9).[3] Nahmanides,[4] differing from Maimonides,[5] includes this in the list of 613 commandments.[6] The commentaries attribute a straightforward purpose to the imperative: to stem the inclination to speak *lashon hara.*

However, this motive would seem to be insufficient basis for a dedicated commandment. There are hundreds of prohibitions in the Torah, and on the whole they exist without need for either cautionary tales or special commandments to remember those tales. The singling out of the prohibition of *lashon hara* for this type of support begs explanation.

In his ethical discourses, Rabbi Yitzḥak Eizik Sher, the spiritual guide of the Slobodka Yeshiva, addresses this question by making reference to broad groups of offenses included in the rubric *lashon*

98:104: *Ḥafetz Ḥayim, Laws of Lashon HaRa, klal* 3, in *Be'er Mayim Ḥayim* 6; and Rabbi Mordekhai Karlebakh, *Ḥavatzelet HaSharon,* Numbers, p. 398.

3. One may consider it ironic that the Torah highlights the dangers of *lashon hara* by appearing to disparage and to perpetuate the memory of the discrediting of Miriam, especially considering her great stature. See Nahmanides to Deut. 25:17, and also Rabbi Aharon Kotler, *Mishnat Rabbi Aharon al HaTorah,* pp. 343–44, and *Ḥiddushei Torah* of the Satmar Rebbe, Deuteronomy, p. 10, as well as *Ḥokhma UMusar* II, 340, and *Daliyut Yeḥezkel* and *Lemaan Aḥai VeRe'ai,* both cited in *Ḥokhmat HaMatzpun,* Deuteronomy (vol. II) pp. 191–93 and *Iyyunim BaParasha,* Leviticus pp. 91–92. See also the discussion of this and related topics in *VaYita Eshel* to Arakhin 96.

   See also Rabbi Nissim Dayan, *Peirot Genosar,* p. 53, regarding the question of why Miriam was punished more severely than Moses himself was for a similar offense (Ex.4:1–7).

4. Deut., 25:17, and glosses to *Sefer HaMitzvot,* positive commandment 7.
5. See Rabbi Tzvi Ryzman, *Ratz KaTzvi,* II, pp. 162–63; Rabbi Yaakov Ḥayim Sofer, *Teranen Leshoni* 19, p. 82, and see also Rabbi Yehuda Tzarum, *Mishnat Yehuda,* p. 300.
6. Note also the rendering of *Targum Yonatan* and the ruling of Maharil, *Sefer Minhagim, Laws of the Ten Days of Repentance* 14, p. 309, and see Rabbi David Zvi Hoffmann, commentary to Deuteronomy. As to the practical implications and the adoption of this position (or lack of same) by halakhic authorities, see Rabbi Tzvi Elimelekh Schapiro, *Benei Yissakhar, Maamarei Ḥodesh Adar, maamar* 3, *derush* 6, no. 9; Rabbi Yosef Greenwald, *Responsa VaYaan Yosef* III, 408:1, and Rabbi Moshe Feinstein, *Responsa Iggerot Moshe,* VIII, *Oraḥ Ḥayim* V, p. 4.

hara under the title of *avak lashon hara*.[7] This category includes not only the intentional disparagement of one's fellow, but even positive statements that unwittingly yield negative interpretations.[8] One might question the fairness of the inclusion of the latter. By definition, the speaker has benevolent intentions. To assume a prohibition in such a case would seem to pose a nearly impossible burden. It is possible, if difficult, to refrain from malicious commenting about others. However, if the speaker is unaware of the negative impact of his statements, how can he avoid the offense?[9]

It is here that the unique risks inherent in speaking *lashon hara* are in evidence, and justify the exceptional focus afforded by additional commandments and cautionary tales. *Lashon hara* is not a transgression one can avoid by simply deciding to refrain from committing the transgression. It is the expression of a mindset, sometimes an active negativity and distortion of judgment, and sometimes a simple insensitivity and lack of appreciation. *Lashon hara* may emerge from insufficient awareness of the unique nature of other individuals; of their particular sensitivities and frailties; of the impact of speech and the differences between the speaker and the listener; or, of the cognitive biases and tendencies that transform our words into weapons by the time they have reached their target.

All of these risks are not offset by a simple commitment. Avoiding the transgression requires forethought, internal reconditioning, training, and practice. There can be no greater reminder of this than the story of Miriam. A great woman of towering stature with the best and purest of intentions, Miriam found herself inadvertently in violation of the prohibition of *lashon hara*. Surely, the rest of us are no better equipped to avoid this transgression. What hope, then, is there for us? Our only advantage is the benefit of the story of Miriam, and all of the Torah literature that surrounds it: a cautionary message that this area of human interaction requires "remembrance," in the sense of extensive advance preparation.[10]

---

7. *Lekket Siḥot Musar* 1, pp. 394–95.
8. *Mishneh Torah, Laws of Personal Development* 7:4.
9. Indeed, as noted earlier, the Talmud (Bava Batra 164b–165a) states that all of us are guilty of at least *avak lashon hara*.
10. R. Reuven Schwartz, in the introduction to his *Emek HaLashon*, notes that while other commandments of "remembering" in the Torah demand discrete acts of

This reality may contribute to an understanding of a difficult comment of the Rabbis.[11] The story of Miriam and her punishment is immediately followed in the Torah by the episode of the spies who spoke negatively of the Land of Israel. The Rabbis comment on the juxtaposition by noting that in their behavior, the spies failed to learn the lesson of Miriam.[12]

The comment is difficult, because it seems to imply there is an argument a fortiori: what Miriam did was bad, what the spies did was worse. However, instinct would point in the other direction; Miriam spoke about a human being, with feelings and emotions, while the spies sinned against land. In fact, the Talmud itself adopts this perspective, stating that the story of the spies teaches us the severity of *lashon hara,* as the punishment of the spies was for disparaging the Land of Israel, and surely to speak badly of humans must therefore be far worse.[13]

It would seem, rather, that the Rabbis are making a different point. Miriam's transgression was indeed, in terms of the victim, worse than that of the spies. The lesson the spies should have learned was not that their disparagement of the Land constituted an even more severe violation. The lesson actually had to do with the extreme complexity and challenges involved in addressing negativity through speech and thought. If Miriam, with her personal greatness and noble intentions, could still run afoul of this value, clearly a program of mental reorientation and proactive attitude adjustment is necessary.

An instructive comparison may come, perhaps unexpectedly, from the laws of Kiddush on Friday night. When this ritual is performed over wine, the practice is to cover the *ḥalla* breads. The Talmud and

---

recitation or the like, the commandment to remember Miriam appears to be a constant imperative of awareness, correlating to the ongoing challenge of *lashon hara.* See *Birkat Reuven Shlomo* to Megillla, no. 24.

11. *Yalkut Shimoni* 11:459, quoted by Rashi in his commentary to the Torah.
12. On this derivation, see *Ḥiddushei HaLev,* Numbers, pp. 76–77.
13. Arakhin 15a. See also Rabbi Naphtali Tzvi Yehuda Berlin, *Haamek Davar* to Deut. 24:9; *Shemirat HaLashon, Parashat Shelaḥ;* Rabbi Moshe Galanti, *Zevaḥ Shelamim, Parashat Behaalotekha* 94; Rabbi Raphael Tzaban, *Nefesh Ḥayya* 11, *Parashat Shelaḥ* 1; Rabbi Avigdor Nebenzahl, *Siḥot LeSefer Bemidbar* 8, 9; and Rabbi Barukh Mordekhai Ezraḥi, in *BeYad HaLashon,* pp. 315–16.

commentators offer a number of possible explanations, one of which seems particularly striking. According to the general rule, we recite the blessing on bread first; in the case of Kiddush, the wine is the object of the first blessing. Accordingly, the *ḥalla* breads are covered so they should not be "embarrassed" by the "honor" accorded to the wine."[14]

This attribution of human feelings to pastry is difficult to understand. Are we truly concerned that inanimate objects will experience humiliation? It seems, rather, that the concern relates to the complexity of human emotion. Determining what will or will not have hurtful consequences to another is a highly involved enterprise, one that does not come easily to the untrained intuition. To assume that undeveloped instinct will rise to the challenge of the moment is dangerous; offense can occur even unintentionally, when the speaker is unpracticed in the nuances of human sensitivity. Thus, even interactions with inanimate objects are viewed as opportunities to hone the awareness necessary to deal with actual people. Being cognizant of a "slight" to *ḥalla* will, it is hoped, instill awareness of the risk involved when a human is in such a situation.[15]

The obligation to remember Miriam, then, calls for training oneself in sensitivity in advance, so that when a situation presents itself, there is a hope that the challenge will be negotiated successfully. This, then, is the lesson that the spies failed to learn. Immediately after Miriam's punishment, the indulgence of a biased negativity in evaluating the Land of Israel was a complete rejection of the moral message.[16]

---

14. The Jerusalem Talmud, cited in *Tur, Oraḥ Ḥayim* 271, and see *Or Zarua, Laws of Shabbat* 11:22.
15. The value of this exercise could thus explain the extensive analyses and hypothetical discussions devoted to the practice of *ḥalla* covering; see, for example, *Responsa Iggerot Moshe*; Rabbi David Rosenberg, *Responsa Minḥat David* 1:2; Rabbi Yisrael David Harfenes, *Nishmat Shabbat* 11, p. 41.
16. On other aspects of the commandment to remember the incident of Miriam, see also Rabbi Tzvi A. Neugroshol in the journal *Kol MeHeikhal* VII (Tevet 5758), pp. 99–101. See also Rabbi Aharon Kotler, *Mishnat Rabbi Aharon al HaTorah*, pp. 342–43, *Ḥavatzelet HaSharon*, Numbers, pp. 390–392; Rabbi Ḥayim Shmuelevitz, *Siḥot Musar* 5732, *Parashot Tazria–Metzora;* and Rabbi Moshe Schapiro, in *BeYad HaLashon*, p. 378.

We have seen that the discussion of *lashon hara* draws heavily on two components, the practice of harmful speech, and the corresponding malevolence of spirit. These two elements possess a sort of negative synergy; the character trait makes the harmful effect more likely, and committing the offense nurtures the malicious nature. While one or the other might dominate as the focus of the prohibition, it is difficult to escape from the interconnectedness of the two.

The commandment to remember Miriam is a reminder of this negative loop. It is impossible to extricate oneself from the behavior of *lashon hara* without addressing its accompanying mentality. The mentality, in turn, is developed and fed by the behavior. Maimonides, who declined to list this obligation as an actual commandment, nonetheless appears to understand it that way, when he details, in the laws of the impurity conferred by *tzaraat,*[17] the nature of *lashon hara* as an escalating pattern, in which one who expresses negativity towards others builds on this tendency until ultimately he disparages God himself.[18]

The authoritative commentary to the code of Jewish law known as the *Magen Avraham* quotes a suggestion that the blessing recited prior to the daily recitation of the *Shema* passage contains allusions to various commandments in the Torah directed at remembering.[19] The commandment to remember Miriam, according to this conception, is hinted at in the words "to offer praiseful thanks to you" (*lehodot lekha*). The *Magen Avraham* expounds that the mouth was created to give praise to God, not to speak *lashon hara.*[20] Another interpretation, though, is that one who indulges in negative attitudes will, as Maimonides warns, grow increasingly cynical, and ultimately lose the instinct to be thankful to God.

It is noteworthy that one interpretation in the Midrash[21] of the commandment to remember Miriam and how it is to be implemented practically is that it constitutes an imperative to study the relevant laws of *lashon hara.*[22] While the notion of study as a form of remembrance

17. *Mishneh Torah, Laws of Contamination from Tzaraat* 16:10.
18. See also Rabbi Moshe Scheinerman, *Ohel Moshe,* Leviticus, pp. 316–17.
19. *Oraḥ Ḥayim* 60:2.
20. See also the journal *Kol HaTorah* LXIV, p 161.
21. *Sifra* to Lev. 26:3 See Nahmanides to Deut. 24:9.
22. See also Rabbi Betzalel Stern, *Responsa BeTzel HaḤokhma* VI:47.

is a recurring theme in the Torah, in this instance it seems to have particular significance. When the Talmud identifies Torah study as the only true corrective, on a personal level, to *lashon hara,* it seems that it is not referring to the general purifying aspects of Torah study that are discussed elsewhere.

Rather, the intent here is to recognize that *lashon hara* can be addressed on both a behavioral level and an attitudinal level. To be successful in this realm, one must work to understand and internalize the principles involved in the prohibition of *lashon hara* and its related precepts. As noted, there were and are Torah scholars who nonetheless stumble in the area of *lashon hara,* despite their great learning. This phenomenon is addressed by some of the prominent authorities who gave written approbations to the volume *Ḥafetz Ḥayim.* They assert that it is not general Torah study that is effective in this role, but specifically the focus on the laws of *lashon hara,* its underlying principles and concepts, coupled with personal commitment, that can bring about the shift in personality that is required.[23]

The mysterious peddler quoted King David as advocating keeping one's lips "from speaking deceitfully" (Ps. 34:14). Rabbi Yosef Tzvi Dushinsky explains the usage here of the word "deceitfully."[24] One will only see the promise of that verse if one is able to bring the mind, the heart, and the mouth into sync with each other. A disconnect between them – a mind that is "deceitfully" judging one's fellow negatively while outwardly praising him – will ultimately express his disparaging sentiment outwardly, even if it is initially concealed.[25]

Thus, this prototypical "Jewish" mitzva is, perhaps also typically, a fusion of personality and practice, one that by its very nature demands an integration of mind, manner, and message. Thus, it is understandable that study has taken such a central role in the realization of this religious precept. The full embodiment of the Torah's vision of a just, responsible

23. See the approbation of the rabbinic court judges of Vilna, Rabbi Yosef and Rabbi Betzalel HaKohen, to *Ḥafetz Ḥayim.* See also Rabbi Yisrael Salanter, *Iggeret HaMusar,* s.v. *hanisgav,* and *Responsa Az Nidberu* XI:42, at length, and *VaYita Eshel* to Arakhin 97.

24. *Torat Maharitz* to Leviticus.

25. See also Rabbi Avraham Yaakov Pam, *Moreh Tzedek,* pp. 175–80.

and compassionate citizen demands a lifetime commitment to learning, understanding, and growing.

Furthermore, the unique demands and balances of *lashon hara* require even greater awareness and sensitivity than is generally necessary to be an observant, pious, and caring individual. As we have seen, making appropriate decisions in this area involves a constant recognition of the competing and sometimes conflicting needs of avoiding malicious speech on the one hand, and the protection of the innocent and the positive functioning and development of society on the other. More often than not, there is no clear-cut, easily provided answer to the quandaries that arise in this area, and no simple guideline or slogan that will reduce the complexity of the issue. A deeply refined appreciation for all of the relevant values and a sophisticated knowledge and understanding of the applicable principles and precepts is a necessary foundation to approaching these areas responsibly.

Much harm is done if those who could protect the innocent fail to because of misguided conceptions of the laws of *lashon hara;* similarly, much devastation can be inflicted by those who would speak with malice or insensitivity, cloaked in either a false or mistaken veneer of purpose and necessity. The fact that either mistake can be defended by pointing to either value – that of speaking out in defense of others and that of observing the laws of *lashon hara* – is irrelevant. In this as with all areas of life, we are responsible for the quality of our judgment calls. This means, in turn, that we are responsible for the substance of our judgment; to ensure that it is built upon solid knowledge, sensitivity, perspective, wisdom, and maturity. To some, this is actually the main lesson of the mysterious peddler; the life that is desired by he who "loves days" is obtained not through simple abstinence, but through the awareness born of constant study.[26] Achieving this level of awareness requires a lifetime of living and learning and is a mission that is never complete.

When the Torah includes the prohibition of talebearing in the same verse as the mandate to protect the victimized, it concludes the verse with the words "I am God" (Lev. 19:16). Rabbinic tradition teaches that there are specific moments when the Torah finds it necessary to

26. See *Birkat Reuven Shlomo, Parashat Metzora.*

remind us of God's presence. It is at those times when nobility of behavior and righteousness of deed is concealed from outside observers, when either poor judgment or maliciousness of intent can be hidden behind a credible excuse, that the actor is told to remember that God is watching. Yes, the verse contains two competing mandates that demand balance and judgment; however, this does not mean that all decisions are equally valid, but rather that the burden is on the actor to ensure that God's wisdom and command are deeply infused into the discretionary process.[27]

In his work of responsa, the great sixteenth-century rabbinic authority Rabbi Shlomo Luria, known as the Maharshal, describes his daily ritual.[28] He notes that every day, immediately after reciting the blessing on learning Torah, he studies a representative selection of passages of Torah content. From Scripture, he recites a passage of three consecutive verses, which he considers "equal to the entire Torah." This set is comprised of the verses beginning with the "peddler verse" and ending with "you shall love your fellow as yourself."

Perhaps, with what we have seen emanating from the "peddler verse," we can understand how even this verse alone may contain principles representative of the entire Torah. The Talmud (Makkot 24a) teaches that the defining values of the Torah are summarized in one verse from the Book of Micah: "It has been told to you, O man, what is good, and what God requires of you: only to do justice, and to love kindness, and to walk modestly with your God" (6:8). The mandate not to go about "as a peddler" gives us directives including all of these principles. It teaches us to respect privacy, the essence of modesty; it teaches us to truly empathize and identify with the needs of others, their uniqueness, and their sensitivities, the essence of compassion; and it teaches us to genuinely weigh all relevant factors, realities, and variables in our judgment of others, and to balance them against the basic needs of the innocent and of society in general, the essence of justice.

The focus that has emerged in recent years on the study of the laws of *lashon hara* is a profound gift. A life devoted to understanding and refining commitment to these principles is a life of ever-expanding

27. See *Pitḥei Teshuva, Oraḥ Ḥayim* 156.

28. *Responsa Maharshal* 64.

sensitivity, of ever-growing awareness, of ever-increasing appreciation of the complexity of humanity. It is a constant attention to the most fundamental needs of others, in all of their diversity and nuance. It is a lifelong course in the finest points of interpersonal interaction. It is a mindset that forces the trivialities of life to recede and to fade, while directing attention towards the genuine priorities of life, whatever they may be. It is a recognition of the endless capacity to grow, to improve, and to transcend a history of mistakes or misjudgments. It is an affirmation that humans must not be painted by the brush of their worst moments, and that the full picture of an individual will always be so much more than any other person can grasp at any moment. It is, in essence, to derive infinite potential through perceiving the infinite potential in others.

We are deeply fortunate to have a tradition of texts and teachings that can guide us in developing the personalities necessary to give expression to these values. We cannot guarantee that our answers will be the right ones, but we can commit to a process that is honest, informed, compassionate, and responsible. We can be the grateful beneficiaries of the legacy that was commanded by the Torah and expressed by King David, King Solomon, the rabbinic literature, the *Ḥafetz Ḥayim*, and all who shared in their vision. As the mysterious peddler promised, if we truly desire a life of love and goodness, there is a path; the first step toward walking on it is to see that it is there, waiting for us.

Halakhic Rulings by Rabbi Hershel Schachter

One who is asked to provide a recommendation for a school must tell the truth about the student. Having a student that is mismatched to the school will be detrimental both to the school and to the applicant. If the student is weak or irresponsible, then the institution must be told, as they would otherwise be harmed.

Dorm counselors are permitted to report on the happenings in the dormitory, so that the administration can correct any issues and make sure that students are getting along.

Teachers may discuss with other teachers if a child cheats on tests, so that the other teachers can be aware and are able to take the proper steps toward the education of this student and other students.

Faculty evaluations by students contain a *to'elet* and do not constitute *lashon hara,* as long as there is no public embarrassment.

If one is asked to comment on a potential *shiddukh,* and the respondent feels that the subject has undesirable attributes, an appropriate method for addressing the question without unnecessarily disparaging the subject is to ask the inquirer what they are looking for in a match, and to then respond that the subject does not fit that description.

If one needs to relate negative information about others in order to unburden themselves psychologically, the spouse may often be the most appropriate confidante.

Rabbi Shachter is the Rosh Yeshiva of the Rabbi Isaac Elchanan Theological Seminary and Rosh Kollel of the Adina and Marcos Katz Kollel.

Halakhic Rulings by Rabbi Mordechai Willig

OBLIGATIONS OF DISCLOSURE IN *SHIDDUKHIM*

In Chapter VI (pp. 107–119), the issue of disclosure regarding potential marriage partners is examined. What must be revealed, when, and by whom? Reference is made (n. 312) to *Kehillot Yaakov* (Yevamot #38, in later editions #44) who distinguishes between merchandise and marriage. In the former instance, the availability of identical unflawed items demands full disclosure of flaws, since one can easily purchase an identical unflawed item. In the latter, one cannot find an identical mate without the flaw. Therefore, it need not be disclosed.

Kehillot Yaakov acknowledges that major issues must be disclosed, but greatly limits their scope. Only an issue so severe that that one would seek a divorce upon discovering after marriage must be revealed.

The Talmudic source for limiting the obligation of disclosure is Yevamot 45a. One whose father is not Jewish may go to a place where his lineage is unknown in order to marry. If they, the *kallah*'s family, would know, they would not agree to the match (Rashi). As noted (n. 44), *Kehillot Yaakov* adds that if a flaw would be revealed early on, it would be nearly impossible to find a *shiddukh*. From this perspective, the flaw should be revealed after the couple has established a relationship. The flaws can then be evaluated in the context of the whole person.

Indeed, *Ḥazon Ish*, brother-in-law and mentor of *Kehillat Ya'akov* (cited by Rav Yitzchak Zilberstein in *Bina LeShiddukh*, p. 534) rules that blemishes, as defined by the community, should be disclosed at the last dates, towards the end of the courtship. It is unwise to hide something that will ultimately be discovered as the deceived party may harbor resentment for a lifetime.

In fact, Rav Elyashiv, *meḥutan* of *Kehillat Yaakov* (cited by his son-in-law Rav Zilberstein, p. 552), rules that one whose father is a non-Jew must reveal this fact. This seems to contradict the aforementioned Gemara (Yevamot 45a) that allows such a person to hide this information.

Perhaps R. Elyashiv accepts the view of the Netziv (*Meshiv Davar* 2:50) and the *Imrei Yosher* (2:214), that in talmudic times, if one travelled to a distant location it would never become known that his father is a non-Jew. Nowadays it will ultimately be discovered and, as *Ḥazon Ish* ruled, must be revealed.

Elsewhere (*Nishmat Avraham* 5, p. 118), R. Elyashiv distinguishes between issues of lineage, which are subjective, and not an intrinsic problem, and a medical issue, which is intrinsic and objective. As such, diabetes, for example, must be disclosed during the second half of the anticipated dating period.

The responsibility of the girl's family to investigate a boy's Torah scholarship exempts not only a third party's involvement (n. 53), but also the boy's family's obligation to disclose a lack of scholarship. *Kehilot Yaakov* suggests that a boy may hide the fact that his father was a non-Jew precisely because the *kallah*'s family did not inquire. He rejects this notion because it was very unusual in Talmudic times for a Jew to have a non-Jewish father. Failure to inquire is not attributed to indifference but rather to a reasonable assumption that the father is Jewish.

Kehillot Yaakov, therefore, returns to his original point, that a problem need not be disclosed if its discovery after the marriage would not lead to divorce. A precedent is found in the Ran (Ketubot 54b) in pages of the Rif. A divorcee need not reveal her status to a Kohen. Even though the marriage is prohibited, the man may find the match pleasing and not seek a divorce. *Ḥazon Ish* (*Even HaEzer* 79:16) adds that a Kohen might choose to marry a divorcee, despite the prohibition, if her status is disclosed just before the wedding, even though he never would have agreed to meet her had he known of it originally.

Potential medical issues are debated by *posekim*. For example, a girl who has not menstruated may be infertile. As such, Rav Zilberstein (p. 551–52) rules that it must be disclosed unless the strong likelihood (presumably over 90 percent) is that she can conceive with intervention. *Iggerot Moshe* (*Even HaEzer* 3:27) allows the issue to be hidden as long as there is a chance that she can conceive. *Iggerot Moshe* requires that the woman agree to receive a *get* unconditionally, if after four years she is unable to conceive. In that case, the man will not have lost too much.

Parents sometimes complain about a flaw disclosed after several dates that causes them to terminate the relationship. Why was it not disclosed initially? My child would have avoided the investment of time and emotion. *Iggerot Moshe*'s ruling should be shared with them. Even Rav Zilberstein, whose ruling seems more correct, allows for non-disclosure of significant flaws until late in the dating process, as mentioned citing *Ḥazon Ish*. The "loss" of one party must be balanced by the gain of the other to potentially find a marriage partner.

Genetic markers can also be controversial. Rav Zilberstein (p. 558) rules that if a girl has the BRCA gene she must disclose it. If her mother has the BRCA gene, the daughter must be tested. Otherwise she is fooling the boy by not telling him that she has a 50 percent chance of having the BRCA gene.

Kehillot Yaakov would certainly disagree. Moreover, if the mother's breast cancer is well known, the obligation to inquire may be with the boy's family, as *Kehillot Yaakov* notes, since it is not unusual for the mother and the daughter to share the BRCA gene. Ironically, then, the more rare and/or secret a condition is, the greater the obligation to disclose.

The question regarding BRCA is just one representative example. Similarly, other genetic conditions, whether affecting men or women, must be evaluated in proportion to the relative statistics, potential harm, and scope of impact, among other factors.

Rabbi Willig is a Rosh Yeshiva of the Rabbi Isaac Elchanan Theological Seminary, Rosh Kollel of the Wexner Kollel Elyon, Segan Rosh Kollel of the Rabbi Norman Lamm Kollel L'Hora'ah, and the rabbi of Young Israel of Riverdale.

List of Sources Cited

Primary Hebrew sources for this book can be found at www.yutorah.org/_materials/lashon-hara-sources.pdf.

Dates and cities listed refer to one edition, not necessarily the first or the most recent. Some dates are approximated from the Hebrew dates. An indented listing is a commentary to the work listed immediately before it.

A. THE BIBLE AND COMMENTARIES

These works are arranged as commentaries to Tanakh.

Akedat Yitzḥak. Rabbi Yitzḥak Arama (ca. 1420–94). Levov, 1868.

Aleinu Leshabeaḥ. Rabbi Yitzḥak Zilberstein (contemporary, b. 1934). Edited by Moshe Michael Stern.

Al Pi HaTorah. Rabbi Yosef Tzvi Adler (contemporary). Jerusalem, 2013.

Asufat Maarakhot. Rabbi Chaim Yaakov Goldvicht (1924–95). Founding Rosh Yeshiva of Yeshivat Kerem B'Yavneh.

Ateret Tzvi. Rabbi Tzvi Hertzka.

Ateret Zahav. Rabbi Eliezer Adirim. Sratuga, 1919.

Ayelet HaShahar. Rabbi Aharon Leib Shteinman (contemporary). Benei Berak, Israel, 2006.

Bad Kodesh. Rabbi Barukh Dov Povarsky (contemporary). Oral discourses edited by students. Benei Berak, Israel: Yeshivat Ponevezh, 2001.

Bikkurei Avraham. Rabbi Avraham Elyashuv (b. 1942). Warsaw.

Birkat Mordekhai. Rabbi Barukh Mordekhai Ezraḥi (contemporary). Jerusalem, 1995.

Brit Olam. Rabbi Moshe David Valley (1696–1777). Jerusalem, 1995.

Commentary to the Penateuch. Rabbi David Zvi Hoffmann (1843–1921). Germany.

Derekh Siḥa. Rabbi Ḥayim Kanievsky. Benei Berak, Israel: Sifrei Or HaḤayim, 2003.

Devar Torah. Rabbi Chaim Shlomo Abraham (contemporary). Brooklyn, New York, 2005.

Divrei Yaakov. Rabbi Yaakov Shechter (1887–1971). Commentary to Proverbs. Jerusalem, 1963.

Ela HaDevarim. Rabbi Eliyahu Shlesinger (contemporary). Jerusalem: Shaar HaMelekh, 1993.

Emet LeYaakov: Iyyunim BeMikra. Rabbi Yaakov Kaminetsky (1891–1986). Edited by Rabbi Daniel Yehuda Neustadt. New York: Makhon Emet L'Ya'akov, 1990. Rosh Yeshiva of Yeshiva Torah VoDaath, Brooklyn, New York. His talmudic lectures have also been published in volumes of the same name, *Emet LeYaakov.*

Haamek Davar and *Harḥev Davar.* Rabbi Naphtali Tzvi Yehuda Berlin (1817–93). Known as the Netziv, he was Rosh Yeshiva of the Volozhin Yeshiva and also authored *Haamek She'ela* to the *She'iltot DeRav Aḥai Gaon, Meromei Sadeh* to the Talmud, and *Shut Meshiv Davar* (see individual listings), as well as other works.

HaKetav VeHakabbala. Rabbi Yaakov Tzvi Mecklenberg (1785–1865). Frankfurt, 1880. Chief rabbi of Koenigsberg, Germany.

HaMidrash VeHaMaase. Rabbi Yeḥiel Libshitz (1862–1932). Petrikev (Piotrkow), 1901.

HaTorah VeHaMitzva. Rabbi Meir Leibush Malbim (1809–79). New York: Torath Israel, 1950.

Ḥavatzelet HaSharon al HaTorah. Rabbi Mordekhai Karlebakh. Jerusalem, 2004.

Ḥiddushei HaLev. Rabbi A. Chenakh Leibowitz. Rosh Yeshiva of Yeshivat Chafetz Chaim in Forest Hills, Queens, New York. Prepared by his students. Jerusalem and Forest Hills, 1987.

Ḥiddushei Torah. Rabbi Yoel Teitelbaum (1887–1979). Satmar Rebbe. Brooklyn, New York: Beit Mischar Sefarim Yerushalayim, 1979.

Ḥokhmat HaMatzpun. Collection of comments by great ethicists arranged in order of the Torah, edited by Rabbi Moshe Avgi. Benei Berak, Israel, 1989.

Ibn Ezra. Rabbi Avraham Ibn Ezra (d. 1167). Printed in standard *Mikraot Gedolot* editions.

Imrei Aharon. Rabbi Aharon HaKohen. France, 1986.

Imrei Barukh. Rabbi Barukh Meir Klein. Munkatsh, 1911.

Imrei Yosher. Rabbi Meir Eisenstat (1786–1852).

Iyyunei Rashi. Rabbi Avraham Yitzḥak Brazil (contemporary). Kiryat Sefer, Israel, 2008.

Iyyunim BaParasha. Rabbi Yehoshua Heschel Ryzman. 2010.

KaMatar Likḥi. Collection of essays by various authors, including many Rashei Yeshiva, arranged by the weekly Torah portion. Edited by Rabbi Yirmiyahu Fraiman. Jerusalem, 2014.

Keli Ḥemda, Rabbi Meir Dan Plotzki (1867–1928). Petaḥ Tikva, Israel: Yeshivat Lomza, 1996. Student of *Avnei Nezer,* he also authored *Ḥemdat Yisrael*.

Ketav Sofer al HaTorah. Rabbi Avraham Shmuel Binyamin Sofer. Tel Aviv: Sinai, 1966.

Kol Yehuda. Rabbi Yehuda Aryeh Klein. Jerusalem, 1970.

Lev Aryeh. Rabbi Aryeh Leib Hoshki. Kiryat Yoel, NY: Broch, 1991.

Lehorot Natan. Rabbi Natan Gestetner (1932–2010) of Benei Berak, Israel. Authored many other works, such as responsa by the same name (see Section G), commentary to Pirkei Avot (see Section L) and the festivals, and *Natan Piryo* to tractates of the Talmud and sections of the *Shulḥan Arukh* (see Section D). A descendant of Rabbi Akiva Eiger, he has also brought to print writings of that scholar.

Lev Tahor. Rabbi Avigdor Parnes (contemporary). Jerusalem, 2002.

Likkutei Siḥot. Rabbi Menachem Mendel Schneersohn (1902–94) of Brooklyn, New York. Brooklyn: Kehot (*Karnei Hod Torah*)

Publication Society. Seventh Rebbe of Lubavitch (Chabad). His ideas are also printed in the form of *Siḥot, Ḥiddushim LeShas, Biurim LePirkei Avot,* and responsa.

Maharil Diskin al HaTorah. Rabbi Moshe Yehoshua Yehuda Leib Diskin (1818–98). Rabbi of Brisk.

Manot HaLevi. Rabbi Shlomo Alkabetz (1505–76). To the Book of Esther. Brooklyn, New York, 1954.

Meshekh Ḥokhma. Rabbi Meir Simḥa HaKohen of Dvinsk. Jerusalem, 1974.

Minḥat Asher al HaTorah. Rabbi Asher Weiss (contemporary). Jerusalem: Makhon Minḥat Asher, 2003.

Mishḥat Shemen. Rabbi Chaim Shaul Kaufman (contemporary). Jerusalem, 2007. Rosh Yeshiva of Tiferet Yaakov of Gateshead, England.

Mishkan Betzalel. Rabbi Betzalel Rudinsky (contemporary). Suffern, New York, 2005.

Mishnat Rabbi Aharon al HaTorah. Rabbi Aharon Kotler (1892–1962). Lakewood, NJ: Makhon Mishnat Rabi Aharon, 2001. Founder and Rosh Yeshiva of Beth Medrash Govoha, Lakewood.

Naḥal Kedumim. Rabbi Aryeh Lubetsky. Brooklyn, New York, 1995.

Nahmanides. Rabbi Moshe ben Nahman (1194–1270) of Gerona, Spain. Also authored *Ḥiddushim* to the Talmud and many other works. In standard *Mikraot Gedolot* editions.

Shalmei Naḥum. Rabbi Naḥum Brobovsky. Jerusalem, 2005.

Nefesh Ḥayya. Rabbi Raphael Tzaban. Netivot, Israel: Makhon Neta Shaashuim, 2007.

Netivot Shalom. Rabbi Shalom Noaḥ Berezovsky (1911–2000). Slonimer Rebbe. Jerusalem: Yeshivat Beit Avraham Slonim, 1994.

Ohel Moshe. Rabbi Moshe Scheinerman. Brooklyn, New York, 2007.

Oraḥ LeḤayim. Rabbi Avraham Ḥayim of Zlotov. Montreal: R. Herzog, 2008.

Or HaḤayim. Rabbi Ḥayim ben Moshe Attar (1669–1743). In standard *Mikraot Gedolot* editions.

Otzar Tehillot Yisrael. Rabbi Yoel Menaḥem Mendel Saḥarov. Commentary to Psalms. Tel Aviv, 1956.

Oznayim LaTorah. Rabbi Zalman Sorotzkin (1881–1966). Known as the Lutzker Rav, he also authored *Moznayim LeMishpat.*

Pardes Yosef and *Pardes Yosef HaḤadash*. Rabbi Yosef Patzanofsky. Commentary to Genesis, Exodus, and Leviticus, containing citations from sources in all areas of Torah study. Loch, 1900. Rabbi David Avraham Mandelbaum (contemporary) has printed a new edition of this work, adding to it his own *Pardes Yosef HaḤadash* to Numbers and Deuteronomy, maintaining the eclectic style of the original and entitling the set *Pardes Yosef HaShalem*.

Perush HaGra to Proverbs. Rabbi Eliyahu ben Shlomo Zalman (1720–97). Petaḥ Tikva, Israel: Yeshivat Ohel Yosef, 1985. Towering scholar known as the *Gaon* of Vilna, or *Gra* (an acronym for *Gaon Rabbi Eliyahu*). Author of more than eighty works.

Rabbi Yehuda Assad al HaTorah. Rabbi Yehuda Assad (1797–1866). Pressburg, 1880, and Benei Berak, Israel, 1985. Rabbi of Rete and Semnitz. Student of Rabbi Mordekhai Benet. Also authored responsa.

Radak. Rabbi David Kimḥi (1160–1235). To the Prophets. In standard *Mikraot Gedolot* editions.

Rashi. Rabbi Shlomo ben Yitzḥak (Yitzḥaki) (1040–1105) of Troyes, France. Printed in most Hebrew editions of the Torah. Preeminent biblical and talmudical commentator; also authored responsa.

Rinat Yitzḥak. Rabbi Yitzḥak Sorotzkin (contemporary). Wickliffe, OH, 1998.

Shaarei Simḥa, Rabbi Simḥa Bunim Sofer (1842–1906), Vienna, 1923.

She'arim Metzuyanim al HaTorah. Rabbi Mordekhai Benedict (contemporary). Jerusalem, 2009.

Siḥot Binyan Av. Rabbi Eliyahu Bakshi-Doron. Former Sephardic chief rabbi of Israel.

Siḥot LeSefer Shemot, Bemidbar. Rabbi Avigdor Nebenzahl (contemporary). Rabbi of the Old City of Jerusalem. Beit El, Israel: Shemuot HaLevi, 1992.

Taam VeDaat. Rabbi Moshe Sternbuch (contemporary) of Johannesburg, South Africa, and Jerusalem. Benei Berak, Israel, 1962. Author of several works, such as *Responsa Teshuvot VeHanhagot*; *Mo'adim UZmanim* (see Section H); *Peshat VeHaIyyun* to the Talmud; and other works.

Targum Yonatan ben Uziel. In standard *Mikraot Gedolot* editions.

Torah Temima. Rabbi Barukh Epstein (1860–1942). New York: Hebrew Publishing, 1925. Biblical commentary intended to display the unity of Oral and Written Torahs, citing most talmudic and midrashic passages relevant to verses and adding a commentary analyzing the relationship. Also authored the biblical commentary *Tosefet Berakha,* and *Barukh She'amar* to *Pirkei Avot* and the prayerbook.

Torat Maharitz. Rabbi Yosef Tzvi Dushinsky (1868–1948). Jerusalem, 1957.

Torat Moshe. Rabbi Moshe Sofer (1763–1830). Rabbi of Pressburg and one of the leading halakhic authorities of his time, he became the son-in-law of Rabbi Akiva Eiger and ancestor to a long line of rabbinic scholars, beginning with his son *Ketav Sofer*. Also authored *ḥiddushim* to the Talmud and *Shulḥan Arukh,* and responsa.

Torat Yaakov. Rabbi Yaakov Ḥayim Sofer. Jerusalem, 2001.

VaYeḥi Yosef. Rabbi Yosef Greenwald. Brooklyn, New York, 1987.

VaYomer Moshe. Rabbi Moshe Yeḥiel Elimelekh (d. 1941) of Libertov. Jerusalem: Makhon Ginzei Maharitz she'al yedei Ḥasidei Bialya, 1985.

VeDarashta VeḤakarta. Rabbi Aharon Yehuda Grossman. Jerusalem, 1995. Also authored responsa.

Zekhut Avot. Rabbi Avraham Duri.

Zera Shimshon. Rabbi Shimshon Ḥayim Naḥmeni (d. 1779). Jerusalem: Wagshal, 1990. Also authored *Toledot Shimshon* to *Pirkei Avot*.

Zevaḥ Shelamim. Rabbi Moshe Galanti.

B. THE TALMUD AND COMMENTARIES – *RISHONIM*

The following commentaries on the Talmud were written by Sages who lived in the medieval era, preceding the *Shulḥan Arukh*.

Aguda. Rabbi Alexander Suslin HaKohen (d. 1349) of Frankfurt.

Aliyot DeRabbeinu Yonah. Rabbeinu Yonah ben Avraham of Gerona (1200–1263). To *Bava Batra*. Also authored a commentary to the Rif.

Maimonides. *Perush Mishnayot*. Rabbi Moshe ben Maimon (see Section E). Commentary to the Mishna. In Vilna editions.

Meiri. Rabbi Menaḥem ben Shlomo HaMeiri (1249–1316) of Provence, France. Talmudic comments in *Ḥiddushei HaMeiri* and *Beit HaBeḥira*.

Mordekhai. Rabbi Mordekhai ben Hillel HaKohen (1240–98) of Germany. In Vilna editions.

Nahmanides. Rabbi Moshe ben Nahman (see Section A).

Raavad. Rabbi Avraham ben David (see Section E). Commentary to the Rif and to *Torat Kohanim.*

Rashbam. Rabbi Shmuel ben Meir (1085–1158) of Troyes, France. Grandson of Rashi. One of the leading Tosafists, a running commentary of his is printed in the Vilna edition of tractates such as Pesaḥim and Bava Batra.

Rashi. Rabbi Shlomo ben Yitzḥak (see Section A). Printed alongside the text in standard Vilna editions.

Rif. Rabbi Yitzḥak Al Fasi (1013–1103) of Fez, Morocco. Authored a code of the halakhically relevant portions of the Talmud.

Ritva. Rabbi Yom Tov ben Ishbilli (1250–1330). Also authored responsa.

Rokeaḥ. Rabbi Eliezer of Worms (1165–1240). One of the Tosafists and student of Rabbi Yehuda HeḤasid.

Rosh. Rabbeinu Asher ben Yeḥiel (1250–1327) of Germany. Code to halakhically relevant sections of the Talmud, and running commentary to Nedarim. Father of the *Tur.*

Maadanei Yom Tov. Rabbi Yom Tov Lipman Heller (1579–1654). Known as the *Tosafot Yom Tov,* after his commentary to the Mishna.

Sefer HaHashlama. Rabbi Meshulam ben Moshe (twelfth century).

Reshit Hashlama. Rabbi Avraham Ḥaputa. Tel Aviv, 1967.

Shiltei Gibborim. Rabbi Yehoshua Boaz. Commentary to the Rif and the *Mordekhai.*

Shitta Mekubetzet. Opinions of many *Rishonim,* compiled by Rabbi Betzalel Ashkenazi (d. 1592).

Tosafot. Talmudic comments of eleventh- and twelfth-century French and German scholars, printed alongside the text in the Vilna Talmud.

Yad Rama. Rabbi Meir ben Todros HaLevi Abulafia (1170–1244).

C. CODES OF MITZVOT AND HALAKHIC CODES OF *RISHONIM* AND *AḤARONIM*

Halakhot Gedolot. Rabbi Shimon Kayyara (ninth century) of Babylonia.

Kol Bo. Rabbi Aharon HaKohen (fourteenth century) of Luneil.

Mivtzar Yisrael. Rabbi Yisrael Moshe Fishelder.

Noam HaMitzvot. Rabbi Naphtali Hertz Kretzmer. Petrikev (Piotrkow), 1905.

Sefer HaḤinnukh. Anonymous, but believed to be by Rabbi Aharon HaLevi of Barcelona.

Minḥat Ḥinnukh. Rabbi Yosef Babad (1800–1875) of Tarnopol.

Sefer HaMitzvot LaRabbi Saadia Gaon. Rabbi Saadia Gaon (882–942).

Biur. Rabbi Yeruḥam Fishel Perlow (1846–1934). Three volumes. Jerusalem: *Keter Keren Sefarim Toraniyyim,* 1973.

Sefer HaMitzvot LaRambam. Rabbi Moshe ben Maimon (see Section E). Printed with most editions of the *Mishneh Torah.*

Nahmanides. Rabbi Moshe ben Nahman (see Section A). In standard editions. Includes additional mitzvot the Rambam omits.

Sefer Ḥaredim. Rabbi Elazar ben Moshe Azkiri. Jerusalem, 1981.

Sefer Ḥasidim. Rabbi Yehuda HeḤasid (1150–1217) of Regensberg. Jerusalem: Mossad HaRav Kook, 1964.

Mekor Ḥesed. Rabbi Reuven Margoliyot (1889–1971). Author of *Margoliyot HaYam* to Sanhedrin, and other works. In above edition.

Milei DeḤasiduta. Rabbi Avraham David Wahrman. New York: Rabbi Shmuel David Katz Friedman, 1995.

Mishnat Avraham. Rabbi Avraham Price of Toronto. Toronto: Yeshivat Torat Chaim, 1955.

Sefer Mitzvot Gadol. Rabbi Moshe of Coucy (early thirteenth century). Known as the *Semag,* this work is divided into two sections, *Lavin* (prohibitions) and *Essin* (positive commandments).

Ammudei Shlomo. Rabbi Shlomo Luria (1510–74) of Prague, 1715. Known as *Maharshal,* he also authored the talmudic commentary *Ḥokhmat Shlomo* and the *Yam shel Shlomo* (see Section D).

Brit Moshe. Rabbi Moshe Ḥayim Weiss of Klein-Varden. Brooklyn, New York: A. Samet, 1959.

Dina DeḤayyai. Rabbi Ḥayim Benveniste (see *Knesset HaGdola,* Section F). Jerusalem, 1970.

Mishnat Avraham. Rabbi Avraham Price. Three volumes. Toronto: Yeshivat Torat Chaim, 1972.

Rabbi Eizek Stein. Rabbi Eizik Stein (1420–95) of Regensherg. Student of *Terumat HaDeshen* (see Section G).

Sefer Mitzvot Katan. Rabbi Yitzḥak ben Yosef (d. 1280) of Corbell. Also known as the *Semak* and *Ammudei HaGola*.

Imrei Yehosef. Rabbi Ḥayim Yehosef Ralbag. Brooklyn, New York.

Sefer Yere'im. Rabbi Eliezer of Metz (ca. 1115–98). A discussion of the mitzvot following the listings of Rabbi Yehudai Gaon and the *Baal Halakhot Gedolot*, divided into seven *ammudim* (pillars). Also known as the *Re'em*. A French Tosafist and student of Rabbeinu Tam.

Toafot Re'em. Rabbi Avraham Abba Schiff. Vilna, 1891.

She'iltot DeRav Aḥai Gaon. Rabbi Aḥai MiShabḥa (680–760).

Haamek She'ela. Rabbi Naphtali Tzvi Yehuda Berlin (see *Haamek Davar,* Section A).

Rabbi Yeshaya Pick. Rabbi of Breslau.

Yalkut Yitzḥak. Rabbi Yitzḥak Zahler. Warsaw, 1895.

D. TALMUD COMMENTARIES – *ACHARONIM*

Commentaries to the Talmud written in the centuries after the *Shulḥan Arukh*.

Arukh LaNer. Rabbi Yaakov Ettlinger. Novellae to several tractates. Jerusalem, 1962.

Beit Leḥem Yehuda. Rabbi Yehuda Meir Devir. To Bava Batra. Jerusalem, 1990.

Beit Shlomo. Rabbi Meir Yeḥiel Weinshtok. To Arakhin. Jerusalem: Machon Torani she'al yedei Yad Kollel Kodashim Lev Aryeh, 1990.

Bikkurei Aretz. Rabbi Avraham Yitzḥak Toker. To Berakhot. Jerusalem, 1973.

Birkat Reuven Shlomo. Rabbi Barukh Reuven Shlomo Shlesinger. Jerusalem: Yeshivat Akiva Yosef, 2002.

Birkat Shai. Rabbi Shemaryahu Yosef Berman. To Sanhedrin. Benei Berak, Israel, 2004.

Diberot Ariel. Rabbi Moshe Ariel Weinberg. To Arakhin. Benei Berak, Israel, 1996.

Divrei Meḥokek. Rabbi Kalonimos Kalman Steinberg. To Arakhin.
Ein Eliyahu. Rabbi Eliyahu Shick. To the *Ein Yaakov* collection of the aggadic material of the Talmud. Vilna, 1869.
Erekh HaḤayim. Rabbi Aharon Elḥanan Neubert. To Arakhin.
Gilyon HaShas. Rabbi Akiva Eiger (see *Ḥiddushei Rabbi Akiva Eiger,* in this section). A terse talmudic commentary, containing questions and references.
Gilyonei HaShas. Rabbi Yosef Engel (1859–1919). Author of many volumes of essays on talmudic topics, and responsa entitled *Porat Yosef.*
Haflaat Arakhin. Rabbi Eliyahu David Reichman. To Arakhin. Kiryat Gat, Israel, 1993.
Ḥashukei Ḥemed. Rabbi Yitzḥak Zilberstein (see *Aleinu Leshabeaḥ,* Section A). 2007.
Ḥatam Sofer. Rabbi Moshe Sofer (see *Torat Moshe,* Section A).
Ḥelkat Yehoshua. Rabbi Yehoshua Bressler. To Arakhin. Lakewood, NJ: Be'er HaTorah, 2010.
Ḥemdat Binyamin. Rabbi Avraham Binyamin Silverberg. To Makkot.
Ḥiddushei Rabbi Akiva Eiger. Rabbi Akiva Eiger (1761–1837) of Eisenstadt, Austria, and Posen, Poland. Expanded edition, Jerusalem, 2005. One of the leading halakhic authorities of his time, he also authored glosses to *Shulḥan Arukh,* as well as the talmudic works *Derush VeḤiddush,* and *Gilyon HaShas.* To Pesaḥim.
Ḥiddushei Rabbi Shlomo. Rabbi Shlomo Heiman (1886–1944). Brooklyn, New York: Otzar HaSeforim, 1975. Rosh Yeshiva of Yeshiva Torah VoDaath, Brooklyn.
Imrei Gedalya. Rabbi Gedalya Finkel. To Ketubot. Jerusalem, 2004.
Kehillot Yaakov. Rabbi Yisrael Yaakov Kanievsky (d. 1985) of Benei Berak, Israel. Known as the "Steipler Gaon" (after the town of Hornsteiple), he authored *Shaarei Tevuna* in his youth, and his *Kehillot Yaakov,* originally a ten-volume collection of essays, was later rearranged, revised, and expanded according to the tractates of the Talmud. Also authored *Birkat Peretz* to the Torah and served as a Rosh Yeshiva in the Yeshiva of Novardok.
Kerem Aryeh. Rabbi Aryeh Mizraḥi. Jerusalem: Makhon Benei Yissakhar, 1997.
Keren Ora. Rabbi Yitzḥak of Karlin. Israel: Orayta, 1977.

Kovetz He'arot. Rabbi Elḥanan Bunim Wasserman (1875–1941). Essays to Yevamot. A student of Rabbi Yisrael Meir Kagan and Rosh Yeshiva of the Yeshiva of Baranovitz.

Kovetz Shiurim. Rabbi Elḥanan Bunim Wasserman. Portions of talmudical lectures (see *Kovetz He'arot,* above).

Kovetz Simḥat Yeḥiel. Rabbi Moshe Chaim Shachna. To Kiddushin. Lakewood, NJ: Machon Be'er HaTorah, 2000.

Maharal, Ḥiddushei Aggadot. Rabbi Yehuda Loew ben Betzalel (1525–1609). Known as the Maharal of Prague, he was the author of many halakhic and philosophical works, including *Netivot Olam, Derekh Ḥayim,* and *Gur Aryeh.*

Maharsha, Ḥiddushei Aggadot, and *Ḥiddushei Halakhot.* Rabbi Shmuel Eidels (1555–1631).

Margoliyot HaYam. Rabbi Reuven Margoliyot (see *Mekor Ḥesed,* Section C). To Sanhedrin. Jerusalem: Mossad HaRav Kook, 1977.

Mishnat Moshe. Rabbi Moshe Blau (b. 1909). Jerusalem, 1972.

Mishnat Yehuda. Rabbi Yehuda Tzarum. Benei Berak, Israel, 1999.

Natan Piryo. Rabbi Natan Gestetner. To several tractates, and sections of *Shulḥan Arukh.* Benei Berak, Israel, 1980 (see *Lehorot Natan,* Section A).

Netivot HaKodesh. Rabbi Avraham Yisrael Moshe Solomon. To Arakhin.

Or Ḥadash. Rabbi Elazar Kalir (1741–1801). To Pesaḥim. Frankfurt, 1776.

Or HaYashar. Rabbi Shmuel Yitzḥak Hillman (d. 1953). Multivolume work covering the Bible, both Talmuds, and the *Mishneh Torah.* Jerusalem, 1977.

Orḥot Yom Tov. Rabbi Yinon Shmueli. To Bava Batra.

Peirot Te'ena. Rabbi Shmuel Rothschild. To Moed Katan. Benei Berak, Israel, 1999.

Penei Moshe. Rabbi Moshe Margolies (ca. 1710–80). Commentary to the Jerusalem Talmud.

Penei Yehoshua. Rabbi Yaakov Yehoshua (1680–1756). Sudylkov, 1834. Subtitled *Apei Zuta* (small face) to differentiate it from the *Responsa Penei Yehoshua* of his grandfather.

Pinat Yakrat. Rabbi Avraham Shmuel Papenheim. To Bava Batra.

Rashash. Rabbi Shmuel Strashoun (1794–1872) of Vilna. Printed in standard Vilna editions of the Talmud.
Sedeh Tzofim. Rabbi Shmuel David Friedman. Brooklyn, New York, 2009.
Shemuot Ḥayim. Rabbi Ḥayim Yudchik. To Arakhin.
Shiurei Maran HaGerish Elyashiv: Berakhot. Lectures of Rabbi Yosef Shalom Elyashiv (1910–2012) of Jerusalem, considered to have been one of the world's leading halakhic authorities.
Shiurei Rabbeinu Meshulam David HaLevi. Rabbi Meshulam David Soloveichik. Jerusalem, 2004. Rosh Yeshiva of the Brisk Yeshiva of Jerusalem.
Teranen Leshoni. Rabbi Yaakov Ḥayim Sofer. To Ketubot. Jerusalem, 1998.
VaYita Eshel. Rabbi Shaul Yudchik. To Arakhin. 2005
Yad Yosef. Rabbi Yosef Jolofsky. To Moed Katan. Lublin, 1911.
Yam shel Shlomo. Rabbi Shlomo Luria (see *Ammudei Shlomo*, Section C). Prague, 1715.
Zaharei Shmuel. Rabbi Avraham Toledanu. To Bava Batra. Jerusalem, 1990.
Zekher Shmuel. Rabbi Shmuel Greineman. To Shabbat. Benei Berak, Israel, 2001.

E. THE RAMBAM'S MISHNEH TORAH AND COMMENTARIES

Rabbi Moshe ben Maimon (1135–1204), known as the Rambam, or Maimonides, authored a codification of the laws in the Talmud, entitled *Mishneh Torah*, or *Yad HaḤazaka*. The latter name is a reference to the organization of the work, which is arranged in fourteen books (the numerical value of the word *yad* is fourteen). The following works are commentaries to the Rambam's code.

Avodat Melekh. Rabbi Menaḥem Krakowski. To *The Book of Knowledge*. Jerusalem: Mossad HaRav Kook.
Be'er Miriam. Rabbi David Yitzḥak Mann (contemporary). To *Laws of Kings*. Kfar Hasidim, Israel, 1981.
Ben Yedid. Rabbi Yedidya Shmuel Tariika (d. ca. 1769). Thessaloniki, 1806.
Benei Binyamin. Rabbi Eliyahu David Rabinowitz-Teomim (1843–1905). Known as the Aderet. Vilna, 1900.

Daat UMaḥashava. Rabbi Moshe Sternbuch (see *Taam VeDaat*, Section A). Benei Berak, Israel, 1980.
Divrei Yirmiyahu. Rabbi Yirmiyahu Loew (1814–74). Munkatsh: Bleier, 1875.
Hagahot Maimoniyot. Rabbi Meir HaKohen (thirteenth century). Rottenberg. Student of Maharam of Rottenberg.
Har HaMelekh. Seven volumes of essays from different authors. Kiryat Malachi, Israel: Naḥalat Har Ḥabad, 1986.
Hasagot HaRaavad. Rabbi Avraham ben David (1120–97) of Posquières, France. Also authored commentaries to the Rif and *Sifra*, and the *Baalei HaNefesh* to the laws of *nidda*. In standard editions of the *Mishneh Torah*.
Kesef Mishneh. Rabbi Yosef Karo (see *Shulḥan Arukh*, Section F). In standard editions of the *Mishneh Torah*.
Kiryat Sefer. Rabbi Moshe MiTrani. New York, 1966.
Leḥem Mishneh. Rabbi Avraham de Baton. In standard editions.
Leḥem Yehuda. Rabbi Yehuda Ayash (1700–1760). Livorno, Italy, 1745.
LiTshuvot HaShana. Rabbi Yisrael Yosef Rappaport. To *Laws of Repentance*. Benei Berak, Israel, 1986.
Maase Rokeaḥ. Rabbi Masud Rokeaḥ (1690–1768).
Maggid Mishneh. Rabbi Vidal Yom Tov (d. 1370) of Tolosa. In standard editions.
Migdal Oz. Rabbi Shem Tov Gaon (b. 1287). First published in 1509.
Mirkevet HaMishna. Rabbi Aharon Alpandari (1701–74). Izmir, Turkey, 1755. (A commentary by the same name was authored by Rabbi Shlomo of Ḥelm (d. 1781).)
Mishnat Yaakov. Rabbi Yaakov Nisan Rosenthal. Haifa, 1986.
Or Avraham. Rabbi Avraham Gurewitz. Jerusalem: Hotzaat Sefarim Or HaNer she'al yedei Yeshivat Ner Moshe, 1985.
Otzar HaMelekh. Rabbi Tzaddok HaKohen of Lublin (1823–1900). Lodz, 1939.
Paraḥ Matteh Aharon. Rabbi Ahron Soloveichik. *Book of Knowledge*. Jerusalem, 1997. Rosh Yeshiva of Yeshivat Brisk of Chicago and at Yeshiva University in New York. His thoughts have been printed in English as *The Warmth and the Light* and *Logic of the Heart, Logic of the Mind* (Genesis Jerusalem Press).
Parashat HaMelekh. Rabbi Yitzḥak Meir Patziner. Jerusalem, 1938.

Peri Etz Ḥayim. Rabbi Peretz Steinberg, New York, 2004.
Sefer HaBattim. Rabbi David ben Shmuel of Ishtila (thirteenth century).
Shaarei De'ah. Rabbi Shabbetai Sofer. New York, 1899.
Shalal David. Rabbi David Muati (1796–1876). Livorno, ca. 1850.
Yad HaKetanna. Rabbi Dov Berish Gottleib (eighteenth century). To the *Books of Knowledge, Love,* and *Times.* New York: *Vaad LeHaramat Keren HaYeshivot,* ca. 1950.
Yeshuot Malko. Rabbi Yehoshua of Kutno. Also contains the glosses *Me'at Tzari.*

F. THE TUR AND SHULḤAN ARUKH AND COMMENTARIES

Rabbi Yaakov ben Asher (ca. 1270–1340) of Germany and Toledo, Spain. The son of the Rosh (see Section B), he authored a codification of Jewish law entitled the *Arbaa Turim* (four rows; see Ex. 28:17), so named because it is divided into four sections: *Oraḥ Ḥayim,* covering daily life, prayer, and festivals; *Even HaEzer,* on marital law; *Ḥoshen Mishpat,* on civil law; and *Yoreh De'ah,* covering the remaining areas of Jewish law, such as *kashrut, nidda,* mourning, vows, and other topics. Two centuries later, Rabbi Yosef Karo (1488–1575), who authored the commentary *Beit Yosef* to the *Turim* (as well as *Kesef Mishneh* to *Mishneh Torah*), earned the title *HaMeḥaber* (the Author) with his *Shulḥan Arukh* (set table), which followed the organization of the *Turim* and took into account the rulings of the Rif, Rosh, and Rambam. However, the rulings are reflective primarily of the Sephardic background of their author, a fact rectified by Rabbi Moshe Isserles (1520–72), known as the Rema and author of *Darkhei Moshe* to the *Turim,* who wrote glosses, known as *Mappa* (tablecloth), to the *Shulḥan Arukh* representing Ashkenazic practice. Together with the Rema's glosses, the *Shulḥan Arukh* has become accepted as the standard text of Jewish law, and the titles listed below are commentaries to that work (or the *Turim,* when indicated as such).

Arukh HaShulḥan. Rabbi Yeḥiel Michel Epstein (1829–1908). Comprehensive code on all sections of the *Shulḥan Arukh,* adding *Arukh HaShulḥan HeAtid* to those areas not covered (ritual impurity, laws of agriculture relevant only in the Land of Israel, sacrificial order, etc.). Warsaw, 1900–1912. Rabbi of Novardok and father of *Torah Temima* (see *Responsa Benei Vanim* 2:8 for a citation of the halakhic authority Rabbi Yosef Eliyahu Henkin concerning the special qualities of this code).

Bayit Chadash (*Baḥ*). Rabbi Yoel Sirkes (1561–1640) of Poland. Commentary to the *Tur*; also author of responsa (see later entries) and talmudic emendations. Rabbi of Belz, Brest-Litovsk, and Krakow, and father-in-law of *Turei Zahav*.

Be'er Heitev. Rabbi Yehuda ben Shimon Ashkenazi (eighteenth century). Amsterdam, 1742.

Be'er Heitev. Rabbi Zekharia Mendel (d. 1706). Commentary digest of earlier authorities. Rabbi of Belz, Poland.

Biur HaGra. Rabbi Eliyahu ben Shlomo Zalman (see *Perush HaGra* to Proverbs, Section A).

Derisha and *Perisha*. Rabbi Yehoshua Falk (1555–1614), of Lublin, Poland, and Lemberg, Germany. Commentaries to the *Tur*. Also author of *Me'irat Einayim* to *Shulḥan Arukh*.

Emet LeYaakov. Rabbi Yaakov Kaminetsky (see Section A). Rabbi Jacob Joseph School Press, 2000.

Ḥatam Sofer. Rabbi Moshe Sofer (see *Torat Moshe*, Section A).

Ḥazon Ish. Rabbi Avraham Yeshaya Karelitz (1878–1953), Benei Berak, Israel. This seven-volume halakhic work actually combines the sections of the Talmud and the *Shulḥan Arukh* and defies easy categorization. Benei Berak, Israel, 1958. Also authored *Emunah UVitaḥon*.

Ḥiddushei Rabbi Akiva Eiger (see section D). Compiled in several editions, printed in various editions of the *Shulḥan Arukh*.

Ḥokhmat Shlomo. Rabbi Shlomo Kluger (1783–1869). Rabbi of Brody, Galicia, and author of several works, including multiple works of responsa.

Kitzur Shulḥan Arukh. Rabbi Shlomo Gantzfried (1802–86). Warsaw, 1901.

She'arim Metzuyanim BeHalakha. Rabbi Shlomo Zalman Braun. New York, 1951.

Knesset HaGdola. Rabbi Ḥayim Beneviste (1603–73). Jerusalem: Keren LeHotzaat Kol Sifrei Knesset HaGdola, 1970.

Magen Avraham. Rabbi Avraham Gumbiner (1637–83) of Poland. In standard editions.

Maḥatzit HaShekel. Rabbi Shmuel HaLevi of Kellin. In standard editions.

Matteh Ephraim. Rabbi Ephraim Zalman Margoliyot (1760–1828). Author of multiple works, including responsa, entitled *Beit Ephraim.* To the laws of the *Rosh HaShana-Yom Kippur* period. Brooklyn, New York: Kol Aryeh Research Institute, 1973.

Me'irat Einayim. See *Derisha* (above).

Mishna Berura. Rabbi Yisrael Meir Kagan (1838–1933) of Radin, Poland. Commentary to the *Oraḥ Ḥayim* section of the *Shulḥan Arukh,* evaluating the positions of earlier authorities and arriving at conclusions. Includes the more in-depth *Biur Halakha* and the *Shaar HaTziyun,* listing sources. One of the preeminent moral authorities of the late eighteenth and early nineteenth centuries, he authored *Ḥafetz Ḥayim* (a name by which he came to be known) and *Ahavat Ḥesed* (see individual listings), as well as many other works, including *Likkutei Halakhot,* a three-part commentary to the talmudical order Kodashim, written in the style of *Mishna Berura.*

Nefesh Ḥayya. Rabbi Reuven Margoliyot (see *Mekor Ḥesed,* Section C). Lvov, 1932.

Netivot HaMishpat. Rabbi Yaakov Loerbaum of Lisa (d. 1832). To *Ḥoshen Mishpat.* Author of several works, including *Ḥavvot Daat, Derekh Ḥayim, Beit Yaakov, Torat Gittin, Emet LeYaakov, Mekor Ḥayim,* and others.

Nimukei Oraḥ Ḥayim. Rabbi Ḥayim Elazar Schapiro (1871–1937). Munczaczer Rebbe and author of *Responsa Minḥat Elazar.* Jerusalem, 1998.

Orḥot Ḥayim. Rabbi Nahman Kahana (1861–1904) of Spinka. A compilation of the views of earlier authorities, with commentary, to *Oraḥ Ḥayim.* Two volumes. Jerusalem: Keter, 1982.

Paamonei Zahav. Rabbi Raphael ben Mordekhai Ankiva (1848–1935). Jerusalem, 1912.

Pitḥei Teshuva. Rabbi Yisrael Isser Isserlein (1827–89). To *Oraḥ Ḥayim.* One of the rabbinical court judges in Vilna.

Shaarei Zevulun. Rabbi Zevulun Shuv. Ramot al yad Yerushalayim, 1992.

Shulḥan Arukh HaRav. Rabbi Shneur Zalman of Liadi (1745–1813). First Rebbe of Lubavitch (Chabad) and author of the *Tanya.*

Turei Zahav (Taz). Rabbi David ben Shmuel HaLevi (1586–1667) of Krakow, Poland. Also authored a commentary to the Torah.

Urim Ve'Tummim. Rabbi Yonatan Eibshutz (1690–1764). To *Ḥoshen Mishpat.* Leading talmudist and halakhist, and author of many works, including *Yaarot Devash, Kereti UFleti, Tiferet Yehonatan,* and others.

G. COLLECTIONS OF RESPONSA AND HALAKHIC AND TALMUDIC ESSAYS

The following works are either responsa, written to answer halakhic inquiries, or collections of essays on topics of halakhic and talmudic analysis. The titles of the works of responsa, are generally preceded by the term "*She'elot UTshuvot*" (lit., questions and answers, rendered in translation as "Responsa,") which is omitted in this listing.

Aderet Tiferet. Rabbi Avraham Duri. Jerusalem, 1993.

Afarkasta DeAnya. Rabbi David Shperber. Jerusalem, 1991.

Afikei Yam. Rabbi Yeḥiel Michel Rabinowitz. Vilna, 1905.

Aḥiezer. Rabbi Ḥayim Ozer Grodzinski (1863–1940). Three volumes. Vol. 1, Vilna, 1922. Vol. 3, New York, 1946. Chief rabbi of Vilna and leading halakhic authority of the pre–World War II era.

Akiva Eiger, Rabbi. Rabbi Akiva Eiger (see *Ḥiddushei Rabbi Akiva Eiger,* Section D). Two volumes of responsa. New York, 1945.

Am KeLavi. Rabbi Shlomo Aviner. Jerusalem, 1983.

Ateret Moshe. Rabbi Moshe Natan Nota Lemberger. Two volumes. To topics pertaining to *Yoreh De'ah.* Benei Berak, Israel, 1990.

Ateret Paz. Rabbi Pineḥas Zeviḥi (Contemporary). Jerusalem.

Ateret Yitzḥak. Rabbi Yitzḥak Eizik Rabinowitz, of Shavel. Jerusalem, 1925.

Avnei Ḥoshen. Rabbi Yitzḥak Zilberstein (see Section A, *Aleinu Leshabeaḥ*). Benei Berak, Israel, 1996.

Avnei Yashpeh. Rabbi Yehoshua Friedlander. Jerusalem: Yeshivat Beit Eliyahu, 1988.

Az Nidberu. Rabbi Binyamin Yehoshua Zilber. Fourteen volumes. Benei Berak, Israel, 1969. Also authored several volumes of *musar,* some anonymously.

Badei HaAron. Rabbi Re'em HaKohen. Jerusalem: Makhon HaTorani Yeshivat Otniel, 2013.

Be'er Sarim. Rabbi Avraham Yafeh Shlesinger (contemporary). Four volumes. Jerusalem: Ḥemed, 1990.

Binyan Av. Rabbi Eliyahu Bakshi-Doron (see *Siḥot Binyan Av,* Section A). Four volumes. Haifa, 1983.

Birkat Avot. Rabbi Barukh Rakovsky. Halakhic essays, many concerning the Patriarchs and pre-sinaitic Judaism in general. Jerusalem, 1990.

Birkat Reuven Shlomo. Rabbi Barukh Reuven Shlomo Shlesinger (see Section D).

Birkat Shlomo. Rabbi Ḥayim Shlomo Abrahams (contempory). Brooklyn, New York: HaMatik Printing, 2000. Also authored a similar volume in the same genre under the title *Divrei Shlomo*.

Benei Vanim. Rabbi Yehuda Herzl Henkin (contemporary) of Beit Shean, Israel. Three volumes. Jerusalem, 1981.

BeOhela shel Torah. Rabbi Yaakov Ariel (contemporary). Makhon HaTorah VeHaAretz, 1997.

BeTzel HaḤokhma. Rabbi Betzalel Stern (d. 1989) of Vienna; Melbourne, Australia; and Jerusalem. Six volumes. Jerusalem, 1967.

Bo Tashiv. Rabbi Yaakov Zeide. 2015

Darkhei Shalom. Rabbi Yeḥiel Michel Leiter. Vienna, 1932.

Devar Tov. Rabbi David Eichenstein (contemporary).

Divrei Malkiel. Rabbi Malkiel Tzvi Tannenbaum of Lomza, Poland. Seven volumes. Vilna, 1901.

Divrei Shalom. Rabbi Shmuel Yudaikin (contemporary). Halakhic essays and sources. Five volumes. Benei Berak, Israel, 1989.

Divrei Shlomo. Rabbi Shlomo Shneider (d. 1995) of Monticello, New York. Three volumes. Brooklyn, New York, 2000.

Divrei Yatziv. Rabbi Yekutiel Yehuda Halberstam. Sanz-Klausenberger Rebbe. Netanya, Israel: Makhon Shefa Ḥayim, 1996.

Divrei Yosef. Rabbi Yosef Aryeh Deutsch. Jerusalem, 1991.

Eretz Tzvi. Rabbi Tzvi Hirsch Frimer. Kozaglover Rav. Student of the *Avnei Nezer* and Rosh Yeshiva of Yeshivat Ḥakhmei Lublin. Lublin, 1939.

Even Pina. Rabbi Ben Tziyon Nesher. Tel Aviv, 1994.

Even Yisrael. Rabbi Yisrael Yaakov Fisher (1925–2003). Jerusalem, 1999.

Halakha LeMoshe. Rabbi Moshe Naiman. Printed together with *Shut Nir LeDavid*, responsa of the author's father, Rabbi David Naiman. Jerusalem, 1981.

Halakhot Ketannot. Rabbi Yisrael Yaakov Ḥagiz (1620–74). Venice, 1704.

Ḥatam Sofer. Rabbi Moshe Sofer (1763–1830). Responsa to the four sections of *Shulḥan Arukh* and additional volumes. Vienna, 1855. (see *Torat Moshe,* Section A).

Ḥavatzelet HaSharon. Rabbi David Menaḥem Manish Babad (1865–1937). Bilgoraj, 1931.

Ḥayim She'al. Rabbi Ḥayim Yosef David Azulai, known as Ḥida (1724–1806). Lvov, 1886.

Ḥayyei HaLevi. Rabbi Yoḥanan Segal Vosner (contemporary). Three volumes, Montreal, 1986.

Ḥelkat Yoav. Rabbi Yoav Yehoshua Weingarten (1847–1922) of Kinsk. Responsa, including the *Kaba DeKashyata,* a collection of 103 talmudic questions that has on its own inspired several books responding to its challenges. Edited, footnoted, and indexed by Rabbi David Avraham Mandelbaum. Jerusalem: Makhon LeHantzaḥat Moreshet Ḥakhmei Polin, 1997.

Ḥikekei Lev. Rabbi Ḥayim Palagi (1788–1869). Thessaloniki, 1840.

Hitorerut Teshuva. Rabbi Shimon (Eiger) Sofer (1850–1944). Four volumes, accompanied by the commentary *Ikvei Sofer* of the author's grandson Rabbi Akiva Menaḥem Sofer. Jerusalem: Makhon Ḥatam Sofer, 1990. Grandson of *Ḥatam Sofer* and son of *Ketav Sofer.*

Ikvei Sofer. Rabbi Akiva Menaḥem Sofer. Glosses to the above by the grandson of the author, printed on the bottom of the page.

Iggerot Moshe. Rabbi Moshe Feinstein (1895–1986) of Luban, Poland, and New York. Eight volumes of responsa, beginning in 1961, New York. Considered one of the leading authorities of the late twentieth century, he was Rosh Yeshiva of Metivta Tiferet Yerushalayim in the Lower East Side of Manhattan and also authored *Diberot Moshe* to several volumes of the Talmud.

Imrei Yosher. Rabbi Meir Arik (1855–1925). Munkatsh. 1913.

Keneh Bosem. Rabbi Meir Brandesdorfer (1934–2009). Jerusalem, 1980.

Ketav Sofer. Rabbi Avraham Shmuel Binyamin Sofer (1815–71). Pressburg, 1873. Son of the *Ḥatam Sofer,* he also authored *ḥiddushim* to the Torah and to Ḥullin.

Kinyan Torah BaHalakha. Rabbi Avraham David Horovitz. From Strassbourg, France, and later a rabbinical court judge in Jerusalem. Eight volumes. Strassbourg, France, 1976.

Kiryat Ḥanna David. Rabbi David HaKohen Sikili. Jerusalem, 1935.

Kol Aryeh. Rabbi Avraham Yehuda Schwartz (1824–83). Brooklyn, New York: Chevra Mefitzei Torah MiMishpaḥat Kol Aryeh, 1983.

Lehorot Natan. See section A.

Lev Avraham. Rabbi Avraham Weinfeld. Monsey, New York: Keren Yeshua, 1977.

Maadanei Yom Tov. Rabbi Yom Tov Zanger (contemporary). Benei Berak, Israel, 2012.

Maharam Mintz. Rabbi Moshe Mintz (1435–85) of Poland and Germany. Krakow, 1637.

Maharam MiRottenberg. Rabbi Meir ben Barukh HaLevi (1320–90) of Rottenberg. Berlin, 1891. Rebbe of the Rosh and the *Mordekhai.*

Maharash Engel. Rabbi Shmuel Engel. Seven volumes. Bardiov, 1926.

Maharashdam. Rabbi Shmuel DiMedina (1506–89). Rabbi of Thessaloniki and cities in Turkey.

Mahari Beruna. Rabbi Yisrael Beruna (1400–1481) of Germany. Student of *Mahari Veil* and *Terumat HaDeshen.* Thessaloniki, 1798.

Maharik. Rabbi Yosef Kolon (1420–80). New York: Y. Ze'ev, 1957.

Maharil. Rabbi Yaakov ben Moshe HaLevi Molin (b. 1427). Krakow, 1881.

Maharil Diskin. Rabbi Moshe Yehoshua Yehuda Leib Diskin. Jerusalem: Ḥedvat Yisrael, 1911.

Maharitatz. Rabbi Yom Tov ben Moshe Tzahalon. Venice, 1694.

Maharitz. Rabbi Yosef Tzvi Dushinsky (1868–1948). Jerusalem, 1955.

Maharshal. Rabbi Shlomo Luria (see *Ammudei Shlomo,* Section C).

Maharsham. Rabbi Shalom Mordekhai Shwadron. Also authored *Daat Torah* to *Shulḥan Arukh.*

Mekom Shmuel. Rabbi Shmuel ben Elkana of Altuna. Altuna, 1738.

Meshiv Davar. Rabbi Naphtali Tzvi Yehuda Berlin (1816–93), known as the Netziv. Rosh Yeshiva of the Yeshiva of Volozhin. Warsaw, 1849. (See *Haamek Davar,* Section A.)

Minḥat David. Rabbi David Rozenberg of Monroe, New York. Four volumes. Brooklyn, New York, 1979.

Minḥat Maḥavat. Rabbi Mordekhai Babad. Jerusalem, 1989.

Minḥat Peri. Rabbi Yeshayahu Pineḥas Rottenberg, Jerusalem, 1994.

Minḥat Yitzḥak. Rabbi Yitzḥak Weiss (1902–89). Ten volumes of responsa. London, 1955. Rabbinical court judge in Manchester, England, and later rabbi of the *Edah HaḤaredit* in Jerusalem.

Mirkaḥat Besamim. Rabbi Shmuel Greenberger. New York: Y. Lichter, 1992.

Mishkenot Yaakov. Rabbi Yaakov Beruḥin of Karlin. Jerusalem: Keren Ora, 1960.

Mishna Shelema. Rabbi Shlomo Gross of Brooklyn, New York. Jerusalem, 1991. Rabbinical court judge of Belzer Hasidim of Boro Park, Brooklyn.

Mishnat Binyamin. Rabbi Avraham Binyamin Silverberg. Rabbi of Pittsburg, Pennsylvania. New York: Moinester, 1948.

Mishnat Yosef. Rabbi Yosef Lieberman. Jerusalem; Makhon Yerushalayim, 1979.

Mishneh Halakhot. Rabbi Menashe Klein. Makhon Mishneh Halakhot Gedolot, 2000.

Mishpat LeYaakov. Rabbi Yaakov Meskin. 1883–1956. New York, 1946.

Mishpatekha LeYaakov. Rabbi Tzvi Yehuda ben Yaakov. Benei Berak, Israel: Makhon Keter Torah Radomsk, 1995.

Netzaḥ Yisrael. Rabbi Yisrael Grossman. Jerusalem, 1986.

Nishmat Shabbat. Rabbi Yisrael David Harfenes. Responsa regarding the laws of Shabbat. Brooklyn, New York, 2005. Author of many other works, including *Yisrael VeHaZemanim* on the rules of time, and additional works of Responsa under different titles.

Ohalei Yehuda. Rabbi Yehuda ben Shlomo HaKohen. Monroe, New York, 1990.

Olat Noaḥ. Rabbi Noaḥ Segal, Tel Aviv, 1947.

Padeh et Avraham. Rabbi Avraham Y. Munseh (b. 1912). Jerusalem, 1995.

Pe'at Sadekha. Rabbi Shmuel David Munk. Jerusalem, 1975.

Peri Yitzḥak. Rabbi Yitzḥak Blazer (1837–1907). Kfar Hasidim, Israel: *Yeshivat Knesset Ḥizkiyahu*, 1975. Known as Rabbi Itzele Peterburger, he was a leading disciple of Rabbi Yisrael Salanter and was equally renowned for accomplishments in *halakha* and in *musar* (see *Kokhvei Or*, Section K).

Rabbeinu Avraham ben Rav Yitzḥak Av Beit Din. Rabbi Avraham ben Yitzḥak. Son-in-law of the Raavad (see Section E under *Hasagot HaRaavad*).

Radbaz. Rabbi David ben Zimra (1479[80?]–1573[89?]). Warsaw, 1862. Chief rabbi of Egypt. Also authored commentary to *Mishneh Torah.*

Rambam. Rabbi Moshe ben Maimon (see Section E). Leipzig, 1859.

Ratz KaTzvi. Rabbi Zvi Ryzman (contemporary). Los Angeles, 2005.

Rav Eliyahu Mizraḥi (Re'em). Rabbi Eliyahu Mizraḥi (ca. 1450–1526). Jerusalem, 1938.

Rema. Rabbi Moshe Isserles (see Section F). Edited by Rabbi Asher Siev. Jerusalem, 1971.

Rivash. Rabbi Yitzḥak ben Sheshet (1326–1407) of Barcelona.

Rivevot Ephraim. Rabbi Ephraim Greenblatt (1932–2014) of Memphis, Tennessee. Ten volumes. Jerusalem, 1975.

Rosh. Rabbi Asher ben Yeḥiel (see Section B).

Salmat Ḥayim. Rabbi Yosef Chaim Sonnenfeld (1848–1932). Benei Berak, Israel, 1982. Rabbi of the *Edah HaḤaredit* of Jerusalem.

Shalmei Simḥa. Rabbi Simchah Elberg. Five volumes, largely dealing with the festivals. Brooklyn, New York: Balshon, 1964. Longtime editor of the journal *HaPardes.*

She'erit Yehuda. Rabbi Yehuda Leib of Yanowitz. Brother of the first Lubavitcher Rebbe. Brooklyn, New York, 2009.

She'elat Rav. Rabbi Ḥayim Kanievsky. Edited by Rabbi Yeḥiel Michel Rothschild. Kiryat Sefer, Israel, 2004.

Shevet HaKehati. Rabbi Shammai Kehat Gross (contemporary) of *Khal Machzikei HaDas* (Belz), Israel. Five volumes. Jerusalem: Orayta, 1987.

Shevet HaLevi. Rabbi Shmuel HaLevi Vosner (1913–2015). Eleven volumes. Benei Berak, Israel, 1969.

Shoel UMeshiv. Rabbi Yosef Shaul Nathanson (1810–75) of Lemberg. Brooklyn, New York: *Harerei Kodesh,* 1994. Also authored *Yad Shaul* to *Shulḥan Arukh* and *Divrei Shaul* to the Torah.

Shoel VeNishal. Rabbi Kalfun Moshe HaKohen (1874–1950). Djerba, Tunisia, 1952.

Shraga HaMeir. Rabbi Shraga Feivel Shneebalg of Stamford Hill, London, England. Eight volumes. Benei Berak, Israel: Friedman, 1972. Also authored *Beit Pineḥas* to the Torah, and other works.

Shevut Yaakov. Rabbi Yaakov Reisher (1670–1733). Lemberg: Salant, 1897. Rabbi of Prague and other cities.

Shivat Tziyon. Rabbi Tziyon Shimon Bognim. 2000.

Siaḥ Naḥum. Rabbi Nachum Rabinovitch (b. 1928). Maaleh Adumim, Israel: Hotzaat Maaliyot she'al yedei Yeshivat Birkat Moshe, 2008.

Siftei Ani. Rabbi Menachem Mendel Schneebalg. Benei Berak, Israel: Friedman, 1993. Rabbi of Congregation Machizikei HaDas, Manchester, England.

Terumat HaDeshen. Rabbi Yisrael Isserlein (1390–1460) of Germany.

Teshuvot VeHanhagot. Rabbi Moshe Sternbuch (contemporary). Three volumes. Jerusalem, *Netivot HaTorah VeHaḤesed,* 1986 (see *Taam VeDaat,* Section A).

Tirosh VeYitzhar. Rabbi Tzvi Yeḥezkel Michaelson (1863–1942). Bilgoraj, 1937.

Toledot Yitzḥak. Rabbi Yitzḥak ben Shoshan. Benei Berak, Israel, 1980.

Torat Yeruḥam. Rabbi Yeruḥam Ciecanaowitz. New York: Twersky Brothers, 1951.

Tov Ayin. Ḥida (see *Ḥayim She'al* in this section). Jerusalem. 1961.

Tzitz Eliezer. Rabbi Eliezer Yehuda Waldenberg (1915–2006). Twenty-one volumes, Jerusalem, beginning 1944.

VeDarashta VeḤakarta. Rabbi Aharon David Grossman (contemporary). Jerusalem, 1996.

Yagel Yaakov. Rabbi Ḥayim Mordekhai Yaakov Gottleib (d. 1936). Brooklyn, New York, 1988.

Yashiv Yitzḥak. Rabbi Yitzḥak Shmuel Schechter (contemporary). Netanya, Israel: Makhon Yashiv Yitzḥak, 1998. More than thirty volumes.

Yeḥaveh Daat. Rabbi Ovadia Yosef (1920–2013). Based on his radio lectures. Jerusalem, 1976. Sephardi chief rabbi of Israel (1973–83) and author of *Responsa Yabbia Omer.*

Yehuda Yaaleh. Rabbi Yehuda Assad. Pressburg, 1880, and Benei Berak, Israel, 1985 (see *Rabbi Yehuda Assad al HaTorah,* Section A).

Yismaḥ Avikha. Rabbi Aharon Kahn. Rosh Yeshiva at RIETS. Brooklyn, New York, 2002.

Yosef Neḥemia, Rabbi. Rabbi Yosef Neḥemia Kornitser of Krakow. Benei Berak, Israel: Yeshivat Ohel Yosef, 1986.

H. WORKS OF HALAKHA

Beit Ḥatanim. Rabbi Moshe Faniri. On the laws of marriage. Jerusalem, 1981.

Ben Ish Ḥai. Rabbi Yosef Ḥayim ben Eliyahu (1834–1909) of Baghdad. Baghdad, 1912.

Darkhei Ḥoshen. Rabbi Yehuda Silman (prepared by his son Rabbi Mordekhai Tzvi Silman). On topics of monetary law. Kiryat Sefer, Israel, 1999.

Derekh HaAtarim. Rabbi Avraham Maimon HaLevi. On topics related to the Internet. Jerusalem, 2014.

Divrei Ḥayil. Rabbi Ḥanina Yisrael Rottenberg. On topics relating to the choice of a spouse. Jerusalem, 1995.

Einei Yitzḥak, Shulḥan Arukh HaMekutzar. Rabbi Yitzḥak Ratzabi. Benei Berak, Israel. 1997.

Emek HaMishpat. Rabbi Yaakov Avraham Kohen. On various topics of civil law, including *Laws of Neighbors.* Netanya, Israel.

HaKatan VeHilkhotav. Rabbi Barukh Rakovsky. On topics relating to minors. Jerusalem, 2004.

Halikhot Shlomo. Rulings of Rabbi Shlomo Zalman Auerbach (1910–95). Edited by Yehuda Trager and Aharon Auerbach. Tel Aviv: Yeshivat Halikhot Shlomo, 1999. Preeminent halakhic authority and author of *Responsa Minḥat Shlomo.*

Hilkhot Ḥag BaḤag: Laws of the High Holy Days. Rabbi Moshe Mordekhai Karp. Jerualem, 2000.

Imrei Yaakov. Rabbi Yeḥiel Michel Stern. On *Laws of Teachers* (*Yoreh De'ah* 245). Benei Berak, Israel, 1995.

Kol Bo. Rabbi Yekutiel Yehuda Greenwald. On mourning. Columbus, Ohio, 1947.

Megillat Sefer. Rabbi Uriel Eisenthal. On the laws of Shabbat. Jerusalem, 1991.

Mesorat Moshe. Rulings of Rabbi Moshe Feinstein. Edited by Rabbi Mordekhai Tendler. Jerusalem, 2013.

Mishpetei HaTorah. Rabbi Tzvi Shpitz (contemporary). Responsa to actual questions in monetary and interpersonal law. Three volumes. Jerusalem, 1998.

Mo'adim UZmanim. Rabbi Moshe Sternbuch. Nine volumes. Jerusalem. On the festivals (see *Taam VeDaat,* Section A).

Netiv Yosher. Rabbi Yehuda Itaḥ. On the laws of commerce. Jerusalem, 1992.

Nishmat Avraham. Professor Avraham Sofer Avraham. On topics relating to medicine. Jerusalem, 2007.

Nitei Gavriel. Rabbi Gavriel Zinner. Jerusalem, 1997.

Nizkei Shekhenim. Rabbi Rephael Stern. On the laws of neighbors. Givat Shmuel, Israel: Beit Vaad LeTorah LeLimud VeLeHaamaka BeDinei Mamonot, 2000.

Om Ani Ḥoma. Rabbi Mordekhai Gros. On sections of *Even HaEzer.* Benei Berak, Israel, 2000.

Orot Yemei HaRaḥamim. Rabbi Shlomo Wahrman. An analytical study of various topics of talmudical law pertaining to the High Holy Days. New York: Fink Graphics, 1994.

Rishumei Aharon. Rabbi Aharon Felder. Rulings of the author's rebbe, Rabbi Moshe Feinstein (see *Responsa Iggerot Moshe*). Philadelphia, 2010.

Sedei Ḥemed. Rabbi Ḥayim Ḥizkiyahu Medini (1832–1904) of Constantinople. Extensive ten-volume collection of halakhic essays, including citations of many contemporaries of the author.

Shalmei Toda. Rabbi Shalom ben Tzion Felman. Benei Berak, Israel, 2001.

Torat HaYoledet. Rabbi Yitzḥak Zilberstein. On topics regarding childbirth (see *Aleinu Leshabeaḥ,* Section A). 1987.

VaYaan Yosef. Rabbi Yosef Greenwald. Appended to the response of the author's father, Rabbi Yaakov Greenwald, *Responsa Mishpatekha LeYaakov.* Jerusalem, 1977.

Yalkut Yosef. Rabbi Ovadia Yosef (see *Yeḥaveh Daat,* Section G). Prepared by Rabbi Yitzḥak Yosef. Jerusalem, 1985.

Zekukei Nura. Rabbi Nissim Dayan, Benei Berak, Israel, 2003.

I. WORKS DEVOTED TO THE LAWS AND CONCEPTS OF *LASHON HARA*

BaYom SheYedubar. Rabbi Mordekhai Menaḥem Veingurt. On the laws of *lashon hara* regarding *shiddukhim.* Jerusalem, 2014.

Bein Shenei Kohanim Gedolim. Rabbi Menaḥem Kempinski. Biographical work about the relationship between the *Ḥafetz Ḥayim* and Rabbi Avraham Yitzḥak HaKohen Kook (1865–1935), the first Ashkenazi chief rabbi of modern Israel; it contains glosses of

Rabbi Kook to the Rambam (*Orot HaRambam*) and to the *Ḥafetz Ḥayim* (*Be'er LaḤai Ro'i*), as well as glosses to the *Ḥafetz Ḥayim* by Rabbi Shlomo Zalman Kook entitled *Mitzva Shelema.* Elad, Israel: Ishim, Makhon Torani, 2008.

BeYad HaLashon. Collection of essays relating to the laws and philosophy of *lashon hara.* Edited anonymously. Jerusalem: VeHigita, 2007.

Emek HaLashon. Rabbi Reuven Schwartz. To *Mishneh Torah, Laws of Personal Development* 7.

Ḥafetz Ḥayim. Rabbi Yisrael Meir Kagan (see *Mishna Berura,* Section F). Classic work to the laws prohibiting gossip (*lashon hara*).

Alei Be'er. Rabbi Shlomo Rozner.

Birkat Yitzḥak. Rabbi Yitzḥak Berakha. Jerusalem: Dorot.

Ḥelkat Binyamin. Rabbi Binyamin Kohen. 2003.

Netivot Ḥayim. Rabbi Moshe Kaufman. Three-tiered commentary comprising *Netiv Ḥayim, Shevili Ḥayim,* and *Zera Ḥayim.* Benei Berak, Israel, 2005.

Ohev Yamim. Rabbi Yosef Yitzḥak Pinter. Lakewood, NJ: Makhon Be'er HaTorah, 2012.

Rigshei Ḥayim. Rabbi Yehonatan Rozler. Benai Berak, Israel, 2015.

Zeh HaShulḥan. Rabbi Shraya Deblitsky. Glosses in the back of a work devoted to other themes of Jewish law. Benei Berak, Israel, 1958.

Ḥut Shani. Rabbi Nissim Karelitz. Benei Berak, Israel: Ḥayim Aryeh Hoḥman, 2010.

Ikkarei Dinim. Rabbi Shmuel Hominer (1913–77). Jerusalem, 1960.

LeḤafetz BaḤayim. Rabbi Shlomo Rozner. Five editions, each adding sections. Jerusalem, 2011.

Marpei Lashon. Journal devoted to topics of *lashon hara,* published by the Vaad Lemaan Shemirat HaLashon, beginning in 1979.

Marpei Lashon. Rabbi Raphael Katz (Hamburger) (1722–1803). Altuna, 1790.

Mishnat Yisrael. Rabbi Yisrael Weinman. Jerusalem, 2009.

Shaarei Avraham. Rabbi Yaakov Bronfman. Lectures on *lashon hara* and other topics of interpersonal relations. Benei Berak, Israel, 2014.

Shemirat HaLashon. Work by the *Ḥafetz Ḥayim* on the conceptual issues related to *lashon hara;* sometimes published with the book *Ḥafetz Ḥayim.*

Shemirat HaPeh KeHilkhato. Rabbi Daniel Ḥayim Orlantzik. Rechovot, Israel: Mifal HaḤafetz Ḥayim Olami, 2014.

Tehor Sefatayim. Rabbi Shlomo Aviner. Beit El, Israel: Sifriyat Ḥavva, 2010.

Tokhaḥat Ḥayim. Rabbi Gershon Robinson. Monograph on the question of purposeful *lashon hara* when conflicting motives are present. Benei Berak, Israel, 1997.

Zekhor LeMiriam. Work by the *Ḥafetz Ḥayim* on the avoidance of *lashon hara* and its consequences. Petrikev (Piotrkow), 1925.

Zikhron David. Rabbi Mordekhai Tzvi Zilber. HaMaarikh, 2014.

J. WORKS OF HALAKHA DEVOTED TO TOPICS OF INTERPERSONAL RELATIONSHIPS

Ketzet HaShemesh BiGvurato. Rabbi Avraham Tovolsky. Part of *Tikkun Sidrat HaMiddot.* This volume concerns the prohibitions against revenge and taking a grudge, and the obligation of forgiveness. 1979.

Kodesh Yisrael. Rabbi Avraham Yosef Ehrman. Essays on laws of interpersonal relationships, printed together with *Halikhot Olam,* a compilation of the relevant laws. Benei Berak, Israel, 1996.

LeRe'akha Kamokha. Rabbi David Ariav (contemporary). A treatment of laws pertaining to interpersonal relations. Includes rulings of Rabbi Ḥayim Kanievsky. Eight volumes. Jerusalem, 2000.

Mishpetei HaShalom. Rabbi Yitzḥak Eizik Silber.

Mitzvot HaLevavot. Rabbi Mordekhai Lichtenstein (b. 1865). Brisk: A. Handler, 1924.

Mitzvot HaShem. Rabbi Yonatan Shteif. Contains one section on faith and one on interpersonal relationships. Monsey, New York, 1980.

Niv Sefatayim. Rabbi Naḥum Yavrov. Essays on the laws of falsehood. Brooklyn, New York, 1980.

Oraḥ Meisharim: Shulḥan Arukh LeMiddot. Rabbi Menachem Troyesh. Sources and commentary concerning matters relevant to the development of character traits. Magenza (Mainz), 1878.

Shaarei Ahavat Yisrael. Rabbi Menachem Mendel Schneerson (Lubavitcher Rebbe). Jerusalem, 2000.

Titten Emet LeYaakov. Rabbi Yaakov Yeḥizkiya Fish. A treatment of the laws of falsehood, including responsa by the author and a section of responsa of earlier authorities. Jerusalem, 1981.

K. WORKS OF *MUSAR* AND PHILOSOPHY

The following titles include works of ethical instruction and inspiration, as well as those of philosophy and homiletic discourses.

Alei Shur. Rabbi Shlomo Wolbe (1914–2005). Jerusalem: Beit HaMusar al shem C. M. Lehman. 1986.

Atara LaMelekh. Rabbi Avraham Yaakov Pam (1913–2001). Rosh Yeshiva of Yeshiva Torah VoDaath. Edited by his students. Brooklyn, New York, 1993.

Daat Ḥokhma UMusar. Rabbi Yeruḥam Levovitz. Brooklyn, New York: Daat Ḥochma UMusar Publications, 1966. *Mashgiaḥ* of the Mir Yeshiva of Jerusalem.

Derashot Ḥatam Sofer. Rabbi Moshe Sofer (see *Torat Moshe,* Section A). Expository discourses.

Derashot Yagel Yaakov. Rabbi Ḥayim Mordekhai Gotlieb. Brooklyn, New York, 1984.

Ḥovot HaLevavot. Rabbeinu Baḥya ibn Pekuda (eleventh century) of Zaragoza, Spain.

Iggeret HaMusar. Rabbi Yisrael Salanter (see *Or Yisrael,* Section M).

Kokhvei Or. Rabbi Yitzḥak Blazer. Jerusalem, 1974 (see *Peri Yitzḥak,* Section G).

Leket Siḥot Musar. Rabbi Yitzḥak Eizik Sher. *Mashgiaḥ* of the Slobodka Yeshiva.

Lev Eliyahu. Rabbi Eliyahu Lopian (1876–1970). Jerusalem: Vaad LeHotzaat Kitvei Maran, 1983.

Menorat HaMaor. Rabbi Yitzḥak Abuhab (fourteenth century). Jerusalem: Makhon HaMidrash HaMevuar, 1988.

Mikhtav MeEliyahu. Rabbi Eliyahu Eliezer Dessler (1892–1953). *Mashgiaḥ* of Yeshivat Ponevezh. Jerusalem, 1963.

Mo'adei HaRe'iya. Rabbi Moshe Zvi Neriah, translated by Pesaḥ Jaffe as *Celebration of the Soul: The Holidays in the Life and Thought of Rabbi Avraham Yitzchak Kook,* Genesis Jerusalem Press, 1992.

Moreh Tzedek. Rabbi Avraham Yaakov Pam. Edited discourses. Jerusalem, 2012.

Netivot Olam. Rabbi Yehuda Loew ben Betzalel (see *Maharal,* Section D).

Or HaTzafun. Rabbi Natan Tzvi Finkel (1849–1927). The "Alter" of Slobodka. Jerusalem: Mossad Haskel al yedei Yeshivat Chevron, 1959.

Orḥot Tzaddikim. Unknown (fourteenth century).

Paḥad Yitzḥak. Rabbi Yitzchak Hutner (1905–80). Philosophical essays arranged according to the festivals, with a volume of "letters and writings." Brooklyn, New York: *Mossad Gur Aryeh*, 1960. Rosh Yeshiva of Yeshiva Chaim Berlin in Brooklyn, New York, and the Kollel Gur Aryeh. In his youth, he authored *Torat HaNazir* to *Mishneh Torah, Laws of the Nazirite*.

Peleh Yoetz. Rabbi Eliezer Papo (1785–1827). Jerusalem: Kerem Shlomo, 1962.

Shaarei Teshuva. Rabbeinu Yonah ben Avraham of Gerona (see *Aliyot DeRabbeinu Yonah*, Section B). Classic ethical work.

BeShaarei HaTshuva. Rabbi Meir Lembrasky. Jerusalem, 2007.

Daltei Teshuva. Rabbi Yitzḥak ben Shoshan. Kiryat Sefer Modi'in, Israel, 2002.

Maor HaShaar. Rabbi Avraham Erlanger. Jerusalem, 1984 (also authored *Birkat Avraham* to many tractates of the Talmud).

Shiurei UPnenei Daat. Rabbi Eliyahu Meir Bloch (ca. 1894–1955). Edited by Rabbi Natan Tzvi Brown. Wickliffe, Ohio: Hotzaat Peninei Da'at, 2005.

Siḥot Ḥokhma UMusar. Rabbi David Kronglass, *Mashgiaḥ* of Ner Israel Rabbinical College, Baltimore, Maryland.

Siḥot Musar. Rabbi Ḥayim Shmuelevitz (1901–79). Recorded discourses from the years 1972 through 1974. The Rosh Yeshiva of the Mir Yeshiva of Jerusalem, his talmudic novellae have been printed as *Shaarei Ḥayim* (to Gittin and Kiddushin).

Torat Eliezer. Rabbi Eliezer Geldzehler. Brooklyn, New York: Machon Torat Eliezer, 2010.

Tzidkat HaTzaddik. Rabbi Tzaddok HaKohen of Lublin (1823–1900). Benei Berak, Israel: Hotzaat Yahadut, 1966. Author of many works of hasidic philosophy, including *Peri Tzaddik* to the Torah.

Yesod VeShoresh HaAvoda. Rabbi Alezander Susskind ben Moshe (b. 1793) of Grodno. Benei Berak, Israel: Makhon LeHotzaat Sefarim Ḥasdei Ḥayim, 1987.

L. COMMENTARIES TO PIRKEI AVOT

The talmudic Tractate Avot (part of Seder Nezikin) is particularly relevant to issues of interpersonal relationships. The following titles are commentaries to that tractate.

Be'er Avot. Rabbi Menaḥem Mendel Frankel-Teomim. Philadelphia: Va'ad Keren Hadfasat Sifrei HaRaMaM Frenkel-Teomim, 1944.

Divrei Daniel. Rabbi Daniel Shteinshneider. Pressburg, 1895.

Etz Yosef. Rabbi Ḥanokh Zundel. Jerusalem, 1993.

Lehorot Natan. Rabbi Natan Gestetner. Benei Berak, Israel, 1985 (see Section A).

MiShel Avot. A compilation by Rabbi Moshe Levi. Benei Berak, Israel, 1992.

Nishba LaAvotekha. Rabbi Barukh Tzvi Moskowitz. Benei Berak, Israel: Beit Midrash Tenuvat Barukh, 1992.

Rabbeinu Yonah. In standard editions of the Vilna Talmud (see Section B).

Sefat Emet. Rabbi Yehuda Aryeh Leib Alter (1847–1905). Gerrer Rebbe. Jerusalem, 1966. Also authored volumes of the same name to the Torah and the talmudic orders of Moed and Kodashim.

Tiferet Yehoshua. Rabbi Yehoshua Belcrovitz. Jerusalem: Makhon Orot HaGnuzim.

Yesodei Yeshurun. Rabbi Gedalyah Felder of Toronto. New York, 1991. Author of works of halakha and other works of the same name.

Zeroa Yamin. Rabbi Ḥayim Yosef David Azulai. Known as Ḥida. Warsaw, 1931.

M. JOURNALS, MEMORIAL AND JUBILEE VOLUMES

Much halakhic discussion is found in periodical journals, often published by yeshivas or rabbinical organizations. Years listed represent the inititiation of the publication.

Aḥrayut Ketuva (Responsibility Inscribed). The Center for Modern Torah Leadership. 2012.

Alim LiTrufa. Published by the Machon Ohr Tzafun of Belz Hasidim. Antwerp, 1995.

Assia. Journal of topics relating to medical matters. Edited by Rabbi Dr. Avraham Steinberg. 1989.

Ateret Shlomo. Devoted to topics of technology and medicine in halakha. Makhon Madai Technologi LeHalakha. 1996.

Beit Aharon VeYisrael. Torah jourmal of the students and faculty of the yeshivas and kollels of the Karlin-Stolin institutions of Israel and the Diaspora. 1986.

Beit Hillel. Journal in memory of Rabbi Hillel Totian. 2000.

Bikkurim. Published by Beit Diskin. 1998.

Dine Israel: Shenaton LeMishpat Ivri VeLaMishpaḥa BeYisrael. Published by Beit Midrash LeMishpat Ivri and the Law Faculty of Tel Aviv University. 1970.

HaBe'er. Published by Sanz Hasidim. 2000.

HaDarom. Torah journal of the Rabbinical Council of America. Rabbi Charles B. Chavel, founding editor. 1957.

HaYashar VeHaTov. Journal devoted to practical issues of monetary law. 2006.

Ḥokhma VeDaat to Bava Batra. Yeshivat Ḥokhma VeDaat, Rechovot, Israel, 2004.

Knesset Yisrael Zikhron Mordekhai. Hitaḥdut HaBogrim of Yeshivat Slobodka of Benei Berak, Israel. In memory of Rabbi Mordekhai Shulman. 2007.

Kol HaTorah. Published by the Education Division of Agudath Yisrael of Europe. 1978.

Kol MeHeikhal. Kovetz Torani Hilkhati MeHeikhalam shel Rabanan Ve'Talmidehon. 2005.

Kol Torah. Torah journal of Agudath Yisrael of Europe. 1977.

Kovetz Shiurei Torah. Beit Shlomo. 1972.

Kovetz Torani Merkazi. Hanhalat Mosdot HaTorah HaMeuḥadim shel Ḥasidei Gur BeEretz Yisrael. 1983.

Morasha Kehillat Yaakov: Essays in Honour of Chief Rabbi Lord Jonathan Sacks. Jerusalem: Maggid Books, 2014.

Nitei Ne'emanim. Lakewood, NJ: Machon Mishnat Rabi Aharon: Ichud Talmidei Kletzk U'Veit Midrash Gavoah. 1998.

Or HaMizraḥ. Dedicated to Torah, People of Israel, and the State of Israel. Published jointly by the Torah Education Department of the World Zionist Organization and Mizrachi/HaPoel HaMizrachi of Canada and of America. 1954.

Or Yisrael. Machon Or Yisrael. Monsey, New York, 1998.

Otzerot Yerushalayim. Rabbinical journal edited by Rabbi Tzvi Markovitch of Jerusalem.

Sefer Zikkaron LeMaran Baal HaPaḥad Yitzḥak. Memorial volume to Rabbi Yitzchak Hutner (see *Paḥad Yitzḥak,* Section K), containing unpublished novellae and biographical information. Jerusalem, 1984.

Shaarei Horaa. Beit Horaa Maarav Benei Berak of Rabbi Shmuel Eliezer Stern, 2002.

Shaarei Tzedek. Journal devoted to practical monetary matters. Kiryat Ono, Israel: Makhon Mishnat HaRambam. 2000.

Shoshanat HaAmakim: BeInyanei Halakha. Journal devoted to topics of medicine and Jewish law. Kollel Halakha URfua.

Sinai. Jerusalem: Mossad HaRav Kook, 1937.

Talpiyot. Quarterly Journal *LeHalakha Agadda UMusar HaYahadut.* 1944.

Teḥumin. Research articles concerning Torah, society, and state. Halakhic monographs concerning the relationship of Torah to modern society. Published by Tzomet (*Tzivtei Madda VeTorah*) Alon Shvut, Israel. 1980.

Tevuna. LeInyanei Hayahadut Pilpulei Orayta VeḤokhmat Musar HaTorah. Kovno, 1922.

Torat HaAdam LeAdam. A collection of Torah essays concerning the relationship of man to his fellow man, published by Makhon Torat HaAdam LeAdam, Safed, Israel.

Tzohar: Kovetz Torani Merkazi MeḤokhmei HaTorah BeInyanei Halakha UMinhag. Published by Makhon Hilkhati Aktuali Derekh Eliezer she'al yedei Makhon Torani Ḥomat Yerusahalayim. 1994.

N. OTHER TORAH WORKS

A'aleh BaTamar. Anonymous collection of citations from the *Ḥazon Ish,* and others. Benei Brak, 2005.

Benei Yissakhar. Rabbi Tzvi Elimelech Schapiro (1783–1841) of Dinov. On the months of the year. Petrikev (Piotrkow), 1884.

Ḥazon Shmuel. Rabbi Shmuel Azrie. On various topics. Ashdod, 2002.

Harḥavat Gevul Yaavetz. Rabbi Dovid Kohn (contemporary). Brooklyn, New York, 2002.

HaMeorot HaGedolim. Rabbi Ḥayim Ephraim Zaichyk. Biographies of major figures of the *Musar* movement. Brooklyn, New York, 1953.

HaSam Orḥotav. Rabbi Ḥayim Kanievsky. Commentary to *Orḥot Ḥayim.*

Ḥiddushei HaRadal. Rabbi David Luria (1798–1855). Commentary to *Midrash Rabba.*

Keriya BaKeriya. Rabbi Moshe Samsonowitz. Essays on Torah topics and advice to yeshiva students. Kiryat Sefer, Israel: Makhon Zikhron Shalom, 2003.

Karyana DeIgarta. Rabbi Yisrael Yaakov Kanievsky (see *Kehillot Yaakov,* Section D). The Steipler Gaon. Benei Berak, Israel, 1985.

Maharzu. Rabbi Ze'ev Wolf Einhorn (d. 1862). Commentary to *Midrash Rabba.*

Maḥzor Vitri. Rabbi Simḥa of Vitri (d. 1105). Student of Rashi. Nuremberg, 1923.

Nefesh HaRav. Rabbi Herschel Schachter, Rosh Yeshiva at RIETS. A halakhic biography of Rabbi Joseph B. Soloveitchik, including many of his positions on matters of Jewish law. Jerusalem: Reshit Yerusahalayim, 1994.

Nefesh Ḥayim. Rabbi Ḥayim Palagi (1788–1869). Thessaloniki. 1842.

Niflaot MiTorat Hashem Yitbaraḥ. Rabbi Tzvi Shlav. Warsaw, 1879.

Rav Lehoshia. Shagiv Amit. Commentary to sections of the *Shulḥan Arukh HaRav.* Beit Shemesh, Israel, 2004.

Sefer HaḤayim. Rabbi Ḥayim ben Betzalel (1530–88). Brother of the Maharal of Prague.

Shenei Luḥot HaBrit. Rabbi Yeshayahu Horovitz (1565–1630). Jerusalem: Zikhron Yehuda, 1993. Work of halakha and Jewish thought.

Tenuat HaMusar. Rabbi Dov Katz. History of the *Musar* movement and its leaders. Tel Aviv: Avraham Tsiyoni, 1954,

Tenuvot Sadai. Rabbi Avraham Rosenberg. Benei Berak, Israel, 1998.

Torat HaKohanim VeAvodat HaBeit HaMikdash VeHaKarbanot. Rabbi Menaḥem HaKohen Rizkov. New York, 1945.

Torat HaOla. Rabbi Moshe Isserles (Rema) (see Section F). On topics relating to the Temple. Keonisgburg, 1854.

VeTziva HaKohen. Rabbi Naftali Katz. Whitefield, 1823.

O. WORKS OF GENERAL LITERATURE

Aboujaoude, Elias. *Virtually You: The Dangerous Powers of the E-Personality.* New York: W. W. Norton, 2011.

Akst, Daniel. *We Have Met the Enemy: Self Control in an Age of Excess.* New York: Penguin, 2011.

Allport, Gordon. *The Nature of Prejudice.* 2nd ed. Reading, MA: Addison-Wesley, 1979.

Andrews, Lori B. *I Know Who You Are and I Saw What You Did: Social Networks and the Death of Privacy.* New York: Free Press, 2012.

Ansolabehere, Stephen, and Shanto Iyengar. *Going Negative: How Political Advertisements Shrink & Polarize the Electorate.* New York: Free Press, 1995.

Appiah, Kwame Anthony. *Experiments in Ethics: What Is Good and Why.* Cambridge, MA: Harvard University Press, 2007.

Ariely, Dan. *Predictably Irrational: The Hidden Forces That Shape Our Decisions.* New York: HarperCollins, 2008.

Ayres, Ian. *Super Crunchers: Why Thinking-by-Numbers Is the New Way to Be Smart.* New York: Bantam, 2007.

Banaji, Mahzarin R., and Anthony G. Greenwald. *Blind Spot: Hidden Biases of Good People.* New York: Delacorte, 2013.

Barash, David. *Payback: Why We Retaliate, Redirect Aggression, and Take Revenge.* New York: Oxford University Press, 2011.

Baumeister, Roy F. *Evil: Inside Human Cruelty and Violence.* New York: W. H. Freeman, 1997.

Bazerman, Max H. *The Power of Noticing: What the Best Leaders See.* New York : Simon & Schuster, 2014

Blau, Melinda, and Karen L. Fingerman. *Consequential Strangers: The Power of People Who Don't Seem to Matter... but Really Do.* New York: W. W. Norton, 2009.

Buonomano, Dean. *Brain Bugs: How The Brain's Flaws Shape Our Lives.* New York : W. W. Norton & Co., 2011.

Brafman, Ori, and Ron Brafman. *Sway: The Irresistable Pull of Irrational Behavior.* New York: Doubleday, 2008.

Breznitz, Shlomo. *Maximum Brainpower: Challenging the Brain for Health and Wisdom.* New York: Ballantine Books, 2012.

Brock, George. *Out of Print: Newspapers, Journalism and the Business of News in the Digital Age.* London: Kogan Page, 2013.

Buell, Emmett H., and Lee Sigelman. *Attack Politics: Negativity in Presidential Campaigns Since 1960.* Lawrence: University Press of Kansas, 2008.

Burton, Robert Alan. *On Being Certain: Believing You Are Right Even When You're Not.* New York: St. Martin's, 2008.

Cain, Susan. *Quiet: The Power of Introverts in a World That Can't Stop Talking.* New York: Crown, 2012.

Carr, Nicholas G. *The Shallows: What the Internet Is Doing to Our Brains.* New York: W. W. Norton, 2010.

Chabris, Christopher, and Daniel Simons. *The Invisible Gorilla.* New York: Crown, 2010.

Davidow, William H. *Overconnected: The Promise and Threat of the Internet.* Harrison, NY: Delphinium Books, 2011.

Dehaene, Stanislas. *Consciousness and the Brain: Deciphering How the Brain Codes Our Thoughts.* New York: Viking Adult, 2014.

DeSteno, David. *The Truth About Trust.* New York: Hudson Street Press, 2014.

DeSteno, David, and Piercarlo Valdesolo. *Out of Character: Surprising Truths About the Liar, Cheat, Sinner (and Saint) Lurking in All of Us.* New York: Crown Archetype, 2011.

DiFonzo, Nicholas. *The Watercooler Effect: A Psychologist Explores the Exraordinary Power of Rumors.* New York: Avery, 2008.

DiSalvo, David. *What Makes Your Brain Happy and Why You Should Do the Opposite.* Amherst, NY: Prometheus Books, 2011.

Dobelli, Rolf. *The Art of Thinking Clearly.* New York: HarperBusiness, 2013.

Dunbar, Robin. *Grooming, Gossip and the Evolution of Language.* Cambridge, MA: Harvard University Press, 1996.

Dutton, Kevin. *Split Second Persuasion: The Ancient Art and New Science of Changing Minds.* Boston: Houghton Mifflin Harcourt, 2011.

Enright, Robert. *Forgiveness Is a Choice.* Washington, DC: American Psychological Association, 2001.

Epley, Nicholas. *Mindwise: How We Understand What Others Think, Believe, Feel and Want.* New York: Knopf, 2014.

Evans, Dylan. *Risk Intelligence: How to Live with Uncertainty.* New York: Free Press, 2012.

Fertik, Michael, and David Thompson. *Wild West 2.0: How to Protect and Restore Your Online Reputation on the Untamed Social Frontier.* New York: Amacom, 2010.

Fox, Elaine. *Rainy Brain Sunny Brain.* New York: Basic Books, 2012.

Freedman, David H. *Wrong: Why Experts* Keep Failing Us – and How to Know When Not to Trust Them; *scientists, finance wizards, doctors, relationship gurus, celebrity CEOs, high-powered consultants, health officials and more.* New York: Little, Brown, 2010.

Freeman, John. *The Tyranny of E-mail: The Four-Thousand-Year Journey to Your Inbox.* New York: Scribner, 2009.

Gardner, Dan. *Future Babble: Why Expert Predictions Are Next to Worthless, and You Can Do Better.* New York: Dutton, 2011.

Gigerenzer, Gerd. *Gut Feelings.* New York: Viking, 2007.

Gino, Francesca. *Sidetracked: Why Our Decisions Get Derailed, and How We Can Stick to the Plan.* Boston: Harvard Business Review Press, 2011.

Goldberg, Robert. *Tabloid Medicine: How the Internet Is Being Used to Hijack Medical Science for Fear and Profits.* New York: Kaplan, 2010.

Gosling, Sam. *Snoop: What Your Stuff Says About You.* New York: Basic Books, 2008.

Greenfield, Susan. *Mindchange: How Digital Technologies Are Leaving Their Marks on our Brains.* New York: Random House, 2015.

Haidt, Jonathan. *The Righteous Mind: Why Good People Are Divided by Politics and Religion.* New York: Pantheon, 2012.

Hammond, Claudia. *Time Warped: Unlocking the Mysteries of Time Perception.* New York: Harper Perennial, 2012.

Heath, Chip, and Dan Heath. *Decisive: How to Make Better Choices in Life and Work.* New York: Crown Business, 2013.

Heffernan, Margaret. *Willful Blindness.* New York: Walker, 2011.

Iacoboni, Marco. *Mirroring People: The New Science of How We Connect with Others.* New York: Farrar, Straus and Giroux, 2008.

Johnson, Clay A. *The Information Diet: A Case for Conscious Consumption.* Beijing: O'Reilly Media, 2012.

Kahneman, Daniel. *Thinking Fast and Slow.* New York: Farrar, Straus and Giroux, 2011.

Kaplan, Michael, and Ellen Kaplan. *Bozo Sapiens: Why to Err Is Human.* New York: Bloomsbury, 2009.

Keen, Andrew. *Digital Vertigo: How Today's Online Social Revolution Is Dividing, Diminishing, and Disorienting Us.* New York: St. Martin's, 2012.

Kida, Thomas. *Don't Believe Everything You Think: The 6 Basic Mistakes We Make in Thinking.* Amherst, NY: Prometheus Books, 2006.

Kovach, Bill, and Tom Rosenstiel. *Blur: How to Know What's True in the Age of Information Overload.* New York: Bloomsbury, 2010.

Kowalski, Robin M., Sue P. Limber, and Patricia W. Agatston. *Cyberbullying: Bullying in the Digital Age.* Malden, MA: Wiley-Blackwell, 2012.

Lehrer, Jonah. *How We Decide.* Boston: Houghton Mifflin Harcourt, 2009.

Levmore, Saul, and Martha C. Nussbaum. *The Offensive Internet: Privacy, Speech, and Reputation.* Cambridge, MA: Harvard University Press, 2010.

Lilienfeld, Scott O., Stephen Jay Lynn, John Ruscio, and Barry L. Beyerstein. *50 Great Myths of Popular Psychology: Shattering Widespread Misconceptions About Human Behavior.* Malden, MA: Wiley-Blackwell, 2010.

Loftus, E., and K. Ketcham. *Witness for the Defense: The Accused, the Eyewitness, and the Expert Who Puts Memory on Trial.* New York: St. Martin's, 1991.

MacKay, Charles. *Extraordinary Popular Delusions and the Madness of Crowds.* New York: Harmony Books, 1980.

Macknick, Stephen, and Susana Martinez-Conde. *Sleights of Mind.* New York: Henry Holt, 2010.

Manjoo, Farhad. *True Enough: Learning to Live in a Post-Fact Society.* Hoboken, NJ: Wiley, 2008.

Marcus, Gary. *Kluge: The Haphazard Construction of the Human Mind.* Boston: Houghton Mifflin, 2008.

Mayer, John D. *Personal Intelligence: The Power of Personality and How It Shapes Our Lives.* New York: Scientific American; Farrar, Straus and Giroux, 2011.

Mayer-Schönberger, Viktor. *Big Data: A Revolution That Will Transform How We Live, Work, and Think.* Boston: Houghton Mifflin Harcourt, 2013.

McCullough, Michael. *Beyond Revenge: The Evolution of the Forgiveness Instinct.* San Franciso: Jossey Bass, 2008.

McRaney, David. *You Are Not So Smart: Why You Have Too Many Friends on Facebook, Why Your Memory Is Mostly Fiction, and 46 Other Ways You're Deluding Yourself.* NewYork: Gotham Books; Penguin, 2011.

McRaney, David. *You Are Now Less Dumb: How to Conquer Mob Mentality, How to Buy Happiness, and All the Other Ways to Outsmart Yourself.* New York: Gotham Books, 2013.

Mlodinow, Leonard. *Subliminal: How Your Unconscious Mind Rules Your Behavior.* New York: Pantheon, 2012.

Mnookin, Robert. *Bargaining with the Devil: When to Negotiate and When to Fight.* New York: Simon and Schuster, 2010.

Morozov, Evgeny. *The Net Delusion: The Dark Side of Internet Freedom (How Not to Liberate the World).* New York: Public Affairs, 2011.

Morozov, Evgeny. *To Save Everything, Click Here: Smart Machines, Dumb Humans, and the Myth of Technological Perfectionism.* New York: Perseus, 2013.

Oakley, Barbara. *Evil Genes.* Amherst, NY: Prometheus Books, 2007.

Ofri, Danielle. *What Doctors Feel: How Emotions Affect the Practice of Medicine.* Boston: Beacon, 2013.

Pariser, Eli. *The Filter Bubble: What the Internet Is Hiding from You.* New York: Penguin, 2011.

Pentland, Alex. *Social Physics: How Good Ideas Spread – the Lessons from a New Science.* New York: Penguin, 2014.

Potter, Andrew. *The Authenticity Hoax: How We Got Lost Finding Ourselves.* New York: HarperCollins, 2010.

Powers, William. *Hamlet's Blackberry: A Practical Philosophy for Building a Good Life in the Digital Age.* New York: Harper, 2010.

Rainie, Lee and Barry Wellman. *Networked: The New Social Operating System.* Cambridge, Mass: MIT Press, 2012

Rosen, Larry D., Nancy A. Cheever, and L. Carrier Mark. *IDisorder: Understanding Our Obsession with Technology and Overcoming Its Hold on Us.* New York: Palgrave Macmillan, 2012.

Rosenberg, Howard, and Charles S. Feldman. *No Time to Think: The Menace of Media Speed and the 24-Hour News Cycle.* New York: Continuum, 2008.

Rosenberg, Scott. *Say Everything: How Blogging Began, What It's Becoming, and Why It Matters.* New York: Crown, 2009.

Rosenzweig, Phil. *The Halo Effect . . . and the Eight Other Business Delusions That Deceive Managers*. New York: Free Press, 2007.
Rosnow, Ralph L., and Gary Alan Fine. *Rumor and Gossip: The Social Psychology of Hearsay*. New York: Elsevier, 1976.
Schacter, Daniel L. *The Seven Sins of Memory: How the Mind Forgets and Remembers*. Boston: Houghton Mifflin, 2001.
Schulz, Kathryn. *Being Wrong: Adventures in the Margins of Error*. New York: Ecco, 2010.
Seife, Charles. *Virtual Unreality: Just Because the Internet Told You, How Do You Know It's True?* New York: Viking, 2014.
Shermer, Michael. *The Science of Good and Evil: Why People Cheat, Share, Gossip, and Follow the Golden Rule*. New York: Times Books, 2004.
Shirky, Clay. *Cognitive Surplus: Creativity and Generosity in a Connected Age*. New York: Penguin, 2010.
Siegel, Lee. *Against the Machine: Being Human in the Age of the Electronic Mob*. New York: Spiegel and Grau, 2008.
Siegfried, Tom. *A Beautiful Math: John Nash, Game Theory, and the Modern Quest for a Code of Nature*. Washington, DC: Joseph Henry, 2006.
Slade, Giles. *The Big Disconnect: The Story of Technology and Loneliness*. Amherst, NY: Prometheus Books, 2012.
Solove, Daniel J. *The Future of Reputation: Gossip, Rumor, and Privacy on the Internet*. New Haven, CT: Yale University Press, 2007.
Sommers, Sam. *Situations Matter: Understanding How Context Transforms Your World*. New York: Riverhead Books, 2011.
Standage, Tom. *Writing on the Wall: Social Media, The First 2000 Years*. New York: Bloomsbury, 2013.
Stanovich, Keith. *What Intelligence Tests Miss: The Psychology of Rational Thought*. New Haven, CT: Yale University Press, 2009.
Steele, Claude. *Whistling Vivaldi*. New York: W. W. Norton, 2010.
Stryker, Cole. *Hacking the Future: Privacy, Identity, and Anonymity on the Web*. New York: Overlook Duckworth, 2012.
Sunstein, Cass R. *On Rumors*. New York: Farrar, Straus and Giroux, 2009.
Surowiecki, James. *The Wisdom of Crowds: Why the Many Are Smarter Than the Few and How Collective Wisdom Shapes Business, Economies, Societies, and Nations*. New York: Doubleday, 2004.

Sunstein, Cass R., and Reid Hastie. *Wiser: Getting Beyond Groupthink to Make Groups Smarter.* Boston: Harvard Business Review Press, 2015.

Taleb, Nassim. *Fooled by Randomness.* New York: Random House, 2005.

Tammet, Daniel. *Embracing the Wide Sky: A Tour Across the Horizons of the Human Brain.* New York: Free Press, 2009.

Tavris, Carol, and Elliot Aronson. *Mistakes Were Made (but Not by Me),* Orlando: Harcourt, 2007.

Thaler, Richard H., and Cass R. Sunstein. *Nudge: Improving Decisions About Health, Wealth, and Happiness.* New Haven, CT: Yale University Press, 2008.

Turkle, Sherry. *Alone Together: Why We Expect More from Technology and Less from Each Other.* New York: Basic Books, 2010.

Vaidhyanathan, Siva. *The Googlization of Everything,* Berkeley: University of California Press, 2010.

Vanderbilt, Tom. *Traffic: Why We Drive the Way We Do (and What It Says About Us).* New York: Knopf, 2008.

Watts, Duncan J. *Everything Is Obvious Once You Know the Answer.* New York: Crown Business, 2011.

Weinberger, David. *Too Big to Know: Rethinking Knowledge Now That the Facts Aren't the Facts, Experts Are Everywhere, and the Smartest Person in the Room Is the Room.* New York: Basic Books, 2011.

Westacott, Emrys. *The Virtue of Our Vices: A Modest Defense of Gossip, Rudeness, and Other Bad Habits.* Princeton, NJ: Princeton University Press, 2012.

Winograd, E., and U. Neisser, eds., *Affect and Accuracy in Recall: Studies of "Flashbulb" Memories.* New York: Cambridge University Press, 1992.

Wittgenstein, Ludwig. *On Certainty.* New York: Harper, 1969.

Zak, Paul J. *The Moral Molecule: The Source of Love and Prosperity.* New York: Dutton, 2012.

Zimbardo, Philip. *The Lucifer Effect.* New York: Random House, 2007.

Zittrain, Jonathan. *The Future of the Internet.* New Haven, CT: Yale University Press, 2008.

Glossary

apei telata: lit. "in front of three"; information that is public knowledge, or inevitably will become public

avak lashon hara: lit. "dust" of *lashon hara*"; a lower degree of *lashon hara*, prohibited either by biblical or rabbinic law, and including statements or gestures that either disparage in a nonexplicit fashion, or encourage others to speak disparagingly

baal lashon hara: lit "master of *lashon hara*," a category innovated by Maimonides to designate one who not only speaks *lashon hara*, but does so with such regularity as to be defined by it

baal teshuva: repentant sinner; in modern usage, often refers to one who takes on religious observance later in life

baalei maḥloket: contentious people

beit din: rabbinic court

devarim hanikarim: supporting evidence that makes the substance of a negative report more credible

genevat daat: deceptive behavior, including evoking an undeserved positive impression

ḥezkat kashrut: presumption of innocence

kabbalat lashon hara: "receiving" of *lashon hara*; variously defined as believing or acting upon negative reports

lashon hara: disparaging speech, sometimes defined as true statements, and sometimes inclusive of true or false statements

lifnei iver: lit. "in front of a blind person [do not place a stumbling block]" (a reference to Lev. 19:14); fig., the prohibition of enabling or causing another to sin

lo taamod al dam re'ekha: the mandate to protect others from harm (a reference to Lev. 19:16)

mefursam lakol: "known to all"; a category of public knowledge more widespread than *apei telata*

mekaḥ ta'ut: mistaken purchase; a transaction conducted under false or mistaken premises and subject to reversal

metzora: one afflicted with *tzaraat*; see below

mitkabbed biklon ḥavero: one who seeks to draw honor through the disgrace of another

motzi shem ra: slander

onaat devarim: lit. verbal oppression; the infiction of emotional pain on another

pesik reishei: an inevitable consequence

raglayim ladavar: lit. "the matter has legs"; factors that give credibility to an allegation

rekhilut: gossip or tale-bearing, sometimes defined as telling another what has been said about them

rokhel or *rakhil*: lit. peddler; in usage, a tale-bearer or gossip, a reference to Lev. 19:16, and other sources

safek: unknown or indeterminate situation

shav: either "unnecessary" or "false"

sheker: falsehood

shiddukh: match, usually a reference to a proposed marriage partner

taromet: grievance

to'elet: purpose; also a reference to the necessity or justification that can allow or mandate the conveying and receiving of negative information

tzaraat: a physical affliction described in the Bible and attributed in rabbinic sources to spiritual causes, including *lashon hara*

Index of Topics and Names

A

A'aleh BaTamar, 33n
Aaron, 87, 106, 148n, 247
Aboujaoude, Elias, 199-200
Abraham, 227n
Abrahams, R. Ḥayim Shlomo, *see Birkat Shlomo*
accepting, 8, 17, 35, 43-44, 76, 106, 162, 167n, 192, 222
 agreeing, 149
 believing, 136, 139-141, 143, 145-146, 242; *see also* credibility
 biblical source for, 134, 145, 147
 covering one's ears, 147n
 equal to or worse than speaking, 133-135, 156, 157n, 242
 listening, 146-151, 192, 242n
 Maimonides on, 156-157
 on internet, 209-212
 protection, 139-140, 141n, 143-145, 150-151, 155n
 repentance for, 242
 verbal objection, 141n, 149n
 violation of *lifnei iver*, 135n
Achiezer, 110n
Aderet Tiferet, 225n
Aderet Zahav, 21n
Adirim, R. Eliezer, *see Aderet Zahav*
Adler, R. Yosef Tzvi *see Al Pi HaTorah*
advertising, 217-218
advice, 107, 113
Afarkasta DeAnya, 176n
Afikei Yam, 103n
Agatston, Patricia W., 200n, 203n, 208n
Akst, Daniel, 68
Al Pi HaTorah, 22n
Alei Be'er, 95n, 128n, 130n, 135n, 147n, 148n, 149n, 163n, 174n, 214n
Alei Shur, 136n
Aleinu Leshabeaḥ, 126n, 236n
Aliyot, 100n, 166n
Alkabetz, R. Shlomo, *see Manot HaLevi*
Allport, Floyd H., 62
Allport, Gordon, 44-45
Alpandari, R. Avraham *see Mirkevet HaMishna*
Altusky, R. Ḥayim Dov, 162n
Am KeLavi, 240n
Amit, Shagiv, *see Rav Lehoshia*
Amsterdam, R. Naphtali, 237, 239n

Index of Topics and Names

Andrews, Lori B., 41n, 204n, 215-216
Ankiva, R. Raphael ben Mordekhai, *see Paamonei Zahav*
Ansolabehere, Stephen, 219n
apei telata, see public
Appiah, Kwame Anthony, 84n
Ariav, David R., *see LeRe'akha Kamokha*
Ariel, R. Azriel, 180n
Ariel, R. Yaakov, *see BeOhala shel Torah*
Arieli, R. Shlomo, 226n
Ariely, Dan, 68n
Arik, R. Meir, *see Imrei Yosher*
Aronson, Elliot, 45n, 48n, 49n, 63n
Arukh HaShulḥan, 128n, 155n, 234n
Arukh LeNer, 167n
Arusi, R. Ratzon, 223n
Asch, Solomon, 69-70, 71
Assad, R. Yehuda, *see Yehuda Yaaleh*
Atara LeMelekh, 106n, 178n
Ateret Moshe, 191n
Ateret Paz, 225n
Ateret Tzvi, 137n
Ateret Yitzḥak, 171n
Auerbach, R. Shlomo Zalman, 107n, 116n, 122n, 126n; *see also Halikhot Shlomo*
avak lashon hara, xvii, 172-176, 179, 213, 225-226, 230n, 249
Aviner, R. Shlomo, *see Am KeLavi*
Aviram, 129n
Avnei Ḥoshen, 113n
Avnei Yashpeh, 96n, 98n, 119n
Avodat Melekh, 12n, 13n, 15n, 135n, 162n, 163n, 166n, 174n
Avraham, R. Avraham S., *see Nishmat Avraham*
Avraham, R. Ḥayim Shlomo, 131n; *see also Devar Torah*
Ayelet HaShaḥar, 22n
Ayres, Ian, 52n
Az Nidberu, 14n, 22n, 125n, 163n, 172n, 176n, 179n, 180n, 192n, 226n, 228n, 230n, 236n, 242n, 253n
Azriel, R. Shmuel, *see Ḥazon Shmuel*
Azulai, R. Ḥayim Yosef David, 22n, 167n, 173n, 192n, 234n

B

baal lashon hara, 13, 20n, 88, 148n
baal teshuva, 123
Babad, R. Mordekhai, *see Minḥat Maḥavat*
Bad Kodesh, 18n
Badei HaAron, 238n
Bakshi-Doron, R. Eliyahu, *see Binyan Av*
Banaji, Mahzarin R., 61
Bar Shalom, R. Eliyahu, 233n
Barash, David, 70-71
Bargh, John, 68
Barron, Robert S., 138
Bartlett, Frederic, 49-50
Baumeister, Roy, 61n, 62
Bayit Ḥadash, 235n
BaYom SheYedubar, 109n, 111n, 113n, 123n
Bazerman, Max H., 47n
Be'er HaAvot, 48n
Be'er LaḤai Ro'i, 17n
Be'er Miriam, 227n
Be'er Sarim, 191n
Bein Shenei Kohanim Gedolim, 17n, 33n, 99n, 123n, 223n, 228n, 247n
beit din, see rabbinic courts
Beit Ḥatanim, 114n
Beit Leḥem Yehuda, 15n, 162n, 165n
Beit Shlomo, 87n
Belcrovitz, R. Yaakov Yehoshua, *see Tiferet Yehoshua*
believing, *see* accepting
BeMareh HaBazak, 126n
Ben Ish Ḥai, 22n
ben Shoshan, R. Yitzḥak, *see Toledot Yitzḥak*
ben Yaakov, R. Tzvi Yehuda *see Mishpatekha LeYaakov*
Ben Yedid, 15n, 175n
Benedict, R. Mordekhai *see She'arim Metzuyanim Al HaTorah*
Benei Binyamin, 175n

Benei Vanim, 94n
Benei Yissakhar, 248n
BeOhala shel Torah, 187n
Berakha, R. Yitzḥak, *see Birkat Yitzḥak*
Berezovsky, R. Shalom Noaḥ, *see Netivot Shalom*
Berkowitz, R. Yitzḥak, 107n
Berlin, R. Naftali Tzvi Yehuda, 15n, 18n, 128, 144n, 177, 250n, 260
Berman, R. Shemaryahu Yosef, *see Birkat Shai*
Berns, Gregory, 71
Berukin, R. Yaakov, *see Mishkenot Yaakov*
BeShaarei HaTshuva, p. 33n
BeTzel HaḤokhma, 125n, 182n, 252n
BeYad HaLashon, 6n, 21n, 32n, 130n, 146n, 155n, 156n, 163n, 169n, 244n, 250n, 251n
Beyerstein, Barry L., 74n
Bialya, R. Shmuel Leiv of, *see Rizma DeḤakhmata*
bias
  ambiguity intolerance, 58
  anchoring, 68-71
  blindness to, 77-82, 147
  confirmation/diagnosis bias, 63-67, 81, 217
  countering, 80-81
  fundamental attribution error, 55-57, 62
  group polarization, 71-75, 196-197, 217
  halo effect, 60-62
  in speaker, 114
  see also truth
Bigdei Yesha, 103n
Bikkurei Aretz, 128n
Bikkurei Avraham, 18n
Binyan Av, 32n, 138n
Birkat Avot, 242n
Birkat Mordekhai, 5n, 32n
Birkat Reuven Shlomo, 13n, 22n, 23n, 87n, 111n, 245n, 250n, 254n
Birkat Shai, 162n
Birkat Shalom, 162n, 163n
Birkat Shlomo, 127n
Birkat Yitzḥak, 104n, 131n, 135n, 148n, 162n, 166n, 167n, 180n, 234n, 242n
Blau, Melinda, 38n, 64-65
Blau, R. Moshe, *see Mishnat Moshe*
Blazer, R. Yitzḥak, 234n-235n, 237
Bloch, R. Eliyahu Meir, 34
Bo Tashiv, 131n
Bognim, R. Tziyon Shimon, *see Shivat Tziyon*
Brafman, Ori, 63-64, 65-66
Brafman, Ron, 63-64, 65-66
Brandeis, Louis, 41
Brandesdorfer, R. Meir, *see Keneh Bosem*
Bratslavsky, Ellen, 61n
Braun, R. Shlomo Zalman, *see She'arim Metzuyanim BeHalakha*
Brazil, R. Avraham Yitzḥak, *see Iyyunei Rashi*
Breisch, R. Yaakov, *see Ḥelkat Yaakov*
Brezakher, R. David Binyamin, 236n
Breznitz, Shlomo, 207n
Brit Moshe, 128n
Brit Olam, 136n
Britt, Thomas, 56n
Brobovsky, R. Naḥum, *see Shalmei Naḥum*
Brock, George, 207n
Brown, Benjamin, 9n
Buell, Emmett, 219n
bullying, 38, 178n; *see also* internet, cyberbullying
Buonomano, Dean, 68n
Burton, Robert Alan, 48n, 77
business, xviii, 124-126, 144-145, 223, 228, 259; *see also* employment

C

Cain, Susan, 52-53, 71-72, 201
Cantril, Hadley, 46-47
Carr, Nicholas G., 197, 216
Carrier, L. Mark, 200n
Chabris, Christopher, 48n, 49n, 52n, 63n, 81-82
Cheever, Nancy A., 200n

Cherlow, R. Yuval, 107n, 190n
children, 119-124
Choshki, R. Yehuda Aryeh Lieb, *see Lev Aryeh*
Ciecanowitz, R. Yeruḥam, *see Torat Yeruḥam*
confidence, 52-54, 75
confidentiality, 126, 130, 165, 182, 186-187
covering the *ḥalla*, 250-251
credibility, 151-158

D

Daat Ḥokhma UMusar, 35n
Daat UMaḥashava, 12n, 20n, 135n, 174n, 179n
Daltei Teshuva, 175n
Darkei Ḥoshen, 97n, 103n, 125n
Darkei Moshe, see Isserles, R. Moshe
Darkhei Shalom, 191n
Datan, 129n
David, 3, 10, 154, 155, 256
Davidow, William H., 196-197, 201n
Dayan, R. Nissim, *see Peirot Genosar; Zekukei Nura*
Deblitsky, R. Shraya, 101, 227n; *see also Zeh HaShulḥan*
Dehaene, Stanislas, 79-80
DeModena, R. Shmuel, 227n
Deichovsky, R. Shlomo, 185n
Derekh Siḥa, 104n
Dessler, R. Eliyahu, 21-22, 236n
DeSteno, David, 28n, 56n, 57n
Deutsch, R. Yosef Aryeh, *see Divrei Yosef*
Devar Torah, 131n
Devar Tov, 234n
devarim hanikarim, 153, 155n
Devoretz, R. Eliezer Zev, 130n
DiFonzo, Nicholas, 28n, 34n, 62, 75, 76-77, 80n, 138-139, 195-196
dignity, 27
Dina DeḤayyei, 182n
DiSalvo, David, 58n, 72, 74n
dishonesty, *see* falsehood
Diskin, R. Yehoshua Leib, 40
Divrei Daniel, 22n
Divrei Ḥayil, 111n
Divrei Malkiel, 191n
Divrei Meḥokek, 173n
Divrei Shalom, 173n, 175n
Divrei Shlomo, 16n
Divrei Yaakov, 4n, 34n, 244n
Divrei Yatziv, see Halberstam, R. Yekutiel Yehuda
Divrei Yirmiyahu, 34n, 173n
Divrei Yosef, 111n, 112n
Dobelli, Rolf, 48n, 56n, 58n, 61n, 63n
Dunbar, Robin, 38n
Duri, R. Avraham, *see Aderet Tiferet; Zekhut Avot*
Dushinsky, R. Yosef Tzvi, 253; *see also Responsa Maharitz; Torat Maharitz*
"dust" of *lashon hara, see avak lashon hara*
Dutton, Kevin, 146n
Dvinsk, R. Meir Simḥa of, *see Meshekh Ḥokhma*

E

eavesdropping, 149n, 185-186
Edelstein, R. Yaakov, *see KaMatar Likḥi*
Ehrentrau, R. Binyamin, 15n
Ehrman, R. Avraham Yosef, *see Kodesh Yisrael*
Eibshutz, R. Yonatan, 242n
Eidels, R. Shmuel, 14n, 20n, 140n, 154n, 171n, 172-173, 176n
Eiger, R. Akiva, 191n; *see also Gilyon HaShas*
Eikenstein, R. David, *see Devar Tov*
Eila HaDevarim, 22n
Ein Eliyahu, 129n
Einei Yitzḥak, 13n, 129n
Eisenstatter, R. Meir, *see Imrei Yosher*
Eisenthal, R. Uriel, *see Megillat Sefer*
Eizenberg, R. Ḥenoch, 148n
Elazar ben Azaria, R., 134
Elberg, R. Simḥa, *see Shalmei Simḥa*
Elimelech, R. Moshe Yeḥiel, *see VaYomer Moshe*

Elyashiv, R. Yosef Shalom, 126, 153n, 229, 236n, 260; *see also Kovetz Teshuvot*

Elyashuv, R. Avraham, *see Bikkurei Avraham*

Emek HaLashon, 4n, 12n, 13n, 15n, 16n, 19n, 20n, 26n, 85n, 88n, 95n, 102n, 142n, 148n, 156n, 163n, 167n, 172n, 174n, 179n, 191n, 225n, 226n, 228n, 244n, 245n, 247n, 249n-250n

Emek HaMishpat, 185n

Emet LeYaakov, 5n, 82n, 105n, 229n, 230n

embarrassment, 167-168, 176n, 178, 238-239, 251

employment, 126, 148; *see also* business

Engel, R. Shmuel, 191n

Engel, R. Yosef, *see Gilyonei HaShas*

Enright, Robert, 105n

Epley, Nicholas, 54, 77n, 78n, 207-208

Erekh HaḤayim, 19n, 245n

Eretz Tzvi, 14n, 21n, 37n

Ettlinger, R. Yaakov, *see Arukh LeNer*

Etz Yosef, 37n

ethics, 83-84, 157

Evans, Dylan, 58-59, 63n, 74

Even Pina, 126n

Even Yisrael, 22n, 104n, 166n

evidence, 154-155

Ezraḥi, R. Barukh Mordekhai, 250n; *see also Birkat Mordekhai*

F

falsehood, 13n, 14n, 16n, 26, 43-44, 54-55, 81-82, 122, 136-137, 147n, 152-153, 169n, 196n, 230, 238n; *see also* slander

Faniri, R. Moshe, *see Beit Ḥatanim*

Fast, Nathaniel J., 73n

Feinhandler, R. Yisrael Pesaḥ, 222n; *see also Avnei Yashpeh*

Feinstein, R. Moshe, 119-121, 130n, 152n, 226n, 248n; *see also Iggerot Moshe*

Felder, R. Gedalya, *see Yesodei Yeshurun*

Feldman, Charles S., 197n

Fertik, Michael, 60, 204n, 209n

Fine, Gary Alan, 49n, 50, 84n

Fingerman, Karen L., 38n, 64-65

Finkel, R. Gedalya, *see Imrei Gedalya*

Finkel, R. Natan Tzvi, *see Or HaTzafun*

Finkenauer, Catrin, 61n

Fish, R. Yaakov Yeḥizkiah, *see Titten Emet LeYaakov*

Fishelder, R. Yisrael Moshe, *see Mivtzar Yisrael*

Fisher, R. Yisrael Yaakov, *see Even Yisrael*

football, 46-47

Fox, Elaine, 63n

Frankel-Teomim, R. Menaḥem Mendel, *see Be'er HaAvot*

Franklin, Benjamin, 37

fraud, *see mekaḥ ta'ut; onaa*

Freeman, John, 200n, 207

Freedman, David H., 52n, 192n

freedom of speech, 29-31

Friedlander, R. Ḥayim, 22n

Friedman, R. Binyamin, 160n

Friedman, R. Shmuel David, *see Sedeh Tzofim*

Frimer, R. Tzvi Hirsch, *see Eretz Tzvi*

G

Galanti, R. Moshe, *see Zevaḥ Shelamim*

game theory, 28

Ganzfried, Shlomo R., *see Kitzur Shulḥan Arukh*

Garden of Eden, 19

Gardner, Dan, 52n, 61n, 63n, 67n, 77n

Garrity, Michael, 56n

Geldzehler, R. Eliezer, *see Torat Eliezer*

Gelernter, R. Alter, 176n

genevat daat, 110, 112n, 117-118, 185-186

Genack, R. Menaḥem, 191n

Genichovsky, R. Avraham, 130n

Gestetner, R. Natan, *see Lehorot Natan; Natan Piryo*

Gigerenzer, Gerd, 84n

Gilbert, Daniel, 146

Gilyon HaShas, 127n, 129n

Gilyonei HaShas, 147n
Gino, Francesca, 57n, 73n, 205
Goldberg, Robert, 206
Goldstein, R. Shlomo, 163n
Goldvicht, R. Chaim Yaakov, 169n
Gosling, Sam, 69-70
gossip
  realistic perspective provided by, 39-40
  essential, 8-9, 27-28, 81, 95
  harm to society, 41, 228, 230
  social bonds formed by, 38
  see also lashon hara; to'elet, protection
Gotlieb, R. Ḥayim Mordechai, *see Yagel Yaakov*
Gottman, John, 61
Greenberger, R. Shmuel, *see Merkaḥat Besamim*
Greenblatt, R. Ephraim, *see Rivevot Ephraim*
Greenfield, Susan, 201n
Greenwald, Anthony G., 61
Greenwald, R. Yekutiel Yehuda, *see Kol Bo* to *aveilut*
Greenwald, R. Yosef, *see VaYaan Yosef; Vayeḥi Yosef*
Greineman, R. Shmuel, *see Zekher Shmuel*
Grodzinski, R. Ḥayim Ozer, 150
Groopman, Jerome, 70
Gros, R. Mordekhai, *see Om Ani Ḥoma*
Gross, R. Shammai Kehat, 23n, 122; *see also Shevet HaKehati*
Gross, R. Shlomo, *see Mishna Shelema*
Grossman, R. Avraham Yehuda, *see VeDarashta VeḤakarta*
Grossman, R. Yisrael, *see Netzaḥ Yisrael*
Grozovsky, R. Reuven, 135n, 141n
Gurewitz, R. Avraham, 170n

H

Haamek Davar, *see* Berlin, R. Naftali Tzvi Yehuda
Haamek She'ela, *see* Berlin, R. Naftali Tzvi Yehuda
Haflaat Arakhin, 171n
Ḥafetz Ḥayim, *see* Kagan, R. Yisrael Meir
Hagahot Maimoniyot, 127n, 155n, 162n, 173n, 223n
Ḥagiz, R. Yaakov, 182; *see also Halakhot Kettanot*
Haidt, Jonathan, 29, 63
HaKetav VeHaKabbala, 43n, 57n, 136n
HaKohen, R. Aharon, *see Imrei Aharon*
HaKohen, R. Kalfun Moshe, *see Shoel VeNishal*
HaKohen, R. Re'em, *see Badei HaAron*
Halakha LeMoshe, 191n
Halakhot Kettanot, 182n
Halberstam, R. Yekutiel Yehuda, 118
HaLevi, Avraham Maimon, 213n
Halikhot Shlomo, 178n, 236n, 238n
Hamberger, R. Raphael, *see Marpei Lashon*
HaMidrash VeHaMaase, 5n
Hammond, Claudia, 48n
HaNegby, Zohar, 177n
Ḥaputa, R. Avraham, *see Reishit Hashlama*
Har HaMelekh, 13n
Harfenes, R. Yisrael David, *see Nishmat Shabbat*
Harḥavat Gevul Yaavetz, 170n
Ḥarif, R. Yitzḥak, 177
Harsch, N., 48n
HaSam Orḥotav, 14n
Ḥashukei Ḥemed, 186n
Hastie, Reid, 72n
Hastorf, Albert, 46-47
Ḥatam Sofer, 22n, 38n, 102n, 128-129, 170n, 175n, 178n, 191n; *see also Torat Moshe*
hate, 20n, 37, 41, 99, 114-115, 156, 180
Ḥavatzelet HaSharon, 32n, 87n, 111n, 129n, 226n, 228n, 248n, 251n
Ḥayim ben Betzalel, R., *see Sefer HaḤayim*
Ḥayim She'al, *see* Azulai, R. Ḥayim Yosef David
Ḥayyei HaLevi, 236n
Ḥazon Ish, *see* Karelitz, R. Avraham Yeshaya

Ḥazon Shmuel, 240n
Heath, Chip, 81
Heath, Dan, 81
Heffernan, Margaret, 72, 79
Heiman, R. Shlomo, 191n
Ḥelkat Binyamin, 16n, 19n, 88n, 96n, 97n, 105n, 107n, 110n, 128n, 135n, 137n, 148n, 153n, 162n, 163n, 165n, 169n, 180n, 214n, 242n
Ḥelkat Yaakov, 111n
Ḥelkat Yehoshua, 228n, 245n
Ḥelkat Yoav, 191n
Heller, R. Yom Tov Lipman, 140; *see also* *Maadanei Yom Tov*
Ḥemdat Binyamin, 21n
Henkin, R. Yehuda Herzl *see Benei Vanim*
Hertzka, R. Tzvi, *see Ateret-Tzvi*
Hertzog, R. Yisrael Isser, 236n
ḥezkat kashrut, 26, 156n
Ḥiddushei HaLev, 250n
Ḥiddushei HaRadal, 7n
Ḥiddushei HaRim, 48n
Ḥikekei Lev, 186n
Hilkhot Ḥag BaḤag, 236n
Hillel, 116
Hillman, R. Shmuel Yitzḥak, *see Or HaYashar*
Hitorerut Teshuva, 191n, 221n, 222n
Ḥiyun, R. Ariel, 94n
Hoffman, R. Dovid Tzvi, 248n
Ḥokhma VeDaat, 165n
Ḥokhmat HaMatzpun, 248n
Ḥokhmat Shlomo, 129n
Hominer, R. Shmuel, *see Ikkarei Dinim*
honesty, *see* truth
Horovitz, R. Yeshaya HaLevi, *see Shenei Luḥot HaBrit*
Horowitz, R. Avraham David, *see Kinyan Torah BeHalakha*
Ḥukkei Ḥayim, 173n
humiliation, *see* embarrassment
Ḥut Shani, 14n, 33n, 111n, 112n, 114n, 115n, 116n, 123n, 135n, 163n, 173n, 190n, 226n, 236n
Hutner, R. Yitzḥak, 33n, 40, 94n, 107n, 126n, 140, 163n, 169n, 175n, 240n, 241, 242n, 247n

I

Iacoboni, Marco, 218-219
Iggerot Moshe, 108n, 111n, 120n, 152n, 176n, 251n, 261
Ikkarei Dinim, 5n, 222
Ikvei Sofer, 222n
Imrei Aharon, 136
Imrei Barukh, 5n
Imrei Gedalya, 149n
Imrei Yaakov, 120n
Imrei Yehosef, 127n
Imrei Yosher, 21n, 111n, 260
informing, 119-120
internet, xix, 8-9, 30, 192, 193, 219;
  accepting *lashon hara* on, 209-212
  accuracy, 194-198, 206, 208-212
  anonymity, 194n, 199-207
  cyberbullying, 202-203, 208
  empathy, 201-202, 216
  hosting, 206, 213
  linking and forwarding, 214
  online disinhibition effect, 198-203, 205
  tone, 207-208
Isaac, 227n
Isserlein, R. Yisrael Isser, 93; *see also* *Pitḥei Teshuva*
Isserles, R. Moshe, 17n, 118, 129n, 155n, 176n, 184n, 192n, 229n, 232, 233n, 243n-244n
Itaḥ, R. Yehuda, *see Netiv Yosher*
Iyengar, Shanto, 219n
Iyyunei Rashi, 136n
Iyyunim BaParasha, 13n, 34n, 248n

J

Jachter, R. Howard, 107n
Jacob, 227n, 244n
Joffen, R. Aharon, 225n
Johnson, Clay A., 66n, 210n

joking, 178-179
Jolofsky, R. Yosef, *see Yad Yosef*
Joseph, 102-103, 244n
journalism, 189-193, 198, 219
judging favorably, 22n, 36-37, 40-41, 47-48, 56, 137, 141n, 169, 247n
Jungreiss, R. Uri, 228n

K

kabbalat lashon hara, see accepting
Kagan, R. Yisrael Meir,
  approbations for the *Sefer Ḥafetz Ḥayim*, 234-235, 253
  biography, xviii, 5-6, 32, 33
  accepting negative speech, 137, 139, 141-142, 143, 145, 147-149, 151-155, 157, 161-162
  conditions permitting negative speech, 97-104, 107n, 110-111, 127-128
  definition of *rekhilut*, 14
  definition of *to'elet*, 95-96
  lashon hara about oneself, 224-225
  objections to methodology of, 9
  obtaining forgiveness for *lashon hara*, 235-239
  public, 171-172
  pioneering work of, xviii, 5-6, 94n
  See also Index of References to the Works of the *Ḥafetz Ḥayim*
Kahn, R. Aharon, *see Yismaḥ Avikha*
Kahneman, Daniel, 54n, 55, 60, 61n, 63n, 67, 81, 146n
Kalir, R. Elazar, 13n
KaMatar Likḥi, 33n
Kaminetsky, R. Yaakov 229; *see also Emet LeYaakov*
Kampinsky, R. Menaḥem Aryeh, 17n
Kanievsky, R. Ḥayim, 111n; *see also Derekh Siḥa; HaSam Orḥotav; She'elat Rav*
Kanievsky, R. Yisrael Yaakov, 117-118; *see also Karyana DeIgarta; Kehillot Yaakov*
Kaplan, Ellen, 47n, 58n
Kaplan, Michael, 47n, 58n
Kaplan, R. Nisan, 130n
Karelitz, R. Avraham Yeshaya, 33, 103, 107n, 141, 147n, 189, 260
Karelitz, R. Nissim, 190; *see also Ḥut Shani*
Karlebakh, R. Mordekhai, *see Ḥavatzelet HaSharon*
Karo, R. Yosef, 12n, 15n, 17n, 162n, 167n, 173n, 183, 213n; *see also Shulḥan Arukh* in Index of Biblical and Rabbinic Sources
Karp, R. Moshe Mordekhai, *see Hilkhot Ḥag BaḤag*
Karyana DeIgarta, 6n
Katan, Hanna, 111n
Katan, Yoel, 111n
Katz, R. Aryeh, 103n, 126n
Katz, R. Dov, *see Tenuat HaMusar*
Katz, R. Eliyahu, *see Har HaMelekh*
Katz, R. Naphtali, *see VeTziva HaKohen*
Kaufman, R. Ḥayim Shaul, 131n, 223n; *see also Mishnat Shemen*
Kaufman, R. Moshe, 123-124, 150, 155; *see also Netiv Ḥayim; Netivot Ḥayim; Zera Ḥayim*
Keen, Andrew, 216
Kehillot Yaakov, 108n, 184n, 259-261
Keli Ḥemda, 127n
Kelley, Harold, 56n
Keneh Bosem, 111n
Kerem Aryeh, 22n
Keren Ora, 20n
Keriya BaKeriya, 101n
Kesef Mishneh, see Karo, R. Yosef
Ketav Sofer, 5n, 191n
Ketcham, Katherine, 48
Kevod Ḥakhamim, 129n
Kida, Thomas, 49n, 52n, 72n
Kinyan Torah BeHalakha, 178n
Kiryat Ḥanna David, 191n
Kiryat Sefer, 12n, 172n
Kitzur Shulḥan Arukh, 94n
Klapper, R. Aryeh, 193n

Klausenberger Rebbe, *see* Halberstam, R. Yekutiel Yehuda
Klein, R. Barukh Meir, *see Imrei Barukh*
Klein, R. Menashe, *see Mishneh Halakhot*
Knesset HaGdola/Be'er Heitev, 186n
Kodesh Yisrael, 13n, 14n, 16n, 94n, 96n, 115n, 143n, 148n, 153n, 154n, 160n, 161n, 167n, 180n, 183n
Kohen, R. Binyamin, 102; *see also Ḥelkat Binyamin*
Kohen, R. Ḥayim Yehuda, 121
Kohn, R. Dovid, *see Harḥavat Gevul Yaavetz*
Kokhvei Or, 237n
Kol Aryeh, 191n
Kol Bo to *aveilut*, 229n
Kol Yehuda, 224n
Kook, R. Avraham Yitzḥak HaKohen, 17n, 33n, 177, 190, 223n; *see also Be'er LaHai Ro'i; Bein Shenei Kohanim Gedolim*
Kook, R. Avraham Yitzḥak HaKohen (of Rechovot), 15n, 101n
Kook, R. Shlomo Zalman, 99n, 123n, 228n, 247n; *see also Bein Shenei Kohanim Gedolim; Mitzvah Shelema*
Koraḥ, 129n
Kornitzer, R. Yosef Neḥemia, 191n
Kotler, R. Aharon, 236, 248n, 251n
Kotler, R. Shneur, 244
Kovatch, Bill, 49n, 198, 210
Kovetz al Yad HaḤazaka, 172n
Kovetz He'arot, 77n, 94n, 127n, 176n
Kovetz Shiurim, 131n
Kovetz Teshuvot, 14n
Kowalski, Robin M., 200n, 203n, 208n
Krakowsky, R. Menaḥem, *see Avodat Melekh*
Kretzmer, R. Naphtali Hertz, *see Noam HaMitzvot*
Kronglass, R. David, *see Siḥot Ḥokhma UMusar*
Kutno, R. Yehoshua, 13n

L

Lafier, R. Shmuel Ḥayim, 16n
Lapkin, Milton, 62
lashon hara
    absence of prohibition of in *Tur* and *Shulḥan Arukh*, 23n
    about groups, 226-227, 234
    about oneself, 224-226
    about the dead, 227n, 228-230
    as desecration of God's name/heresy, 17, 29, 33, 35, 252
    biblical source for,11-12, 16-19, 36, 43, 87, 88, 93, 95, 134, 169, 254
    character vs. behavior-based view of, 85-89, 93, 113, 121, 142, 156-157, 161, 162-163, 174n-175n, 180, 221-223, 224-225, 230, 240, 241, 244, 252
    collecting damages for, 85-86, 232-233, 240
    condemnation of, 7, 19-23, 25, 34
    corrolation with seminal events in history, 19-20, 23
    definition of, 13n, 14-15, 35, 86-87, 168
    distinguished from *motzi shem ra*, 14n, 18n, 25
    distinguished from *rekhilut*, 15, 35, 97n, 161, 240-241
    forgiveness for, 87, 233-242
    harm to receiver, 35, 76, 133, 156, 157n
    harm to speaker, 31-35, 41, 86, 88, 133, 156, 157n, 241, 243
    harm to society, 35-41, 228, 230
    harm to subject, 4, 25-28, 31, 35, 37, 41, 76, 86, 88, 95, 97, 98, 133, 137, 143-144, 175-176, 180, 223, 227, 235, 238n, 240, 242, 243
    in public, *see* public
    intent, 33-34, 99-101, 103, 123, 171-172, 179-180, 222-223, 249
    listening to, *see accepting lashon hara*
    no names, 221-223
    other precepts contravened during, 17, 30, 33

permitted/obligatory circumstances, *see to'elet*
presence/permission of subject, 138n, 151, 166, 167-172, 178n, 179, 223
preventing oneself from speaking, 73, 81, 245n, 249, 252-253
protesting, 142
punishment for, 19, 21-22
rabbinic prohibition, 141n, 147, 182n, 229-230
repeating, 161-162
repentance for, 22n, 31, 231, 241, 243-246, 253
subjectivity in, 44-46, 111, 112n, 113
violating privacy, 182, 184-185, 215-216
written, 191-192
see also gossip

leadership, 150-151
Lemberger, R. Moshe Natan Nota, *see Ateret Moshe*
Lembrasky, R. Meir, *see BeShaarei HaTshuva*
LeḤafetz BaḤayim, 96n, 97n, 98n, 100n, 105n, 106n, 112n, 113n, 114n, 116n, 119n, 121n, 123n, 125n, 127n, 131n, 141n, 148n, 149n, 153n, 154n, 164n, 167n, 180n, 222n, 225n, 227n, 236n, 242n
Leḥem Yehuda, 12n
Lehorot Natan, 5n, 6n, 48n, 129n, 191n
Lehrer, Jonah, 61n
Leiter, R. Yeḥiel Michel, *see Darkhei Shalom*
LeRe'akha Kamokha, 94n, 115n, 135n, 153n, 180n, 193n, 233n, 238n
Lev Aryeh, 244n, 245n
Lev Tahor, 19n
Lev Tov, 175n
Levine, R. Aaron, 122
Levmore, Saul, 30, 72n, 164n
Libshitz, R. Yeḥiel, *see HaMidrash VeHaMaase*
Lichtenstein, R. Mordekhai, *see Mitzvot HaLevavot*
Lieberman, R. Yosef, *see Mishnat Yosef*
Lifshitz, R. Tzvi, 232n
Likkutei Siḥot, *see* Schneerson, R. Menachem Mendel
Lilienfeld, Scott O., 74n
Limber, Sue P., 200n, 203n, 208n
Lior, R. Dov, 180n
LiTeshuvat HaShana, 239n
lo taamod al dam re'ekha, 95-96, 103, 113, 140, 254-255
Loew, R. Yehuda, *see* Maharal of Prague; *Netivot Olam*
Loftus, Elizabeth, 48, 49n
Long, R. Menaḥem, 230n
Lopian, R. Eliyahu, 234n
love your fellow, 37, 56, 104, 109n, 140, 146, 183, 185, 241, 255; *see also* Leviticus 19:18 in the Index of Biblical and Rabbinic Sources
Lubavitcher Rebbe, *see* Schneerson, R. Menachem Mendel
Lubetsky, R. Aryeh, *see Naḥal Kedumim*
Lubetzky, R. Yeḥiel Michel, 171n
Luria, R. Shlomo, 37n, 154n, 171n, 255
lying, *see* falsehood
Lynn, Stephen Jay, 74n

M

Maadanei Yom Tov, 140n
Maarkhei Lev, 87n
Maase Rokeaḥ, 173n
Macknick, Stephen, 50n
Magen Avraham, 127n, 157n, 175n, 182n, 234n, 238, 239n, 252
Maggid, R. Meir Menaḥem, 152n
Maharal of Prague, 168-170; *see also Netivot Olam*
Maharitatz, 166n
Maharsha, *see* Eidels, R. Shmuel
Maharshal, *see* Luria, R. Shlomo
Maharsham, 111n, 192n
Maharshdam, 227n
Maharzu, 6n
Maḥatzit HaShekel, 127n, 239n

Maimon, R. Moshe, *see Lev Tov*
Malbim, R. Meir Leibush, 20n
Malone, Patrick S., 146n
Mandelbaum, R. David, *see Pardes Yosef HeHadash*
Manjoo, Farhad, 46-47
Mann, R. David Yitzḥak, *see Be'er Miriam*
Manot HaLevi, 38n
Maor HaShaar, 127n, 237n
Marcus, Gary, 48n, 61n, 63n, 68n
Marcus, R. Yaakov Avraham, 33n
Margoliyot, R. Reuven, 13n, 110n
Marpei Lashon, 22n, 245n
marriage, *see* spouse
Martinez-Conde, Susana, 50n
Matteh Ephraim, 234n
Mayer, John D., 28n, 57
Mayer-Schönberger, Vikor, 67, 145n
McCullough, Michael, 28
McKay, Charles, 74
McRaney, David, 37n, 51n, 56n, 58n, 61n, 66n, 68n, 105n, 199n
Mecklenberg, R. Yaakov Tzvi, *see HaKetav VeHaKabbala*
Medini, R. Ḥayim Ḥizkiyahu, *see Sedei Ḥemed*
Megillat Sefer, 149n
Meiklejohn, Alexander, 30
mekaḥ ta'ut, 110, 116-117
Mekom Shmuel, 167n
Meltzer, R. Isser Zalman, 5n
memory, 48-52, 211-212
Menaḥem Yisrael, 4n
Mephiboshet, 154
Merkaḥat Besamim, 191n
Merkaz HaRav (Yeshiva), 177
Mesharet Moshe, 173n
Meshekh Ḥokhma, 17
mesiaḥ lefi tumo, 153
Meskin, R. Yaakov, *see Mishpat LeYaakov*
Mesorat Moshe, 226n
metzora, *see tzaraat*
Michaelson, R. Yeḥezkel, 142; *see also Tirosh VeYitzhar*
Michella, John, 56n
Michtav MeEliyahu, *see* Dessler, R. Eliyahu
Miernik, R. Moshe, 169n
Migdal Oz, 13n
Milei DeḤasiduta, 127n
Mill, John Stuart, 30
Minhagei Yisrael, 177n
Minḥat Asher, 5n, 22n, 94n, 121n, 184n
Minḥat David, 250n
Minḥat Elimelekh, 236n
Minḥat Ḥinnukh, 95n, 135n
Minḥat Maḥavat, 237n
Minḥat Peri, 163n, 222n, 223n, 226n
Minḥat Yitzḥak, 111n, 135n
Miriam, 18, 87, 106, 148n, 169-170, 247-252
Mirkevet HaMishna, 15n
Mirsky, R. Shmuel K., 163n
Mischel, Walter, 57
Mishel Avot, 48n
Mishḥat Shemen, 128n, 223n
Mishkan Betzalel, 4n, 5n
Mishkenot Yaakov, 95n
Mishna Shelema, 191n
Mishnat Avraham, 22n, 127n
Mishnat Binyamin, 191n
Mishnat Moshe, 102n
Mishnat Yaakov, 162n
Mishnat Yehuda, 248n
Mishnat Yisrael, 88n, 117n, 160n, 163n, 171n, 234n, 236n, 237n, 239n, 241n, 242n
Mishnat Yosef, 227n, 237n
Mishneh Halakhot, 111n
Mishpat LeYaakov, 129n
Mishpatekha LeYaakov, 14n
Mishpetei HaShalom, 99n, 101n, 110n, 111n, 112n, 115n, 147n, 180n, 228n
Mishpetei HaTorah, 96n, 108n, 116n, 186n
mitkabbed biklon ḥavero, 34
Mitzvah Shelema, 19n
Mitzvot HaLevavot, 127n
Mitzvot Hashem, 127n
Mivtzar Yisrael, 147n
Mizraḥi, R. Aryeh *see Kerem Aryeh*

Mlodinow, Leonard, 48n, 49-50, 80n
Mnookin, Robert, 56n
Mo'adei HaRe'iya, 177n
Mo'adim UZmanim, 148n, 178n, 237n, 238n, 239n
Moreh Tzedek, 21n, 173n, 253n
Morozov, Evgeny, 203n, 209, 211-212
Moses, 18, 19, 87, 106, 129n, 169-170, 226n-227n, 247, 248n
Moskowitz, R. Barukh Tzvi, *see Nishba LaAvotekha*
motzi shem ra
  biblical source for, 16n, 17
  distinguished from *lashon hara*, 14n, 18n
  linguistic relation to *metzora*, 18n
  see also slander
Munk, R. Meir, 120
Munk, R. S. D., *see Pe'at Sadekha*
Munseh, R. Avraham Y., *see Padeh et Avraham*
Munsterberg, Hugo, 49

N

Naḥal Kedumim, 136n
Naḥmani, R. Shimshon Ḥayim, *see Zera Shimshon*
Natan Piryo, 21n, 87n
Nathanson, R. Yosef Shaul, *see Shoel UMeshiv*
Nebenzahl, R. Avigdor, 33n, 35n, 36n, 156n, 244n, 250n
Nefesh HaRav, 224n
Nefesh Ḥayim, 21n
Nefesh Ḥayya, 250n
Neisser, Ulric, 48, 49n
Neriah, R. Moshe Tzvi, 177
Netiv Ḥayim, 96n, 105n, 119n, 128n, 135n, 149n, 150n, 151n, 155n, 227n, 242n, 247n
Netiv Yosher, 96n, 228n
Netivot HaKodesh, 19n, 228n
Netivot HaMishpat, 184n
Netivot Ḥayim, 148n, 165n
Netivot Olam, 4n, 32n, 147n, 168n
Netivot Shalom, 36n
Netzaḥ Yisrael, 176n
Neubert, R. Aharon Elḥanan, *see Erekh HaḤayim*
Neugroshol, R. Tzvi A., 251n
newspapers, 153, 180, 190-192, 207; *see also* journalism
Niflaot MiTorat Hashem Yitbarakh, 136n
Nimukei Oraḥ Ḥayim, 230n
Nir LeDavid, 135n, 193n
Nishba LaAvotekha, 22n
Nishmat Avraham, 126n, 260
Nishmat Shabbat, 251n
Nitei Gavriel, 237n
Nizkei Shekhenim, 182n
Noam HaMitzvot, 36n
Nussbaum, Martha C., 30, 72n, 164n
Nussbaum, R. Naphtali, 117n
Nyhan, Brendan, 66

O

Oakley, Barbara, 63n
Ofri, Danielle, 70
Oḥayon, R. Yosef, 5n
Ohalei Yehuda, 132n, 140n, 223n
Ohel Moshe, 252n
Ohev Yamim, 96n, 116n, 128n, 131n, 135n, 187n, 230n, 242n
Om Ani Ḥoma, 107n
onaa, 117
onaat devarim, 110, 178n, 201, 228n, 235, 239-240
Openheimer, R. Yosef Aharon, 135n
Or HaḤayim, 88n, 98n, 182n
Or HaTzafun, 147n
Or HaYashar, 173n
Oraḥ LeḤayim, 36n, 145n
Oraḥ Meisharim, 14n, 26n, 135n, 137n, 147n, 175n, 230n, 245n
Orḥot Yom Tov, 160n
Orot Yemei HaRaḥamim, 237n
overhearing, 149n; *see also* eavesdropping
Oznayim LaTorah, 147n

P

Paamonei Zahav, 129n
Padeh et Avraham, 102n
Paḥad Yitzḥak, *see* Hutner, R. Yitzḥak
Palagi, R. Ḥayim *see Nefesh Ḥayim*
Paltin, R. Yisrael Zissel, 102n
Pam, R. Avraham Yaakov 105-106, *see also Atara LeMelekh; Moreh Tzedek*
Papenheim, R. Avraham Shmuel, *see Pinat Yakrat*
Papo, R. Eliezer, *see Pele Yoetz*
Paraḥ Matteh Aharon, 237n
Parashat HaMelekh, 20n, 163n, 173n
Pardes Yosef, 48n
Pardes Yosef HeḤadash, 13n, 147n
parents, 123-124, 130
Pariser, Eli, 47n, 80n, 196n
Parnes, R. Avigdor, *see Lev Tahor*
Patzanofsky, R. Yosef, *see Pardes Yosef*
Patziner, R. Yitzḥak Meir, *see Parashat HaMelekh*
Pe'at Sadekha, 141n, 155n
peddler, image of, 3-7, 10, 11, 18n, 22n, 88-89, 163-164, 168-169, 182, 253, 255, 256
peddler verse, *see* Leviticus 19:16 in the Index of Biblical and Rabbinic Sources
Peirot Genosar, 248n
Peirot Te'ena, 129n
Pele Yoetz, 227n
Penei Moshe, 185n, 234n
Penei Yehoshua, 16n, 102n
Pentland, Alex, 55n
perception, 46-47
Peretz, R. Meir, 17n
Perkins, David, 63
Perlow, R. Yeruḥam Fishel, 96n
Peri Eitz Ḥayim, 173n
pesik reishei, 149n
Pik, R. Yeshaya, 247n
Piltz, R. Eliezer, 146n
Pinat Yakrat, 87n, 163n
Pinter, R. Yosef Yitzḥak, *see Ohev Yamim*
Piskei HaRashbetz, 144n
Pitḥei Teshuva, 93n, 255n
Plato, 29, 199
Plotski, R. Meir Dan, *see Keli Ḥemda*
politics, 217-219
positive speech, 173-174, 230n, 249
Post, Robert C., 26-27
Potash, R. Mordekhai, 22n
Potter, Andrew, 39, 214-215, 218
Povarsky, R. Barukh Dov, *see Bad Kodesh*
Powers, William, 201n
Pribelsky, R. Zelig, 48n
Price, R. Avraham, *see Mishnat Avraham*
privacy, 41, 99n, 181-87, 215-216, 255; *see also* confidentiality
public, 159-172, 190;
  Maimonides on, 161-164, 166, 213n
  mefursam lakol, 180
  Rabbeinu Yonah on, 166n
  Rashi on, 165-166
  speech likely to be more positive in, 172
  Tosafot on, 170-172, 212, 213n
  see also journalism
Purim, 38, 176-180
purpose, *see to'elet*

R

rabbinic courts, 14, 51-52, 84, 129n, 137-138, 147-148, 157n, 166, 232-233
Rabinovitch, R. Nachum, *see Siaḥ Naḥum*
Rabinowitz, R. Gamliel, 23n
Rabinowitz, R. Yeḥiel Michel, 102-103; *see also Afikei Yam*
Rackover, Naḥum, 229n, 233n
raglayim ladavar, 143
Rainie, Lee, 210n
Rakovsky, R. Barukh, *see Birkat Avot; Sefer HaKatan VeHilkhotav*
Rappaport, R. Ḥayim, 33n
Rashash, 161n
Ratz KaTzvi, 248n
Ratzabi, R. Yitzḥak, *see Einei Yitzḥak*

Rav Lehoshia, 225n
rebuke, 102, 119, 149n
receiving, *see* accepting
recommendations, 257
Reifle, Jason, 66
Reischer, R. Yaakov, 190; *see also Shevut Yaakov*
Reishit Hashlama, 160n
rekhilut
and peddler of elixir of life, 5, 11-12
definition, 12, 14-15, 16n, 35
distinguished from *lashon hara*, 15, 35, 97n, 161, 240-241
limitation on prohibition, 131
possible examples, 130, 165
relating conversations to original subject 14-15, 131
revealing secrets, 181, 183, 185
Rema, *see* Isserles, R. Moshe
reputation, 21, 26-29, 41, 56-57, 60, 80, 82n, 130-131, 143, 145, 225
Responsa Maharitz, 178n
Responsa Rabbeinu Avraham Ben Rav Yitzḥak Av Beit Din, 175n
reviewing, 125
Rigshei Ḥayim, 33n, 96n, 101n, 135n, 214n, 225n
Rinat Yitzḥak, 140n, 214n
ring of Gyges, 29
Rishumei Aharon, 130n
Rivevot Ephraim, 13n, 123n
Rizkov, R. Menaḥem Mendel HaKohen, *see Torat HaKohanim VeAvodat HaBeit HaMikdash*
Rizma DeḤakhmata, 135n
Robinson, R. Gershon, 100; *see also Tokhaḥat Ḥayim*
Romin, Daniel T., 146n
Rosen, Larry D., 200n
Rosenberg, R. Avraham, *see Tenuvot Sadai*
Rosenberg, R. David, *see Minḥat David*
Rosenberg, Howard, 197n
Rosenberg, Scott, 204n
Rosensteil, Tom, 49n, 198, 210
Rosenthal, R. Yaakov, *see Mishnat Yaakov*
Rosenzweig, Phil, 60n
Rosnow, Ralph L., 49n, 50, 84n
Ross, Lee, 56n
Roth, R. Aharon, 222n
Rothchild, R. Ephraim Natan, 132n, 169n
Rothschild, R. Shmuel, *see Peirot Te'ena*
Rothstein, R. Yeḥiel, 149n
Rottenberg, R. Ḥanina Yisrael, *see Divrei Ḥayil*
Rottenberg, R. Yeshayahu Pineḥas, *see Minḥat Peri*
Royzman, Edward B., 61n
Rozin, Paul, 61n
Rozler, R. Yehonatan, *see Rigshei Ḥayim*
Rozner, R. Shlomo, 131 164; *see also Alei Be'er; LeḤafetz BaḤayim*
Rudinksy, R. Betzalel, see *Mishkan Betzalel*
rumor, 62, 72n, 75-76, 154-155
Ruscio, John, 74n
Ryzman, R. Tzvi, *see Ratz KaTzvi*
Ryzman, R. Yehoshua Heshel, *see Iyyunim BaParasha*

S

safek, 113, 141n
Saḥarov, R. Yoel Menaḥem Mendel, see *Menaḥem Yisrael*
Salanter, R. Yisrael (Lipkin), 34, 234-236, 238-241, 253n
Salmat Ḥayim, 191n
Samḥon, R. Avraham ben, *see Bigdei Yesha*
Samsonowitz, R. Moshe, *see Keriya BaKeriya*
Sandler, R. Deror Binyamin, 127n
Satmar Rebbe, *see* Teitelbaum, R. Yoel
Schachter, R. Hershel, 107n, 257-258
Schapiro, R. Avraham, 180n
Schapiro, R. Ḥayim Elazar, *see Nimukei Oraḥ Ḥayim*
Schapiro, R. Moshe, 32n, 163n, 169n, 251n

Schapiro, R. Tzvi Elimelech, *see Benei Yissakhar*
Scheinberger, R. Tzvi Hirsch, 236n
Scheinerman, R. Moshe, *see Ohel Moshe*
Schneebalg, R. Menaḥem Mendel, *see Siftei Ani*
Schneerson, R. Menachem Mendel, 19n, 36n
Schneider, R. Shlomo, *see Divrei Shlomo*
Schulz, Kathryn, 48n, 54n, 66-67, 80n
Schwab, R. Moshe, 87n
Schwartz, R. Avraham Yehuda, *see Kol Aryeh*
Schwartz, R. Reuven, *see Emek HaLashon*
secretary, 126
Sedeh Tzofim, 95n, 153n
Sedei Ḥemed, 6n, 13n, 22n, 163n
Sefat Emet, 48n
Sefer HaBatim, 12n
Sefer HaḤayim, 38n
Sefer HaKatan VeHilkhotav, 122n
Sefer Hashlama, 165n
Sefer Kovetz al Yad HaḤazaka, 172n
Sefer Me'irat Einayim, 100n-101n, 129n, 184n, 232n
Seife, Charles, 196n
Seigel, Lee, 204
self, 46, 214-215
Shaarei Ahavat Yisrael, *see* Schneerson, R. Menachem Mendel
Shaarei Avraham, 16n, 98n, 107n, 123n, 126n, 131n, 135n, 137n, 140n, 141n, 148n, 156n, 175n, 180n, 185n, 223n, 225n, 226n, 239n
Shaarei De'ah, 221n
Shaarei Simḥa, 7n
Shaarei Zevulun, 15n, 104n, 149n, 163n
Shaarim Metzuyanim Al HaTorah, 22n, 244n
Shabbat, 149n
Shachter, Daniel L., 51-52, 80n
Shaḥna, Moshe Hayim, *see Simḥat Yeḥiel*
Shalmei Naḥum, 19n, 88n
Shalmei Simḥa, 191n
Shalmei Toda, 238n, 242n
Shapiro, R. Moshe David, 223n
Shapiro, R. Shalom Tzvi, 22n
shav, 17, 43, 94, 134, 136-137, 147n, 214n
Shavel, R. Yitzḥak Isaac of, *see Ateret Yitzḥak*
She'arim Metzuyanim BeHalakha, 94n
Shechter, R. Yaakov, *see Divrei Yaakov*
Shechter, R. Yitzḥak Shmuel, *see Yashiv Yitzḥak*
She'elat Rav, 221n, 225n
She'elat Shmuel, 236n
She'erit Yehuda, 154n
sheker, *see* falsehood
Shema, 52n, 252
Shemirat HaPeh KeHilkhato, 99n, 123n, 129n, 131n, 148n, 153n, 156n, 223n, 230n
Shemuot Ḥayim, 20n, 77n, 128n, 157n, 176n, 244n, 245n
Shenei Luḥot HaBrit, 18n, 88n
Sher, R. Yitzḥak Eizik, 248
Shermer, Michael, 38n
Sheshet, R., 134-136
Shevet HaKehati, 122n, 123n, 191n
Shevet HaLevi, 111n
Shevilei Ḥayim, 107n, 131n, 135n, 148n, 149n, 152n, 242n
Shevut Yaakov, 190n
Shick, R. Eliyahu, *see Ein Eliyahu*
shiddukh, *see* spouse, information about prospective
Shiltei Gibborim, 186n
Shirky, Clay, 56n
Shiurei Rabbeinu Meshulam David HaLevi, 167n, 228n
Shiurei UPninei Daat, see Bloch, R. Eliyahu Meir
Shivat Tziyon, 191n
Shlav, R. Tzvi, *see Niflaot MiTorat Hashem Yitbarakh*
Shlesinger, R. Barukh Reuven Shlomo, *see Birkat Reuven Shlomo*

Shlesinger, R. Eliyahu, *see Eila HaDevarim*
Shmuel ben Elkana of Altuna, R., *see Mekom Shmuel*
Shmuelevitz, R. Ḥayim, *see Siḥot Musar*
Shmueli, R. Yinon, *see Orḥot Yom Tov*
Shneebalg, R. Shraga Feivel, *see Shraga HaMeir*
Shoel UMeshiv, 129n, 140n, 144n
Shoel VeNishal, 223n
Shoshan, R. Yitzḥak ben, *see Daltei Teshuva*
Shoshanat HaAmakim, 126n
Shperber, R. David, *see Afarkasta DeAnya*
Shpitz, R. Tzvi, *see Mishpetei HaTorah*
Shraga HaMeir, 191n
Shteif, R. Yonatan, *see Mitzvot Hashem*
Shteinman, R. Aharon Leib, *see Ayelet HaShaḥar*
Shteinshneider, R. Daniel, *see Divrei Daniel*
Shulḥan Arukh HaRav, 154n
Shuv, R. Zevulun, *see Shaarei Zevulun*
Siaḥ Naḥum, 106n, 187n
Siegfried, Tom, 28n
Siftei Ani, 191n
Sigelman, Lee, 219n
Siḥot Ḥokhma UMusar, 21n, 37n, 244n, 248n
Siḥot Musar, 251n
Sikili, R. David, *see Kiryat Ḥanna David*
Silber, R. Yitzḥak Eizik, *see Mishpetei HaShalom*
Silman, R. Yehuda, 125; *see also Darkei Ḥoshen*
Silverberg, R. Avraham Binyamin, *see Ḥemdat Binyamin; Mishnat Binyamin*
Simḥat Yeḥiel, 104n
Simons, Daniel, 48n, 49n, 52n, 63n, 81-82
Slade, Giles, 207n
slander, 229-230;
  definition, 6-7, 13, 44
  governmental limits on, 30
  distinguished from *lashon hara*, 13, 25
Smith, Adam, 201
social media, *see* internet
social network theory, 164n
Sofer, R. Avraham Shmuel Binyamin, *see Ketav Sofer*
Sofer, R. Ḥayim Yaakov, *see Teranen Leshoni*
Sofer, R. Moshe, 22n, 128-129; *see also Ḥatam Sofer; Torat Moshe*
Sofer, R. Shabbetai, *see Shaarei De'ah*
Sofer, R. Shimon (Eiger), *see Hitorerut Teshuva*
Sofer, R. Simḥa Bunim, *see Shaarei Simḥa*
Sofer, R. Yaakov Ḥayim, 22n; *see also Torat Yaakov*
Solomon, 3, 256
Solomon, R. Avraham Yisrael Moshe, *see Netivot HaKodesh*
Solomon, R. Matisyahu, 34n, 35n
Solove, Daniel, 27, 28n, 39n, 45-46, 73n, 76n, 109, 164n, 194-195
Soloveichik, R. Ahron, 234n, 237; *see also Paraḥ Matteh Aharon*
Soloveichik, R. Meshulam David, *see Shiurei Rabbeinu Meshulam David HaLevi*
Soloveitchik, R. Joseph B., 224
Sommers, Sam, 56-57
Sonnenfeld, R. Yosef Chaim, *see Salmat Ḥayim*
Sorotzkin, R. Yitzḥak, *see Rinat Yitzḥak*
Sorotzkin, R. Zalman, *see Oznayim LaTorah*
speech, power of, 32, 105n, 191n, 249
Sperber, R. Daniel, 177n
spies, 20, 87, 228, 250
spouse
  information about prospective, xviii, 59, 107-119, 257-258, 259-261
  "merchandise model," 117-118, 259
  speaking *lashon hara* to, 106-107, 258
  see also to'elet, timing of speech

Standage, Tom, 194n
Stanovich, Keith, 77-78
Steblay, N., 78n
Steele, Claude, 227
Stein, R. Yitzḥak Isaac, 163n
Steinberg, R. Kalonimos Kalman, *see* *Divrei Meḥokek*
Steinberg, R. Peretz, *see Peri Eitz Ḥayim*
Steipler Gaon, *see* Kanievsky, R. Yisrael Yaakov
Stern, R. Betzalel, *see BeTzel HaḤokhma*
Stern, R. Rephael, *see Nizkei Shekhenim*
Stern, R. Yeḥiel Michel, 120; *see also Imrei Yaakov*
Sternbuch, R. Moshe, 94, 121, 237n; *see also Mo'adim UZmanim*; *Taam VeDaat*; *Teshuvot VeHanhagot*
Strahilowitz, Lior Jacob, 164n
Stryker, Cole, 203n
Student, R. Gil, 180n
subconscious, 55, 58, 74
Sunstein, Cass, 55, 58n, 68n, 72n
Surowiecki, James, 74
Susskind, R. Alezander ben Moshe, *see Yesod VeShoresh HaAvodah*

T

Taam VeDaat, 22n, 95n, 243n
Tafarodi, W., 146n
Tal Ḥayim, 129n
Taleb, Nassim, 73n
Tammet, Daniel, 39n, 146n
Tarfon, R., 144n
taromet, 124-125
Tavris, Carol, 45n, 48n, 49n, 63n
Taz, 100n-101n
teachers, 164, 257; *see also to'elet*, educational settings
Tehor Sefatayim, 96n, 107n, 122n, 123n, 124n, 128n, 178n, 180n, 190n, 223n, 226n, 227n
Teitelbaum, R. Yoel, 248n
Tenuat HaMusar, 224n
Tenuvot Sadai, 237n
Teranen Leshoni, 248n
Teshuvot VeHanhagot, 21n, 94n, 107n, 111n, 112n, 121n, 125n, 140n, 150n, 191n, 236n, 237n
testimonial dinner, 175
Thaler, Richard, 55, 58n, 68n
therapy, 104-105
Thompson, David, 60, 204n, 209n
Thorndike, Edward, 60
Tiferet Yehoshua, 48n
Tirosh VeYitzhar, 142n
Titten Emet LeYaakov, 122n
To'afot Re'em, 168n, 175n
Tobolsky, R. Avraham, 224n
to'elet
- *baalei maḥloket*, 127-130
- certainty, 97-98
- definition, 93-94
- educational settings, 119-124, 222-223, 229, 257
- excluded from or overriding prohibition of *lashon hara*, 95-96, 97, 103
- intent, 99-101, 103, 104, 166
- limit damage to subject, 98-99, 105-106
- necessity, 98, 112-113, 140, 150-151, 166
- protection, 96-97, 99n, 101-102, 103-104, 113, 121, 124, 187, 193
- relationships, 101-102
- straightforwardness, 98, 103, 114
- timing of speech, 108-110
- *see also* business; spouse, information about prospective; therapy; venting

Tohar HaLashon, 171n
Toker, R. Avraham Yitzḥak, 167n; *see also Bikkurei Aretz*
Tokhaḥat Ḥayim, 100n, 101n, 112n, 120n
Toledanu, R. Avraham, *see Zaharei Shmuel*
Toledot Yitzḥak, 240n
Torah Temima, 129n, 182n, 191n
Torat Eliezer, 34n, 245n
Torat HaKohanim VeAvodat HaBeit HaMikdash, 154n

Torat Maharitz, 5n, 22n, 253n
Torat Moshe, 19n, 22n, 129n, 175n
Torat Yaakov, 16n
Torat Yeruḥam, 191n
Tov Ayin, *see* Azulai, R. Ḥayim Yosef David
Troyesh, R. Menaḥem, *see Oraḥ Meisharim*
truth
- as defense of speaking about others, 7, 43, 97-98, 169n
- false impact of, 44, 77, 81, 82, 137-138, 143, 147, 211
- free speech as a way of arriving at, 30
- included in prohibition, 8, 12-13, 14n, 26, 43-45, 82, 136-137, 195, 230
- limited by bias and perception, 43-47, 54, 57-58, 60, 75, 80, 147, 155

Turkle, Sherry, 202, 204n
Turtzin, R. Avraham Yeshayahu, 129n
Tzaban, R. Raphael, *see Nefesh Ḥayya*
Tzadok HaKohen, R., 5n
Tzahalon, R. Yom Tov ben Moshe, *see Maharitatz*
tzaraat, 18, 36, 135n, 243, 245, 247, 252
Tzarum, R. Yehuda, *see Mishnat Yehuda*
Tzimerman, R. Moshe, 130n
Tzitz Eliezer, 17n, 111n, 126n

U

unconscious, 78, 79

V

Vaidhyanathan, Siva, 209
Valdesolo, Piercarlo, 57n
Valley, R. Moshe David, *see Brit Olam*
Vanderbilt, Tom, 56
VaYaan Yosef, 248n
Vayeḥi Yosef, 4n
VaYita Eshel, 88n, 228n, 244n, 245n, 248n
VaYomer Moshe, 37n
VeDarashta VeḤakarta, 88n, 99n, 185n, 186n, 226n
Veingert, R. Mordekhai Menaḥem, *see BaYom SheYedubar*
Veinman, R. Yisrael, *see Mishnat Yisrael*
venting, 105-106, 258
VeTziva HaKohen, 129n
Vilna Gaon, 39n, 176n, 181n, 227n, 245n
Vital, R. Ḥayim, 12n
Vohs, Kathleen, 61n
Volozhin Yeshiva, 177
Vosner, R. Yoḥanan Segal, *see Ḥayyei HaLevi*

W

Wachtfogel, R. Yitzḥak Yaakov, 191n
Wahrman, R. Avraham David, *see Milei DeḤasiduta*
Wahrman, R. Shlomo, *see Orot Yemei HaRaḥamim*
Waldenberg, R. Eliezer Yehuda, 126; *see also Tzitz Eliezer*
Warren, Samuel, 41
Wasserman, R. Elḥanan Bunim, *see Kovetz He'arot; Kovetz Shiurim*
Watts, Duncan J., 60n-61n, 63n, 68n
websites, *see* internet
Weinberger, David, 72n, 198
Weingarten, R. Yo'av Yehoshua, *see Ḥelkat Yoav*
Weinman, R. Yisrael, *see Mishnat Yisrael*
Weinshtok, R. Meir Yeḥiel *see Beit Shlomo*
Weiss, R. Asher, 121; *see also Minḥat Asher*
Weiss, R. Yitzḥak, *see Minḥat Yitzḥak*
Wellman, Barry, 210n
Westacott, Emrys, 27n, 194n
Willig, R. Mordechai, 259-261
Winograd, E., 48n
Winter, R. Elimelekh, *see Minḥat Elimelekh*
Wittenstein, Ludwig, 145n
Wolbe, R. Shlomo, *see Alei Shur*
Wosner, R. Shmuel, *see Shevet HaLevi*

Y

Yad Eitan, 173n
Yad HaKettana, 136n, 166n
Yad Yosef, 129n
Yafe-Shlesinger, R. Avraham, *see Be'er Sarim*
Yagel Yaakov, 22n, 191n
Yalkut Yitzḥak, 21n, 229n
Yalkut Yosef, 112n, 116n, 163n, 237n
Yannai, R., 3-4, 6n
Yashiv Yitzḥak, 118n
Yeḥaveh Daat, 95n, 178n, 187n
Yehuda ben Beteira, R., 229n
Yehuda Yaaleh, 182n
Yesod VeShoresh HaAvoda, 37n
Yesodei Yeshurun, 48n
Yismaḥ Avikha, 234n
Yom Kippur, 21, 100, 236-238
Yosef, R. Ovadia, *see Yalkut Yosef; Yeḥaveh Daat*
Yuchik, R. Shalom, *see VaYita Eshel*
Yudaikin, R. Shmuel Yitzḥak Gad HaKohen, *see Divrei Shalom*
Yudchik, R. Ḥayim, *see Shemuot Ḥayim*

Z

Zaharei Shmuel, 160n
Zahler, R. Yitzḥak, *see Yalkut Yitzḥak*
Zak, Paul J., 28n, 201
Zaks, R. Hillel, 148n, 156n
Zanger, R. Yom Tov, 234n
Zeh HaShulḥan, 94n, 223n
Zekher Shmuel, 141n, 163n
Zekhut Avot, 225n
Zekukei Nura, 22n
Zevaḥ Shelamim, 250n
Zera Ḥayim, 105n, 110n, 111n, 112n, 115n, 123n, 137n, 140n, 141n, 148n, 150n, 163n, 165n, 169n, 172n, 178n, 179n, 214n, 228n
Zera Shimshon, 127n
Zeroa Yamim, *see* Azulai, R. Ḥayim Yosef David
Zide, R. Yaakov, *see Bo Tashiv*
Zikhron David, 12n, 14n, 20n, 33n, 86n, 135n, 141n, 229n
Zilber, R. Binyamin Yehoshua, 179; *see also Az Nidberu*
Zilber, R. Michel, 244n
Zilber, R. Mordekhai Tzvi, *see Zikhron David*
Zilberberg, R. Yitzḥak Yosef, 160n
Zilberstein, R. Yitzḥak, 106, 126n, 130n, 132n, 184n, 186, 187n, 260, 261; *see also Aleinu Leshabeaḥ; Avnei Ḥoshen*
Zimbardo, Philip, 199
Zittrain, Jonathan, 84n
Zlotov, R. Avraham Ḥayim of, *see Oraḥ LeḤayim*
Zundel, R. Ḥanokh, *see Etz Yosef*

Index of Biblical and Rabbinic Sources

Bible

Genesis
- 27:46, p. 98n
- 37:2, pp. 102-103

Exodus
- 4:1-7, p. 248n
- 7:8-9, p. 182n
- 23:1, pp. 17, 43, 87, 94, 134, 137, 147-148
- 23:7, p. 137
- 25:2, p. 182n

Leviticus
- 1:1, pp. 181n, 182n
- 12:11, p. 18n
- 13:3, p. 48n
- 13:46, p. 36
- 13-14, p. 18
- 19:15, p. 36
- 19:16, pp. 5, 11-12, 16, 19n, 36, 87, 88, 95-96, 169, 181, 254-255
- 19:17, pp. 37, 149n
- 19:18, pp. 57n, 183
- 25:17, p. 17

Numbers
- 12:1-15, p. 247
- 13-14, p. 20
- 16:14, p. 129n
- 24:5, p. 183
- 32:14, pp. 226n-227n
- 32:22, p. 224

Deuteronomy
- 23:10, p. 16
- 23:14, p. 147n
- 24:8, p. 18
- 24:9, pp. 18, 179n, 248

Joshua 7, p. 98n

I Samuel 20:38, p. 99n

II Samuel 9, 16, 19, p. 154

I Kings 1:14, p. 127n

Jeremiah
- 6:28, p. 169
- 41:9, p. 140n

Micah 6:8, p. 255

Zechariah
- 7:10, p. 222
- 8:16, p. 222n

Ecclesiastes
- 1:8, p. xvii
- 10:11, p. 32n

Proverbs
- 4:3, p. 4n
- 11:13, pp. 14n, 181
- 12:25, p. 104

15:4, p. 245n
18:21, p. 32
21:23, p. 3
27:14, p. 176n
Psalms
1:1, p. 38
12:4, p. 13
12:4-5, p. 30
34:14, p. 253
34:14-15, p. 3
34:15, p. 37n

Mishna
Avot
1:6, p. 36, 48n
1:8, p. 82n
4:13, p. 26

Tosefta
Avoda Zara ch. 1, p. 173n

Talmud
Babylonian Talmud
Arakhin
15a, pp. 20, 250n
15b, pp. xix, 19, 20, 25, 34n, 133, 167, 245n
16a, pp. 36, 159-160, 173, 243
16b, pp. 36, 120
Avoda Zara 19b, p.4n
Bava Batra
39a, pp. 100n, 159-160
59b, p. 184n
60a, p. 183
164b, pp. 173, 175n, 249n
165a, pp. xvii, 40, 172, 249n
Bava Kamma 90b, p. 225
Bava Metzia 58b, pp. 17, 167
Bekhorot 36a, p. 152
Berakhot 19b, p. 27n
Eiruvin 41b, p. 27n
Gittin 36b, p. 152
Ketubot
5a, p. 147n
17a, p. 116
36b, p. 156n
46a, p. 16n
Kiddushin
50a, p. 110
81a, p. 155n
Makkot
23a, p. 21n
24a, p. 255
Megilla
3b, p. 27n
25b, p. 155n
28a, p. 34n
Mo'ed Katan 16a, pp. 126n, 129n
Nidda 61a, pp. 139, 140n, 144n
Pesaḥim
113b, pp. 152, 233n
118a, pp. 13n, 17n, 21n, 134n
Rosh HaShana 22b, p. 152
Sanhedrin
11a, p. 98n
26a, p. 38
29a, pp. 162n, 164
31a, pp. 12n, 14, 162n
73a, 95n
97a, p. 122n
Shabbat
33b, p. 13n
54b, p. 149n
55a, p. 8
55b, p. 102n
56a, p. 153, 154n
81b, p. 27n
94b, p. 27n
96b-97a, p. 229n
108b, p. 147n
127b, p. 36n
Shavuot 31a, p. 137n
Sota
5a, p. 34n
21a, p. 246
35a, p. 13n
42a, p. 20

Sukka 46b, p. 122
Taanit
7b, p. 20n
8a, p. 32n
Yevamot
45a, pp. 259-260
65b, pp. 16n, 112n, 122, 149n
Yoma
4b, p. 181n
9b, p. 20n
19b, pp. xvii, 144n
23b, p. 152
72b, p. 245n
75a, p. 104
85b, p. 235
86b, p. 39n
Zevaḥim 88b, pp. 21, 243

Jerusalem Talmud
Bava Kamma 8:7, p. 223n
Ḥagiga 2:1, p. 34n
Pe'ah 1:1, pp. 12n, 16n, 20n, 127, 129n, 185
Taanit 1:1, p. 245n
Yoma 5:3, p. 244n

Midrash and Biblical Translations
Avot DeRabbi Natan 7:3, p. 106
Midrash Rabba
Genesis
1:5, p. 34n
20:1, p. 19n
Exodus 1, p. 19n
Leviticus
16:1, p. 18n
16:2, pp. 4n, 6n
16:6, p. 21
16:13, p. 7n
Pirkei DeRabbi Eliezer ch. 52, p. 20n
Shoḥer Tov mizmor 42, p. 21n
Sifra
Leviticus 26:3, p. 252n
Beḥukkotai 1, p. 18n
Kedoshim 40, p. 12n
Tanḥuma
Vayeshev, p. 102n
Shemot 10, p. 19n
Mishpatim 1, p. 37n
Metzora 2, pp. 18n, 30n
Targum Onkelos
Genesis 2:7, p. 32
Exodus 23:1, pp. 43, 136n
Leviticus 19:16, p. 11n
Targum Yonatan 25:17, p. 248n
Yalkut Shimoni
1:565, p. 170n
1:933, p. 37n
11:459, p. 250n
11:767, p. 4n
13:87, p. 13n

Ge'onim and Rishonim
Aguda, Sukka 45a, p. 176n
Aḥai Gaon, R., 15n; *see also She'iltot*
Arama, R. Yitzḥak, 6n
Eliezer of Metz, R., 168; *see also Sefer Yere'im*
Ḥovot HaLevavot, 21
Ibn Ezra, Proverbs 11:13, p. 181n
Kol Bo, 186n
Maharam Mintz, 186n
Maharam MiRottenberg, 186n
Mahari Beruna, 130n, 155n, 167n, 170n
Mahari Kara, 1 Samuel 20:38, p. 99n
Maharik, 156n
Maharil, 18n, 148n, 248n
Maḥzor Vitri 531, p. 231
Maimonides, 9, 15, 84-85, 127n, 155, 156-157, 161-164, 167n, 174-175, 178-179, 182n, 213n, 226n, 232, 242, 249, 252
Mishnah Commentary: Pirkei Avot
1:6, p. 36n
1:16, p. 174
1:17, p. 13n
Mishneh Torah
Laws of Contamination from *Tzaraat*, 18n, 35, 252n
Laws of Injury and Damage, 232n

Laws of Personal Development, 12n, 20n, 26n, 34n, 85n, 86n, 87n, 135n, 136n, 148n, 161n, 167n, 173n, 174n, 175n, 178n, 182n, 221n, 223n, 249n
Laws of Repentance, 34n, 231n, 242n
Laws of the *Sanhedrin*, 14n, 17n, 134n, 137n, 155n, 157n
Laws of the Virgin Maiden, 17n
Sefer HaMitzvot
negative commandment 297, p. 95n
Responsa, 231n
Meiri, R. Menaḥem, 40-41, 182n, 185n
Menorat HaMaor, 147n, 245n
Mordekhai, 176n, 226n, 227n, 229n, 223n
Nahmanides, 184-185
Bible Commentary
Genesis 2:9, p. 19n
Genesis 37:2, p. 103n
Leviticus 19:16, pp. 11n, 88
Numbers 13:31, p. 13n
Deuteronomy 23:10, pp. 16-17, 36
Deuteronomy 24:9, pp. 179n, 248, 252n
Deuteronomy 25:17, p. 248n
Talmud Commentary
Bava Batra 59b, p. 184n
glosses to Sefer HaMitzvot
positive commandment 7, pp. 19n, 248n
Or Zarua, 251n
Orḥot Tzadikim, 21n
Raavad, 15, 26n
Rabbeinu Gershom, 166n, 186
Rabbeinu Tam, 144n
Rabbeinu Yonah of Gerona, 30, 86, 100, 136, 166, 174-175, 181n, 213, 226n, 235-236; *see also Shaarei Teshuva*
Rabbi Yehudah HeḤasid, 105-106; *see also Sefer Ḥasidim*
Radak, II Chronicles 13:20, p. 226n
Radbaz, 15, 95n
Ran
Ketubot 54b, p. 260
Yoma 6a, p. 231n
Rashbam, 161
Bava Batra 164b, pp. 173n, 175n
Bava Batra 165a, p. 176n
Pesaḥim 118a, pp. 134n, 139n
Rashi
Torah Commentary
Genesis 37:2, p. 102n
Exodus 2:14, p. 19n
Exodus 23:1, pp. 43, 136n
Leviticus 19:15, pp. 36n, 89n
Numbers 13:1, p. 250n
Numbers 16:14, p. 129n
Talmud Commentary
Arakhin 15b, pp. 26n, 176n
Arakhin 16a, pp. 36, 165n, 173n, 175
Bava Metzia 52b, p. 125n
Megilla 25b, 155n
Mo'ed Katan 16a, p. 153n
Nidda 61a, p. 144n
Sanhedrin 103a, p. 13n
Shabbat 118b, p. 13n
Sukka 40b, p. 172n
Taanit 7b, p. 13n
Yevamot 45a, p. 259
Rif, Yoma 6a, p. 231n
Ritva, 165n
Rokeaḥ, 241n
Rosh, 232
Bava Kamma 8:2, p. 232n
Bava Kamma 8:15, p. 27n
Nidda 9:5, p. 140n
Sukka 45a, p. 176n
Yoma 8:18, p. 231n
Sefer HaḤinnukh
16, p. 84
74, p. 137
231, p. 242n
236, pp. 12n, 157n
364, p. 231n
Sefer Ḥaredim
negative commandments, ch. 4, p. 95n
3:3, p. 147n
12, p. 37n
54, p. 37n

Sefer Ḥasidim
64, p. 174n
92:1, pp. 22n, 105
388, p. 112n
482, p. 226n
507, p. 110n
613, p. 223n
631, pp. 127n, 223n
Sefer Mitzvot Gadol
negative commandment 9, pp. 12n, 157n, 182n
negative commandment 10, pp. 127n, 128n, 154n
positive commandment 16, p. 223n
Sefer Mitzvot Katan 8, p. 127n
Sefer Yere'im
6, p. 32n
39, p. 37n
191, pp. 168n, 175n, 228n
Shaarei Teshuva
1:52, p. 231n
3:58, p. 127n
3:200, p. 33n
3:203-9, p. 20n
3:207, p. 235n
3:216, pp. 85n, 100n
3:218, p. 36n
3:218, p. 100n
3:226, pp. 174n, 213n
3:228, pp. 100n, 116n, 171n, 225n
She'iltot, 141n, 144n, 165n, 182n
Shulḥan Arukh, 232
Oraḥ Ḥayim 606:3, p. 229n
Ḥoshen Mishpat 1:6, p. 232n
Ḥoshen Mishpat 19:1, p. 14n
Ḥoshen Mishpat 15, p. 155n
Terumat HaDeshen, 233n
Tosafot
Arakhin 15b, p. 26n
Bava Batra 39b, p. 170n
Nidda 61a, pp. 140n, 144n
Sukka 45a, p. 176n
Taanit 7b, p. 13n
Yevamot 109b, p. 4n
Tosafot Ḥakhmei Anglia, Nidda 61a, p. 140n
Tur, 232
Oraḥ Ḥayim 271, p. 251
Ḥoshen Mishpat 19:1, p. 14n
Ḥoshen Mishpat 420, p. 232n
Yad Rama, 173n
Yisrael of Beruna, R., 130-131; *see also* *Mahari Beruna*

Index of References to the Works of the Ḥafetz Ḥayim

Mishna Berura
53:15, p. 156n
606:3, pp. 238-239

Sefer Ḥafetz Ḥayim
introduction, 20n, 32, 172n
positive commandments
Be'er Mayim Ḥayim
2, p. 137n
prohibitions
4, p. 135n
6, pp. 32n, 66n
Be'er Mayim Ḥayim
3, p. 135n
Laws of Lashon HaRa
klal 1
1:1, p. 13n
1:4, p. 20n
1:6, p. 148n
1:8, p. 191n
Be'er Mayim Ḥayim
4, p. 88n
6, p. 20n
13, p. 123n
14, p. 214n
15, p. 224n
klal 2, p. 169n
2:1, p. 160n
2:2, p. 171n
2:5, p. 162
2:6, p. 164n
2:8, p. 166n
2:10, p. 160n, 164n
2:12, p. 88n
2:13, pp. 182n, 223n
Be'er Mayim Ḥayim
1-2, p. 171n
3, pp. 162n, 163n, 165n
4, p. 163n
15, p. 162n
28, p. 223n
klal 3
3:1, p. 167n
3:3, p. 178n
3:6, p. 226n
3:7-8, p. 36n
Be'er Mayim Ḥayim

5, p. 172n
6, pp.15n, 248n
7, p. 86n
klal 4
4:7, p. 39n
4:11, pp. 112n, 226n
4:12, p. 235n
Be'er Mayim Ḥayim
29, p. 245n
30, p. 39n
33, p. 77n
41, p. 180n
48, pp. 236n, 241n
49, p. 245n
klal 5
5:7, p. 228n
klal 6
6:1, p. 139n
6:2, p. 147n
6:3, p. 135n
6:4, pp. 104n, 151n
6:5, p. 149n
6:9, pp. 135n, 149n
6:25, p. 156n
Be'er Mayim Ḥayim
1, p. 143n
2, p. 147n
klal 7
7:1, p. 152n
7:10-11, p. 154n
Be'er Mayim Ḥayim
8, pp. 153n, 156n
10, p. 156n
14, p. 153n
26, p. 154n
klal 8
8:8, p. 127n
8:10, pp. 106n, 107n
8:11, p. 119n
Be'er Mayim Ḥayim
1, p. 247n
17, p. 128n
25, p. 102n
klal 9
9:3, p. 225n
9:4, pp. 148n, 149n
klal 10
10:2, pp. 97n, 98n, 100n
10:4, p. 125n
10:5, p. 131n
10:12, p. 226n
10:14, pp. 100n, 104n
10:17, pp. 130n, 131n
Be'er Mayim Ḥayim
10, p. 100n
11, p. 98n
30, p. 128n
43, p. 130n
Laws of Rekhilut
introduction
Be'er Mayim Ḥayim, 86n
klal 1
1:8, p. 16n
klal 2, p. 171n
klal 4
4:3, p. 241n
Be'er Mayim Ḥayim
4, p. 241n
klal 6
6:7, p. 152n
6:9, p. 154n, 155n
Be'er Mayim Ḥayim
16, p. 152n
20, p. 154n
klal 9, pp. xviii, 110n
9:1, p. 95n
9:2, pp. 97n, 98n
9:10, pp. 96n, 97n
9:12, p. 100n
Be'er Mayim Ḥayim, 99n
3, p. 100n
14, p. 119n
27, p. 96n
28, p. 100n
35, p. 98n
36, p. 153n

Index of References to the Works of the Ḥafetz Ḥayim

Sefer Shemirat HaLashon
Shaar HaZekhira
1, p. 32n
7, pp. 21n, 245n
12, p. 137n
Shaar HaTevuna 15, p. 172n
Shaar HaTorah, p. 245n
II:14, p. 102n
II:19 (*Parashat Shelaḥ*), 250n
II:20:9, p. 244n

Zekhor LeMiriam
25, p. 99n

About the Author

RABBI DANIEL Z. FELDMAN is a Rosh Yeshiva at the Rabbi Isaac Elchanan Theological Seminary at Yeshiva University, an instructor in the Syms School of Business and the Wurzweiler School of Social Work, and Executive Editor of the RIETS initiative of YU Press. An alumnus of Yeshivat Kerem B'Yavneh, he was ordained (Yoreh Yoreh and Yadin Yadin) at RIETS, where he was a fellow of the Wexner Kollel Elyon.

Rabbi Feldman is the author of *The Right and The Good: Halakhah and Human Relations*, and *Divine Footsteps: Chesed and the Jewish Soul*, and three volumes of talmudic essays entitled *Binah BaSefarim*. He is the co-editor of more than ten volumes, serves on the editorial board of *Tradition*, and has written for publications including *Jewish Action*, *The Orthodox Forum*, and the *Oxford Handbook of Judaism and Economics*. Rabbi Feldman lectures frequently throughout the United States and abroad.

Rabbi Feldman is the spiritual leader of Ohr Saadya of Teaneck, NJ, where he resides with his wife Leah and their children.

Maggid Books
The best of contemporary Jewish thought from
Koren Publishers Jerusalem Ltd.